P9-APU-458

TOGETHER
Communicating
Interpersonally

A Social Construction Approach

Sixth Edition

**John
Stewart**

**Karen E.
Zediker**

**Saskia
Witteborn**

University of Dubuque   *University of Puget Sound*   *University of Washington*

A comprehensive Instructor's Manual/Testing Program is available

COMPLIMENTARY
COPY
Not for Resale

Roxbury Publishing Company

Los Angeles, California

Library of Congress Cataloging-in-Publication Data

Stewart, John Robert, 1941–
Together: communicating interpersonally—6th ed. / John Stewart,
Karen E. Zediker, Saskia Witteborn.
    p.   cm.
Various multi-media instructional aids are available to supplement
the text.
Includes bibliographical references and index.
ISBN 1-891487-97-3
1. Interpersonal relations. 2. Interpersonal communication.
I. Zediker, Karen E., 1963– II. Witteborn, Saskia, 1971– III. Title.

HM1106S764 2004
302—dc22   2003064641
                                                          CIP

**TOGETHER: COMMUNICATING INTERPERSONALLY: A SOCIAL
CONSTRUCTION APPROACH, Sixth Edition.**

Copyright © 2005 Roxbury Publishing Company. Previous edition published by McGraw-Hill. All rights reserved under International and Pan-
American Copyright Conventions. No part of this publication may be reproduced, stored in a retrieval system, or transmitted in any form or by
any means, electronic, mechanical, photocopying, recording, or otherwise
without prior written permission of the publisher.

Publisher: Claude Teweles
Managing Editor: Dawn VanDercreek
Production Editors: Jim Ballinger and Renee Ergazos
Copy Editor: Pauline Piekarz
Production Assistants: Josh Levine and Carla Max-Ryan
Proofreaders: Jackie Estrada and Cheryl Adams
Cover Design: Marnie Kenney
Typography: Pegasus Type, Inc.

A comprehensive Instructor's Manual/Testing Program is available.

Printed on acid-free paper in the United States of America. This book
meets the standards of recycling of the Environmental Protection Agency.

ISBN 1-891487-97-3

ROXBURY PUBLISHING COMPANY
P.O. Box 491044
Los Angeles, California 90049-9044
Voice: (310) 473-3312 • Fax: (310) 473-4490
Email: roxbury@roxbury.net
Website: www.roxbury.net

Table of Contents

Part II
Inhaling and Exhaling

Part III
Relating Together

Preface

Together: Communicating Interpersonally is written primarily for students in basic undergraduate interpersonal communication classes. Like other books designed for this audience, Together includes discussions of basic communication theory; verbal and nonverbal cues; object and person perception; listening; self-expression and disclosure; friendship, family, and dating relationship development and decay; conflict management, betrayal, aggression, and harassment; as well as relating in cyberspace. Unlike most other basic interpersonal texts, Together integrates this material into a unified and practical approach that gives the book a sense of consistency and wholeness. Every chapter of this Sixth Edition has been revised to keep the best of earlier editions while weaving cutting-edge theory and research into a student-tested, user-friendly whole.

Together begins with a five-part explanation of human communication followed by a simple but powerful definition of what makes communication "interpersonal" and an explanation of the close connection between quality of communication and quality of life. Each chapter's discussion of a basic feature or skill is in connection to this definition and approach. This is the primary distinctive feature of the book: *A consistent overall approach translated into applicable skills.* This overall approach can be used to understand and cope with just about every conceivable communication challenge, including those not directly discussed in this book. In addition, since this simple but strong theoretical focus is anchored in an account of what it means to be a person, it can help the basic interpersonal course be a cornerstone of a liberal education while still focusing on practical skills to increase communication competence.

This means that Together can be part of a course that does more than train students to be technically effective perceivers, listeners, and managers of self-disclosure and conflict. This book does offer tools for listening well, developing relationships, and managing conflict. But it also emphasizes how communication choices affect both who we are and the emerging and changing identities of the people around us. Readers are encouraged to develop a maximum amount of communication flexibility, so they can adapt sensitively to different situations. But they are also urged always to remember that communication is more than just a set of skills for "winning friends and influencing people." How people communicate affects the kind of persons they become. Who we are emerges in how we talk and listen.

Beginning with the first edition in the mid-1970s, this text has focused on what happens between communicators, rather than on messages that one communicator sends to another or meanings that communicators allegedly have "in their heads." This was the original reason for the title. *Together*.

Especially since the early 1990s, writers who call themselves "social constructionists" have been developing and testing accounts of communication that complement and extend the one traditionally developed in *Together*. This Sixth Edition appropriates what its authors believe are the best features of social constructionism as they are found in the writings of such communication researchers and teachers as Leslie Baxter, Barbara Montgomery, John Shotter, Barnett Pearce, Bill Rawlins, Kenneth Gergen, Sheila McNamee, Stanley Deetz, and the theorists they cite—Mikhail Bakhtin, Martin Buber, Hans-Georg Gadamer, Ludwig Wittgenstein, and others.

Since this is a basic text, this cutting-edge theory has been translated and simplified. Hundreds of students in first-year interpersonal communication classes read and responded to early drafts of these chapters, and their feedback resulted in many additions, expanded or shortened explanations, simplifications, and organizational changes to increase teach-ability. Partly as a result of the students' input, this edition maintains its conceptually integrated approach, but presents it more descriptively and less prescriptively. There are expanded discussions of the advantages of interpersonal communicating, and there are also many challenging " 'But . . .' A Student Responds" questions in each chapter, increased emphasis on ethics and culture, a more thorough discussion of identity, and a treatment of communicating in cyberspace. Now teachers and students can more easily apply *Together*'s relational approach not only to "warm and fuzzy" encounters but also to such "cold and prickly" experiences as deception, betrayal, harassment, codependence, and relational breakup.

Like earlier editions, this one draws from a broad range of substantive literatures. Communication theorists and philosophers contribute to the basic definitions. Social scientific research is cited to develop and support discussions of all the major concepts and skills. Chapters also integrate ideas and behavioral guidelines from clinical psychology and applied linguistics. Importantly, all these contributions are translated into concepts and skills that can be easily understood by first-year students and presented in a style that speaks directly to the student-reader. *Together*'s language is readily accessible and there are realistic examples to illustrate every major point, many of which have been provided by student readers. Comprehension checks within chapters, reference lists for each chapter, a complete glossary, extensive indexes, and a full *Instructor's Manual* facilitate student and teacher use of the book. The plan of the book, its new features, and the authors are all introduced in Chapter One.

Besides the dual emphases on ethics and culture—also discussed in Chapter One—the book combines the advantages of a text and a reader by providing a short selection at the end of each chapter to illustrate one of the chapter's main points. Along with the presence of three authors and the input from students, these readings function to make the text multivocal. We know that readers hear authorship differently and learners respond to varied voices. You will not find one, authoritarian, white male voice in *Together*. You will hear from women and men of several generations, and persons speaking from non-Caucasian standpoints. We believe that this multivocality will enhance the accessibility and applicability of what's here.

Instructor's Manual

A complete **Instructor's Manual** is available for adopters. Like all good manuals, it includes sample syllabi for a variety of course formats, chapter outlines, in-class activities, individual, partner and group assignments, paper assignments, and exam questions. A unique feature is the "words of wisdom" section that included advice and the shared experience of each of the authors regarding teaching from a social construction approach. The activities included in the manual have been field tested by the authors and experienced instructors, many of whom who have used several editions of *Together* in their classrooms.

Acknowledgements

Although we claim ownership for our biases and for our "errors and omissions," we want to express our appreciation to some of the people who have contributed most to this edition of *Together*.

Several colleagues helped us sharpen our understanding of basic concepts and how to talk about them. John Shotter's writing and conversations strongly influenced our theorizing, along with that of his New Hampshire colleagues, Kenneth E. Gergen and Sheila McNamee. Conversations with colleagues Gerry Philipsen, John Gastil, Valerie Manusov, Lisa Coutu, Laura Black, Theresa Castor, Fred Korn, M. Lane Bruner, Robyn Penman, Sallyann Roth, Joanna Brook, Todd Kelshaw, Cindy King, and Crispin Thurlow all helped our thinking and teaching.

We are especially grateful to the teachers and students in the basic interpersonal communication classes who tested early versions of these chapters and provided a wealth of feedback. Their teachers were

Laura Black, Jody Koenig, Andi Zamora, Cindy King, Eve-Anne Doohan, Jaelle Dragomir, and Joanna Brook. Several reviewers provided insightful comments for the Sixth Edition, including Vincent L. Bloom (California State University—Fresno), Steve Duck (University of Iowa), Krista M. Hirschmann (Penn State Berks-Lehigh Valley College), Kimberly Pearce (De Anza College), Penni Pier (Wartburg College), C. Thomas Preston, Jr. (University of Missouri—St. Louis), Dennis L. Wignall (Saginaw Valley State University), Andi Zamora (Whatcom Community College), and Brooke Zimmers (Shoreline Community College). To all of you, thank you.

Furthermore, we would like to thank our undergraduates, Christa Robinson and Evan Newton, who contributed to this book through their research and their questions about interpersonal communication.

John would also like especially to thank Dale Reiger, Sue Dyer, and John Angus Campbell for long and fruitful friendships. Karen would like to thank Tim and Logan for their unfaltering support and Julie Benson-Rosston for her enduring friendship. And Saskia expresses gratitude to Tim for his love and his patience and to Joanna Brook for being a friend and a colleague. ✦

Part I

Understanding Communication

Chapter One

Introduction to the Authors and the Text

You may have noticed that the title of this first chapter, "Introduction to the Authors and the Text," is not a typical one. Students who have read earlier editions of *Together* tell us that there are many things about this book that are different from the texts they generally read, and that one of the most significant differences is that they feel as if they get the chance to know something about the authors. So, in this edition of the book, we decided to dedicate a short chapter to self-introductions. In some courses, the text authors' identities may not be all that important, but in this one it makes a difference because our approach to interpersonal communication focuses on the *persons* involved, and we are three of these persons. You, your classmates, and your teacher are some other parts of the mix.

In a nutshell, we understand communication to be a process of collaboratively creating meaning. We understand interpersonal communication to be a subset of this process that emphasizes what we call *the presence of the personal*. In this book we contrast interpersonal communicating with impersonal communicating, and we identify how the choices people make between the two on a daily, hourly, and even moment-by-moment basis affect their identities and their relationships with family, friends, coworkers, and even the person they may be randomly assigned to sit next to on an airplane. Before we develop this basic understanding of interpersonal communicating, we'd like to tell you a little about ourselves. After you have the chance to learn something about each of us, we'll introduce you to the layout of this text and some of its unique features.

John Stewart

Hello! I am writing this at a cabin in the San Juan Islands in Washington State where I am vacationing with Kris, my wife, and our 11-

year-old son, Lincoln. Although we are natives of the Pacific Northwest and really love its salt water, mountains, and green landscape, we now live where I work, as the dean of the undergraduate college at the University of Dubuque, a small Presbyterian school in northeast Iowa.

I actually began work on this book in 1973, and I'm willing to bet that you might not even have been alive then. That makes me the "old guy" of this author team. I had come to the University of Washington fresh out of graduate school to direct an innovative course called Interpersonal Communication. Back then it was a blend of psychology, sociology, and communication that was becoming the fastest-growing course on U.S. college campuses. I was excited to begin my new job and frustrated that there were almost no texts available. A publisher's representative who visited my office suggested that a colleague and I write one, so we did.

From that day to this one, my main goal for this text has been to help people with one of the most important things we do as humans: connect with others. I strongly believe, as one communication philosopher put it, that "all real living is meeting" (Buber 1958, 11). In other words, no human is "an island." Our bodies and our experiences make us individuals, but we become who we are as we experience contacts with others. People who mostly experience abusive or impersonal contacts don't have the same opportunity to realize their human potential as people who experience positive attention, support, and love.

Many contacts have helped make me who I am. My mother's hearing impairment made me realize very early on how important and difficult it can be to communicate interpersonally. When my daughters were born during my junior and senior years in college, I experienced the incredible magic, mystery, and terror of being a parent. In the 1970s, a divorce removed any vestiges I had of interpersonal innocence, and later I learned with Kris what it's like as an adult to fall in love and build a long-term relationship. Teaching connected me with stimulating colleagues, enthusiastic and challenging undergraduates, and graduate students who taught me more and more. Kris and I were blessed with two grandkids in the 1980s and, when our son Lincoln was born in 1992, I started my second set of adventures as a parent, one that I'm still experiencing.

After over 30 years at the University of Washington, I moved in 2001 to the University of Dubuque. I still teach interpersonal communication, but many of my professional contacts are now with faculty from across the college, administrators, and trustees. It's still true for me, though, that—as we put it in Chapter Three—there's a direct relationship between the quality of my communication and the quality of my life. In other words, for humans, contact is crucial.

Karen, Saskia, and I got together to write this book because we each have a little different take on the importance of contact. In the next few paragraphs each of them will tell you a little about herself and the special emphasis she brings to this book. From where I sit, our collaboration is really exciting, not only because it's a joy to work together, but also because the three of us are developing an approach to interpersonal communication that embodies the most crucial elements of this study in the twenty-first century: contact, ethics, and culture.

Karen Zediker

So hi! I'm glad to have the chance to share with you a little about who I am and about my role in this edition of *Together*. I agree wholeheartedly with John about the importance of contact and the point that the quality of our communication influences the quality of our lives. And I'd add that each of us makes ethical choices about the kinds of contact we encourage or discourage. Some of these choices are carefully considered, and others seem to get made by default. Our life histories, cultural norms, and socially prescribed roles shape what seems possible in relationships, *and* I believe that we can, in the context of our lived experience, make choices that enhance the potential for the kinds of interpersonal contact that enhance the quality of our lives. We might not realize until some time later how our choices and the choices of others will shape us, but they do.

As an undergraduate student, I chose to major in Interpersonal Communication after exploring a variety of other majors (Theater, English Literature, and Nursing). I have to admit that, like many of you, when I started college I didn't even know there *was* a discipline of communication. But I found an intellectual home in the Department of Interpersonal Communication at the University of Montana. Through assigned readings I was introduced to John Stewart's orientation to interpersonal communication, and as a master's student I used his work to form the basis of a paper I wrote for a philosophy of religion course. Little did I know, then, that my choice to study and teach interpersonal communication would lead me to study with John as a doctoral student at the University of Washington (UW) or to teach under his supervision from earlier versions of *Together*. For the past several years I have been on the faculty at UW and have served as the course supervisor for a new group of graduate students who teach from this text. I have enjoyed the ongoing conversations with a new group of teacher/ scholars and many more students as they explore the ideas presented here.

The primary emphasis I bring to this version of *Together* is a focus on communication ethics. I define ethics as the set of standards used to evaluate beliefs, values, and communicative actions perceived to be good or bad, right or wrong, appropriate or inappropriate. As a third-generation preacher's kid, I've been immersed in conversations about ethical and moral dilemmas my whole life. I learned early on that an individual's communication choices and actions significantly influence others. The first time I remember seeing my dad cry provided one of those learning opportunities. I was 5 years old. When I asked him why he was crying, he told me that someone had just shot and killed a very good man. Did he know the man? Not personally, but that didn't matter. The man shared my dad's hope and vision for a united and loving world, and dad was mourning his loss. By observing my dad's response to the assassination of Martin Luther King, Jr., I learned that difference can unite as well as divide; that the risks of speaking your convictions can pay off in unexpected ways, even when the speaker is shot and killed; and that human beings can choose responses of empathy and action over hatred and fear. I also learned that it's possible to choose to put into practice one's moral and ethical standards even in the face of personal grief and social upheaval. Now I try to put this understanding into practice and help others to develop their own abilities to negotiate the tensions of ethical dilemmas in their own lives. .

Two people who help me to practice what I profess are Tim and Logan. Tim and I have been married since 1987. One of the things that brought us together and keeps our life interesting is our commitment to engage each other on controversial issues. We don't always agree with each other, but we try very hard to listen and understand where each of us is coming from. And that's not easy when you have two opinionated persons in one relationship! Together we have a wonderful son, Logan, who teaches me as much about the importance of contact as I teach him. He is a sensitive and caring being who has already learned to talk about his observations about communication and continues to learn what it means to be responsible for his choices. Often, he reminds me to take responsibility for mine.

The process of working with John and Saskia on this edition of *Together* has been a rewarding one. We really believe in the approach to interpersonal communication that we write about and have indeed collaboratively constructed the ways we talk about the communication theories and skills presented in the chapters to come. We have chosen to write in a unified voice, but not as if there were only one author for this book. You are likely to hear each of us in the pages that follow, and we hope that as our voices blend, there will be more harmony than discord. I find that our working relationship has been an illustration of the way that differences in culture, perspective, and priorities can inform and enhance the meaning-making process called communication. I trust that what we have to say will resonate with you.

Saskia Witteborn

Welcome! I cannot agree more with Karen and John that contacts with other human beings and with our environment shape how we see others and ourselves. And I also agree that we make ethical choices about the contacts that we encourage and discourage. I'll tell you briefly about the choices that others and I have made. As a master's student in Germany I chose to study English linguistics, literature, and business. During my studies, I became more interested in human communication, especially culture and communication, and made the choice to come to the University of Washington as a doctoral student. My parents, grandparents, and brother Sebastian were proud of me but very sad at the same time that I would go so far away. I was sad, too, and it was a great relief when my partner Tim, who is from Germany too, decided to join me. I'm still thankful to him that he made that decision.

Once at the University of Washington, I took a class with John Stewart and thought, "Great stuff, wanna know more." I started to teach with *Together* under Karen's supervision and have since then enjoyed the long conversations with Karen, John, and students about the concepts of the book.

What I bring to *Together* is a focus on the relationship between interpersonal communication and culture. I think about culture as a system of beliefs, values, norms, and meanings that have a significant influence on how people communicate. Thinking about culture and experiencing cultural similarities and differences became a very important part of my life from early on.

I was born in the former East Germany, which used to be a pretty homogeneous society. However, I was lucky enough that my parents always encouraged me to travel and to show respect for other cultures. Through my travels I learned that different cultures have different ways of dealing with time, work, and relationships, and have different approaches to spirituality. I also learned that all these things influence how people talk and listen to each other. I'll give you an example. When I was 14, I traveled with my mom to Baku in Azerbaijan, a former republic of the Soviet Union. There, I learned that taking one's time and having close relationships are more important than rushing from one appointment to the other. One day, my mom and I went to a mosque. I had never been in a mosque before, and the concept of having a women's room was not familiar to me. We sat down with the other women, who welcomed us, drank tea, and chatted in broken Russian and German for a long time. We sat there for hours. I was getting a little nervous because of all the other things that we wanted to see in town. But for the women there was no rush. Relationships and having conversations together were more important than the clock.

Another example of how cultural beliefs can influence communication was my experience in the jungle of Ecuador, where I spent two weeks with a shaman family, living, gathering herbs, and trying to find my way through the jungle. As you may know, a shaman is a tribal adviser and healer. In the jungle I learned about the differences between

Western and non-Western views about whether you can communicate with nature. For the shaman family, nature was filled with spirits. These spirits talk to humans and the other way round. Sometimes the shaman would get up around 4 A.M. to walk 20 miles through the jungle to his sacred mountain to pray. And although I did not understand some things that were going on around me, I felt the human connection between me, the shaman, and his family. I respected their privacy and their way of life, and I could see that they trusted me because they asked me to stay.

What I want to say is that I was able to connect with the people in different cultures by being aware and respecting the different value and belief systems. These stays also helped me to reflect on my own worldview and what I think are appropriate and inappropriate communicative choices and behaviors.

Why am I telling you all about this? You might think, yeah, interesting, but that sounds too much like let's make the world a happy family. This is not what John, Karen, or I want to say. What we are saying is that we want to encourage you to think about how your cultural background, your view of what is right and wrong in the world (with some more shades of gray in between), and the choices that you make based on these views influence your interpersonal encounters with other people and the relationships that you engage in. If I had decided to make fun of the shaman and his family for their beliefs, I would have not gained their trust. If I had decided not to go into the mosque because I was raised as a Protestant by my grandparents and parents, I would not have been able to explore the beauty of the relationship among the women. Together with John and Karen, I believe that how you engage in interpersonal communication is influenced by your cultural lenses and the ethical choices you make. And we also believe that the more you know about the choices and different cultural worldviews, the more you'll be able to have satisfying human contacts. *Viel Spass beim Lernen* (have fun learning).

Together

Now that we have briefly introduced ourselves to you, we want to introduce the book itself. This is the sixth edition of *Together* and, as we've said, it continues the book's traditional emphasis on contact and adds two additional areas of focus: ethics and culture. In each chapter there are opportunities to reflect on issues of ethical and cultural concerns. You may find it a useful practice to respond to these questions as you read.

Ethical concerns are central to all aspects of human communication. The National Communication Association has recently approved an ethical credo, and the emphasis on ethics in the discipline is evident in the presence of an annual ethics conference, an online newsletter dedicated to the study of communication ethics, and the growing number of ethics papers at national, regional, and local conferences. All this is happening because countries, corporations, educational institutions, families, and relational partners continue to face the challenges of figuring out how to best make ethical choices in an increasingly complex world.

In the pages that follow, we argue for an ethical standard that is multivocal and that honors competing views. We are not advocating a situational ethics in which prevailing winds guide communicative action. Our perspective is anchored in a clear understanding of what it means to be a person and the most humane qualities of human contact. You will notice that this emphasis on ethics surfaces in each chapter in discussion of ethical dilemmas and conversations about the choices and consequences for choices in communicative relationships that maximize the presence of the personal.

Communication and culture are also part of our daily lives. Today, a person might well go to school and talk to fellow students in the technical language of their subject fields, follow certain rules of politeness when talking to professors or asking for directions from a stranger, and chat over the Internet with a friend who is an exchange student in London. They might also talk in the afternoon to a neighbor who has just arrived from Ghana and apply knowledge of Spanish during an afternoon job as a bank teller. Globalization, technological development, and migration have changed demographics in the United States and have also changed our communicating. Those people who have access to technology use e-mail, the Internet, and cell phones to transcend time and space, and individuals around the globe are exposed to situations where they interact with people who have differing norms for speaking and for engaging in conversations.

In this interpersonal communication textbook we integrate communication and culture because we recognize the importance of cultural situatedness. This means, first, that only by giving the time and taking the risk to become aware of one's own cultural positions can people cope effectively with the challenges of communicating in a diverse world. It also means that we believe that the approach taken in this book is culturally situated and therefore limited by our cultural blinders, so that people need to become aware that, for example, verbal and nonverbal cues, listening, and relational systems might work differently in different cultures. Culture does not always mean national culture, but can also refer to gender, ethnic, occupational, or religious identities *or* speech communities. You won't find a separate chapter about culture and communication in this text because we integrate into every chapter comments, explanations, and examples that provide

Notice how contact, ethics, and culture are present here. Contact—and the lack of it—are obvious. Cultural elements include age, ethnicity, and the culture of youth baseball. Ethical issues arise when parents like these get caught up in the competition.

opportunities to relate knowledge about interpersonal concepts to different cultural contexts.

In addition, throughout this book you'll find questions and comments made by students like yourselves. (Yes, they really are from actual students—we didn't just make them up.) The student responses are titled " 'But . . .' A Student Responds." Each of these is an opportunity to introduce additional voices into the development of the ideas in the text. As you read along, you may experience these as interruptions to the flow of the text. While some of you may find yourself skipping over them, we encourage you to take a moment to reflect on the questions and contributions of others along the way.

Another feature of this text that you are bound to notice is the inclusion of a short reading at the end of each chapter. These readings highlight one of the main points of the chapter. We include them because we are committed to multivocality (many voices) and know that it can help to have complex ideas discussed by different people. We call these readings "In Other Words." They are here to give you another perspective on one of the central ideas of each chapter. These snippets offer you another way to think about communication concepts and practices, and may serve as the basis for discussions in class.

The text as a whole is divided into three parts: Understanding Communication, Inhaling and Exhaling, and Relating Together. Part I, "Understanding Communication," consists of the first four chapters and introduces you to the ideas that the rest of the book develops. After this, Chapter Two, "Communication and Meaning," provides you with an overview of the communication process and introduces you to a central concept in this text that we call *worlds of meaning*. You will notice as you move through the text that the seven dimensions that constitute an individual's world of meaning are interwoven throughout. In Chapter Two we also explain further why *Together* includes an explicit focus on both ethics and culture. Finally, we introduce you to the important skill of nexting (yep, we know that sounds like a strange word, but trust us for now—it fits) and explain why this may be one of the most important concepts you can learn from us.

Chapter Three, "Interpersonal Communicating," responds to a couple of important questions many of you may already be asking: "What is interpersonal communication?" and "Why should I study it?" In this chapter we introduce you to the impersonal◀──▶interpersonal scale and five features that help to distinguish between its poles. We also explain the important link between the quality of your communication and the quality of your life. We believe that when you develop your communication flexibility and interpersonal communication competence, you can notice a difference in the quality of your life.

Chapter Four, "Constructing Identities," helps you understand how communication affects your identity. This chapter explores human selves as socially constructed and introduces you to some of the choices that each individual has when collaboratively constructing meaning with others.

Part II is called "Inhaling and Exhaling." The breathing metaphor is meant to echo several features of the simultaneously taking-in and giving-out process of communicating. Chapter Five, "Inhaling: Perception," provides you with an overview of the perception process, discusses the development of cognitive schema and scripts, and focuses your attention on how people perceive people. The chapter discusses attributions, stereotypes, and impressions as important parts of how you "take in" others and how they may be "taking in" you. Chapter Six, "Inhaling: Listening," begins with some of the challenges of listening and then overviews four different ways to listen, including reflectively, analytically, empathically, and dialogically. Our goal is to give you a balance between theoretical grounding in listening research and practical ways to put the theories into practice in your own communication.

Chapters Seven, "Verbal Dimensions of Talk," and Eight, "Nonverbal Communicating," shift the focus from what you take in to what you give out. We have decided to divide verbal and nonverbal aspects of communication into two chapters, not because we believe they can be divided in actual communicative practice but because students have told us that it is easier to study them this way. In Chapter Seven we distinguish between oral/non-oral and verbal/nonverbal aspects of communicating, introduce you to the view of language as a way of being, and briefly discuss ways you may choose to improve how you express ideas. In Chapter Eight we share some of the research on nonverbal communication, and discuss the ways nonverbal and verbal cues interact and the ways nonverbal communication is also linked to identity. We strongly encourage you to explore the connections between these two chapters, recognizing that each chapter summarizes one part of the whole of language.

Part III, "Relating Together," consists of the final four chapters and gives you a chance to see how the ideas presented in the first two parts of the book intertwine in communicative practice. Chapter Nine, "Constructing Relational Systems: Friends, Partners, and Families," introduces you to the theory and practice of relationship formation and maintenance and how relationships come apart. In this chapter we explore how your "inhaling " others and "exhaling" yourself work together to form, reshape, and even collapse relationships. We describe three different models for understanding relationships with romantic partners, friends, and family members.

In Chapter Ten, "Relating Through Problems," we address the reality that even relationships that are riddled with problems are collaboratively constructed. We do not dismiss the responsibility that communicators have when deception, betrayal, aggression, and even relational violence are present, but instead we challenge you to think about the ways in which relational problems as well as relational success are collaboratively constructed.

Chapter Eleven, "Managing Conflict Effectively," defines interpersonal conflict, identifies some of the risks and benefits of engaging in conflict, and provides you with an overview of the theories of conflict styles. Again, in this chapter we strive to strike a balance between theoretical insights and some very practical strategies to manage the conflicts that will inevitably occur. You will find that many of the ideas presented throughout the book come to fruition in this chapter. Your perception and listening skills, ability to communicate verbally and nonverbally, and understanding of response options and differences in worlds of meaning are all important if you hope to develop your competence in relating in conflict.

Finally, Chapter Twelve, "Relating Interpersonally in Cyberspace," takes the study of interpersonal communication to issues of relational development online. This chapter reviews the variety of forms of mediated communication that can and likely will influence your communication in the days, months, and years to come. We also introduce you to the current research on interpersonal communication in cyberspace and guide you to reflect on the ways meaning, identities, and relationships are collaboratively constructed there.

So that's what's coming! It's been exciting for us to put these ideas together, and we look forward to your responses.

References

Buber, M. 1958. *I and Thou*. Trans. R. G. Smith. New York: Charles Scribner's Sons. ✦

Chapter Two

Communication and Meaning

Chapter Objectives

By the end of this chapter you should be able to do the following:
- Define communication.
- Explain what it means to say that communication is a socially constructed process.
- Describe how fault and blame are linked to the message transmission view of communication.
- Identify seven features of your world of meaning.
- Reflect on the ethical standards that influence your communication choices.
- Discuss the role of culture in collaborative meaning making.
- Define the term "nexting."

Chapter Preview

So here you are in the first "regular" chapter of this interpersonal communication text. The fact that you are reading these pages means that you have decided—or someone has decided for you—to learn more about communicating interpersonally. If you are enrolled as a full-time student, you may also be studying chemistry, English, political science, or psychology. The content of some of those courses may seem obvious by their titles, but most every one begins by orienting you to the subject matter through definitions. This text does, too. So what is interpersonal communication?

Our response to this question is likely to be more involved than you might expect. And before we are done, some of you might even be asking yourselves, "When are they going to get to the part I should memorize for the test?" Others might be thinking that you know what communication is because you've been doing it in one form or another since the day you were born, so what's the point of some elaborate definition?

Our answer is, first, that this whole book essentially develops the two definitions that are explained in this chapter and the next, "communication" and "interpersonal communication." And second, we don't want to take the risk of assuming that everybody starts with the same understanding when our experiences tell us that students come to this course with different cultural and individual experiences of communication that shape all their contacts with others. So definitions matter.

Fundamentally, *communication* is a general term used to label the processes through which humans collaboratively construct meaning. Meaning is what makes the human world different from the spaces inhabited by other living beings—worms, dogs and cats, and even, so far as we now know, dolphins and chimpanzees. Since humans live in worlds of meaning—rather than worlds made up only of objects, or "things"—the process of constructing and modifying these worlds goes on literally *all* the time. This is why communication is such a major part of human living.

To understand what we mean when we say that humans live in worlds of meaning, consider the part of your world that's your "home." What's most important about it is not how many square feet it has, how tall it is, where it's located, or the color of the bedroom walls (objective features), but what it *means* to live in a place this small or this big, how the wall color affects you, and what it *means* to live where your home is located. Similarly, the transportation part of your world is significant not simply because you travel by bike or on a bus, in your own old or new car, on foot or on a motorcycle, but because of what it *means* in your family, neighborhood, and culture to get around this way. And the meanings of all these parts of our worlds get established and changed in communication—the written and oral, verbal and nonverbal contact people have with each other.

When each human being is born, this process of collaborative meaning-making is already going on around us. Even before we have developed our abilities to be articulate in our family's language, we enter a number of ongoing conversations. In some ways, we enter our world kind of like a chunk of potato is plopped into a pot of simmering soup. The soup of human meaning-making will be simmering all the time we are alive, and communication processes will continue after we die. Of course, individuals and groups affect their worlds a lot more than a chunk of potato affects a pot of soup. In fact, much of this book is about the ethical choices and cultural responses communicators make, and how these affect their worlds. But although the element of choice is present in every communication event, it is also important to keep in mind that the communication process is not one that any individual can completely control. Communication is something that we do collectively, *together*, as the title of this book suggests. All the time, everywhere, in all the contacts that make us social animals, humans are constructing meaning together, and *communication* is the name given to this ongoing process.

Interpersonal communication is a subset of this broader process, a particular quality or type of communication. We develop our definition of interpersonal communicating in the next chapter. But before we do, there are enough important points about the process of communication in general to fill the rest of this chapter.

As we noted, our goal in this chapter is to lay the foundation for the rest of the book. We provide you with an up-to-date, research-anchored, and experientially relevant understanding of what human communication is and how it works. This will prepare you for the similarly important definition of interpersonal communication in Chapter Three.

Views of Communication

Most people don't go around asking themselves or each another, "What is communication anyway?" or "How do you define human communication?" This activity is generally reserved for those of us who write textbooks. But every day, all of us do say and do things that *indirectly* indicate how we would answer these questions if asked. In other words, definitions of communication "leak out" in the ways people engage in or avoid communication with others. The way you understand communication—your definition—leaks out in your communicating too.

For example, when your parent or supervisor at work tells you that you made a mistake, you might think—or say—"You never told me to do that!" Your parent or supervisor might respond, "You weren't listening!" Here you understand communication as the primary responsibility of the "sender," and they are defining it as a process that depends most on the "receiver." In addition, both of you are defining communication as a cause-effect process, because the problem is caused by one person's actions/inactions or the other's.

Each of you has a way of understanding communication, a lens that you look through as you plan how to communicate and respond to communication problems. It's possible that the view of communication we present in this text may be different from other views you've learned about or experienced in your own life. Our definition or lens is anchored in a contemporary scholarly tradition. Social construction is its name, and we are convinced that it is both theoretically sound and practically useful. We are also convinced that learning to use a social construction lens will empower you to understand some things about interpersonal communication that you may not have recognized before. So let's start by briefly reviewing a common—and incomplete—way of understanding communication.

Communication as Message Transmission

One commonly held definition of communication is that it is the process in which ideas are formulated by one person and then conveyed to another. This view has been labeled the *message transmission* view of communication. From this perspective the success of a communicative exchange is judged by how well the message in one person's head is transmitted into the other person's head. The word *fidelity* is the term used to label how well message sent equals message received. You can tell that this view exists in your culture when people say to one another "That's not what I meant!" or "Perhaps I wasn't clear, let me try again." Deborah Tannen's (1990) book about communication between men and women, *You Just Don't Understand!*, reinforces several aspects of this perspective, including the assumption that understanding is an individualistic process and that one of the partners can be blamed if mutual understanding is not achieved.

The message transmission view of communication is grounded in the practices of public speech, radio, television, and film. People who look at communication through this lens contend that, to be an effective communicator, one must construct a message in such a way that it can be clearly and easily conveyed to an awaiting audience or listener. The bulk of the responsibility for communicative "success" lies with the person who sends the message. It is her responsibility to analyze her audience and determine the most appropriate channel for sending her message. Some people call this the "hypodermic" view because it assumes that one person "injects" her ideas into the other person's head like a hypodermic needle injects drugs into a vein or muscle.

There are advantages to viewing communication through this lens. First, it encourages communicators to think about their messages and meanings ahead of time, and to adapt them to the needs and concerns of their audiences. This view of communication also draws attention to the variety of different message elements and modes, including verbal cues, nonverbal cues, e-mail, face-to-face, telephone, and broadcast. It is a tidy way of conceptualizing communication. Participants can assess "where things went wrong" and then make choices about how they might change their patterns of communicating to "fix" the problem.

One significant disadvantage of this view of communication, however, is embedded in this very talk about "communication breakdowns" and "fixing things." Communication is much more complicated than the message transmission view suggests. Human interaction does not consist of mechanistic parts that can simply be replaced

In the message-transmission view, this kind of event becomes the model for interpersonal communicating. What are some problems with this move?

when something doesn't seem to be running smoothly. Communication happens between unique individuals who constantly make choices influenced by their cultural experiences and individual value systems. These choices, sometimes reflective and more often reactive, help to shape the course of a conversation with other choice making, culturally influenced persons. In other words, the two problems with the message transmission view are that it is oversimplified and that it treats communication as a linear and causal process. *Linear* means in-a-line (from one person's head into the other's), and *causal* means that the process obeys the laws of cause and effect like a rocket engine or lever.

When people define communication as message transmission, they tend to believe that communication challenges are the fault of, or can be blamed on, one of the participants, just as you might blame your parent or supervisor for being unclear, and they say that it is your fault that you didn't "get it" because you weren't listening. To say that a problem is somebody's "fault" is to say that they *caused* it, like the wind causing a door to slam shut. This view assumes that human communicating is governed by the laws of cause and effect.

Children of all ages invoke the message transmission view of communication when they assign blame as a way of relieving themselves of responsibility for what happens. You can hear them say, "It's not my fault—he started it!" The pattered response is often something like, "Uh-uh! She hit me first." And then, "But you looked at me funny!" The problem then is to figure out where a misunderstanding *started* so the "cause" can be determined and the "effect" evaluated.

The resulting circle of fault and blame is almost never very productive or satisfying for the people involved—except, possibly, for the child who "wins." The reason is that, as we said, human communication is much more complicated than the message transmission view says it is. We will say more about the fault and blame problem in a few more pages. At this point, you can hopefully see that definitions make a difference, and that oversimplified definitions create problems.

The definition of communication we develop in this chapter includes six main points:

1. *Meaning*: Humans live in worlds of meaning, and communication is the process of collaboratively making these meanings.

   Implication 1: No one person can completely control a communication event, and no single person or action causes—or can be blamed for—a communication outcome.

2. *Choice*: All communication involves choices, some of which we actively consider and others that follow cultural norms and seem almost automatic.

   Implication 2: The choices communicators make reveal their ethical standards and commitments.

3. *Culture*: Culture and communication are intertwined. Ethnicity, gender, age, social class, sexual orientation, and other cultural features always affect communication and are affected by it.

   Implication 3: Your cultures, and ours, affect what we say about communication in this book and how you respond to it.

4. *Identities*: Some of the most important meanings people collaboratively construct are identities. All communicating involves negotiating identities or selves.

   Implication 4: Identity messages are always in play.

5. *Conversation*: The most influential communication events are conversations.

   Implication 5: The most ordinary communication events are generally the most significant.

6. *Nexting*: The most important single communication skill is "nexting."

   Implication 6: Whenever you face a communication challenge or problem, the most useful question you can ask yourself is, "What can I help to happen next?"

Communication as Collaborative Meaning-Making

We understand communication to be the continuous, complex, collaborative process of verbal and nonverbal meaning-making. This is our definition of communication. It's continuous because humans are always making meaning—figuring out, making sense of, or interpreting what's happening—even when we're asleep. It's complex because it involves not just words and ideas but also intonation, facial expression, eye contact, touch, and several other nonverbal elements, and it always includes identity and relationship messages, culture and gender cues, more or less hidden agendas, unspoken expectations, and literally dozens of other features that usually become apparent only when they create problems. It's collaborative because we do it with other people. This definitely isn't to say that people always *agree*, but only that we don't communicate alone.[1] Even prizefighters collaborate, because they show up at the same time and abide by the rules. Co-labor-ating just means engaging an issue together, and collaboration can be as anonymous as obeying traffic laws and speaking the local language or as intimate as attending to your partner's lovemaking preferences.

> **1. Meaning: Humans live in worlds of meaning, and communication is the process of collaboratively making these meanings.**

Worlds of Meaning

By *worlds of meaning* we mean the more-or-less coherent spheres of sense, significance, or interpretation that each human inhabits. You might want to think about your world of meaning as your "reality," or your overall view of the way things are. Each of us has his or her own world of meaning that has been, and continues to be, collaboratively constructed in relation to others. May people notice that their worlds of meaning overlap in many ways, *and* each is as unique as the individual who inhabits it. We use the term *world of meaning* to indicate that there is a wholeness to the sphere of out understanding. The geographical world (that is, the earth) is roughly shaped like a sphere, and the sphere is an ancient symbol for wholeness. Even though the human's world of meaning changes, potentially with each new communication encounter, people experience their worlds of meaning as relatively whole.

The following image (Figure 2.1) illustrates the complexity of our worlds of meaning. You'll note that, like models of the physical world, it is also shaped like a sphere. In our model, the sphere has seven overlapping, intertwining ellipses that represent each of the seven dimensions of the worlds of meaning construct: physical environment, time, relationships, spirituality, vocation, language, and technology. Each el-

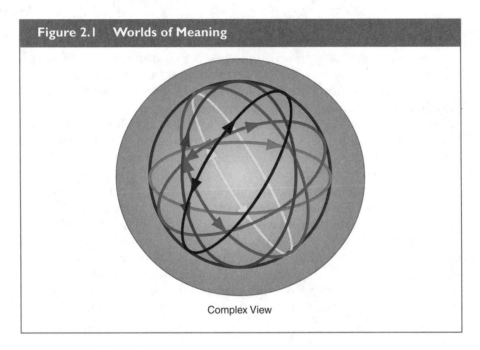

Figure 2.1   Worlds of Meaning

Complex View

lipse is a different shade, and each is always in flux. We'll show you a less complex version of the model in a bit that may help you focus on the common characteristics of each dimension, but for now, let's focus on the model as a whole. The purple field surrounding the sphere in this model indicates that the dimensions of one's world of meaning are not floating free, but suspended within, and influenced by, the cosmos in which it develops. We'd like to make the case that two of the primary elements of the cosmic "stuff" that surrounds and imbues worlds of meaning are ethics and culture. The purple overlay here can be understood as the intermingling of ethics (red) and culture (blue).

Whether we simply inherit or actively choose the ethical standards that guide our lives, the choices we make about right and wrong, good and bad, what's appropriate and inappropriate all shape our world of meaning. We interpret our experiences through the lens of our ethical standards. The meaning-making process is also embedded in and influenced by our cultural identities. Together, ethics and culture influence an individual's world of meaning and each person's world. For example, the cultural norms and ethical standards for someone raised in the heart of the Bible Belt of the southern United States are almost certainly different from the cultural and ethical norms of someone raised in the rainforests of New Guinea. Even when ethical and cultural elements are shared in common, each person's individual world of meaning will be as unique as their life experiences.

What difference does it make if you understand that people have uniquely constructed worlds of meaning? Each person's world of meaning influences the way he or she communicates with others. As two people communicate, their worlds of meaning are present in the conversation, shaping their interpretations of one another. Imagine if you will a conversation between two classmates about whether the death penalty should be imposed on teenagers convicted of first degree murder. If the classmates assume that their worlds of meaning overlap significantly—that their worldviews generally align—it is likely that they will spend less time explaining the details of their perspectives to one another. If their worlds of meaning are assumed to be less in sync, they may have to spend more time and energy coming to understand one another.

The degree of alignment of our worlds of meaning can both help and hinder our ability to communicate effectively. Sometimes, when you assume that your communication partner views the world in the same way as you do, you can be surprised when you don't see eye to eye. Actual similarity can be helpful, but assuming similarity is present can hinder your quest for understanding and being understood. In the same way, differences in worlds of meaning can both hinder and help communication between people. If we have different ethical standards and come from dramatically different cultures, we may have challenges finding common ground. On the other hand, acknowledging differences in perspective provides the opportunity to learn a new way of seeing and to collaborate in creating new understanding. Whatever the initial alignment between worlds of meaning, each person's world is molded and shaped in by each communication encounter.

You may find that some dimensions of your world of meaning align with your communicative partner better than others. That's why we believe it is helpful to look at each dimension individually and in relation to one another. But before we break the model down into smaller pieces, keep in mind that, while a smaller piece of the model allows you to understand aspects of each of the seven dimensions in more detail, we don't want you to let go of the complexity of the world of meaning. You can, productively, view each dimension independently or explore the ways in which two or more dimensions are shaped in relation to one another—and they are always part of a dynamic and interrelated whole.

Applying What You Know

Think for a moment about someone in your class who you think views the world in similar ways as you. Then identify someone else who you imagine has a really different perspective.

After you have read through the seven dimensions that follow, take the opportunity to talk to at least one of them and compare at least three of the seven dimensions. Make note of your similarities and differences.

Figure 2.2   Single Dimension

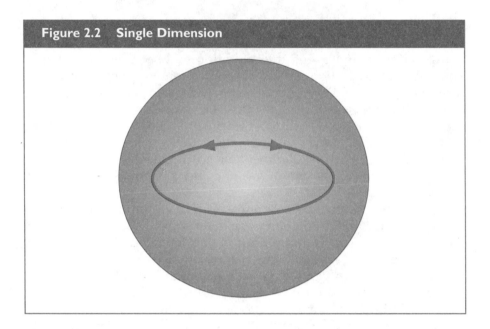

In the next few pages, we develop each of the seven dimensions of the worlds of meaning that are included in the previous complex image (Figure 2.1): physical environment, time, relationships, spirituality, vocation, language(s), and technology. Remember that each dimension is present in an individual's world of meaning, but the relative significance of each dimension can differ from person to person. And keep in mind that similarities and differences in ethical standards and cultural norms influence each dimension and the world of meaning as whole.

Earlier we noted that each dimension of your world of meaning can be viewed as an ellipse. You'll see that in the illustration above (Figure 2.2) of a single dimension there are two arrows pointing in opposite directions. Those arrows are meant to indicate tensionality. We'll get back to that concept in a moment. First, we'd like you to imagine that the ellipse on the page is elastic. Imagine that you could stretch it like a rubber band, making the ellipse larger or smaller, sometimes even distorting its shape. Each dimension of your world of meaning is individually in flux, if not fluid, then at least elastic. Your understanding of each dimension has developed and changed over your life time and will continue to be stretched and shaped by your interactions with others. No one dimension of your world of meaning is static.

And each dimension is tensional which takes us back to those arrows in the model of the single dimension. It is reasonable for you to be asking about now, "What do you mean by tensionality?" We're not talking about the pain of a tension headache, or the pressure of a tension rod to hold your shower curtain in place. Both these images do offer in-

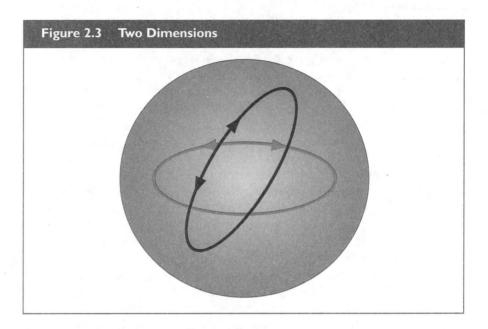

Figure 2.3   Two Dimensions

sight into what we are getting at, though. For most people, a tension headache consists of the sensation of pain pulling between the base of their neck and the top of their forehead. The tension rod in your bathroom stays on the walls because it simultaneously pushes out in opposite directions. What we're getting at with the word *tension* us that each dimension of your world of meaning is dynamic or in flux, and that understanding the whole requires paying attention to both ends at once. People who study humans agree, for example, that although each of us is born with primary sex characteristics, we are a blend of male and female. The most feminine woman has some male features and the most macho guy has some female features. Male and female are *in tension* in each of us.

Once you have a sense of one dimension as tensional, things get more complicated as additional dimensions come into play. For example, your understanding of your physical environment can be influenced by your relationships. If you live in a dorm room with someone you enjoy and respect, the space you share may seem more than enough. But, on the other hand, if you and your roommate don't get along, your room may feel cramped or even stifling. As you read about each of the seven dimensions in the next several pages, take some time to think about the ways that they are interconnected in your world of meaning.

Physical Environment. The first dimension (ellipse) we discuss is physical environment. Think for a minute about your world's physical environment. How big is your living space or your bedroom? How big would you *like* it to be? How cold or warm is it? How light or dark?

These are parts of the physical environment of your world, and there are many others. The meanings you have for hot and cold, light and dark are tensional in nature. Hot is understood in relation to cold, and this understanding is different for different people. For example, Karen's friends recently returned to Washington State from a trip to Arizona. They were amazed to hear people in Seattle complaining about the unbearable heat of 90 degrees. For them, 90 felt cool, since they were used to temperatures averaging 110 degrees. Light is also understood in relation to dark. If you live in Alaska, the land of the midnight sun, the meaning of dark differs dramatically between summer and winter. How crowded or roomy is the campus, neighborhood, or community where you're currently living? Do you think that everybody in this campus, neighborhood, or community believes it's as crowded or roomy as you do? This may well be one of the ways your world of meaning differs from those of others. When you think of a relative or family member who lives "a long way from here," how many kilometers or miles separate the two of you? (In other words, what does a long way from here *mean* to you?) Does everyone you know think of this distance in the same way? What are some communication events where the spatial parts of your world are particularly relevant? Looking for a place to live? Interviewing for a job? Negotiating with a roommate? Each of us inhabits a world that's partly spatial, and its meaning is built in communication.

There is also more to your environment than physical space. If you live in a war zone or in a part of the country with a large number of military installations and public venues that may be targets of terrorist attacks, your communicative world will be affected. If you live in a rural community with mountains and rivers in sight, the physical parts of your world of meaning are likely to be very different from that of someone who lives in a many-storied apartment building with hundreds of other people, views of other buildings, and elevated transit, as well as being surrounded by the sounds of the city.

Time. Time is another dimension of every person's world of meaning. Different individuals and cultures view time differently, and these differences are significant in shaping collaborative meaning. While a friend of ours was in the Peace Corps, she experienced dramatic differences in what it meant to meet someone "after lunch." Lisa made arrangements to meet a student enrolled in her English-language class after lunch on a Saturday. He had invited her to meet his family and she was eager to do so. She arrived at the place where they agreed to meet at 11:30 in the morning, so that she would not be late. Then she waited for several hours, growing more and more frustrated. She felt she was wasting her day off and that the student was very inconsiderate for not even leaving a message that he would be late. When he finally showed up, happy to see her and ready to take her to meet his family, he was surprised that she was annoyed. He had finished the midday meal with his family before rapidly walking several miles to town. He felt as if he had rushed to meet her. Obviously, their meanings for "after lunch" were very different.

What about your meaning of time? When you're put on hold on the telephone, how long are you willing to wait? How quickly do you feel it is necessary to respond to an e-mail message? How fast do you walk and talk, and does everybody walk and talk at the same speed you do? What time is "really early" in the morning for you, and what time is "really late" at night? What are some of the meanings of time in your culture? For example, if your boss at work asks to meet with you at 9 A.M., how late can you arrive before you have to apologize—9:03? 9:10? 9:20? How close in age do you believe intimate partners or spouses should ideally be? As you've matured, how has your sense of time changed? Is it easier to wait for something exciting than it used to be? What communicating has most affected these time-related parts of your world? When are the time dimensions of your world most relevant? When you plan a weekend with a friend? When you register for classes? When you make a commitment at work?

Relationships. It's easy to understand how important relationships are to creating meaning in a human's world. Each of us has been molded most of all by our relationships in our family of origin—the people we lived with in our early years. People's senses of themselves as women and men emerge in relationships with parents, as do our definitions of what it means to be a husband, mother, wife, and father. Children with many siblings inhabit a world that's different from the world of an only child. Family relationships are where we learn how to act—how to express (or hide) anger, deal with money, be polite, tell the truth and lie, work, and relax.

What is the difference in importance and intimacy between your relationship with your mom and the relationship with your dad? How are you affected by relationships with sisters or brothers? With grandparents? Godparents? What nonfamily relationship affected you most when you were growing up? How about in your life now? In what ways does your relationship with your roommate influence your relationships with others? If you're married or intimately partnered with someone, how does this relationship reflect the way you got along with your mom or dad?

Spirituality. For many people, spiritual or religious principles and practices also help shape their world. Identities, both individual and collective, are nurtured in relation to others who share your spiritual values and beliefs. They are also molded in contrast to others with different belief structures. Growing up Buddhist, Muslim, Jewish, Christian, or atheist will have an impact on your world of meaning. So will discovering and developing a spiritual journey as an adult. For many, the spiritual or religious dimension of their world influences the activities they engage in and the range of relationships in their lives. Are you

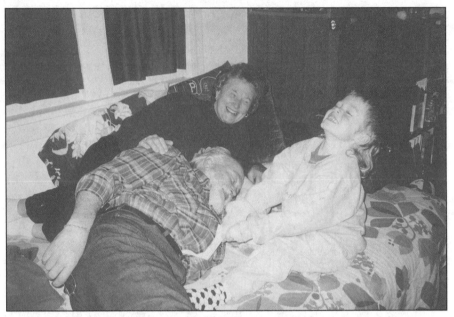

Logan's relationships with 'grammy and papa' help shape his world of meaning—and theirs.

likely to date or marry someone who does not share your spiritual views? What difference does it make if members of your family do not share your beliefs? What communicative practices—such as designated times for prayer, confession, and attending religious services—are encouraged and which are discouraged—dancing, drinking alcohol, premarital sex? How does your belief system influence your communication with others in your classes? Living groups? Work life?

Vocation. Most adults also inhabit a world of work, at least part of the time, and the worlds of these people can be strongly influenced by the tasks that occupy a major part of their day-to-day efforts. Not all people receive monetary compensation for their employment, however. Interns often work for the opportunity to learn about an interesting field and to make contacts for future employment. Some people volunteer their time to work in the public school system or for charitable organizations. Still others work one job so they can afford to live out their sense of vocational calling. Paid or unpaid, many people think of their work as a major part of who they *are* rather than simply something they *do*. So they introduce themselves with "I'm a stay-at-home mom," "I'm in real estate," "I work in construction," or "I'm at Microsoft." Family members' worlds are also affected by the work of primary breadwinners. Consider the differences between the worlds of the spouses and children of doctors, lawyers, accountants, and other professionals, on the one hand, and those of laborers, on the other.

Work affects our worlds in other ways, too. For example, the people who hire and supervise us in our first part-time and full-time jobs significantly affect our definitions of ourselves as competent, trustworthy, creative, and intelligent—or their opposites. In addition, work helps determine whom we spend time with. Some police officers complain that their work forces them into constant contact with people who are at their worst, nurses spend most of their time with people who are sick and needy, and summer jobs can require college students with grand intellectual ambitions to get along with career truck drivers.

Language(s). The language or set of languages you learn throughout your life has a profound effect on your world of meaning. The rules for grammar, words, and meaning of utterances differ from language to language and culture to culture. For example, German speakers understand the sun to be female and the moon male. In Spanish, though, the sun is *el sol* (masculine). To Saskia, whose first language was German, the sun means warmth and strength, two characteristics that are culturally attributed to women. Karen and John do not share Saskia's perception of the moon as male, but both relate to the fictionalized image of the "man in the moon." As you learn a second or third language, you learn another way of viewing and valuing the world you live in. Your language also influences the relationships you are likely to form and maintain. Although it is not impossible to communicate with someone who does not share linguistic and grammatical rules, it is challenging. This is because each organization and academic community has linguistic characteristics that are understood by members of the community and serve as boundaries to include some and exclude others.

Technology. Another dimension of each human's world of meaning is the technology that affects him or her. As the three of us work together on this edition of the book, we recognize how our own differences in technological proficiency influence our collaborative understanding of goals and ideas. For instance, Saskia is the most comfortable using what John and Karen would call *new media.* She has tried to coax John and Karen into the world of online editing and document sharing. Karen has recently mastered attaching and exchanging documents through e-mail and is improving her ability to edit at the computer. John still prefers to have hard copy of texts in front of him and to edit with pen in hand.

Think for a few minutes about how your world of meaning is shaped by technology. You may communicate with friends and family through e-mail on a regular basis. Does this mean that you don't write or receive letters through conventional mail? How many of you find that your course syllabus requires students to turn off cell phones and pagers? For many of you, surfing the Web was easier to learn than riding a bike. But for others, the idea of using a search engine to find information is as foreign as dialing 411 on a cell phone to find out times and locations of current movies or the closest Thai restaurant.

'But . . .' A Student Responds

If you say that we co-construct our worlds, then how come I have different worlds of meaning than the person sitting next to me in class—or even from other members of my family?

Your world of meaning is shaped by the interactions you have had with others and by your ethical commitments and cultural experiences. The person next to you may share some of these experiences, so it is likely that you have overlapping understanding. But each of you also has life experiences and responses to your environment that are unique. Growing up in the same family does not guarantee that your patterns of communication will match those of your sibling or your cousin. Living in the same community or going to the same school or synagogue cannot ensure that all the ways you collaborate with others to co-construct your worlds of meaning will be the same.

As you can tell from our description of these seven dimensions, human worlds are not objectively given but interpreted; they're not made up of objects but of peoples' *responses* to objects, which we're calling meanings.[2] And these meanings are negotiated in communication. Each of us develops a relatively whole sense of "reality" that we call our "world," and it can be thought of as made up of the physical environment, time, relationships, spirituality, vocation, language, and technology.

Rashad Versey, an African-American friend of John's from a rough urban neighborhood, applied this idea when, as a high-school peer counselor, he talked to friends about the power of what he calls their "mindset." When he was arrested for armed robbery, Rashad was shocked into seeing the difference between a mindset that gave him a world of hopelessness, hostility, and aggression, and a mindset that gave him a world marked by hope and ambition. He also recognized how he'd built his aggressive mindset (world) in his communication with hostile, hopeless, and aggressive friends. The most important parts of Rashad's mindset at the time were the physical environment (disrepair, litter, and crowding), relationships (older boys dared him to commit the robbery), and vocation (he couldn't figure out what to do with his life).

After Rashad's arrest and jail time, the objective features of his neighborhood and situation didn't change much. He still lived in a rough part of the community and continued to suffer from the racism of U.S. culture. But the way he *interpreted* these objective features— their *meaning*—did change. While he was out on bail, on trial, and even in jail, he spent time with people with hope and ambition, and this communicating helped change his world. He returned to school, and in his communication as a peer counselor, Rashad tried to be one of these people with hope and ambition so he could help change the mindset of others.

As with all of us, significant parts of Rashad's world were and are beyond his control. Each of us is born into a family, culture, language, physical setting, and set of gender patterns and power relationships that can be limiting and even abusive. Television, movies, computer games, and other media also affect how we see ourselves, define others, and interpret our experiences. But the responses we make that grow out of our communication with others also significantly determine the shape of our world. Rashad's message to high schoolers is that they can change the people they communicate with, and what and how they communicate, and this process can change what we are calling their "world."

Rashad's experience also highlights one more feature of each person's world—namely, that human worlds are *both partly stable and always changing*. Each dimension—space, time, relationships, etc.—has some solid features, *and* each is always in transition. For example, as we've already suggested, our senses of time and space change as we grow up. Patience is part of maturity (our sense of time changes as we get older), and spaces that looked huge when we were 5 or 6 years old seem smaller now. In addition, people pay attention to and learn various physical laws at different times of their lives, cultural identities shift, relationships grow and deteriorate, and our world of work is also continually in flux. We use the term *tensional* to label this feature. Our sense of space is both stable and changing; relationships are both predictable and frustratingly surprising; technology is both familiar in many ways and always new. Each dimension of your world of meaning is in tension between stability and change.

In Summary So Far

Humans live in worlds of meaning that are made up of at least seven dimensions: physical environment, time, relationships, spirituality, vocation, language(s), and technology.

Each human's world of meaning looks something like the figure to the right.

Communication is the process of collaboratively making these meanings.

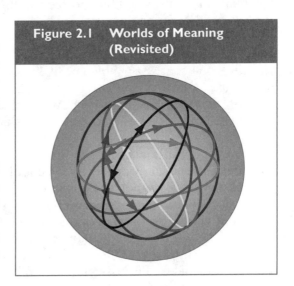

Figure 2.1   Worlds of Meaning (Revisited)

Implication 1: No One Person Can Completely Control a Communication Event, and No Single Person or Action Causes—or Can Be Blamed for—a Communication Outcome

This is the main implication of our first point, that humans live in tensional worlds of meaning that are collaboratively made in communication. Many people who take classes like the one you are enrolled in believe that it is their instructor's responsibility to teach them to "do it right." Understandably, they want to know how to *solve* the communication problems they experience—to get their parents off their backs; eliminate misunderstandings with roommates, coworkers, or dating partners; deal with a critical and complaining boss; end a painful relationship; or become a masterful salesperson. In the training workshops we lead it is not unusual for participants to want us to teach them the surefire techniques that will give them control over their communication lives. These people are disappointed, and some are even angry, when we tell them, "It isn't that simple" and "There's more to it than that." They are even more uncomfortable when we explain that it's an illusion to believe that such surefire techniques even exist! As philosopher William Barrett (1978) put it over 30 years ago in his book *The Illusion of Technique*, "Technical thinking cannot deal with our human problems."

We're obviously not saying that technical thinking is hopeless. We've developed the ideas in this book out of our own and others' research, teaching, and everyday experience, and they continually help us in the practicalities of our personal and professional lives. But one direct implication of the recognition that communication is a *collaborative* process is that no one person can completely control any communication event, and that no technique or set of communication moves can determine its outcome.

Regardless of how clearly I write or speak, you may still interpret me in a variety of different ways. Regardless of how carefully I plan a meeting, one or more people are likely to have agendas very different from mine. Even if I'm a successful dictator whose orders are consistently followed, I can't control how people respond verbally and nonverbally to my demands. And as we—Saskia, Karen, and John—know, even though we're relatively well-informed and skillful communicators, we still experience problems in our relationships with family members, friends, coworkers, and acquaintances, difficulties that we cannot completely predict or control.

We believe that your development as a communicator will be enhanced if you try to manage your expectations about control and perfection. The more you understand how communication works and the more communication skills you develop, the more effective and competent you will be. It is possible to learn how to give and take criticism gracefully, to manage conflict effectively, and to develop relationships smoothly. But not 100 percent of the time. Hugh Prather put it very well when he wrote these lines:

> *Ideas are clean.*
> *They soar in the serene supernal.*
> *I can take them out and look at them,*
> *they fit in books, they lead me down that narrow way.*
> *And in the morning they are*
> *there. Ideas are straight—*
> *But the world is round, and a*
> *messy mortal is my friend.*
> *Come walk with me in the mud.*
> (Prather 1970)

As we have already mentioned, cause-effect, fault-blame thinking is one of the oversimplifications people often fall into. One implication of the view of communication developed and applied in this book is that, when thinking and communicating about communication, we need to give up our comfortable reliance on linear causality and the accompanying constructs of "fault" and "blame."

Problems obviously happen in communication, and the choices and actions of the people involved help create, maintain, worsen, and solve these problems. But when you understand that communication is *continuous, complex,* and *collaborative,* you cannot coherently blame one person or one set of actions for the problem. For one thing, fault and blame ignore the continuousness of communication. In order to say someone is "at fault," you need to assume that whatever happened began with the guilty person's action. But all the people involved have been engaged in communication literally since before they were born and have developed and reinforced each other's ways of speaking, listening, and interpreting since at least the time they met. In order to assign fault, you have to ignore or set aside all this history of continuous communicating. So the person who you say is at fault because he didn't call you back to confirm the meeting may be remembering your complaints about "getting all those annoying calls" and your insistence that it's only necessary to call if meeting plans change.

Fault and blame also ignore the fact that communication is collaborative. When directions are unclear, for example, it's due to both the direction-giver and the direction-receiver. Did the receiver ask about what confused her? Did the giver check the receiver's understanding? It may have seemed perfectly legitimate to one person to assume that everybody understood that the meeting was at 8 P.M. and not 8 A.M., for example, or that the entire work team should be told about the policy change, or that the family would gather for the holiday dinner just like they had in the past. But others might have radically different assumptions that lead to significantly different interpretations.

Does this mean that when there are problems, "nobody's responsible"? Have we given up any possibility of accountability? No, not at all.

Individual responses still make a difference, and some are definitely more ethical, culturally appropriate, and humane than others. But we are trying to replace the oversimplified and distorted notions of fault and blame with a broader focus on both or all sides of the communication process. We do not mean to replace "It's his fault" with "It's her fault," "It's both of their faults," or "It's nobody's fault." Instead, we encourage you to give up the notion of fault altogether, at least when you're thinking or talking about human communication.

'But . . .' A Student Responds

If we give up fault and blame as you suggest, how are we supposed to hold anyone accountable for their actions? People need to be able to know who's to blame so that the guilty can be punished, and so we can ensure that bad stuff won't happen again.

This is another question that we could discuss for a long time! We are not suggesting that people are not accountable for their actions, but that fault and blame are generally unproductive communication strategies in relationships. Also, since communication is an ongoing and responsive process, it is difficult if not impossible to figure out how far back to go when assessing blame or determining who is at fault.

Even our legal system assesses partial responsibility to a variety of sources when something illegal or tragic happens. Take the Enron collapse as one example. While there are a lot of people blaming one another, it is difficult to determine who is most responsible for the corporate wrongdoings. Is the blame to be placed on the CEO? On the accounting firm? On Congress for creating laws with so many loopholes? On the individuals who didn't monitor their investments? On the companies and lenders who negotiated deals with Enron? And how about a plane crash resulting from a broken part? Who is at fault? The pilot? The maintenance crew? The airline? The company that built the airline? While the legal system does help assess degrees of accountability and impose punishment for choices that break the law or result in tragedy, and victims may feel that a sense of justice has prevailed, placing fault and blame does nothing to restore relationships or ensure that these practices will not happen again.

Applying What You Know

Your Picture of Communication

Think about your last disagreement with someone. Did either of you treat it as somebody's fault? Whose?

Did the two of you agree about whose fault it was?

Here's the most important question: *How did the assignment of fault contribute to resolving the disagreement?*

What, if anything, does this experience tell you about fault and blame?

Our point is, since communication is a collaborative activity, no one person can be held individually accountable for the meanings that are co-constructed. If you choose to reframe your accounts of interactions in such a way that fault and blame are not part of the equation, we believe that your communication with others will be less contentious and more productive.

---

2. Choice: All communication involves choices, some of which people actively consider, and others that follow cultural norms and seem almost automatic.

Human worlds are inherently ethical because they involve choices. Individually and collectively, humans create and abide by guidelines for evaluating actions as right or wrong, good or bad, and appropriate or inappropriate. These ethical standards influence people's actions but do not always determine them. In the next chapter we develop the idea that interpersonal communication involves reflective and responsive choices. At this point, we want to emphasize that, because humans are ethical beings, they are capable of making choices and that these choices reflect and affect their worlds of meaning.

Some of the choices people make each day don't feel much like choices. For example, shaking hands and bowing are two culturally influenced actions that one may choose to engage in when meeting another person for a business lunch. Although decisions about how long or firmly to shake a hand or how deep a bow is appropriate for this particular person's status, may be a choice you actively consider, the initial behavior of shaking or bowing may not. You may not actively choose the tone you use with your sibling in the same way you may consider how to talk with your best friend, because the norms for interaction in your family culture may be taken for granted but not in your friendship. If you are a member of the Deaf culture, you may not think anything about communicating in sign language, but if you are a hearing person who encounters a group of hearing-impaired tourists, you might actively consider your mode of communicating.

Implication 2: The Choices Communicators Make Reveal Their Ethical Standards and Commitments

Take the issue of stealing food from the local grocery store, for example. Many people admit to shoplifting a candy bar as a kid—a choice made for the thrill, as a response to peer pressure, or just because they wanted one and didn't have any money at the time. They might have had an ethical standard that stealing was wrong and another competing standard that said that adrenaline rushes, fitting in with friends, or immediate gratification was good. They had to make a choice between competing standards, and in this case the "stealing is wrong" ethic carried less weight. Other people cannot understand how anyone could ever decide to steal. They have never considered swiping anything— ever! For these people, the stealing-is-wrong ethical standard is more heavily weighted, perhaps in response to explicit lessons from family, teachers, or a religious community. But whether you would or would not have stolen something from a grocery store, how would you evaluate an individual who had been unemployed for months, exhausted the limited resources of the local food bank, and decided that the only way members of her family would eat today would be if she took a loaf of bread and a jar of peanut butter without paying for them? In this case, is stealing right or wrong? A good or bad choice? An appropriate or inappropriate action?

Our point is that there are always competing forces in our lives, and that part of what it means to be human is to make meaningful choices between them. If communication is a collaboratively constructed activity, no one individual has complete control over its outcome. All of our choices are made within the context of our personal experience and are evaluated in accordance with cultural norms and expectations. And, standards for evaluation (assessment of our values) can differ from person to person, family to family, and culture to culture over time.

> **3. Culture: Culture and communication are intertwined. Ethnicity, gender, age, social class, sexual orientation, and other cultural features always affect communication and are affected by it.**

When many people think about culture, they envision a group's customs, cooking, and clothing, but there's much more to it than that. In a very general sense, culture provides you with means to make meaning in your life worlds. One way to talk about culture is to say that *culture means shared norms, values, and beliefs related to how people live and how people communicate verbally and nonverbally with each other.* These shared values, norms, and beliefs influence how people communicate in their relationships, how people talk about time and their work, or how they view communication technology. As we said earlier, culture is a central element of the cosmos in which our worlds of meaning are socially constructed. Dating, for example, is one context in which the ways culture and communication are intertwined can be observed. In some cultures, dating is a means to an end—a way to select a life partner. And who you date is your business—you don't need parental or community permission or approval. In other cultures, however, it would be inappropriate to bring someone home to meet the folks. The "folks"—parents, community members, or tribal leaders will have already made arrangements for marriage and the concept of dating to determine compatibility is not part of the broader picture. In either case, cultural norms influence the kinds of communication possible and preferable with both family members and dating partners.

When you think about culture as a way of meaning making, you'll realize that culture is much more than just national identity, that is, being U.S. American or French or German. *People who share ways of living and speaking* can belong to different ethnic groups (Arabs, African Americans, Latinas or Asian Americans) and also be part of the same national group (citizen of the Unites States). Likewise, people can belong to cultural groups associated with religion and/or groups defined by members' sexual orientation. Contemporary communication theory underscores that studies of culture should not focus on just one feature—like ethnicity—but should consider "interlocking and overlapping modes of identity" (Moon, 1996). Such an understanding of culture helps to illustrate how two members of the same family (a heterosexual brother and his lesbian sister) inhabit different cultures, and thus different worlds of meaning.

What we want you to understand is that culture becomes manifest or concrete mainly in a group's *ways of communicating*. Cultures are marked primarily by special ways of speaking, verbal and nonverbal, including terms for important things and people, ways of being polite or resolve conflicts, use of formal or informal terms of address, use of silence, specific attire and adornments, gestures, ways of touching, and so on. Silence, for example, is important in Apache culture. Many Apache ridicule white men because they talk so often, so loudly, and so much (Basso 1992).

Which cultural groups do you identify with? Ethnic groups? Groups with particular sexual orientations? Groups that are characterized by their physical abilities? Social class? Gender? Religious groups? The three of us share cultural identities as teacher-scholars, middle-class, gendered heterosexuals. John and Karen share identities of English-speaking, married, parents, raised in the Pacific Northwest of the United States, while Saskia is multilingual and was raised in East Germany. We span three different generations, and one of us is a grandparent, one a preacher's kid, and one was socialized in a musician's family. Our cultural experiences and identities, along with the values cultivated within each of our cultural groupings, are continually being worked out in the way we live. And as we negotiate these tensions we constitute and re-constitute our worlds of meanings. Each cultural feature has emerged and taken on its meaning for us as we have communicated with the people who've helped define us. Sometimes these as-

What might it mean to belong to this culture and to engage in these activities together? Notice, among other things, dress, gender, and seating arrangement.

pects of our world stay in the background, but they are none-the-less central parts of our communicating.

Especially today, with the increasing globalization of sports, music, media, business, education, and religion; with the explosion of international communication via the internet and the World Wide Web; and with the growing recognition among managers that diversity in organizations is a strength rather than a threat, culture is on almost everybody's mind. This is partly why we make the point that culture figures prominently in communication.

But there is a more basic reason: As we've already said, culture becomes concrete in communication. The shared ways of living can be observed in a group's way of relating to each other—that is, in their communicating. What it *means* to belong to a culture is to communicate in certain ways—as we said, to use certain expressions that members of other cultures don't use, to honor certain styles of speaking, to maintain certain distances, to touch certain ways, and so on (Gudykunst, Ting-Toomey, and Chua 1988).

Implication 3: Your Cultures—and Ours—Affect What We Say About Communication in This Book and How You Respond to It

Throughout this book, we'll be describing implications of this point. For example, when we discuss the verbal and nonverbal features of talk, we'll identify some ways cultures differ in their vocabulary, gestures, vocal inflections, and touching patterns. When we describe how identities are constructed in conversation, we'll be noting differences between male and female gender identities. When we discuss conflict, we'll identify some cultural differences in conflict management styles.

Importantly for us as textbook writers—and for you as our readers—our culture is present in our communicating, too. And this is especially true because this textbook is not about calculus, chemistry, or biology but about communication, through which cultures are socially constructed.

We've already identified several of our cultural identities. We did that in part to help you think of some of your cultural identities but also to help you understand that our communication content and style in this book will embody these cultural features (and potentially others we may not be aware of). If you identify yourself culturally as different from us in any one or more of these ways, you may legitimately ask, "How's this book relevant to me? If culture and communication are so intertwined, what can I—an African American, perhaps, or Latino, 20-year-old, gay or lesbian, engineering or chemistry student—learn from this book?"

Enough, we hope, to keep you reading. We're going to offer some knowledge and skills about communication that are supported by evidence from a variety of cultures, and we're going to speak from our position in some cultures with fairly large memberships and wide ranges of influence. If you are not a member of one or more of the cultures we belong to, this text can still be useful to you in at least two ways: (1) You can test the generalizations we make against your experience in your own cultures to determine which apply both here and there, and (2) when the points we make *don't* apply in one or more of your cultures, you can use them to enhance your ability to communicate with people in the cultures we inhabit.

For example, our first three claims about human communication are that humans live in worlds of meaning that are constructed in communicating, that ethical choices matter, and that culture figures prominently in all communication. We believe that there is ample evidence to demonstrate that these points are true about all people in all cultures. Do you? We encourage you to test them against your own experience and to discuss the results with your instructor and classmates. At various points in the book we will make similarly broad generalizations about communication, and we encourage you to test them, too.

On the other hand, when we discuss nonverbal communication, we will say that in *our* cultures (Karen's, John's, and Saskia's), there are no positive meanings for too little eye contact. The meaning of too little may vary, but whenever people notice that someone is not looking them in the eye "enough," they will infer something negative—that the person is lying, frightened, distracted, shy, or something else. This may not be exactly the way it works in one or more of the cultures you belong to. You may have learned that it is disrespectful to look a superior in the eye, or that direct eye contact is reserved for intimates. If so, combine your understanding of your own culture with what we say about ours and use this knowledge about eye contact in our cultures to enhance your ability to communicate outside your own culture with people in some of the cultures we inhabit.

And notice that you can do this without being coopted. If you feel culturally different from us, you don't have to give up your distinctiveness to profit from what's here. You can operate like a global businessperson. People who have to serve customers or work with producers outside their own cultures routinely learn how to adapt to these other cultures, but from their own position of strength—as a representative of their business. These people want to do business in another culture, so their adaptation is based on that foundation; it doesn't mean that their values or morals are coopted. Regardless of the culture you enter or the adaptations you may choose to make, you can do so from a position of confidence and strength.

> **4. Identities: Some of the most important meanings people collaboratively construct are identities. All communicating involves negotiating identities or selves.**

As worlds of meaning are collaboratively constructed in communication, so are identities. Communication theorist and teacher John Shotter emphasizes how our

> ways of being, our "selves," are produced in our . . .ways of interrelating ourselves to each other—these are the terms in which we are socially accountable in our society—and these "traditional" or "basic" (dominant) ways of talking are productive of our "traditional" or "basic" psychological and social [identities]. (Shotter 1993, 180)

In other words, who people are—their identities—gets built in communicating. We come to each encounter with an identifiable "self," but it has been developed in communication and, *as we talk*, we adapt ourselves to fit the topic we're discussing and the people we're talking with, and we are changed by what happens to us as we communicate.

The way communication and identity are closely related became especially apparent in a conversation John had with a friend who was going through a painful divorce. "Mary Kay is not the person she used to be," Dale said. "Sometimes I hardly know her. I wish we could communicate and enjoy each other like we did when we were first married."

The times Dale was remembering were before Mary Kay was a mother, before she completed medical school, before she suffered through her residency in an urban hospital 2,000 miles from home, before she joined a prestigious medical clinic, and before she became a full-fledged practicing physician. They were also before Dale was a dad, before he started his import-export business, before he became active in his state professional association, and before he began attending church regularly. Dale was forgetting that Mary Kay could not possibly still be "the person she used to be." Neither could he. Both of them have experienced many relationships that have changed them decisively. Mary Kay has been treated like a medical student—required to cram scientific information into her head and spout it on command—and like a first-year resident—forced to go without sleep, stand up to authoritarian doctors, and cope with hospital administrators. Now nurses obey her, many patients admire her for her skills, and prestigious doctors treat her like an equal. Plus she's treated as a mom by her son. Dale has also experienced many different relationships, and he's changed, too. He's treated as a boss by his employees and as "a respected American businessman" by his Japanese customers. Because of the contacts both have experienced, each is a different person. And the process continues as both Mary Kay and Dale continue to be changed by their communication.

Obviously, these identity changes are limited. Most people don't change their gender or ethnicity. But some changes are inevitable over time, and others can happen in the short term. For example, a woman can communicate in ways that say she is more feminine—or more masculine—than her conversation partner, and as a person with greater or less authority or power than her conversation partner has. The other person's responses will contribute to the identity as it's negotiated verbally and nonverbally.

Consider the difference, for example, between "Shut the door, stupid!" and "Please close the door." The command implies the identity of a superior speaking to a subordinate. On the other hand, the request identifies the speaker as an equal to the person being addressed. The person who's told to "Shut the door, stupid!" may silently comply, in which case he or she is reinforcing part of the speaker's identity. Or the person may respond, "Shut it yourself!" which is a different negotiation move. This response says, in effect, "I don't agree with or accept the identity you're claiming. You're not my superior; we're equals."

Many treatments of communication have missed or underemphasized the identity-construction part of human communication. These books and articles treated the process of communication as if it mainly consisted of transmitting ideas, content, or information. When "selves" were discussed, they were treated as static entities that communicators brought with them into their contacts, where they were hid or revealed. Many communication researchers now see selves as primarily constructed in communicating (Davies and Harré 1992). We say more about this in Chapter Four.

Implication 4: Identity Issues Are Always in Play

The practical implication of the fourth point is that whenever you communicate—on the telephone, via e-mail, face-to-face, in meetings, even in front of the television—part of what is happening is identity negotiation. In other words, *identity-negotiation or the collaborative construction of selves is going on whenever people communicate.* It isn't the *only* thing that's happening, but it's one of the very important processes, and it often gets overlooked. When it does, as we'll explain in later chapters, troubles usually result. By contrast, people who are aware of relationship messages and identity-negotiation processes can communicate more effectively and successfully in many different situations.

Communication content is important too, and sometimes problems can be solved only when the parties involved have more or better information. Policies may be out of date, data may be incomplete, and people may have misread or misheard key instructions. In these cases, the people involved may need to complete, refine, or recalibrate the information they're working with.

But as we noted, effective communicators understand and manage what they're verbally and nonverbally "saying" about *who they are* to the people they're communicating with. Grooming and dress obviously contribute to this process, as people offer definitions of themselves using nose rings and other body piercing, colorful tattoos, starched white shirts or blouses, and conservative business suits. Tone of voice and facial expressions are also identity-defining. Some people foster misunderstanding by unknowingly sounding like they're skeptical, hostile, or bored, and facial expressions can help define a person as attentive, careful, positive, or their opposites.

Especially when you're troubleshooting—or just trying to live through—a disagreement or conflict, it usually works best to start by understanding the identities that are in play. By the time you've worked through this book, you should have a wealth of ideas and practical skills for constructively managing how you define yourself and how others define you.

---

5. Conversation: The most influential communication events are conversations.

If you had to identify one event that humans all over the world engage in characteristically—because they're humans—routinely, naturally, and almost constantly, what would it be? We all breathe, but so do other animals. We eat and drink, but not constantly, and again, other animals do too. The one activity that marks us as human and that occupies, in one form or another, a large part of our personal and occupational lives is conversation, verbal and nonverbal exchange in real time, either face-to-face or mediated by some electronic medium (e.g., the telephone).

For a long time, people who studied communication and language tended to overlook this point. Language scholars focused on rules of grammar and syntax, dictionary definitions, and other features of writing, and speech research and teaching paid primary attention to public speaking and deliberation in law courts and legislatures. But in the last half of the twentieth century, an increasing number of scholars and teachers have shown how written and formal kinds of communicating are derived from the most basic human activity, informal conversation. Recently, for example, two well-known psychologists from Stanford University began a report of their National Science Foundation-supported research with the following words:

> Conversation is the fundamental site of language use. For many people, even for whole societies, it is the only site, and it is the primary one for children acquiring language. From this perspective other arenas of language use—novels, newspapers, lectures, street signs, rituals—are derivative or secondary. (Clark and Wilkes-Gibbs 1986, 1)

Another respected scholar puts it more simply. "Conversation," he writes, "is sociological bedrock" (Schegloff 1995, 186–187), the absolute foundation or base for everything humans do as social beings. This explains the sense of the title of one of communication theorist John Shotter's (1993) books, *Conversational Realities: Constructing Life Through Language*. Shotter's book explains in detail how human realities get constructed in communication—our point 1, above—and emphasizes that the most characteristic form of this communication is *conversation*. Some of the largest companies in the United States have also profited from the services of Susan Scott, author of the best-selling book, *Fierce Conversations: Achieving Success at Work and in Life, One Conversation at a Time* (Scott 2002). Scott emphasizes that "Business is fundamentally an extended conversation . . . What gets talked about in a company and how it gets talked about determines what will happen." And if you're tempted to think that conversations at work are just "small talk," realize this: "While no single conversation is guaranteed to change the trajectory of a career, a company, a relationship or a life, any single conversation can" (Scott 2003, C2).

Implication 5: The Most Ordinary Communication Events Are the Most Significant

The reason we highlight this idea as one of the six main points we make about human communication is that it justifies paying close attention to something common and ordinary. The fact that humans engage in conversation so constantly, and so often almost without thinking, is part of what makes the process so important. Along with Susan Scott, organizational theorist and trainer Peter Senge and his coauthors argue that effective conversation is "the single greatest learning tool in your organization—more important than computers or sophisticated research" (1994, 14). Whether in a living group, a family-run shop, a small work team, or a multinational corporation, the real organizational structure and rules—as contrasted with what's on the organizational chart—get defined in the subtleties of verbal and nonverbal conversation. Superior and subordinate status get negotiated in face-to-face contacts. Key decisions are heavily influenced by brief informal contacts in the bathrooms and halls as much as they are by formal presentations in meetings. And when the organization needs to change and there are feelings about rights or two worthwhile principles in conflict, the only options available are some form of authoritarianism or some form of problem-solving conversation. Similarly, conversation is the primary way families have of making decisions and negotiating differences. And children become effective participants in play groups, classrooms, sports teams, and their own families by learning how to converse well.

We believe, in short, that one very important way to improve your communication competence is to pay close attention to the most common, everyday kind of communicating—conversation. When you do, you'll discover that you already have a great deal of experience with many of the concepts and skills this book discusses. This means that you have a solid foundation to build on. Even if you don't believe you're very good at conversation, you've done it often and well enough, and it's going on around you so much, that you can build on the experiences you have.

> **6. Nexting: The most important single communication skill is 'nexting.'**

Nexting is a strange term, we admit. But it's the best one we've come up with for the skill we have in mind. If, as you read this book, you come up with a better one, please let us know.

By "nexting" we mean doing something helpful next, responding fruitfully to what's just happened, taking an additional useful step in the communication process. If you've grasped how we've described communication in this chapter, this is the most important single skill you can build on this understanding. Here's why:

Since you realize that communication is complex, continuous, and collaborative, you'll always recognize that, no matter what's happened before and no matter how bad things currently look, you always have the option to take a fruitful *next* step. No matter how many times the same insult has been repeated, the next response can be creative rather than retaliatory. No matter how long the parties have not been speaking to each other, the next time they meet, one of them could speak. No matter how ingrained and toxic the pattern is that two groups are caught in, the next move one side makes could be positive. No matter how much you feel "thrown" by what the other person just said and did, if you give yourself a little time to regroup, you can make a next move that could help get the relationship back on track. No matter how little power the system gives you, your next communication choice can maximize the power you have. Even when it is very difficult not to strike back, your next comment could conceivably be encouraging rather than abusive. Conversely, no matter how well things are going, the next communication move can introduce a problem. No matter how smooth the water, people's next responses can help make it rough.

When you understand that communication is continuous and collaborative, you'll recognize the potential value of what you do next. Why? Because since no one person determines all the outcomes of a communication event, you can help determine some outcomes, even if you feel almost powerless. Since no one person is 100 percent to blame or at fault, and all parties share accountability, your next contribution can affect what's happening. Since all communication is collaborative—remember, even prizefighters are co-labor-ating—your next communication move can make a change in the situation.

As our friend John Angus Campbell puts it, this understanding of communication can help you carry around the constant recognition that "history isn't over yet." You and the people you're communicating with are continually constructing (modifying, adding to, deconstructing) your worlds, and this means that the *next* actions can be as influential and powerful as the best and worst of the previous actions. Just as no playing of the World Series or the Super Bowl finishes the games of baseball or football, no communication move permanently defines a situation or a relationship.

Implication 6: Whenever You Face a Communication Challenge or Problem, the Most Useful Question You Can Ask Yourself Is, 'What Can I Help to Happen Next?'

You can apply the skill of nexting by refusing to believe that any human system is ever cast in stone. Regardless of how well things are going between you and someone else, remember that what you do next will help maintain or destroy the relationship. Regardless of how badly things are going between your group and another, you can look for something positive to do next.

If you were the state police officer, what would be your most likely next response? Can you imagine a nexting move that could shift this contact from confrontation to conversation?

It almost goes without saying that in some cases you may not *want* to try to improve a bad situation or to maintain a good one. You may have tried to make positive contributions and have been continually rebuffed, and you may be out of patience, resources, or caring. You may in this particular case decide not to make a positive, supportive, or conciliatory move. You may also decide to let silence remain, to keep your distance, or to let the hostility fester. These are examples of nexting, too. But if you remember how communication works to construct human worlds, you can understand these options for what they are—*responses*, choices, decisions about what you are going to do *next*. They have their benefits and their consequences, just as other responses do.

To put it simply, people who understand communication to be the kind of process we've outlined in this chapter are not generally thrown off balance by communication difficulties. They understand that the most important thing to consider is what they are going to do *next*.

'But . . .' A Student Responds

The idea of going directly to "nexting" when you are in the middle of difficult communication seems kind of weird to me. And I'm sure that my friends and family would think I was a little crazy if I asked them to stop for a minute while I think about what do to next. Shouldn't I just think about the situation and make a plan or develop a strategy beforehand?

It *is* important to be thoughtful and to plan ahead. On the other hand, in a real-time situation (face-to-face or on the telephone, for example), time marches on whether we do or not. A long pause will be perceived as your "next" move, even if you're using the pause to plan or strategize. In order to clarify what's happening, you might want to frame the pause with something like, "Okay, let's figure out together what we can do next." In this chapter, our main point about nexting is that you adopt the attitude or perspective that, no matter what's happened up to this point, something different can still happen next, and you can help it to happen.

Another way to put this point is to say that this view of communication redefines what "responsibility" means. Traditionally, being responsible means that you *caused* something to happen, that it was your "fault." But from this book's perspective, responsibility means *ability to respond*, not taking fault, blame, or credit. It means *response-ability*. You are response-able when you have the willingness and the ability to contribute in some way to how things are unfolding, rather than ignoring what's going on or dropping out of the event. "Irresponsible" people are not responsive; they act without taking into account what else is going on or how their actions may affect others. Responsible (response-able) actions consider the larger wholes that they help make up. As you will see in the next chapter, the notion of response-ability is related to the basic skill of nexting.

Chapter Summary

This chapter describes the general process of communicating. We start by noting that communication is a general term used to label the process through which humans collaboratively construct meaning. We make the point that humans don't live in worlds of objects but in worlds of meaning, more or less coherent spheres of understanding or sense that develop throughout our lives. Then we further define communication as the continuous, complex, collaborative process of verbal and nonverbal meaning-making, the process humans use to construct and modify our worlds.

We describe seven dimensions of the worlds of meaning that humans construct in communication—physical environment, time, relationships, spirituality, vocation, language(s), and technology. We note that each of these dimensions is tensional, which means that each is both stable and changing. We offer a figure of a sphere made up of seven ellipses with arrows on them to model, or graphically represent, these ideas. This model emphasizes the points that human worlds of sense can be thought of as made up of at least seven dimensions; that these are worlds of meaning; that the meanings are tensional; that these worlds are inherited, constructed, modified, and molded in communication; and that ethics and culture overlay the whole picture. One main implication of this set of ideas is that no one person can completely control any communication event and that the causal notions of fault and blame can't accurately be applied to humans communicating.

Our second point is that all communication involves choices between competing ethical standards. Some of the choices are made after reflection and others seem more instinctive or automatic. In either case, there are always competing forces in play, and part of being human is making meaningful choices between them.

Our next point is that culture figures prominently in all communicating. We explain that culture means much more than ethnicity and that each of us can have multiple cultural identities. We also discuss how you might respond to what's here if you experience yourself as culturally different from us. The implication we emphasize is that culture is affecting what we write in this book and how you read and respond to it.

The fourth main point we make about communication is that it always involves co-constructing identities or selves. Every time people communicate, they are verbally and nonverbally offering definitions of themselves and responding to the ways others define them. This isn't the *only* thing that's going on when humans communicate, but it's a very important process that many discussions of communication overlook. You'll hear much more about it in Chapter Four.

We also say that the most influential communication events are conversations. Our point is that this everyday, common experience we all have—of exchanging ideas with others face-to-face or on the telephone or e-mail—is what one author called sociological bedrock and can thus be the anchor experience for a study of interpersonal communication. Even though it's common, it's important and can be taken seriously—thought about and studied. There's lots to learn *from* and *about* everyday conversation.

Finally, we say that if you think of communication in the ways we talk about in this chapter, you can see that the single most important communication skill is what we call nexting. Since communication is complex, continuous, and collaborative, the most useful response to any difficult or problematic communication situation is the question "What can I do next?"

In Other Words

In the next couple of pages, you will be introduced to Lia Lee and her family. Lia is the child of a Hmong father and Hmong mother who lived in Merced, California, at the time when the text was written. They came to the United States from Laos in 1980 as refugees. Historically, Hmong people have populated the mountainous regions of southeastern China, Vietnam, Laos, and Thailand. Many Hmong, like the Lee family, escaped from Laos after 1975 when the country became controlled by communist forces and lived in a Thai refugee camp before coming to the United States. Lia Lee was born in the United States and diagnosed with epilepsy when she was a baby. This excerpt talks about Lia's first episode of epilepsy and introduces you to some of the beliefs and values of Hmong culture, such as the meanings attached to epilepsy, shamanism or child rearing practices. We can only show you a brief excerpt here but if you are interested in more, we suggest that you read the whole fascinating book. The author, Anne Fadiman, spent many months in the late 1980's with the Lee family. In the rest of the book she describes some of the conflicts between the worldviews of the Hmong family and those of the US doctors, particularly as these worldviews affect decisions about how to treat Lia's epilepsy.

After reading this excerpt, you should have a better idea what we mean when we say that people live in "worlds of meanings." You should be able to respond to the following questions:

1. What are some dimensions of worlds of meanings of the Hmong family that strike you most? Pick at least two.

2. How are the meanings that these dimensions have for the Hmong family similar to or different from the meanings that they have for you?

3. What are some of your cultural assumptions about such illnesses as epilepsy that contrast with assumptions that the Hmong family make about this illness?

✳ ✳ ✳

The Spirit Catches You and You Fall Down

Anne Fadiman

When Lia was about three months old, her older sister Yer slammed the front door of the Lees' apartment. A few moments later, Lia's eyes rolled up, her arms jerked over her head, and she fainted. The Lees had little doubt what had happened. Despite the careful installation of Lia's soul during the *hu plig* ceremony, the noise of the door had been so profoundly frightening that her soul had fled her body and become lost. They recognized the resulting symptoms as *qaug dab peg*, which means "the spirit catches you and you fall down." The spirit referred to in this phrase is a soul-stealing *dab*; *peg* means to catch or hit; and *qaug* means to fall over with one's roots still in the ground, as grain might be beaten down by wind or rain.

In Hmong-English dictionaries, *qaug dab peg* is generally translated as epilepsy. It is an illness well known to the Hmong, who regard it with ambivalence. On the one hand, it is acknowledged to be a serious and potentially dangerous condition. Tony Coelho, who was Merced's congressman from 1979 to 1989, is an epileptic. Coelho is a popular figure among the Hmong, and a few years ago, some local Hmong men were sufficiently concerned when they learned he suffered from *qaug dab peg* that they volunteered the services of a shaman, a *txiv neeb*, to perform a ceremony that would retrieve Coelho's errant soul. The Hmong leader to whom they made this proposition politely discouraged them, suspecting that Coelho, who is a Catholic of Portuguese descent, might not appreciate having chickens, and maybe a pig as well, sacrificed on his behalf.

On the other hand, the Hmong consider *qaug dab peg* to be an illness of some distinction. This fact might have surprised Tony Coelho no less than the dead chickens would have. Before he entered politics, Coelho planned to become a Jesuit priest, but was barred by a canon forbidding the ordination of epileptics. What was considered a disqualifying impairment by Coelho's church might have been seen by the Hmong as a sign that he was particularly fit for divine office. Hmong epileptics often become shamans. Their seizures are thought to be evidence that they have the power to perceive things other people cannot see, as well as facilitating their entry into trances, a prerequisite for their journeys into the realm of the unseen. The fact that they have been ill themselves gives them an intuitive sympathy for the suffering of others and lends them emotional credibility as healers. Becoming a *txiv neeb* is not a choice; it is a vocation. The calling is revealed when a person falls sick, either with *qaug dab peg* or with some other illness whose symptoms similarly include shivering and pain. An established *txiv neeb*, summoned to diagnose the problem, may conclude from these symptoms that the person (who is usually but not always male) has been chosen to be the host of a healing spirit, a *neeb*. (*Txiv neeb* means "person with a healing spirit.") It is an offer that the sick person cannot refuse, since if he rejects his vocation, he will die. In any case, few Hmong would choose to decline. Although shamanism is an arduous calling that requires years of training with a master in order to learn the ritual techniques and chants, it confers an enormous amount of social status in the community and publicly marks the *txiv neeb* as a person of high moral character, since a healing spirit would never choose a no-account host. Even if an epileptic turns out not to be elected to host a *neeb*, his illness, with its thrilling aura of the supramundane, singles him out as a person of consequence.

In their attitude toward Lia's seizures, the Lees reflected this mixture of concern and pride. The Hmong are known for the gentleness with which they treat their children. Hugo Adolf Bernatzik, a German ethnographer who lived with the Hmong of Thailand for several years during the 1930s, wrote that the Hmong he had studied regarded a child as "the most treasured possession a person can have." In Laos, a baby was never apart from its mother, sleeping in her arms all night and riding on her back all day. Small children were rarely abused; it was believed that a *dab* who witnessed mistreatment might take the child, assuming it was not wanted. The Hmong who live in the United States have continued to be unusually attentive parents. A study conducted at the University of Minnesota found Hmong infants in the first month of life to be less irritable and more securely attached to their mothers than Caucasian infants, a difference the researcher attributed to the fact that the Hmong mothers were, without exception, more sensitive, more accepting, and more responsive, as well as "exquisitely attuned" to their children's signals. Another study, conducted in Portland, Oregon, found that Hmong mothers held and touched their babies far more frequently than Caucasian mothers. In a third study, conducted at the Hennepin County Medical Center in Minnesota, a group of Hmong mothers of toddlers surpassed a group of Caucasian mothers of similar socioeconomic status in every one of fourteen categories selected from the Egeland Mother-Child Rating Scale, ranging from "Speed of Responsiveness to Fussing and Crying" to "Delight."

Foua and Nao Kao had nurtured Lia in typical Hmong fashion (on the Egeland Scale, they would have scored especially high in Delight), and they were naturally distressed to think that anything might compromise her health and happiness. They therefore hoped, at least most of the time, that the *qaug dab peg* could be healed. Yet they also considered the illness an honor. Jeanine Hilt, a social worker who knew the Lees well, told me, "They felt Lia was kind of an anointed one, like a member of royalty. She was a very special person in their culture because she had these spirits in her and she might grow up to be a shaman, and so sometimes their thinking was that this was not so much a medical problem as it was a blessing." (Of the forty or so American doctors, nurses, and Merced County agency employees I spoke with who had dealt with Lia and her family, several had a vague idea that "spirits" were somehow involved, but Jeanine Hilt was the only one who had actually asked the Lees what they thought was the cause of their daughter's illness.)

Within the Lee family, in one of those unconscious processes of selection that are as mysterious as any other form of falling in love, it was obvious that Lia was her parents' favorite, the child they considered the most beautiful, the one who was most extravagantly hugged and kissed, the one who was dressed in the most exquisite garments (embroidered by Foua, wearing dimestore glasses to work her almost microscopic stitches). Whether Lia occupied this position from the moment of her birth, whether it was a result of her spiritually distinguished illness, or whether it came from the special tenderness any parent feels for a sick child, is not a matter Foua and Nao Kao wish, or are able, to analyze. One thing that is clear is that for many years the cost of that extra love was partially borne by her sister Yer. "They blamed Yer for slamming the door," said Jeanine Hilt. "I tried many times to explain that the door had nothing to do with it, but they didn't believe me. Lia's illness made them so sad that I think for a long time they treated Yer differently from their other children."

During the next few months of her life, Lia had at least twenty more seizures. On two occasions, Foua and Nao Kao were worried enough to carry her in their arms to the emergency room at Merced Community Medical Center, which was three blocks from their apartment. Like most Hmong refugees, they had their doubts about the efficacy of Western medical techniques. However, when they were living in the Mae Jarim refugee camp in Thailand, their only surviving son, Cheng, and three of their six surviving daughters, Ge, May, and True, had been seriously ill. Ge died. They took Cheng, May, and True to the camp hospital; Cheng and May recovered rapidly, and True was sent to another, larger hospital, where she eventually recovered as well. (The Lees also concurrently addressed the possible spiritual origins of their children's illnesses by moving to a new hut. A dead person had been buried beneath their old one, and his soul might have wished to harm the new residents.) This experience did nothing to shake their faith in traditional Hmong beliefs about the causes and cures of illness, but it did convince them that on some occasions Western doctors could be of additional help, and that it would do no harm to hedge their bets.

Excerpted from *The Spirit Catches You and You Fall Down* by Anne Fadiman, copyright © 1997. Reprinted with permission of Farrar, Straus, & Giroux. All rights reserved.

Endnotes

1. Some people call talking to yourself or thinking out loud "intrapersonal communication" or communication "within" one person. We prefer to reserve the term "communication" for what happens between two or more people. The main reason is that "common," or "commune," is the root of "communication," and you can't make something common that's not divided or separated. Although any one person obviously has various "parts" or "sides," we think it's most useful to understand the human as a whole, a unity captured by such terms as "I," "me," or "the person." Talking to yourself and thinking out loud are important processes, but they are fundamentally different from connecting with an *other*, someone who is not you. As we'll explain later in this chapter, we also want to emphasize that humans are first and foremost "social animals," relational beings. Humans become who we are in our contacts with others, not as a result of thinking and talking to ourselves.

2. Notice that when we emphasize how fundamental meanings are, we are not claiming that there are no such things as objects. Meanings emerge as people contact aspects of their worlds. Some of these aspects are concrete, material, solid. But, as we clarify in Chapter Five, humans constantly *interpret* these objects; we don't perceive them directly. And the results of interpretation are meanings.

References

Barrett, W. 1987. *The Illusion of Technique: A Search for Meaning in a Technological Civilization.* Garden City: NY: Anchor Doubleday.

Basso, K. 1992. *Portraits of the "Whiteman": Linguistic Play and Cultural Symbols Among the Western Apache.* Cambridge: Cambridge University Press.

Clark, H. H., and Wilkes-Gibbs, D. 1986. "Referring as a Collaborative Process." *Cognition,* 22: 1.

Davies, B., and Harré, R. 1992. "Contradictions in Lived and Told Narratives." *Research on Language and Social Interaction,* 25: 1–36.

Gudykunst. W. B., Ting-Toomey, S., and Chua, E. 1988. *Culture and Interpersonal Communication.* Newbury Park, CA: Sage.

Moon, D. G. 1996. "Concepts of 'Culture': Implication for Intercultural Communication Research." *Communication Quarterly,* 44: 76.

Prather, H. 1970. *Notes to Myself.* Lafayette, CA: Real People Press. Reprinted by permission.

Schegloff, E. A. 1995. "Discourse as an Interactional Achievement III: The Omnirelevance of Action." *Research on Language and Social Interaction* 28: 186–187.

Scott, S. 2002. *Fierce Conversations: Achieving Success at Work and in Life, One Conversation at a Time*. New York: Viking.

——. 2003. "Executing Epiphanies: Companies, Careers Built or Lost One Conversation at a Time." *Seattle Post-Intelligencer,* October 6, 2003, C1–2.

Senge, P. M., Keiner, A., Roberts, C., Boss, R. B., and Smith, B. J. 1994. *The Fifth Discipline Fieldbook: Strategies and Tools for Building a Learning Organization*. New York: Doubleday.

Shotter, J. 1993. *Conversational Realities: Constructing Life Through Language*. Thousand Oaks, CA: Sage.

Tannen, D. 1990. *You Just Don't Understand: Women and Men in Conversation*. New York: Morrow. ✦

Chapter Three

Interpersonal Communicating

Chapter Objectives

After reading this chapter, you should be able to do the following:

- Distinguish between impersonal and interpersonal contact.
- Describe how uniqueness, unmeasurability, responsiveness, reflective-ness, and addressability are parts of *personal* identity.
- Explain how giving and receiving uniqueness, unmeasurability, respon-siveness, reflectiveness, and addressability can construct *interpersonal communicating*.
- Explain the connection between quality of communication and quality of life.
- Explain what communicative flexibility is and why it's important.
- Distinguish among expressive, rule-governed, and negotiation stages of communication development.
- Tell why those who've developed to the negotiation stage can be more flexible than those who haven't.

Chapter Preview

In the last chapter we defined communication as the collaborative process of meaning-making that constructs human worlds of mean-ing. We said that this process is continuous and complex, we empha-sized its ethical and cultural aspects, and we explained how all human communicating involves identity management and negotiation. We also focused on conversation as the most typical communication event. We identified one important implication of each of the six fea-tures of this view of communication and emphasized the skill we call *nexting.* Interpersonal communication, the focus of this book, is a subset of what we explained in Chapter Two, a particular type or kind of human communication.

This chapter defines and describes *interpersonal* communicating primarily by comparing and contrasting it with impersonal communicating. We provide a simple model and an explanation of how interpersonal communicating works. We also respond to the question "Why should anybody study interpersonal communication anyway?" Our response is that it's important to study interpersonal communicating because, we believe, the quality of your communication is directly connected to the quality of your life.

What Is 'Interpersonal' Communicating?

Interpersonal communicating doesn't happen all the time, but it can occur in families, between friends, during an argument, in business situations, and in the classroom. It can also happen on the telephone, in cyberspace, among jurors, at a party, across a bargaining table, in work group and committee meetings, and even during public speeches or presentations. The main characteristic of interpersonal communicating is that the people involved are contacting each other *as persons*. This may sound pretty straightforward but, as you will hear from us more than once, it's more complicated than that.

Think about your typical communication day. When you get up in the morning you may turn on *Good Morning America* or your favorite radio program. You may argue with your roommate about the clutter, or with your spouse about the kids, or you may talk about an upcoming party or your plans for the weekend. Some people also read part of the morning newspaper. Breakfast may find you in a cafeteria, coffee bar, or fast-food restaurant with 20 or 30 strangers where you wait in line, balance your plastic tray, and smile with appreciation or boredom at the cashier and the predictable food. Telephone conversations, some with people you know and others with nameless businesspeople, may fill part of your morning. You may also spend time online answering your e-mail or in a chat room. You may visit a convenience store or bank, where you make brief contact with the clerk or teller. Over lunch you may have a conversation with an acquaintance you believe could be a closer friend because on first impression he or she seems a lot like you in age, ethnicity, and social class. You may also listen to a lecture or give a presentation yourself. As part of your job, you may tell someone how to perform a complex task, or you may participate in the efforts of a committee to make an important decision. In the afternoon you may spend time online playing computer games with folks you interact with regularly but have never met face-to-face. Or you may be part of a basketball game or an aerobics class, and you might notice again how it's easier to relate to the strangers in the group who are culturally similar. At various times during the day you may pause to talk with a close friend, or as you walk or ride to an appointment, you may maintain a comfortable silence, thinking about the events of the day. In the evening you may hang out with a close friend or lover and talk about your feelings, fears, or hopes for the future. You may also go clubbing or spend an intimate evening at home.

While you're in a crowded restaurant, convenience store, bank, aerobics class, and even a party, you may feel more like an animal in a herd than a person. The cashier, teller, instructor, or host greets you with what seems like the same smile everyone gets, each statement is programmed by the business you're doing, and many encounters may end with a mechanical "Have a nice day!" This isn't always unpleasant. In fact, you may really appreciate the anonymity you have in the middle row of your aerobics class.

But the conversations with people close to you are very different from your herd experiences. The two, three, or four of you have *personal* contact as you focus with interest on each other, and you feel what it's like to be treated as a unique person, someone with feelings and someone who matters. You may have some of this same positive experience during the committee meeting, at the party, as you listen to the lecture or presentation, or even during an argument. The committee chair may be very committed to the work the group is doing together, and all the group members may be sincerely interested in each person's best ideas. The argument may be an opportunity to air some of each person's real fears about the relationship. Or in the presentation, the speaker may actually converse with you and the other audience members, talking about his or her personal experience with the topic and encouraging each listener to respond to the ideas presented in the talk.

One way to describe the various events that make up your communication day is to place them on a continuum or sliding scale that runs from "Impersonal" at one end and "Interpersonal" on the other. The sliding scale looks like this:

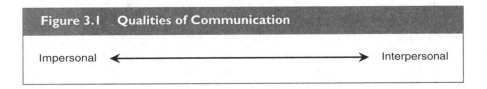

Figure 3.1   Qualities of Communication

Impersonal ⟵──────────────────────⟶ Interpersonal

The left side of the continuum, the impersonal side, is characterized by communication that is based on social roles and exchanges that minimize the presence of the communicators' personal identities. Impersonal communication is the label we use to describe your typical communication at the bank, convenience store, fast-food restaurant, and in front of the television. In these situations people usually connect in ways that emphasize their *social roles*—teller/customer, buyer/seller, server/diner, and so on. Even though human beings are obviously involved, they all function pretty much like interchangeable parts of the situation, something like the interchangeable parts of an automobile or computer. So long as the teller, buyer, or server knows his or her job (social role), and so long as the customer, seller, or diner remains in his or her role, it doesn't matter much who they are as individuals. We call this quality of communication *impersonal* because it's the most generic kind of human contact. The people involved don't know or care much about each other beyond what social roles each is playing. There is human association but little or no close human contact.

Often, of course, this is exactly the best kind of communication to have. For one thing, it's efficient. Nobody wants to wait in line while the Burger King cashier has a personal chat with each customer. It's also often the most appropriate kind of communicating. We don't ordinarily approach bank tellers, ticket sellers, or driver's license clerks expecting or wanting to have a deep conversation.

However, not all impersonal communication takes place with people we hardly know. It is not unusual to engage in efficient, issue-centered communication with people we know well and care about. We also engage in generic greeting rituals with our best friends and family members as well as strangers. It is not uncommon to hear parents invoke role-based communication patterns with their children that do not explicitly acknowledge the uniqueness of the participants ("Because I'm the mom, that's why!"). The important point is that impersonal communication can and does occur between people who would define their overall relationships as *personal*. Impersonal communicating is common, normal, useful, and often the most appropriate in a given situation.

Remember, too, that no one's communication life can be packaged into neat boxes. That's why we use a sliding scale. In fact, one philosopher describes the movement between impersonal and interpersonal communicating like the shifting of the tide. Tidal movement is constant; it is "all the way out" or "all the way in" for only a moment—and what counts as low or high tide changes from day to day. Your communicating moves similarly between the impersonal and interpersonal poles. The main difference between impersonal and interpersonal communication is that the former suggests a lack of personal contact and the latter implies contact between *persons*.

Definition of Interpersonal Communicating

We define interpersonal communication as the *type or kind of communication that happens when the people involved talk and listen in ways that maximize the presence of the personal.* You might notice that our definition is not based on the number of people involved or whether or not they are in the same place. Instead, our definition is based on the kind, type, or quality of their contact. We believe it is possible to communicate interpersonally in groups and even when your contact is mediated (for example, through mail carriers, phone lines, or the World Wide Web). When communication emphasizes the persons involved rather than just their roles or stereotypical characteristics, interpersonal communication is happening.

These two snapshots capture some elements of communicating that maximize the presence of the personal. What looks more interpersonal to you here than impersonal?

So what counts as the "personal"? Many philosophers, anthropologists, and communication scholars have defined what it means to be a person and how persons differ from other kinds of animals. One widely recognized description was created by a philosopher of communication named Martin Buber. Buber argued that humans have two ways of being in the world, and he labeled them based on two ways of communicating: "I-It" and "I-Thou."[1]

When engaging in I-It communicating, at least one of the communication partners speaks and listens in ways that imply that the other is more like an object or generic thing than a unique human being. In I-Thou communicating, the people involved recognize and actively acknowledge the unique personal characteristics and contributions of the other. Buber's description forms the basis for our distinction between impersonal and interpersonal communicating.

Buber also suggested that there are five qualities or characteristics that distinguish persons across many—though not all—cultures: uniqueness, measurability, reflectiveness, responsiveness, and addressability.[2] These five will define what we mean by "the personal" throughout this book, and we will use the five and their opposites to distinguish *impersonal* from *interpersonal* communicating. The five features can identify what communicators are giving out (later we call this *exhaling*) and taking in (we call this *inhaling*).

Five Features of the Personal

Unique. Uniqueness means noninterchangeability. Persons *can* be treated as if they are interchangeable parts, but each of us can also be thought of as unique in a couple of ways, genetically and experientially. Several years ago John heard a geneticist on National Public Radio say that, given the complexity of each individual's makeup of genes and chromosomes, the probability that two persons other than identical twins would have the same genetic materials is one in 10 to the 10,000th power. That's less than one chance in a billion trillion!

But even when two persons who are identical twins have the same biological raw material, each is still unique because each experiences the world differently. Karen had identical twin sisters in a couple of her courses recently. It turns out that they have taken every one of their college classes together and even have the same GPA. Although Natalie and Alyssa earned the same grades in Karen's courses, it was obvious from the papers they wrote, their engagement in class discussions, and their responses on exams that each experienced the course content differently. As Eleanor Roosevelt put it,

> Since everybody is an individual, nobody can be you. You are unique. No one can tell you how to use your time. It is yours. Your life is your own. You mold it. You make it. All anyone can do is to point out ways and means which have been helpful to others. (Roosevelt 1960, 45)

When people are communicating with each other *impersonally,* they're overlooking most of this uniqueness and focusing on the similarities among all those who play a given social role. Although you may notice and even acknowledge that the person you are communicating with is distinct, his or her distinct features are not central to your interaction. When you focus on the function or purpose of your interaction, you minimize the presence of the personal and maximize the presence of the social roles and expectations. As a result, communicators view one another as interchangeable.

So the first feature that distinguishes *persons* is experiential and, in most cases, genetic *uniqueness.* Some cultures downplay this feature, but most Western cultures emphasize it. The more vividly this feature is involved in your communicating, the farther your communication is toward the right-hand side of the impersonal←——→interpersonal continuum.

> ### 'But . . .' A Student Responds
>
> *When I go to the grocery store and use my debit card to pay for things, the clerk usually thanks me by name (they read it on my receipt) and in that way they are acknowledging that I am unique, aren't they?*
>
> To some extent, yes, but the reality is that the clerks have been trained to call you by name to make you feel that you are unique—they are using addressability (keep reading, we'll be explaining this term shortly) strategically to make you feel singled out and valued as a customer. Many of our students who work in retail say that their personalized greeting is as much of a ritual as asking if you found everything you needed. They often feel awkward calling people they really don't know by name, and they only do it because their managers tell them that market research indicated it may increase repeat business.

Unmeasurable. The second feature that distinguishes interpersonal from impersonal communicating is acknowledgment of the fact that people are ultimately *unmeasureable*. Even if your doctor accurately identifies your height, weight, temperature, blood pressure, serum cholesterol level, hemoglobin count, and all your other data right down to the electric potential in your seventh cranial nerve, she still will not have exhaustively accounted for the person you are because there are parts of you that can't be measured. Many scientists, social scientists, philosophers, and theologians have made this point. Some cognitive scientists, for example, include in their model of the person components they call *schemata,* or *cognitive patterns*, that don't have any space-and-time (measurable) existence but can be inferred from observations of behavior. Others call the unmeasurable elements of a person the *human spirit, soul,* or *psyche*. But whatever you call it, it's there.

Emotions or feelings are the clearest observable evidence of this unmeasurable part of us. Although we can measure things related to feelings—brain waves, sweaty palms, heart rate, paper-and-pencil responses—what the measurements record is a long way from the feelings themselves. "Pulse 110, respiration 72, Likert rating 5.39, palmar conductivity 0.036 ohms" may be accurate, but it doesn't quite capture what's going on in you when you encounter somebody you can't stand or greet somebody you love.

One other thing: These emotions or feelings are *always* a part of what we are experiencing. Psychologists and educators agree that it's unrealistic to try to separate the "intellectual" or "objective" aspect of a person or a subject matter from the "affective" or "emotional" parts. This is because humans are always thinking and feeling. As one writer puts it, "It should be apparent that there is no intellectual learning without some sort of feeling and there are no feelings without the mind's somehow being involved" (Brown 1971).

Even though feelings are always present, some communication acknowledges them and some communication doesn't. When people are communicating interpersonally, the unique emotions and feelings of the participants are likely to be acknowledged and in play. This does not mean that you have to "wear your heart on your sleeve" to communicate interpersonally. It just means that when people are making interpersonal contact, some feelings are appropriately acknowledged and shared. *Impersonal* communication is characterized by the practice of masking or denying emotions and feelings. Even if you are having a lousy day, for example you might respond to the question "How's it going?" with a socially scripted "Fine, thanks." You have probably learned that bringing your feelings to work or your personal opinions and experiences to the classroom is not always valued or deemed appropriate, so you choose to engage in communication that is more on the impersonal end of the continuum.

Reflective. A third distinguishing characteristic is that persons are reflective. Being reflective means not only that are we aware of what's around us, but also that we can be *aware of our awareness.* As one author puts it, "No matter how much of your self you are able to objectify and examine, the quintessential, living part of yourself will always elude you, i.e., the part of you that is conducting the examination" (Buechner 1973, 4)—the reflective part. Wrenches, rocks, and rowboats aren't aware at all. Dogs, cats, armadillos, and giraffes are all aware of their environments, but we don't have any evidence that they are aware of their awareness. So far as we know, only humans compose and save histories of their lives, elaborately bury their dead, create libraries, explore their extrasensory powers, question the meaning of life, and speculate about the past and future. And only humans are aware that we do all these things.

Reflection is not a process that affects only philosophers and people who know that they don't have long to live. Healthy "ordinary" people reflect, too. The three of us each wonder from time to time whether we're spending our work time wisely, and John and Karen often reflect on whether we're making the right parenting decisions with our sons Lincoln and Logan. Sometimes you probably wonder what you'll be doing five years from now. Before you make an important decision, you ask questions of yourself and others about priorities and probable consequences. On clear days you may notice the beauty of the landscape around you and reflect on how fortunate you are to live where you do. Like all persons, you ask questions and reflect.

Questions can be a clear indicator that a person is reflecting. Someone who is seriously reflecting will almost always be asking questions. In addition, the reflective person will often express reservations and qualifications about his or her opinions and beliefs rather than maintain a rigid position or communicate with absolute certainty about an issue—"I think this is the right thing to do in this situation, but to be honest, I'm not absolutely sure." Or "I know I don't want to lie to him about my feelings, but I'm not sure that this is the best time to talk about it." Reflective communicators are aware that multiple perspectives are always in play in communication encounters, and they make use of their human abilities to explore the relevance of positions that are different from their own. Reflective communicating helps to maximize the presence of the personal by highlighting this unique characteristic of human beings. Reflecting can also lead to interpersonal communication as the perspectives and views of all participants are invited into the collaborative construction of meaning.

When people ignore the fact that persons are reflective, their communication usually shows it. For example, you may stick with superficial topics—the weather, recent news items, gossip. You'll also probably miss noticing how your communication is affected by the way you see yourself, the other person's self-image, and what the other person believes that you think of him or her (see Chapter Five). On the other hand, when you're aware of your own and another's reflectiveness, you can respond to more of what's going on as you communicate.

Responsive. Reflective communicating not only helps tip the scale to the interpersonal end of the continuum, it also makes space for the fourth feature of persons identified by Buber: responsiveness. People, unlike objects, can choose to respond rather than simply react. Objects cannot choose what to do next. Automatic pilots, photoelectric switches, personal and industrial robots, thermostats, and computers can sometimes seem to "operate on their own" or "turn themselves off and on," but they too are dependent on actions initiated outside them. The computers and robots have to be programmed, and the thermostat reacts to temperature, which reacts to the sun's rays, which are affected by the earth's rotation, and so on. Similarly, a ball can go only where it's kicked, and if you were good enough at physics calculations, you could figure out how far and where it would go on the basis of weight, velocity, aerodynamics, the shape of your shoe, atmospheric conditions, and so on.

But what if you kick a person? It's an entirely different kind of activity, and you cannot accurately predict what will happen. The reason you can't is that when persons are involved, human *choice* intervenes between cause and effect, stimulus and response. That's the difference, as we suggested in the last chapter, between the *reactions* of objects and the *responses* of persons. If you tap my knee, you may cause a reflex jerk—the movement. But the feelings that occur are not completely predictable, and the behavior or actions that accompany my reflex may be anything from giggles to a slap in the face. This happens because persons choose how to respond to words and actions. If your ideas about abortion are different from mine, I may decide not to listen when you discuss biological evidence about when life begins. Or you may give me simple directions to the theater, but I respond by traveling a different route. In short, humans do have physiological reactions, like the knee-jerk reflex. But our behavior is also responsive. Even when it seems like we have no choice, we're *responding*.

Whereas reflectiveness manifests itself in questions, responsiveness is manifest in choices. Each person's range of choices is limited, of course. There are personal, political, cultural, and practical issues that restrain our responses. We can't instantly change sex, make someone love us, or memorize the contents of the Library of Congress. But we can decide whether to use a conventional word or an obscene one, how to prioritize our time commitments, and, as we'll discuss in later chapters, feelings are also responses.

In fact, the more you realize your freedom and power to respond rather than simply react, the more developed a person you can be. Sometimes it's easy to get out of touch with this freedom and power. You feel like "I *had* to shout back; he was making me look silly!" "I just *couldn't* say anything!" or "Sure, I withdrew, but she made me—she was always on my back about something!" All of these statements make it sound like you don't have any choice, like what you do is completely *caused* by what another person does. But if you remember the discussion of fault and blame in Chapter Two, cause-and-effect reasoning doesn't apply well to human interaction. Our point there and here is that, even when circumstances are exerting pressure, you still have some freedom and power to choose how to respond to the pressure. It may mean resisting a culturally rooted preference or breaking some well-established habit patterns, and it may take lots of practice, but it's possible to become aware of your responses and, when you want to, to change them. This is what we've called *nexting*. The reason it's important to learn this skill is that when you believe you're just reacting, you've lost touch with part of what it means to be a person. Persons are responsive, and the more you remember and act on this fact, the more interpersonal your communicating can become.

A person can spend a great deal of time asking questions and exploring options (reflecting) and never get around to making choices (responding). John calls this process "analysis paralysis." Perhaps some of you have been afflicted by it. You spend more time thinking about what you could have, should have, or would have done than you do making a choice and following through on it. One can also react without asking questions (reflecting), but people who do run the risk of making unethical and/or inappropriate choices.

'But . . .' A Student Responds

It seems to me like the idea of nexting is related to the theme of ethics you identified as important to this approach. And I wonder if I am unethical if I don't choose to respond and I simply react out of habit?

That's an important observation and a great question! We agree that there is a direct connection between ethical communicating and nexting. You always have a choice about what you will do or say next in a given situation, and that choice has ethical dimensions. And when you ask if you are being unethical when you react habitually, you highlight some of the complexity of ethical communicating. If you understand unethical communicating as the kind that violates norms and standards of right and wrong, it is quite possible that your habitual response doesn't do that. Perhaps all of your automatically ingrained reactions are consistent with individual and cultural norms for right and wrong. In that case, you could have an ethical reaction. If, however, you believe as we do that every choice has ethical dimensions, and you choose to ignore them, you could be perceived as less than ethical. We would argue that when you choose to respond, you have more of an opportunity to assess the appropriateness of your next contribution to the communication and that taking the moment to reflect increases the likelihood that you'd make an ethical choice.

When individuals maximize their human potential for both reflective and responsive communication, they are likely to communicate verbally and nonverbally in ways that maximize the presence of the personal—at the interpersonal end of the continuum.

Addressable. A fifth important feature of humans is that we are addressable. Addressability is tied to linguistic responsiveness. Beings who are addressable can recognize when they are addressed, that is, when they are called or spoken to in language and can also respond in language. Addressability is what makes the difference between talking *to* and talking *with*. Neither baseball bats nor dogs and cats are addressable; you can talk to them, but not with them. You can call them, curse them, scold them, and praise them, but you cannot carry on a mutual conversation with them. We acknowledge that some of us engage in the practice of personification, in which we project human characteristics onto our pets and inanimate objects. In fact, children regularly carry on "conversations" with their toys and stuffed animals, responding for them, but the toy itself is not actually talking for itself. Our point here is that, as a feature of the personal, humans are able to address others and understand that they are being addressed.

One student described what addressability meant to her by recounting her experience as a child with her imaginary playmate, "Sharla." Mary said that Sharla went everywhere with her and was always dressed appropriately. Sharla was also (in Mary's mind) always sympathetic to what Mary was doing and feeling. Mary would talk *to* Sharla constantly, telling her how she felt, complaining about her parents and older sister, and sometimes making elaborate plans. Occasionally Mary would talk *about* Sharla to her friends or her mother. But of course Sharla never responded out loud. She never talked back.

Mary could talk *to* and *about* Sharla, but not *with* her. Sharla was not addressable; she wasn't a person.

Communication theorist John Shotter talks about this feature of human communication under the heading of "addressivity," which he defines as "the quality of being directed toward someone" (Shotter 1993, 176). "Addressed" speech is directed or "aimed" speech, and one characteristic of persons is that they can recognize address and respond in kind. Shotter gets the idea from Mikhail Bakhtin, a Russian theorist who emphasized that *all* writing and speaking is *a response* to circumstances that precede and frame it. As Bakhtin put it,

> any utterance . . . always responds (in the broad sense of the word) in one form or another to others' utterances that precede it. The speaker is not Adam, and therefore the subject of his speech itself inevitably becomes the arena where his opinions meet those of his partners . . . or other viewpoints, world views, trends, theories, and so forth. (Bakhtin 1986, 94)

This quality of addressivity is unique to *human* communication because addressability is one distinctive feature of humans.

Addressability is a feature of interpersonal communication because when we acknowledge the individuality of another, we are in effect helping to maximize the presence of the personal. If, on the other hand, we speak to or at others, we treat them as if they are interchangeable—more like objects than people. This can happen in the classroom, in the workplace, and even in the bedroom. If the other we address is not acknowledged as an individual person capable of making, and even expected to make, a response, the scale tips toward the impersonal end of the continuum.

Recall and Applications

Your Personal Qualities

As a check of your understanding of this section, respond briefly to the following questions:

1. What are two ways that you are unique?
2. List one unmeasurable feature of who you are right now.
3. What is one way that you've been reflective in the last 24 hours?
4. Identify one response (choice) you made in the last two hours.
5. If you were to talk with someone right now, what is one way that you could ensure that your speech was "addressed" or "aimed"? How might that person acknowledge your addressability?

In this chapter we're saying that when communicators give and receive or talk and listen in ways that maximize their uniqueness, unmeasureability, reflectiveness, responsiveness, and addressability, then we'd label the communication between them as *interpersonal*. When they listen and talk in ways that highlight their generic, interchangeably measurable aspects, and unconsidered reactions, we'd identify their communication on the "impersonal" end of the sliding scale.

Every day, your communication shifts back and forth along this continuum more often than you imagine. Some of your communication with others may be predominately at one end or the other, but even in the most impersonal of communication events, you may notice that your identity as a person has been reinforced, or that in your most intimate relationships you feel that your communication partner does not really acknowledge *you*. An important point we want to make is that in *every* communication encounter there is the potential for impersonal communicating as well as interpersonal communication, and the odds are that both are happening. Then why a continuum that distinguishes between them, you might ask? Because we find that the overall quality of communicating at one end of the continuum is significantly different from the quality of communicating at the other end— and that, as we will explain in just a minute, the quality of your life is influenced by the quality of your communicating. Whereas both impersonal and interpersonal communication are appropriate ways of engaging with others, most people report that their lives are more fulfilling when they engage in more interpersonal contact. This is why we have spent so much time describing these differences. The communication continuum or sliding scale now looks like this:

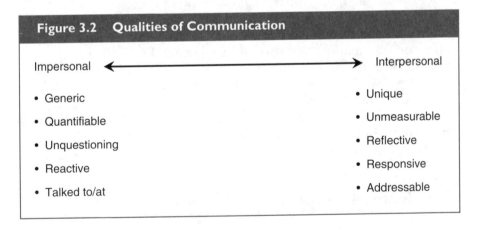

Figure 3.2   Qualities of Communication

Impersonal ←——————————————→ Interpersonal

- Generic
- Quantifiable
- Unquestioning
- Reactive
- Talked to/at

- Unique
- Unmeasurable
- Reflective
- Responsive
- Addressable

So two persons who stick to their (interchangeable) role definitions—"I'm the teacher and you're the student"—ignore feelings, and behave as if they're controlled by outside forces (reacting rather than responding) will be communicating more impersonally than interpersonally. One way to describe their communication would be to place it near the left end of the sliding scale. A student and teacher who both identify themselves culturally as female and Taiwanese, and who recognize each other's characteristically female and Taiwanese feelings and responses, but who are still "teacher" and "student" to each other, and who know little of each other's uniqueness, will be communicating somewhere nearer the middle of the continuum.

On the other hand, a different student and teacher might both acknowledge each other's unique features, affirm relevant feelings, actively respond rather than react, and show they're aware of their own perspectives by questioning or being tentative about some of their ideas. When they both speak and listen in ways that reflect these qualities, their communicating would fit nearer the right-hand, interpersonal end of the continuum.

Interpersonal communication is easiest when there are only two of you and you already know and trust each other. But it can also occur early in a relationship—even at the first meeting—and, as we've already mentioned, it can occur over the telephone, during an argument, on the job, in group meetings, and even in public speaking or presentation situations. The important thing is not how many people there are or where they're located, but the individuals' willingness and ability to choose personal over impersonal communication attitudes and behaviors.

So our basic definition of interpersonal communication is pretty simple: It's the counterpart of impersonal communication. But as you'll see, we base our entire approach to the topic on this simple definition. The rest of the chapters in this book describe more specifically how to distinguish the impersonal from the interpersonal, how to decide when to move in one or the other direction on the continuum, and how verbal and nonverbal cues can promote impersonal or interpersonal communicating. We also discuss how to listen for uniqueness, feelings, reflectiveness, responsiveness, and addressability; how to express your own uniqueness, feelings, reflectiveness, responsiveness, and addressability; how to build interpersonal relationships; how to cope interpersonally with conflict; and impersonal-interpersonal contacts online. But before we move on to these topics, we need to address the second major question.

Why Study Interpersonal Communication?

Our basic answer is this: because *there's a direct link between the quality of your communication and the quality of your life.*

After high school, John attended a community college for two years and then transferred to a four-year college to finish his degree. He took a basic speech course at both schools, and noticed that in each something was missing. The teachers encouraged students to think about and work on their communicating, and they emphasized how to inform others and persuade them to do what you want. They showed the class how to outline ideas, how to gesture effectively, and how to use vocal variety to keep their listeners' attention. Students were required to write papers and give speeches to demonstrate that they'd mastered these skills. But the courses seemed to overlook something even more important. Neither the textbooks nor the instructors said anything about the connection between the quality of your communication and the quality of your life.

Other texts and teachers did. In his literature and anthropology classes John read that "no human is an island" and that "the human is a social animal." Psychology books reported studies of infants who were deprived of touch, talk, or any other kind of contact and who suffered profoundly. A philosophy text made the same point in these words:

> . . . [C]ommunication means life or death to persons. . . . Both the individual and society derive their basic meaning from the relations that exist between [persons]. It is through dialogue that [humans] accomplish the miracle of personhood and community. (Howe 1963)

This outing enhances the quality of the lives of the many families who participate, not mainly because of the place, but because of the interpersonal communicating. Which of your communication experiences most affect the quality of your life? (They won't all be as warm and fuzzy as the ones in this picture.)

The speech communication texts and teachers promised students that they could help them learn to make ideas clear, be entertaining, and persuade others to agree with them. But they seemed to miss the communication impact of the point being made in literature, anthropology, psychology, and philosophy. If humans really are social beings, *then communication is where humanness happens.* In other words, although communication is definitely a way to express ideas, get things done, and entertain, convince, and persuade others, it's also more than that. It's the process that defines who we are. *If we experience mainly impersonal communicating, we're liable to miss developing interpersonally, and if we experience mainly interpersonal communicating, we're likely to develop more of our human potential.* This is how the quality of your communication affects the quality of your life.

One reason the three of us choose to teach interpersonal communication is because we recognized the truth of this idea. This same point has motivated our writing of this book. We've also been impressed with some research that supports this reason for studying interpersonal communication.

Quality of Communication and Quality of Life

Medical doctors have done some impressive studies linking communication with health. James J. Lynch has been codirector of the Psychophysiological Clinic and Laboratories at the University of Maryland School of Medicine. He introduces one of his books with these words:

> As we shall see, study after study reveals that human dialogue not only affects our hearts significantly but can even alter the biochemistry of individual tissues at the farthest extremities of the body. Since blood flows through every human tissue, the entire body is influenced by dialogue. (Lynch 1985, 3)

In other words, the quality of your communication affects the *physiological* quality of your life. One of Lynch's important discoveries is that blood pressure changes much more rapidly and frequently than we used to believe, and that some of the most radical blood pressure changes occur when we speak and are spoken to. Computerized instruments permit Lynch and other medical researchers to monitor blood pressure constantly and to map the effects of a person entering the room, nonverbal contact, reading aloud, and conversation. Speech appears to directly affect blood pressure; in one study the mean arterial pressure of healthy nurses went from 92 when they were quiet to 100 when they "talked calmly" (Lynch 1985, 123–124). Listening has the opposite effect. Rather than just returning to baseline when a person stops speaking, blood pressure actually drops below baseline when one concentrates on the other person (Lynch 1985, 160). And this happens only when we talk with people; conversation with pets does not produce the same result (Lynch 1985).

In an earlier book, Lynch discusses some of the more global effects of essentially the same phenomenon. There he reports the results of literally hundreds of medical studies that correlate loneliness and poor health. For example, people with few interpersonal relationships tend to die before their counterparts who enjoy a network of family and friends (Lynch 1977). In fact, a study by two Swedish doctors of identical twins found that smoking habits, obesity, and cholesterol levels of the twins who had heart attacks were *not* significantly different from the twins with healthier hearts. But there were some other important differences, one of which was what the doctors called "poor childhood and adult interpersonal relationships." The twins with heart disease were the ones who had experienced more unresolved conflict, more arguments at work and home, and less emotional support (Liljefors and Rahe 1974). What conclusions can we draw from evidence like this? Lynch puts it this way:

> Human companionship does affect our hearts, and . . . there is reflected in our hearts a biological basis for our need for loving human relationships, which we fail to fulfill at our peril. . . . The ultimate decision is simple: we must either learn to live together or increase our chances of prematurely dying alone. (Lynch 1977, 14)

If we go beyond physiological quality of life, the same point can be made even more strongly. In fact, nonmedical people have been talking about the link between the quality of your communication and the quality of your life for many years. For example, Martin Buber wrote that

> the unique thing about the human world is that something is continually happening between one person and another, something that never happens in the animal or plant world. *Humans are made human by that happening.* That special event begins by one human turning to another, seeing him or her as this particular other being, and offering to communicate with the other in a mutual way, building from the individual world each person experiences to a world they share together. (Buber 1965, 203, italics added)

Psychologist John Powell puts the same idea in simpler terms: "What I am, at any given moment in the process of my becoming a person, will be determined by my relationships with those who love me or refuse to love me, with those I love or refuse to love" (Powell 1980, 43).

"Okay," you might be saying, "I don't disagree with the lofty ideals expressed by all these people, and I can see how quality of life and quality of communication are related. But let's be a little *practical.* It's not always *possible* to treat everybody interpersonally, and it's not always *wise.* Plus, you sure can't expect other people to treat you interpersonally all the time. So you can't realistically expect your communication always to be at the interpersonal end of the continuum."

We agree. We can't realistically expect that, and we don't. As we've already said, impersonal communication works best in many situations, and a number of factors make interpersonal communication difficult or even impossible. Role definitions, status relationships, cultural differences, physical surroundings, and the amount of time available all can be obstacles to interpersonal contact. Lack of awareness and lack of skills can also limit interpersonal communicating.

One person may want to "tune into" another person's choices and feelings but may simply not know how to listen that way.

In still other situations it may be possible, but as you say, it may not be wise. The power relationships or the level of hostility may make it too risky. For example, we know a man who used to teach interpersonal communication as part of a Living Skills class in a work-release facility. The facility and the program he worked in are parts of the prison system. Eric also worked there as a guard. His power as a guard—he had the authority to send people back to the county jail—drastically affected what he could accomplish as an interpersonal communication teacher. Some people in his classes responded openly to his efforts to develop interpersonal contacts. Others, however, were hardened enough by their years in various prisons that they focused only on maintaining their own power in the convict hierarchy and getting out as soon as possible—legally or otherwise. It simply didn't make good sense for Eric to try to communicate with all the persons in his class in consistently interpersonal ways.

Flexibility: Expressive, Rule-Governed, Negotiation

To repeat: There is often nothing inappropriate or "bad" about communicating impersonally. This is sometimes the best way to deal with a situation because of expectations, time constraints, or a multitude of other factors. But it is important not to be "stuck" at any one point on the impersonal←——→interpersonal continuum. Sometimes you'll want to be able to help move your communicating toward the left-hand side, and sometimes you'll want to go in the other direction, to help your contact be more interpersonal. In order to do this, *it is important to develop some communication flexibility*. This means being skilled enough as a communicator to make choices about the appropriateness of moving your communication in either direction on the impersonal←——→interpersonal continuum, depending on the situation. And importantly, when you increase your flexibility as a communicator, you are increasing your awareness of the *responses* you're making.

Recent research specifies what it means to have communication flexibility and why it's important. According to these studies, communication flexibility leads to enhanced sensitivity to personal and cultural differences, the willingness to explore alternatives to familiar patterns, and the ability to adapt to changing conditions. So you're flexible when you can *sense differences* and when you're both *willing* and *able* to make changes. Several studies indicate that communicators normally develop through three general stages, from being less to being more flexible.

Stage one is called *expressive*, stage two *rule-governed*, and stage three *negotiation* (O'Keefe 1988). At the first level of development people view communication as a way to *express thoughts and feelings*. At this stage, effective communication is communication that openly and honestly signals where the person's coming from. A crying baby is the simplest example of purely expressive communicating. The baby pays no attention to the context or communication situation; it simply expresses its internal state "openly and honestly." A person communicating expressively would say things like "I'm having a great day! I really like being here" or "That outfit is really ugly! And you look stupid with that hairstyle!" This person obviously has very little awareness of the collaborative nature of communication because he or she operates as if only one set of choices counts: his or her own.

At the second, *rule-governed* stage of development, the person views communication as a game played cooperatively by social rules. At this stage, communication is perceived to be effective to the degree that it appropriately controls the social resources and gets the desired response. A person communicating in rule-governed ways notices and responds to all the participants' social rights and obligations and does whatever he or she can to have people abide by the social rules. So one feature of this stage is that the speaker's view of the context controls what happens. Barbara O'Keefe, the researcher who first outlined these three stages, describes rule-governed communicating this way:

> Speakers cooperate in playing the game by doing the things they are obligated to do, refraining from doing the things that the social conventions say they should avoid, and following the rules that specify what counts as an appropriate way to achieve their ends in the immediate context. Hearers cooperate in playing the game by paying attention to the significant conventions or rules in the context, cooperatively inferring the speaker's intention, and by responding in ways consistent with their current social position. (O'Keefe 1988, 86)

The person communicating expressively knows that one way you get others to understand your thoughts and feelings is to express them. The person communicating in a rule-governed way understands that point, and he or she also understands a second important idea—namely, that you can more effectively get people to go along with you by referring to and using the social rules. This person understands that communication is collaborative, but he or she thinks that the joint action is determined by social rules. So this is how stage two represents a higher level of development than stage one: The understanding that rule-governed communication is based on and encompasses or subsumes the understanding that expressive communication is based on.

Stage-three communicating—*negotiation*—represents an even higher level of development. A person operating at this level sees communication as the "negotiation of social selves and situations" (O'Keefe 1988, 85). In other words, a person at this level recognizes that "who we are to each other" (our social selves) and "what we're doing here" (the situation) *emerge out of the communication that's going on.* This means that social selves and situations are not entirely set beforehand. This person understands that words, gestures, and facial expressions initially mean something to each person communicating, but also that their meaning for the people *together* is *constructed in the communication.* In other words, people operating at this level of development understand the description of communication that we developed in Chapter Two. They recognize that communication is complex, continuous, and collaborative, and that it is the way people construct their worlds together.

Effective communication from this stage-three perspective is communication that achieves interpersonal alignment on a mutually shared set of goals. Importantly, *alignment* is not the same as *agreement.* Even though the people communicating may not agree on all the topics they're discussing, they can still all be reading from the same music. So even though they may disagree, they understand at some level that they're both or all "in conflict," "trying to negotiate a compromise," or "problem solving." In other words, they can be aligned on some general topics even when they may be in conflict about some specifics.

There's also another important difference. At the rule-governed stage, context is seen as controlling the communication, but at the negotiation stage the people involved negotiate the context. So, for example, a teacher and a student operating at the negotiation stage could transcend their role definitions and could talk as "friends," or they

Imagine you are one of the people in this picture. How might you move beyond expressive or rule-governed to negotiated contact? How might you overcome the gender rules operating here? The rules of business culture?

could negotiate roles and redefine the situation so that the student would be "teaching" the teacher. Or two persons who had been "friends" for years might be doing something together that they've always done as friends and discover that they both want their relationship to develop toward romantic intimacy. In this case, the two don't just let personal history or the situation govern who they are to each other. As they communicate, they redefine the familiar context into a new one and also become more to each other than who they've been before. Using another term we introduced in Chapter One, they both practice effective nexting.

In summary, this research program indicates that people normally move through three stages in the development of their communication knowledge and skills. At stage one, people see themselves as communicating mainly to express thoughts and feelings. When people develop to stage two, they know that communication can express, but they also know how to adapt their expressions to the social rules and the situation. Then the most highly developed communicators know about expressing and following social rules, but they also realize that both selves and situations can be *negotiated by the communicators*, actually defined-as-they-happen by the ways people talk and listen to each other.

And here's the central point: *People communicating at stage one have the least flexibility and people communicating at stage three have the most flexibility.* Why? Because those at stage one know only how to handle communication in one way, but those at stage three know *three ways* in any given situation. In addition, people at level one notice few differences and aren't particularly willing or able to adapt to them, whereas people at level three are sensitive to both cultural and personal differences, are willing to adapt, and know how to do it. Even more important, not only do they know how to adapt to the situation, but they also know how to negotiate the selves and situation to adapt to them.

Evidence from several empirical studies illustrates the usefulness of this approach to communication. The results show that generally, as persons develop from one stage to another, they become more sophisticated in their reasoning about the way communication works and about interpersonal relationships. The more sophisticated the person communicating, the more likely that he or she will be seen as interpersonally competent (Applegate and Delia 1980). There are also specific differences. For example, those able to communicate at stage three have been found to be more effective than those at the other stages in "regulative" communication—getting others to complete an assigned task. They are also *liked* more than persons communicating at stage one or two, and are judged by peers to be more *competent*. In addition, group or committee members led by people who are at the third stage of development are more satisfied than those led by expressive or rule-governed communicators (O'Keefe and McCornack 1987). Other studies have suggested that pharmacists can improve the effectiveness of their communication by adapting messages to patients' levels of development (Lambert and Gillespie 1994), and that nurse managers at the negotiation stage work more effectively with the nurses they manage than those at the expressive and rule-governed stage (Peterson and Albrecht 1996). In short, several studies show that increased flexibility can mean increased effectiveness. This is why we talk a lot about flexibility in this book. The communication skills these chapters will help you develop are all designed to increase your flexibility.

Chapter Summary

This chapter defines interpersonal communication—the topic of this book—and explains why we believe it's important to study it. We use the term *interpersonal* to label a kind, type, or quality of communication that occurs when the people involved choose to talk and listen in ways that maximize the presence of the personal.

We clarify what this means by discussing the features that characterize the personal. The first is *uniqueness;* every person is virtually a genetic one-of-a-kind, and even identical twins, who share the same genetic makeup, have unique experiences. A second characteristic has to do with how *measurable* persons are. Objects can be completely described in space-and-time terms. Humans are partly measurable, too, but we also have some important unmeasurable features. The most common ones are emotions or feelings.

The third characteristic of persons is that we are *reflective,* which means that we are not only aware but also aware that we are aware. No other object or animal we know of has invented philosophy, science, or religion, and only humans spend as much time as we do wondering about and questioning ourselves and others. Questioning, in fact, is a primary indicator of reflectiveness. Directly linked to reflectiveness is the fourth distinctive feature, *responsiveness.* Persons are not completely controlled by outside forces; we can and do choose what to think, feel, and do. It's true that our responses are often limited, sometimes by circumstances and sometimes by our own lack of awareness. But our present is never completely determined by our past or future.

Addressability is the final distinctive feature of the personal. Addressability means the ability not only to talk *to* but also to talk *with* and to be talked with. These five characteristics taken together fairly clearly define what we call the personal.

These features also clarify what it means to say that interpersonal communication *maximizes the presence of the personal.* When you treat others as generic, interchangeable objects; ignore their feelings, their questions, and their choices; and talk at rather than with them, and when they treat you similarly, the communication between you will be more impersonal than interpersonal. On the other hand, when you treat others and are treated by them as unique, unmeasurable, reflective, choosing, and addressable, your communication will be closer to the right-hand end of the continuum—more interpersonal.

Why is it important to learn about impersonal and interpersonal communicating and to develop your communication skills? Because there's a direct link between the quality of your life and the quality of your communication. Medical research shows how unresolved conflict and poor relationships affect your blood pressure, susceptibility to cancer and heart disease, and general physiological health. Philosophers and psychologists also argue that many nonphysiological aspects of human life—level of personal satisfaction, serenity, centeredness, personal sense of well-being—are "determined by my relationships with those who love me or refuse to love me, with those I love or refuse to love" (Powell 1980, 43).

Close relationships obviously can't and don't happen all the time. It is not always possible to communicate interpersonally with everybody, and sometimes it is definitely not wise. Hopefully you won't hear us saying that if everyone would just love each other, the world's problems would dissolve and we could all hold hands and walk into the sunset together. We're not that naive. We do believe, though, that people can develop a better understanding of the distinctions between impersonal and interpersonal communicating so they can make choices that enhance their flexibility. Ultimately we believe that more human communicating could be interpersonal than it now is, and if it were, human lives would be the better for it.

Because of the connection between quality of communication and quality of life, we believe that the most important practical task is to develop flexibility. The most successful, satisfied, and competent communicators—and the ones who are most appreciated and well liked— are those with the broadest repertoire of knowledge and skills. They are the people who can not only effectively *express* their thoughts and feelings and obey the social and cultural *rules* but who can also *negotiate* "who we are" and "what's going on here" *in their communicating*.

In Other Words

In this reading, Patricia talks about how you can identify where a relationship is on the impersonal←—→interpersonal continuum by the terms people use in conversation. In her case, the use of "Pat" by her schoolteacher—which was likely perceived by her teacher and others in her school as a more familiar term of address—demonstrated distance in her relationship rather than closeness. From Patricia's perspective, her new teacher denied the uniqueness of her heritage and sense of identity. As a result, the relationship between Patricia and her teacher was limited to their roles of teacher and student.

After you have read this selection, you should be able to respond to the following questions:

1. When are terms of address or endearment more likely to demonstrate interpersonal communication rather than impersonal communication?

2. How are reflectiveness and responsiveness linked to terms of endearment?

3. Does anyone call you something that you wish they wouldn't? Which features of the impersonal←——→interpersonal continuum are most relevant in determining where you would place your relationship with that person?

4. To what extent do you feel addressable in your class? How addressable is your teacher?

* * *

Of Endearment and Other Terms of Address: A Mexican Perspective

Patricia Covarrubias

"This old man, he played two, he play knick-knack on my—" The singing jerked to a halt. It was my first day of school in my new country. As the school principal and I entered the third-grade classroom, Mrs. Williams ceased her piano playing and came toward me. With a hand on my shoulder, she steered me to face the children who were sitting on small wooden chairs in a large circle. "Class, this is *Pat.*" With that introduction I had been rechristened. In one unexpected and infinitesimal moment, all that I was and had been was abridged into three-letter, bottom-line efficiency: *Pat.* Mrs. Williams could not have imagined that her choice of address, imposed on me in 1960, just two weeks after my mother, my brother, and I immigrated to the United States to join my father, would be a name I would revile for the rest of my life.

Yet I am not ungrateful to Mrs. Williams. She facilitated, inadvertently, an important pivotal point in my life. In calling me *Pat,* in that hair-splitting instant, she prompted what became one of my primary life themes: understanding the profound and enduring personal and social consequences of the terms people use to address one another. As a recent doctoral student in communication, I join those who suggest that address forms are unique vocabularies in and through which people strategically align themselves in reference to other people. But in that fractional childhood moment, all I could understand was that with a simple *Pat* Mrs. Williams had crammed me into a space I did not fit. I was suddenly at the mercy of a word that did not describe me. With a single syllable she invaded a private way of being and made it accessible publicly, on her terms. I knew I was not *Pat,* but I did not know enough English to defend myself.

From the moment I stepped into my new American world the alien separated me not only from myself but also from the classmates who would make up so much of my social life through elementary, junior high and high school. For weeks, months, years I struggled to convey who I "really" was using the most direct channel available to humans: speech. But I continually failed. I lacked the lexicon. I lacked the syntax. I lacked the defiance. Like a mute patient who holds the solution to a crime and wants to speak but is unable to do so I gagged on my urge to argue for my real name, for the real me. By the time I had acquired enough English and enough courage to assert my personhood I was off by too much to catch up. Over time, the people who composed so much of my social world had formed impressions of the person they thought I was. *Pat* became a composite of my awkward utterances, their imaginations, and some destructive stereotypes.

During those early years I was in some in-between space, some hollow whose depth I did not comprehend for decades. Yet I realized from the beginning that I could not surrender to the gap that alienated me from myself and from everyone else. I sensed early on that integration and reintegration would come at a cost, but that they would come. I did not lose hope. I did not stop giving. Nor did I stop hearing my parents' admonitions for grit. Instinctively and by design, I set out to recover that which had been overtaken, without losing entirely the moment at hand.

Curiously, it was in the public sphere that the reintegration of my intimate real self began to occur. Reintegration crystallized recently when I returned to Mexico for seven months to conduct ethnographic fieldwork for my doctoral dissertation. Since we left in December 1959 I had returned to Mexico only four or five times and only for brief visits. One absence lasted 16 years. Moreover, I had never returned alone. It was only against the backdrop of my recent stay that I have finally been able to answer my own questions: "What specifically did *Pat* take away from me?" and "Can I finally make peace with her?" For me to understand what I had lost, I first had to find out what I had possessed prior to our immigration.

My given name is Patricia Olivia Covarrubias Baillet and I was born to a world shaped, in great measure, by what people call themselves and each other. Titles, first names, surnames, nicknames, terms of endearment, terms of estrangement—they all reflect and constitute a particular Mexican way of being. In my childhood world, people used terms of address not only to point to particular people but also to form particular relationships and to evoke complementary emotions.

As a child I was seldom called *Patricia*. To address someone by his or her first name *a secas* (literally "dryly" but connoting "alone") is perceived by most Mexicans as cold and distant. First names alone are generally reserved for reprimand or censure or to underscore formality. Therefore, in most conversations a variety of pointing terms are used to personalize one's communication with another and to affirm intimacy, friendship, esteem, and *confianza*, which is a blend of trust, respect, confidentiality, and unity.

In keeping with the Mexican penchant for avoiding formal names in favor of more personalized address when *confianza* is desired, at school and elsewhere in my world I was *Pati, Paty,* or *Patty* (the Spanish diminutives for *Patricia*). Only on formal occasions, such as at the presentation of school diplomas, are students addressed by their full names. All Mexicans have at least two last names, the first for their father's family name and the second for their mother's. As the Mexican expression goes, people have **two parents**. In the Maddox Academy annuals for 1958 and 1959, I am listed as *Covarrubias Baillet, Patricia Olivia.*

My grandmothers and great-grandmother were generous deployers of nicknames and other terms of endearment. They cajoled, hugged, bathed, dressed, played with me, took me to school, sang and read to me. They lathered me also with an abundant array of forms of address. To my paternal grandmother and great-grandmother, with whom I lived for a time, I was *Patricita, Pato* (duck), *Patita* (little duck or little foot), *la Patricita, la niña* (the girl), la chiquita (the little one). My mother's mother had her own selection. In addition to *Paty* and *Patricita,* she called me *mi rosita de Castilla* (my rose of Castille), *mi rosita de Jericó* (my rose of Jericho), *mi orquídea* (my orchid). I, in turn, had a term for these women who were additional mothers to me: *mamá.* My maternal grandmother was *Mamá Mary* or *Mamita Mary* (*mamita* is the diminutive for *mamá* and *Mary* is the diminutive for *María*). My paternal grandmother was *Mamá Lupe* (*Lupe* is the diminutive for *Guadalupe*). . . .

In the Mexico of my early childhood, terms of address and of reference were an integral part of my history. Whether I was at school or at home, my name assured me a place in the universal continuum. I was *Patricia* because *Mamá Lupe* wanted it so; the *Mamá Lupe* who more than 20 years before my birth had left the town of Cárdenas to participate in the presidential campaign of Lázaro Cárdenas. I was *Olivia* because that was *Mamá Mary's* choice; the *Mamá Mary* whose family ranch had been confiscated by the government during the Revolution of 1910 and whose family was disbanded forever in the ensuing chaos. I had a father, *Covarrubias,* whose ancestors had come from northern Spain and settled in Mexico City. I had a mother, *Baillet,* whose father's family emigrated from France and settled in Puebla and who had served in the Mexican military until his death.

Having a name does not grant me claims to idealism. My Mexican childhood was not perfect, but I had a secure cultural footing. In the network of rituals, myths, and traditions that has characterized many Mexicans from ancient to modern times, I held appointed office, I was daughter, granddaughter, great-granddaughter, sister, niece, cousin, pupil, Catholic, playmate. I lived in a world where public and private domains routinely exchanged places. This, while I had a generalized public function as defined by my status and role, I also had a differentiated intimate space. It was in this intimate space that my uniqueness was largely shaped and sustained by the banquet of terms of address that were meant exclusively for me. So it was for the first eight years of my life.

A few days before Christmas 1959 I experienced a concentrated outpouring of address forms unlike any other I had yet known. In a nervous stream, the sounds from my grandmothers' lips overflowed: *"Patricita," "Patty," "Paty," "Patita," "mi rosita," "mi orquídea," "mi niña," "mi niñita."* We had gathered at the train station for a final good-bye and it would be my last feast of spoken endearments for a long time.

I didn't know it at the time, but I was just a few days away from a pivotal moment. Two weeks after our final parting from Mexico City, I was introduced to Mrs. Williams and her third-grade class in California. "Class, this is *Pat*." I still cannot hear that phrase without my stomach cramping. With a single turn of the tongue, my mother's and my father's surnames vanished, my first name and its variations were razed, and the affect and history associated with them were dimmed. For the next eight years—in elementary, junior high, and high school—I was *Pat*. When last names were required I was *Pat C.* because others could not or would not try to pronounce *Covarrubias*. . . .

Excerpts pp. 9–11 and 12–13 from *Among Us: Essays on Identity, Belonging and Intercultural Competence*, edited by M. W. Lustig and J. Koester. Copyright © 2000 by Addison Wesley Longman, Inc. Reprinted by permission of Pearson Education, Inc.

Endnotes

1. The word *Thou* strikes many as a religious term, but in German it translates as "you." Buber's distinction is between addressing another as an object or "it" versus addressing the other as a person or "you."
2. Buber was an international citizen—an Austrian Jew who lived for 30 years in Israel, spoke half a dozen languages, and traveled widely. His major book has been translated into over 20 languages. So he believed his definition of the person applied across cultures. Many people agree, but others argue that his view of the person is in some ways more Western than Eastern. Some people in cultures that emphasize *group* identity (Japan, for example) believe that Buber's emphasis *on the individual* is misplaced. But most people in Western cultures think that his description fits their experience very well. And in Japan, Buber is one of the most popular Western authors. What do you think? See Martin Buber, *I and Thou,* translated by Walter Kaufmann (New York: Scribners, 1970).

References

Applegate, J. S., and Delia, J. G. 1980. "Person-Centered Speech, Psychological Development, and the Context of Languages Usage." In R. S. Clair and H. Giles (eds.), *The Social and Psychological Context of Language.* Hillsdale, NJ: Erlbaum.

Bakhtin, M. M. 1986. *Speech Genres and Other Late Essays.* Translated by V. W. McGee. Austin: University of Texas Press. (Originally published 1953.)

Brown, G. I. 1971. *Human Teaching for Human Learning: An Introduction to Confluent Education.* New York: Viking.

Buber, M. 1965. *Between Man and Man.* New York: Macmillan.

Buechner, F. 1973. *Wishful Thinking: A Theological ABC.* New York: HarperCollins.

Howe, R. 1963. *The Miracle of Dialogue.* New York: Seabury.

Lambert, B. L., and Gillespie, J. L. (1994). "Patient Perceptions of Pharmacy Students' Hypertension Compliance-Gaining Messages: Effects of Message Design Logic and Content Themes." *Health Communication,* 6: 311–325.

Liljefors, E. A., and Rahe, R. H. 1974. "Psychosocial Characteristics of Subjects with Myocardial Infarction in Stockholm." In E. K. Gunderson and R. H. Rahe (eds.), *Life Stress Illness.* Springfield, IL: Charles Thomas.

Lynch, J. J. 1977. *The Broken Heart: The Medical Consequences of Loneliness.* New York: Basic Books.

——. 1985. *The Language of the Heart: The Body's Response to Human Dialogue.* New York: Basic Books.

O'Keefe, B. 1988. "The Logic of Message Design: Individual Differences in Reasoning About Communication." *Communication Monographs,* 35: 80–103.

O'Keefe, B., and McCornack, S. A. 1987. "Message Design Logic and Message Goal Structure: Effects on Perceptions of Message Quality in Regulative Communication Situations." *Human Communication Research,* 14: 68–92.

Peterson, L. W., and Albrecht T. L. 1996. "Message Design Logic, Social Support, and Mixed-Status Relationships." *Western Journal of Communication,* 60: 291–309.

Powell, J. 1980. *Why Am I Afraid to Tell You Who I Am?* Chicago: Argus Communication.

Roosevelt, E. 1960. *You Learn by Living.* Philadelphia: Westminster Press.

Shotter, J. 1993. *Cultural Politics of Everyday Life: Social Constructionism, Rhetoric and Knowing of the Third Kind.* Toronto: University of Toronto Press. ✦

Chapter Four

Constructing Identities

Chapter Objectives

When you complete this chapter, you should be able to do the following:
- Define "identity" or "self" and describe some parts of your own.
- Explain what it means to say that your self is not something that you *are* but something you *do*.
- Explain basically how people construct identities through communication.
- Describe how the process of constructing identities is collaborative.
- Explain how selves are relational rather than individual, responsive, multidimensional, and changing.
- Describe and give an example of the response called closed stereotyping.
- Describe and give an example of the response called closed sensitivity.
- Describe and give an example of the response called open stereotyping.
- Describe and give an example of the response called open sensitivity.
- Explain how each response option, when combined with the responses made by those you communicate with, affects where your communication is on the interpersonal◀——▶impersonal continuum.

Chapter Preview

As you already know, your self or identity is who you are: male, female, outgoing, shy, curious, careful, optimistic, realistic, musical, mechanical, athletic, sarcastic, funny, serious, Hawaiian, Hispanic, Muslim, Methodist, and hundreds of other features. You were born with some parts of your identity—for example, the chromosomes that determine your primary sex characteristics. But you develop most of the qualities of your self—including your gender identity—as you interact with family members, friends, and other culturally influential people.

In many ways, there is no more important topic than identity. Who we are affects everything we do. That's why this chapter is so important. In these pages we explain how humans build and rebuild identities as they communicate. We want you to understand that your self or identity is not something that you simply *are* but something that you *do*. Human selves are not just entities that are always there, because they are negotiated as we communicate with others. The chapter identifies four main response options that communicators choose as they participate in the identity-construction process. And the final section of the chapter shows how different responses affect where communication lands on the impersonal◄──►interpersonal scale.

What Is Identity or Self?

Notice what happens in the following conversation:

Alia: Hi, just wanted to introduce myself. I'm Alia. I'm your new roommate. Just switched universities. Kind of sucks to move in your senior year, but well. . .

Cheryl: Cool. I'm Cheryl. Nice to meet you, finally. I just knew that a girl named Alia—how do you pronounce your name?—would be my new roommate, that's all. Anyways, good to meet you. Any preference in terms of where you wanna sleep?

Alia: Not really.

Cheryl: I'm just asking because I just got back from Germany. Exchange student, you know? I was sleeping in a dorm there and was glad that my roommate let me sleep by the window. I'm kind of claustrophobic. Ha-ha. Don't worry; otherwise I'm pretty much together. Let me guess where you're from. Honestly, you don't quite look as if you were from around here.

Alia: Well, whatdaya think?

Cheryl: Greece. Oh no, Italy.

Alia: Naaa.

Cheryl: Spain or South America?

Alia: Wrong again. Born in Chicago, my parents are from Iraq. Where are you from?

Cheryl: Born in Detroit and raised in Oregon.

Alia: So you are American, too?

Cheryl: Absolutely, although it's not that important to me, really. No kidding. Could have sworn you were from Greece. My best friend in Germany looks like you, and she's Greek. Well, I feel stupid to ask this, but . . . aren't you supposed to wear a scarf?

Alia: Guess what? I am a Christian, Chaldean to be exact. Not all Arabs are Muslims, and not all Muslims are Arabs. Islam's the biggest religion in the Arab world, but there're also lots of Christians.

Cheryl: Wow. Let's talk more about that. That's exciting. I'm living with an Iraqi woman.

Alia: Iraqi American is better. I was born here. Chicago, remember?

Cheryl: You're right, I'm sorry I went off on this cultural thing. I'm really, really glad to finally live with someone who is from another culture. I'm still in a kind of culture shock, coming back to the States from Germany. That's why I'm so glad about you.

Alia: Sure, but first, if you don't mind, could you show me around here? I need to register before classes start.

Cheryl: Yep, no problem. I'm sorry if I talked too much. Let's start with the library.

Cheryl and Alia are constructing themselves together. At first, Cheryl gives Alia a national identity that Alia does not identify with. Cheryl does this mainly because of how Alia looks. For a minute Cheryl restricts Alia's self to her nationality and religion. Alia is the "Iraqi woman," even though she would probably have liked to be the *person* Alia first, or the senior who is new to the university. Cheryl, on the other hand, constructs herself as a curious and outspoken young woman, a student, and someone who has been exposed to different cultures.

This conversation shows how identities or selves are outcomes of conversations and something that we do, rather than are. Cheryl and Alia move from negotiating their student identities when they talk about being a senior and an exchange student, to negotiating their national and ethnic identities, and back to negotiating their student selves again. Alia does not want to be known only as an Iraqi and an Arab. She wants Cheryl to recognize her multiple identities as a woman, a student, a Chaldean Christian, and an Iraqi American. Cheryl also emphasizes that her national identity is not that important to her. At that moment, she wants to be perceived as a knowledgeable and open person and a possible friend, and not just as an American. As you can see, identities are fluid, not static. No one wants to be put in an ethnic, national, or gender box, especially at the beginning of a relationship.

Here is another example of how identities are constructed in verbal and nonverbal talk:

Conversation 2:

Jan: Hey, how's it goin'?

Heather: (Silence and a scowl)

Jan: What's the matter?

Heather: Nothing. Forget it.

Jan: What are you so pissed about?

Heather: Forget it! Just drop it.

Jan: Well, all right! Pout! I don't give a damn!

Here, even though Jan and Heather are not talking about any specific object, issue, or event, they are definitely constructing identities together. In this conversation Heather's definition of herself and of Jan goes something like this:

> Right now I identify myself as independent of you (Silence. "Nothing. Forget it."). You're butting into my space, and you probably think I'm antisocial. But I've got good reasons for my anger.

On the other hand, Jan's definition of herself and of Heather is something like this:

> Right now I identify myself as friendly and concerned ("Hey, how's it goin'?" "What's the matter?"). I'm willing to stick my neck out a little, but you're obviously not interested in being civil. So there's a limit to how long I'll *stay* friendly and concerned. ("Well, all right! Pout! I don't give a damn!").

We want to emphasize that nobody in these conversations is constructing identities perfectly or poorly, right or wrong. In one sense, there is no right or wrong way to participate in this process. There are just *outcomes* of how you do it, *results* that you may or may not want.

We also want to emphasize that none of the people in these conversations could avoid constructing selves. It's a process that happens whenever people communicate. As we said in Chapter Two, some of the most important meanings we collaboratively construct are our identities, and all communicating involves constructing identities or selves. No matter how brief or extended the contact, whether it's written or oral, mediated or face-to-face, impersonal or interpersonal, the people involved will be directly or indirectly constructing definitions of themselves and responding to the definitions offered by others. Radio talk show hosts and television newscasters are continually building identities. The person who writes a letter longhand on colorful stationery is defining him- or herself differently from the person who writes the same letter on a word processor. The person who answers the telephone, "Yeah?" is defining him- or herself differently from the one who answers, "Good morning. May I help you?"

Research on intercultural communication shows how identity construction occurs in different cultures. For instance, Bailey (2000) shows how young Dominican Americans negotiate their cultural identities by switching between Spanish and English. Speaking in Spanish indicates solidarity with their peers who are similar in cultural background. In another study, Hegde (1998) shows how immigrants from India navigate between their Indian identity and their new American identity. Saskia has also studied Arab identities and has found that people of Arab descent enact multiple national and religious identities and feel more or less strongly Arab at various times, but it really depends on the context. For instance, some people say that they call themselves Arab American mostly when they have to fill out official forms, and that they feel Arab rather than Arab American when they talk about families because family is so important in the Arab world. As Scotton (1983) summarizes, in various cultural contexts, speakers use language choices "imaginatively . . . a range of options is open to them within a normative framework, and . . . taking one option rather than another is the *negotiation of identities.*"

So two reasons why it's important to understand the process of identity construction are (1) that you're doing it whenever you communicate—and everybody else is, too—and (2) that the process affects who you are in relation to others. The third reason why it's important is that *your negotiation responses also affect where your communication is on the impersonal*◄——►*interpersonal continuum.* As we'll explain in the final section of this chapter, some responses just about guarantee that your communication will be impersonal. Others lead to more interpersonal communicating. So if you want to help change the quality of your contacts with your dating partner, employer, roommate, sister, or parent in either direction on the continuum, you'll probably want to learn as much as you can about this process.

Definition of Identity

As identity or self is made up of interlocking features that mark how we behave and respond to others, identities are constellations of labels that establish social expectations that we have of ourselves and others. These social expectations can include roles that we want or have to play in specific situations and the languages or dialects we speak and expect others to speak. When you enter a classroom in the United States, you expect your instructor to talk and behave in certain ways. For instance, most North Americans expect that a person enacting the identity of an "instructor" should normally stand in front of the class, speak in a loud and intelligible voice, have control in the classroom, and, unless it's a foreign language class, express him- or herself in some form of English. And in order to enact the role of instructor, this person needs students who enact their role. Notice how we say "enact." This is another way of emphasizing that identities are something that we *do* rather than what we *are* (Collier and Thomas 1988; Hecht, Jackson, and Ribeau 2003). You are not born to be a student for all of your life, but you are socialized into this identity, and it becomes salient in different times and places.

Old Versus Current Views of Identity

It may sound weird to you to say that identities or selves are co-constructed in verbal and nonverbal talk. You might think of your *self* as fairly stable, identifiable, and clearly bounded. If so, you're not alone. Most people in Western cultures have been taught to think of their selves as individual containers that enclose their unique essence. As one book puts it,

> There is an individualist mode of thought, distinctive of modern Western cultures, which, though we may criticize it in part or in whole, we cannot escape. . . . This inescapable cultural vise has given us—or, at least, the dominant social groups in the West—a sense of themselves as distinctive, independent agents who own themselves and have relatively clear boundaries to protect in order to ensure their integrity and permit them to function more effectively in the world. (Sampson 1993, 31)

Most members of dominant social groups in the Western world think of the boundary of the individual as the same as the boundary of the body, and that the body houses or contains the self. Common metaphors reflect this view, as when people say that a person is *"filled* with anger," "unable to *contain* her joy," *"brimming* with laughter," or "trying to get anger *out of our system"* (Lakoff 1987, 383). Some theories of psychology reinforce this view of identity or the self. Psychologists influenced by the famous therapist Sigmund Freud, for example, think of society as made up of individual selves who are each working out their inner tensions. One Freudian insisted that a student revolt against university administrators was caused by the students' unresolved conflicts with their fathers. In his view,

> protestors were taking out their inner conflicts with parental authority by acting against the authority represented by the University. It was as though there were no legitimate problems with the University; it only symbolized protestors' unresolved Oedipal conflicts with the real source of their troubles, their fathers. (Sampson 1993, 44)

For this psychologist, selves were individual and internal.

But in the last decades of the twentieth century, the development of space travel, satellite television, and the World Wide Web; the globalization of music and business; and the end of the Cold War have all helped Westerners understand that this view of the person as a bounded individual is, as one anthropologist puts it, rather "peculiar" (Geertz 1979, 229). For centuries, people in many cultures outside the West have not been thinking this way. For example, if a North American is asked to explain why someone financially cheated another person, the North American's tendency will be to locate the cause in "the kind of person she is." A Hindu, by contrast, is more likely to offer a social explanation—"The man is unemployed. He is not in a position to give that money" (Miller 1984, 968). This is because many members of the Hindu culture don't think of identity or the self as individual, but as social or communal. For them, identity is a function of cultural or group memberships. Or, to take another example, in a study of U.S. and Samoan child care workers, U.S. preschool teachers tended to help children socialize by developing their individuality, whereas Samoan caregivers' efforts "were directed towards helping the children learn how better to fit into their in-group" (Ochs 1988, 199). In their broader culture, Samoans in this study also recognized the central role of other people in events that were deemed worthy of praise or compliments. So one researcher reported that when a Samoan passenger complimented a driver with language that translates, "Well done the driving," the driver typically responded, "Well done the support." "In this Samoan view, if a performance went well, it is the supporters' merit as much as the performers" (Ochs 1988, 200). Many Japanese understand the person in a similar way. In Japan, one author notes, "The concept of a self completely independent from the environment is very foreign" (Kojima 1984, 972). Rather, Japanese think of individuals in terms of the social context they fit into—their family, work group, and so on. The United States, Canada, Australia, Great Britain, and some other Western cultures have a strong belief in the individual self, but many European countries (e.g., Spain, Austria, and Finland) and most Asian and Latin American cultures understand identities or selves as social, relational, or group-oriented (Hofstede 1980).

It's easier to understand how identity construction works—and how to manage your own identity constructing—if you adopt what has historically been a more Eastern perspective. This doesn't mean that you have to change cultures or religions, or to pretend to be somebody you're not. In fact, this understanding is being accepted by communication scholars, psychologists, anthropologists, and other students of human behavior all over the world. Especially in the final decade of the twentieth century, many of these scholars and teachers recognized that selves or identities are relational from birth, or maybe even before. They began taking seriously what Lev Vygotsky and George Herbert Mead, two very influential human development researchers, said several decades ago: namely, that infants are first *social* beings and only later in life learn to see themselves as *individuals*. As psychologist Edward Sampson explains,

> Both Vygotsky and Mead clearly emphasize the necessary social bases of human thinking, cognition, and mindedness. Indeed, rather than viewing the individual's mind as setting forth the terms for the social order, the reverse describes the actual event: the social process—namely, dialogue and conversation—precedes, and is the foundation for, any subsequent psychological processes that emerge. (Sampson 1993, 103)

In short, the English terms, *self* and *identity* and their meanings are only about 300 years old. Studies of history and of other cultures illustrate that the Western definition developed over the last 275 of these 300 years is very narrow. Today, this idea that selves are individual containers is being revised as communication scholars and psychologists are recognizing how much our selves are developed in communication with others. Westerners increasingly recognize that identities or selves are multidimensional and that they change in response to the people and institutions we connect with. Each of our identities has athletic, artistic, ethnic, gendered, occupational, scientific, political, economic, and religious dimensions, and all of these shift in content and importance as we move from situation to situation.

Four Characteristics of Identities or Selves

This understanding of identities or selves can be summarized in four primary characteristics.

1. Identities Are Multidimensional and Changing

One feature of selves is that we're complex. On the one hand, each of us is characterized by some stabilities or patterns. A person's genetic makeup is stable, and your ethnic identity also probably hasn't changed and probably won't. Someone who's known you all your life can probably identify some features you had when you were 4 or 5 years old that you still have, and as you look at old photographs of yourself, you might recognize how the identity of the person in the picture is in some ways "the same" as who you are today.

On the other hand, you are different in at least as many ways as you are the same. Think, for example, of who you were at age 9 or 10 and who you were at age 14 or 15. Adolescence is a time of *significant* change in our selves. Or, if it fits you, think of your self before you were married and after, or your identity before and after you had children.

Some researchers broadly classify identities or selves into personal, relational, and communal features (Hecht, Jackson, and Ribeau 2003). *Personal* identity is all the characteristics that you think make you a unique person, such as being friendly, helpful, disciplined, hard work-ing, beautiful, and so forth. *Relational* identities are based on relation-ships you have with others, such as mother-daughter, teacher-student, or employer-employee. *Communal* identities are usually related to larger groups, such as ethnicities, race, religion, gender, or nationality.

2. Selves Are Responders

We've already introduced this second feature of selves in Chapter Three when we said that responsiveness is one of the five features that makes each of us a person. Our main point there was to contrast re-sponding with simply reacting. Now we want to build the meaning of this idea by noting that responding implies both *choice* (not just react-ing) and *connection* with what's already happened.

To say that selves are responders is to say that we grow out of and fit into a context of actions and events that we behave-in-relation-to. On the one hand, this is just another way of saying that selves are relational or social. Remember how Alia responded to Cheryl's ques-tion about where she is from and how they both constructed their student and ethnic/national identi-ties? They responded to each other. In one instance, Cheryl might be regarded as just reacting when she asks about Alia's absent scarf. However, in most in-stances, both women are responding to each other, which includes reflecting about what the other per-son just said. Responding means that all human ac-tion is joint action. No human starts behaving from ground zero, so that everything we do, from the very beginning, is in reply or answer to something else.

Humans begin respond-ing from the first moment

The woman in this photo is simultaneously negotiating her personal identities (helpful, competent, professional), her relational identities (mom, mentor), and her communal identity (conference attendee). How might she have pre-sented herself two minutes earlier before her children ran to her? Five minutes later in her family's hotel room?

we develop any awareness, which, as we noted earlier, probably happens before birth. Every baby is born into a world of verbal and nonverbal talk, family relationships, gender patterns, ongoing activities, and social and political events. This is the sense in which no person is, "after all, the first speaker, the one who disturbs the eternal silence of the universe." Since none of us is Adam or Eve, all of our actions more or less effectively connect with or fit into the activities and language systems that surround us (Bakhtin 1986, 69).

3. Identities Are Developed in Past and Present Relationships

The reason selves change over time is that we develop who we are in relationships with the people around us. Some of the most important parts of each person's identity are established in one's family of origin, the people with whom you spend the first five to seven years of your life. One of your parents may have consistently introduced you to new people from the time you were old enough to talk, and today you may still find it easy to make acquaintances. Or you may have moved around a lot when you were young, and today you feel secure only when you have your own "place" and you prefer to spend holidays close to home. You may treasure a wonderful relationship with your dad, or you may have had the opposite kind of experience. Your family is the role model for many types of relational, religious, or ethnic identities. For instance, you learn what it means to be a good friend or a good neighbor, a good brother or sister or mother or father, or perhaps not such a good one:

> My father is an alcoholic. He has never admitted to that fact. He and my mom used to get in lots of fights when I lived at home. The six of us kids were used as pawns in their war games. I always wondered whether or not I was responsible for his drinking. When the fights were going on, I always retreated to my room. There I felt secure. Now, I am 22, and have been married for two years. I have this affliction that, whenever the slightest thing happens, I always say I am so sorry. I am sorry when the milk is not cold, sorry that the wet towel was left in the gym bag. I just want to take the blame for everything, even things I have no control over. (Black 1982, 9)

Many current studies about dysfunctional families emphasize how people with addictions to alcohol, cocaine, prescription drugs, and other chemicals developed the communication patterns that reinforce these addictions in their families of origin (Fuller et al. 2003). Other research focuses on how addictions affect the children or other family members of addicted persons. One review of studies about adult children of alcoholics concludes that, regardless of gender, socioeconomic group, or ethnic identity, these people develop 13 common features. For example, many adult children of alcoholics "have difficulty following a project through from beginning to end," "lie when it would be just as easy to tell the truth," "judge themselves without mercy," "take themselves very seriously," "constantly seek approval and affirmation," and "are extremely loyal, even in the face of evidence that the loyalty is undeserved" (Beatty 1989). These books and articles illustrate how much our family of origin contributes to the response patterns that we follow in identity construction. We talk about one of these patterns, codependence, in detail in Chapter Ten. But our main point here is that past relationships contribute a great deal to the patterns that help make up our present selves.

Present relationships are also important. When you realize that a new friend really likes you, it can do great things for your self-definition. Getting a top grade from a teacher you respect can affect how you see yourself. At work, a positive performance evaluation from your supervisor or a raise can improve not only your mood and your bank account but also your perception of yourself. And again, the reverse can obviously also happen. The point is, genetic makeup does not determine your identity, and we call the communication process that produces these identities *identity construction.*

Recall and Application

Family of Origin and Communication Patterns

In the left-hand column, list some important communication pattern in your family of origin. For example, your parents might have been unusually active in the community or church, or even famous. One of your parents might have emphasized the importance of being a good listener or of always speaking logically and clearly. Your family might have valued its privacy strongly or always shown its feelings openly. Perhaps they argued loudly but lovingly with each other or held a grudge for a long time. Social events might always have been accompanied with lots of alcohol, or none. Write down a few of what you think are your family's most important communication patterns.

Then, across from each feature, list some characteristics of your communication that connect with the items in column 1. What ways of communicating did you learn in your family of origin?

Family Communication Patterns	My Communication Patterns
1.	1.
2.	2.
3.	3.

4. Identities Can Be Avowed and Ascribed

Finally, identities or selves can be ascribed and avowed. *Ascribed* means that others assign you an identity that you may or may not agree with; *avowed* means that you personally assign yourself an identity and act it out. People also try to negotiate this avowal and ascription process. Remember the conversation between Cheryl and Alia? Cheryl ascribed to Alia a somewhat stereotyped national and religious identity that Alia did not accept as her main identity in that particular situation. During the conversation they both put their student and cultural identities on the table (being from Detroit and growing up in Oregon can imply two different regional identities) and reached somewhat of an alignment on how they wanted to be perceived in this initial encounter. However, sometimes when people stereotype, they rigidly stick with their opinions about people and make them one dimensional. For instance, sometimes people talk slower when they realize that English is Saskia's second language or start immediately to talk about beer when they hear that Saskia is from Germany. It can be entertaining for a while, but then Saskia wants to be perceived as Saskia or a woman or an instructor and not only as German. Rigid ascription of identities can become a problem for the person who is ascribed the identity. This is also true for many African Americans, Latinas, or Asian Americans. People are often judged on their looks and language and not who else they are or want to be. The question of ascription and avowal will come up again when we talk about response options.

This woman is protesting an ascribed identity.

Applying What You Know

On one side of a piece of paper write the words, "I am." On the other side, write the words "I am not." Then write down as many different ways you can finish each statement. Review your lists to determine which of your identity statements are ascribed and which are avowed. Which of your statements best describe who you have been, who you are now, and who you would like to be?

Characteristics of How We Construct Identities

Now that you have an idea of what identities are and four of their characteristics, it's time to describe how these selves get constructed. Overall, we want to highlight four characteristics of the identity construction process:

- Identities are constructed collaboratively in verbal and nonverbal talk.
- The outcomes of this process cannot always be anticipated.
- Identities are constructed by what communicators give out and take in.
- The construction and negotiation of identities happen both intentionally and unintentionally.

1. Identities Are Constructed Collaboratively in Verbal and Nonverbal Talk

Throughout this book we're emphasizing how verbal and nonverbal talk *construct* the worlds we inhabit. As we've said before, when we say "construction," we mean "co-construction." You can't do it by yourself. It takes at least two. It happens between people, and, as we have said, identities are something that you do rather than what you are. You might say, for example, that you're a friendly, patient person and that's part of the self who you "are." We would say, yes, this is probably a part of you, *and* recall the time a friend observed an interaction between you and another person and commented, "You were really rude to him, do you know that?" Perhaps you answered, "No way, I thought that I was being really friendly. I'm not a rude person. But you're right, he turned away and I didn't know why." In the interaction you unintentionally gave out verbal and nonverbal cues that you thought were friendly but that the other person interpreted as rude.

We've also noted that "collaborate" doesn't mean "agree." It just means "labor together." Think again of the difference between *alignment* and *agreement*. Two individuals or groups can be *aligned* (collaborating) in that they are moving in a similar direction, even though they *disagree* about how to get there or who should get there first. One implication of the fact that the process of constructing selves is collaborative is that you cannot control it yourself. Your responses make up no more than one half of the process.

2. The Outcomes of the Process Cannot Always Be Anticipated

Since your part is only half of the identity construction process, you have to "stay tuned" to see what the outcomes are going to be (remember nexting from Chapter Two). It's also likely that they'll change. Here's an example. Your mom calls you and tells you that she wants to talk with you about some important things. You sigh and assume immediately that she wants to do the "mom" thing, which is to remind you about your spending habits, your grades, and especially your new boyfriend. You call and try to be happy, friendly, and polite. Basically you do what you think a good daughter is supposed to do on the phone. But you cannot really take the sharp edge out of your voice. Then, five minutes into the talk, you realize that your mom really just wants to have a chat with you. She is easygoing and actually talks just like a friend, rather than a mom. The sharp edge comes out of your voice, and instead of reminding your mom to mind her own business, you have a great talk with her. This outcome was not anticipated. Or imagine you start a new job after only talking with your new boss on the phone. He had a strange and harsh voice, and you assumed the worst. The next day, you meet him and find out that he had a very stressful day the day before, and that he's actually a very friendly person who is concerned about his employees. You did not expect that either. One of his personal identities emerged in the telephone conversation. However, he is more than that. You can expect that during another stressful day, he might respond to you as he did on the phone. But that's okay because you know that you can be grumpy as well when you're stressed.

3. Identities Are Constructed by What Communicators Give Out and Take In

As we've said earlier in this book, people are exhaling and inhaling all the time, and identities emerge from this two-part, or bidirectional, process. The *inhaling* parts of this process include what you perceive, how completely and carefully you listen, how much you are distracted by your own agendas, the extent to which you stereotype the people you're communicating with, and so on. What we call the *exhaling* parts include all the cues or messages you give out, including your appearance and dress, tone of voice, facial expression, word choice, eye behavior, amount of talk, and so on.

4. Identity Construction Happens Both Intentionally and Unintentionally

Many communicators don't even realize that this process is going on all the time. They think that communication deals only with information or content, and they don't notice how selves and relationships are constantly being constructed. One main goal of this book is to reduce the number of these people. We believe strongly that everyone should know about identity construction. But this doesn't mean that you need to focus on it all the time. In many situations, people aren't aware of the identity construction process because it's not creating any problems. If everybody agrees about whom they are to each other there's no reason to pay much attention to how selves are being collaboratively defined.

But effective communicators are aware of the process when they need to be. They realize how the process works and are flexible enough to adapt the ways they participate in it. They understand what's happening in a situation like the conversation between mother and daughter, and they know what they can do about it. They are aware of the four main responses we are about to describe and they can choose the one that best fits the situation, their values, and their own needs.

'But . . .' A Student Responds

This chapter ignores individual integrity. The most important parts of who I am are determined individually, not between me and someone else. In fact, it's not good for one person to let somebody else define who he or she is. Only weak people with low self-esteem let themselves be affected by others that much.

We believe individual integrity is important, too. This is why we emphasize how important your individual *responses* are. Human identity is not just a knee-jerk *reaction* to surrounding forces. But it's also true that no person is an island. No human determines his or her identity entirely on their own. For example, your ethnic or racial identity grows out of the relationships you have with others. So two college students might both be Chinese by looks, but one might be ethnically more Caucasian—relating to her parents and family as Caucasians do, preferring western food, attending a western Christian church—while the other is ethnically more Chinese—relating to her parents in appropriately Chinese ways, preferring Chinese food, attending a Buddhist temple. Each developed his ethnicity in contacts with the people around him. Similarly, some people who are born African American learn pride, strength, and self-respect from the African Americans in their family of origin and the Latinos, whites, and others they relate with. Other African American children grow up without strong role models, experience continual racism, and develop weaker or angrier self-definitions. Still others are raised to be at home in a dominant power structure and develop identities almost indistinguishable from their Caucasian and Asian colleagues and friends. Even more importantly, many African Americans in each of these groups *change* their self-definitions at some points in their lives. How? By changing the ways they relate with others.

At the same time, deep-rooted habits and patterns that have become part of your "core self" certainly don't change every time you talk with someone new. In fact, even when you want to alter them, they can be incredibly resistant. But each of us is so multidimensional that important parts of who we actually are can and do change from one communication situation to the other. Our discussion of identity construction focuses on exactly this dynamic of change.

Understanding the Process: Response Options

In order to understand how identity construction happens, follow us along through three steps. First recall again the impersonal ⟷ interpersonal communication scale from Chapter Three. Second, recall the distinction we've made between inhaling and exhaling, what you take in and what you give out. Third, have a look at the following diagram.

Each of us sometimes responds to a communication situation by exhaling or expressing mainly impersonal information about the roles we play, such as being a cook, retail sales clerk, or telemarketer. In other situations we respond by giving out not only impersonal but also personal information about our uniqueness, unmeasurability, reflectiveness, responsiveness, and addressability.

At the same time, we respond to some communication situations by inhaling or perceiving other peoples' role identities, which are their impersonal characteristics. And in other situations, we're aware of not only impersonal but also personal features of the person(s) with whom we're communicating.

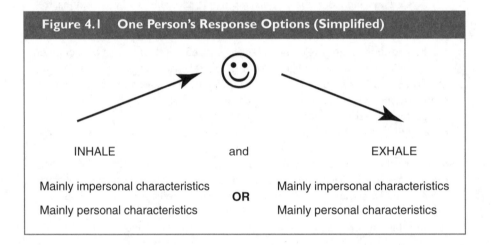

Figure 4.1   One Person's Response Options (Simplified)

INHALE   and   EXHALE

Mainly impersonal characteristics   Mainly impersonal characteristics

                          OR

Mainly personal characteristics   Mainly personal characteristics

As this simple diagram shows, each individual participates in the identity construction process by making one of four possible responses:

1. Exhaling impersonal characteristics and inhaling impersonal characteristics.

2. Exhaling impersonal characteristics and inhaling personal characteristics.

3. Exhaling personal characteristics and inhaling impersonal characteristics.

4. Exhaling personal characteristics and inhaling personal characteristics.

Notice that each of these responses is made up of two parts: what you receive, or inhale, and what you express, or exhale. For example, when talking with a store clerk you may choose only to *express* (exhale) impersonal information—"I'm a customer (just like most of the other customers you've helped today)"—and to *perceive* (inhale) the clerk only as a filler of that role. This would be an example of Choice 1, "inhaling" and "exhaling" mainly impersonal characteristics. Or when talking with a close friend, you might choose to be sensitive to your friend's feelings and to express some of your feelings at the same time. This would be an example of Choice 4, because you'd be inhaling some personal characteristics and also exhaling some personal characteristics.

Also notice that the ways you engage in this process change from impersonal to personal and back again. As the communication unfolds, your inhaling and exhaling choices change. In order to track these changes more clearly, we introduce some new labels for your four response options:

- Closed stereotyping.
- Closed sensitivity.
- Open stereotyping.
- Open sensitivity.

Exhaling: Closed or Open

The term *closed* can be used to mean both "hands over ears" (closed to input) or "hands over mouth" (closed to output). We use it in the second sense. *Closed* means willing and able to exhale (present or express) mainly impersonal information or characteristics. It follows that *open* means willing and able to present or express some personal characteristics. When you respond by verbally and nonverbally presenting only your role identity or other interchangeable aspects of who you are, we're calling that *closed*. But when you reveal or talk about part of who you are as a person, for example your unique features, feelings, or uncertainties, we're calling that *open*.

Inhaling: Stereotyping or Sensitivity

The second word of each label—"stereotyping" or "sensitivity"—designates what you're receiving, perceiving, or inhaling. When you're primarily aware of the other's impersonal characteristics—his or her role identities or other interchangeable features—we're labeling that choice *stereotyping*. Stereotyping is a common coping mechanism in a complex world, and we all do it to a certain extent. As we note in Chapter Five, especially when interacting with people in their social roles, we fall back on scripts and former interactions that we had with people in the same roles. However, people have to be careful not to let stereotypes become rigid or fixed. This is especially true when we're around people with different ethnic, religious, or gender identities.

On the other hand, when you perceive, notice, or listen for the other's personal characteristics (uniqueness, unmeasurable parts, reflectiveness, responsiveness, addressability), we call this choice *sensitivity*. So, each time you interact with another person, you make choices between these four response options, and each choice makes a difference in your conversation and relationship. At the same time you are making choices about your own response options, so is your communication partner. As you might imagine, this process gets more and more complicated as more people join in. At a basic level you can visualize your response options in the following way.

Figure 4.2	**Response Options**	
Inhaling the other's social roles and impersonal characteristics	**1. Closed Stereotyping**	**3. Open Stereotyping**
Inhaling the other's personal characteristics	**2. Closed Sensitivity**	**4. Open Sensitivity**
	Exhaling your social roles and impersonal characteristics	Exhaling your personal characteristics

We recognize that these labels sound value loaded. It might sound to you as if "closed stereotyping" is always bad and "open sensitivity" is always good. *Please try not to jump to this conclusion.* We chose the terms in part because they are simple and direct. Instead of "closed," for example, we could have used "limited," "restrained," partial," or "restricted." But we chose the simpler word in the hope that it would be clearer. It is important to realize, as we've said several times, that you are not "failing" or "making a mistake" when you respond by expressing your impersonal characteristics or paying most attention to the other's impersonal characteristics. Often this is entirely appropriate for the situation you're in. But even though stereotyping can be natural and unavoidable, it still limits your ability to contact the person with whom you are communicating. And there are many situations where it is appropriate to limit how much you share of yourself—to primarily express your impersonal characteristics. But this is still a closed response that limits the extent to which others contact you as a person. Both of these communication choices tend to have the predictable consequence of maintaining social roles and reducing the potential to move toward the interpersonal end of the communication continuum. This is why we label the responses as we do.

'But . . .' A Student Responds

Are you saying that when I'm in a group of five or six people, each of us actually develops a definition of how each other person views us?

Yes. Again, the definitions often operate below the level of awareness, but your definition of each person (and of yourself in relation to that person) becomes important as you turn to talk with him or her. If you had a videotape of yourself in that group, you'd notice the differences—sometimes subtle ones and sometimes obvious ones. You do not communicate with any two persons in exactly the same way, and the differences reflect differences in how you define yourself, how you define them, and what you think they think of you.

Take an obvious example. Your facial expression and tone of voice change when you move from talking with a person you define as interested, attractive, and informed to talking with someone you define as bored and uninformed about the topic. These are visible and audible changes. And they directly reflect different identities, different definitions of self and other.

Closed Stereotyping

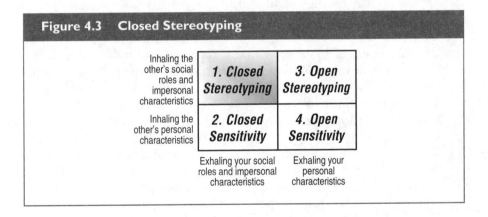

Figure 4.3   Closed Stereotyping

	Exhaling your social roles and impersonal characteristics	Exhaling your personal characteristics
Inhaling the other's social roles and impersonal characteristics	*1. Closed Stereotyping*	*3. Open Stereotyping*
Inhaling the other's personal characteristics	*2. Closed Sensitivity*	*4. Open Sensitivity*

Consider the first response. Whenever you choose this one, your response is *closed* in the sense that you give out primarily impersonal information, and it is *stereotyping* in the sense that you are aware primarily of the other person's impersonal characteristics. This supervisor-subordinate exchange is an example of closed stereotyping by both persons.

Supervisor: As I tell all my people, Mr. Bennett, your job is to learn these tasks as quickly as you can and then work toward the production level the company has set for a person in your position.

Subordinate: I appreciate the clarity. I understand what I'm supposed to do, and I realize that you've got a lot of people in my position to deal with.

In this situation, each person identifies him- or herself and the other primarily as a filler of a role, one who is virtually interchangeable with every other person in that role. Each expresses mainly impersonal aspects of him- or herself, and acknowledges the impersonal aspects of the other: "I'm a supervisor and I see you as a subordinate." "I'm a subordinate and I see you as my supervisor." So each person selects choice 1, closed stereotyping. One or both of them could conceivably be aware of some personal characteristics. For example, the supervisor may have noticed that Bennett dresses nicely or has bad breath. But none of this surfaces in her talk. The communication between them clearly embodies closed stereotyping on both parts.

Closed stereotyping also occurs when you are approached by a Jehovah's Witness or a person of Mormon faith and you immediately say no, you are not interested in talking with them because you are Catholic and already have your faith. You are closed because you inhale only the religious identity of the other person and as a response you exhale your religious identity without talking further about it. You perceive and respond only to one social identity or role without responding to other personal characteristics.

Sometimes people who choose this option express many of their impersonal features instead of just a few. For example, since John's wife is an attorney, he sometimes finds himself in the role of "spouse" at a party or other gathering populated by many attorneys and clients he doesn't know. Sometimes he'll have a moderately intense 10- or 15-minute conversation with one or two of these people, but their communication seldom moves far beyond role relating. Many topics get discussed—differences between being a professor and being a lawyer, the fortunes of the local sports teams, the state of the economy, and so on. But John tends to perceive most of these people generally as "lawyers" or "clients," and they tend to perceive him as "spouse of an attorney" and "a professor." Because of the situation, John also usually responds only by expressing impersonal parts of himself, and the other person responds similarly. So even though they converse for a relatively long time, they are both inhaling and exhaling social role information, and thus their communication doesn't move much beyond closed stereotyping.

As we've already noted, there's nothing wrong with this. Both John and his conversation partner help keep the party going smoothly, each makes a new acquaintance, and each learns something, both about the topics they discuss and about the other person. They establish a connection that may get renewed or developed beyond closed stereotyping in future business or social contacts.

Disconfirmation

On the other hand, one especially powerful and often damaging kind of closed stereotyping is called *disconfirmation.* This occurs when a person communicates in such a way to deny the other person's existence or significance. This response is closed because it only expresses the disconfirming person's negative judgment of the other, and it's stereotyping because it labels the other person as simply not worth contacting. In its most extreme form, disconfirmation almost halts the identity construction process. This is because if you deny someone's existence or significance, you're in effect refusing to continue communicating with him or her. Even though you may be in the same space with the other person, you're behaving almost as if he or she wasn't there. So there's almost no communicating between you. The only message is "You don't count" or "You're a zero." We say almost because, first, that message can be very significant and, second, even the slightest attention minimally confirms a person's presence. So it is virtually impossible to disconfirm someone absolutely.

As a matter of fact, disconfirmation usually occurs in partial, episodic, or even momentary ways. At a party, for example, you may include someone in a conversation for a while and then ignore her while you focus on someone else, as if the first person suddenly didn't exist. But even momentary or partial disconfirmation can create problems. For example, in their discussion of an important business decision, some senior executives might ignore the contributions of a junior executive because they assume that the junior executive's questions or suggestions are naive or uninformed. Young children are also disconfirmed when adults talk about them as if they weren't even present or when they respond to the child's excited "Hey! Look at this neat frog!" with "Watch out for that clean floor and go wash your hands!" It can also be disconfirming to respond to someone's "Hi!" with avoidance or a blank stare.

Research indicates that there are at least three different ways disconfirmation occurs: "denial of presence," "avoiding involvement," and offering only an "unrelated response." Psychiatrist R. D. Laing illustrates denial of presence by describing a young man named Peter.

> A peculiar aspect of [Peter's] childhood was that his presence in the world was largely ignored. No weight was given to the fact that he was in the same room while his parents had intercourse. He had been physically cared for in that he had been well fed and kept warm, and underwent no physical separation from his parents during his earlier years. Yet he had been consistently treated as though he did not "really" exist. Perhaps worse than the experience of physical separation was to be put in the same room as his parents and ignored, not malevolently, but through sheer indifference. (Laing 1961, 119)

Which of the three kinds of disconfirmation are occurring here? What leads you to this conclusion?

Extreme cases like this one are rare. But less intense kinds of disconfirmation can also create feelings of alienation, frustration, and lowered self-worth—"avoiding involvement," for example. Ken Cissna and Evelyn Sieburg are two interpersonal communication researchers and teachers who have described several ways people help create disconfirmation. One is avoidance of eye contact. As you'll read in the chapter on nonverbal communication, especially in most Western cultures, lack of eye contact is often experienced as disconfirming. Another is "avoidance of physical contact except in ritualized situations such as hand-shaking" (Cissna and Sieburg 1981, 263). Again, the common element among all these examples is that they are experienced as saying, in effect, "You're insignificant," "You don't count," or, in its most extreme form, "You don't even exist."

Another way communicators sometimes disconfirm is by responding "irrelevantly" or "tangentially." An irrelevant response is one that is unrelated or only minimally related to what the other person has just said. As Cissna and Sieburg point out, "The person whose topic is repeatedly ignored may soon come to doubt his or her very existence, and at best will feel that he or she is not heard, attended to, or regarded as significant" (Cissna and Sieburg 1981). A weaker version of this same kind of experience can occur when someone responds tangentially by making only a slight connection with what the other has said, and then immediately going off on a tangent by shifting to a different topic. Consider how you'd respond, for example, if you were Marcelo in this exchange:

> *Marcelo*: I can't believe it! I spent three entire days researching an answer to the "very important" question my boss asked me to "get right on," and when I went to give him my report, he told me he didn't need the information any more! This organization is so screwed up. I don't know how they stay in business!

> *Tom*: Wow. I've been trying to figure out whether to take my vacation time in weekends or in one two-week stretch this year. What are you going to do?

If you were Marcelo, it's likely that Tom's comment would at least lead you to wonder whether he has wax in his ears. If this kind of thing happened consistently, it would be difficult for you to feel valued, important, *confirmed*.

Some counselors and therapists believe that constant disconfirmation is the most devastating experience a human can have. If you are disconfirmed often enough, you actually begin to wonder who you are or, worse yet, *if* you are anybody at all. As psychologist William James put it, the worst possible punishment any human could experience would be to be "turned loose in society and remain absolutely unnoticed" (Laing 1969, 98).

On the other hand, sometimes it's just fine to be ignored. Many people enjoy living in a large city precisely because they can be anonymous when they want to be. This is especially important in crowded cultures such as some places in Japan, where a couple can make love with only a rice-paper screen separating them from others and can feel alone because they know that their neighbors have learned to ignore them completely. It can also be helpful to be able to effectively ignore another person. For example, disconfirmation can provide some protection from an aggressive panhandler on the street or someone else who is being abusive or persistently offensive.

In short, the first of the four main identity-construction responses is closed stereotyping, and it can be positive or negative, helpful or toxic. The most extreme form, disconfirmation almost stops communication in its tracks.

Closed Sensitivity

When you respond with option 2, you are still unwilling or unable to exhale or express much about who you are as a person, but you are aware of or are inhaling some of the other person's human features (Figure 4.4). Persons in the helping professions—counselors, lawyers, accountants, nurses, psychologists, teachers—often respond in this way. They develop their abilities to be sensitive to the personal characteristics of their client, student, patient, or counselee, but they avoid

Figure 4.4   Closed Sensitivity

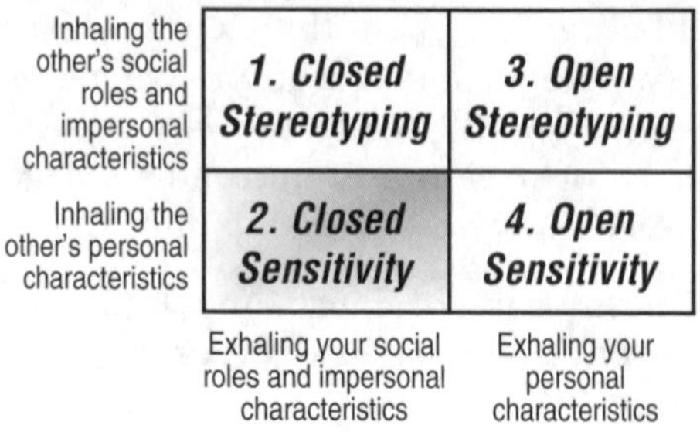

expressing much of who they are as a person. They try to stay in their role as adviser, educator, or facilitator, sometimes revealing a little of their professional self but usually going into detail only about their client's or patient's life and problems. You may have experienced this kind of communicating where *your* uniqueness, feelings, choices, and so forth are very important but the other's personal characteristics are out of bounds.

People choose closed sensitivity in other contexts, too.

> *Shopper*: This luggage is a piece of junk! I took it on only three trips, and it's already falling apart! Why do you sell this kind of garbage? When I pay over $200 for a suitcase, I don't expect to get cardboard and cheap plastic!

> *Clerk*: I'm sorry that happened. I realize you're upset. I know that it's frustrating to have to return something you expected to last for years. But the store's objective is to satisfy all our customers, and our policy says you can return this item up to a year after you bought it. So if you're within the time period, I'll write out a refund.

Here the clerk is sensitive to some of the shopper's feelings (personal information) but responds only in terms of the role as clerk (social identity).

Open Stereotyping

The third response option is *open* in the sense that you express some of your personal characteristics, but it still involves *stereotyping* because you're receiving and responding only to the other's social features (Figure 4.5). For example, a manager choosing option 3 might be upset with her boss's excessive authoritarianism and let her boss know her feelings. She might say something like, "I feel frustrated because you're pushing me a lot harder than I believe you've got any right to.

| | Figure 4.5 | Open Stereotyping | |

Inhaling the other's social roles and impersonal characteristics	**1. Closed Stereotyping**	**3. Open Stereotyping**
Inhaling the other's personal characteristics	**2. Closed Sensitivity**	**4. Open Sensitivity**
	Exhaling your social roles and impersonal characteristics	Exhaling your personal characteristics

My whole group is working as hard as we can, but it seems like you hardly even notice." In this case, she's revealing some feelings (open), but she is aware only of the role identity of her boss (stereotyping).

Unfortunately, sometimes a divorced parent will fall into open stereotyping when talking with his or her child. When the parent is acutely feeling the pain of the divorce, he or she is often looking for someone to talk to but is hesitant to "unload" on a person outside the family. So, especially if there's a child who's near college age or above, the parent will sometimes talk with the child at great length about the pain and misery of divorce. Most children are uncomfortable when they're put in this position because they don't feel they can be a parent for their own mom or dad. If parents were aware of the discomfort, they'd probably stop. But the problem is created when the parent in pain needs to be open with "someone who understands," and, in the parent's eyes, the child qualifies. In these situations the parent is clearly being open, in that he or she is talking about feelings and reflections. But the choice is also stereotyping, because the parent only sees the child as "a family member" or "a willing ear," and isn't sensitive to his or her discomfort.

The so-called "stranger on the train" (or plane) phenomenon can be another example of this identity construction response option. Has it happened to you yet? A person takes the seat next to you, finds a conversational opening, and launches into a monologue about his or her personal life and problems. Before the trip is over you have learned some of the most intimate details of the person's eating habits, health struggles, sex life, and work successes and failures. This person is obviously very open. But often he or she is stereotyping you, in that you are simply someone who is unassertive or patient enough to sit there and listen. From this person's perspective, the primary thing that qualifies you as a listener is that you have the adjoining seat. Almost anybody in that seat would have gotten the same treatment.

Open Sensitivity

When you respond with option 4 you make available some of your personal characteristics while also perceiving and responding to the other as a person (Figure 4.6). The counselor Carl Rogers wrote that he tried to choose this option with the people who came to him.

> I enter the relationship as a subjective person, not as a scrutinizer, not as a scientist. I feel, too, that when I am most effective, then somehow I am relatively whole in that relationship, or the word that has meaning to me is "transparent." To be sure there may be many aspects of my life that aren't brought into the relationship, but what is brought into the relationship is transparent. There is nothing hidden. Then I think, too, that in such a relationship I feel a real willingness for this other person to *be what he [or she] is.* I call that "acceptance." I don't know that that's a very good word for it, but my meaning there is that I'm willing for him [or her] to possess the feelings he [or she] possesses, to hold the attitudes he [or she] holds, to be the person he [or she] is. (Rogers 1965, 169–170)

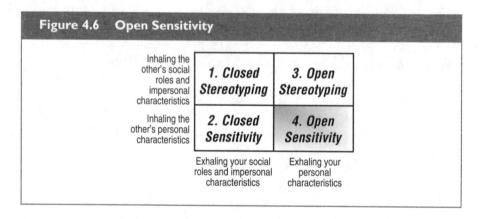

Figure 4.6   Open Sensitivity

	Exhaling your social roles and impersonal characteristics	Exhaling your personal characteristics
Inhaling the other's social roles and impersonal characteristics	*1. Closed Stereotyping*	*3. Open Stereotyping*
Inhaling the other's personal characteristics	*2. Closed Sensitivity*	*4. Open Sensitivity*

This response is definitely not restricted to the communication between a professional counselor and a client or patient. It's also not necessary that the persons involved agree with each other. In fact, *open sensitivity is not always marked by everybody feeling warm and fuzzy.* For example, even though the following conversation involves disagreement, we think it comes quite close to open sensitivity (Bach and Wyden 1968).

Frank: Honey, why don't you clean up the kitchen before you go to bed?

Ellie: I don't think it makes any difference. I get it done in the morning.

Frank: No. When I come down in the morning, it makes the house feel depressing.

Ellie: Really? Why don't you clean it up yourself, then?

Frank: Okay, I'm willing to help. But it seems that we could work together on it, and it would be easier the night before.

Ellie: Does it actually bother you that much?

Frank: Yeah—I really feel that the whole house looks messy when the kitchen's cluttered with dirty dishes.

Ellie: Well, I guess I'm just used to it—my dad never seemed to mind.

Frank: Yeah, I bet.

Ellie: Don't tell me you want to have a fight about this!

Frank: Okay. That was a cheap shot. I don't especially want to fight. I'd just like you to help me clean it up in the evening.

Ellie: So you don't have to live in a lower-class house, huh—like the one I lived in before I met you?

Frank: Wait a minute! I've told you and told you that I *love* your family!

Ellie: So why do you mind getting the kitchen cleaned up in the morning instead of at night when I want to relax?

Frank: When it would only take us a few minutes?

Ellie: Okay. I guess it *is* kind of silly—if it means that much to you. But you've got to do something for me, too.

Frank: Okay. What?

Ellie: I wish you'd try not to be so unpleasant in the morning.

Frank: Okay, okay. I'm not *that* bad. But I'll try.

Frank is responding *openly* to Ellie in that he expresses his feelings—for example, his disagreement, his depression, and his regret over his "cheap shot." In addition, he makes available to her some of the tensions that make him unique—he does want to raise this issue, but he doesn't want to fight, and he is willing, though a little resistant, to change himself. At the same time, Frank is *sensitive* to some of Ellie's personal characteristics. He sees and hears her desire to relax in the evening and her protectiveness toward her family. Ellie is also responding relatively openly and sensitively. For example, she is aware of both Frank's anger and his apology. She is also willing to express her reasons for choosing to leave kitchen cleaning until the morning.

Supervisor-subordinate or student-teacher communication can also move beyond role-relating when one or both parties respond with open sensitivity. For example, both persons in the following conversation seem willing to express some of their personal characteristics and to attend to some of the other's personal characteristics.

Student: I don't know how to say it, but it bothered me in class today when you talked about diversity but did not mention hearing-impaired people or people with disabilities for one moment.

Teacher: I'm very sorry about that, I didn't mean to ignore them. Tell me more about what exactly bothered you.

Student: Well, in the first place I always have the feeling that people talk about diversity and mean ethnicity or religion or gays and lesbians. But I am working with deaf people and can tell you that they have their own culture and are very proud of it.

Teacher: I am glad that you mention that. I have a friend who's an American Sign Language interpreter and he's told me about Deaf culture and that many deaf people do not regard themselves as disabled. Thanks for coming and reminding me about this. You're right. Sometimes we forget some groups of people because they don't fit our initial image of a category or group.

Student: I didn't mean to offend you. I'm glad that you had some contacts with Deaf culture. If you're interested, I have some great reading stuff on this subject.

Teacher: Absolutely. I'd like to know more about your involvement. Could we get together and talk?

Student: Sure. I'm busy today, but tomorrow would work. I also have a lot going on in my family at the moment.

Teacher: Do you wanna talk about that?

Student: If you don't mind. Can we talk tomorrow?

Teacher: Sure. Thanks again for speaking up. I wish more students would do that. In fact, I'd really like to make sure that I'm not the only one to hear your important addition. Would you be willing to talk about your experiences in our next class?

Student: Sure—that would be fun. Plus, I would like to come talk with you about the other stuff that's going on with me right now. I'll see you tomorrow in your office hours—okay? And thanks for listening.

Teacher: See ya tomorrow.

The teacher is responding openly to the student in that he expresses his feelings, for example, his regret over his not including Deaf culture or the cultures of the disabled. He makes available to the student some of the characteristics that make him unique: He is willing to learn from the student and to read more about these cultures. These are ways he displays open characteristics. In addition, he is sensitive to

What response options are possible and likely here? How might the presence of media encourage closed rather than open responses? Stereotyping rather than sensitivity?

the student. He is offering to talk about the student's family problems. He hears the student's desire to talk. The student is also responding relatively openly and sensitively. He is expressing his concern about professors being offended and he addresses his family problems. At the same time, he is sensitive to the professor and offers him material to read about Deaf culture.

It's important to note that open sensitivity is relatively rare in superior-subordinate relationships, like between professor and student or employer and employee. In most of these interactions, power is involved, and responding with open sensitivity means giving up power to a certain degree. It means being vulnerable and giving the other person a glance into your more private identities.

'But . . .' A Student Responds

What happens when I reveal some of who I am as a person and also perceive the other as a person, but she still treats me as a role-filler? In other words, what happens when I choose open sensitivity but the other chooses closed stereotyping?

That can hurt. Or at least be frustrating. As we've said, the communication occurs between you and the other person; it's collaborative. This means that you cannot control it by yourself. The quality of your communication is affected by the choices *both* of you make.

Remember, though, that your responses and the other person's are interdependent. Her responses are affected by yours and yours are affected by hers. If you keep responding with open sensitivity, especially in the face of her closed stereotyping, *this will often affect her response.* When you express some question you have, a vulnerability, or some other feeling, this will often encourage her to do the same thing. When you show that you are aware of who she is as a person, that can influence how she perceives you. But you cannot *determine* her responses. The bottom line is that you can't make interpersonal-quality communication happen by yourself, but you can *help* it happen. And you can also stop it from happening.

Recall and Application

What Choices Did You Make?

Recall the last time you experienced something like the event described. Think about how you felt and what you said and did. Then label the negotiation choice you made: closed stereotyping, closed sensitivity, open stereotyping, or open sensitivity.

1. The last time your employer or supervisor criticized your work, what response option did you choose to use first?

   _____.

2. The last time you were introduced to a person you thought was very attractive, what was your response option of choice?

   _____.

3. The last time one of your parents criticized you for the way you managed money, which response option did you choose?

   _____.

4. The last time someone you love complimented you or told you what he or she loves about you, what was the response option you used?

   _____.

5. The last time you were around a young person who had been pestering and interrupting you, and he or she insisted that you pay attention or "Watch me!" which choice of response options did you make?

   _____.

Constructing Selves and the Impersonal⟷Interpersonal Scale

At the beginning of this chapter we made the point that your identity-construction responses affect where your communication is on the impersonal⟷interpersonal continuum. The examples we've given of each of the four responses suggest how this happens. When one person responds in a given way, it's reflected verbally and nonverbally in everything he or she does until the response changes. In this way, one person's responses affect the other persons involved. And as communication proceeds, each person's identity construction responses are continuously being reflected in verbal and nonverbal behavior. The process continues interdependently, with each person's responses being *reflected in* and *influencing* the other person's.

For example, in the midst of studying for an exam, Angela calls her good friend to ask if she has the notes for the day of class Angela missed. The conversation goes something like this:

Angela: SanDee? This is Angela.

SanDee: Oh. Hi, Angela.

Angela: Hey, like everybody else, I'm trying to cram for Butler's exam tomorrow, and I need the notes for last Tuesday, when I was gone. Have you got them?

SanDee: Yeah, I think so. Hold on and let me look. Yeah, I do. A bunch of people copied them. You want them, too?

Angela: Yeah. Can I come by right away?

SanDee: No problem.

This exchange is between good friends, there is both inhaling and exhaling, and a task is accomplished. But the communicating stays impersonal rather than interpersonal. Angela notices almost nothing about SanDee but the role she fills as a fellow student in Butler's class. At the same time, Angela expresses only student-in-Butler's-class characteristics. SanDee responds the same way. Although their friendship is almost certainly based on a mutual liking of each other's personal features, none of those aspects comes into play in this conversation. Both respond with option 1, closed stereotyping. So this particular communication event *between* the two is more impersonal than interpersonal. This conversation would look something like this if we diagrammed the two persons' individual response options:

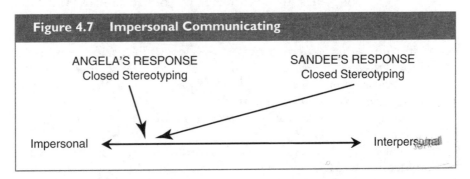

Figure 4.7   Impersonal Communicating

ANGELA'S RESPONSE
Closed Stereotyping

SANDEE'S RESPONSE
Closed Stereotyping

Impersonal ⟵—————————————————⟶ Interpersonal

We say "something like this," because it's impossible to tell exactly where their communicating would fall on the continuum without having a lot of details about what each person does verbally and nonverbally. Therefore, don't regard the arrows as pointing at an exact place on the continuum. Remember, the continuum is a flexible and fluid construct, and you can move back and forth on it when you communicate. When two people both respond with closed stereotyping, the communication between them will end up somewhere near the left-hand end of the continuum, and when they select some combination of the four choices, the communication between them will end up somewhere in the middle of the continuum.

By the same token, when both persons respond with open sensitivity, the communication between them will be somewhere near the right-hand end of the continuum. So if Angela and SanDee's conversation shifted to include expressions of Angela's feelings about her mom's breast cancer treatments (the reason Angela missed the class in the first place) and SanDee's responses of emotional support and sharing about how she coped when her sister was diagnosed with leukemia, then the communication between them would look more like this:

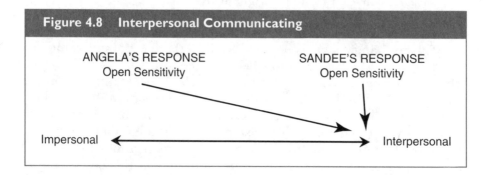

Figure 4.8   Interpersonal Communicating

ANGELA'S RESPONSE
Open Sensitivity

SANDEE'S RESPONSE
Open Sensitivity

Impersonal ← ————————————→ Interpersonal

This is how your identity-construction responses affect the quality of communication between you and others. As we've said throughout the book, there is no one, general "right" or "wrong" choice to make. There are only *outcomes*, results affected by your responses. Moreover, you don't have 100 percent control over where your communication is on the continuum, but your responses do make a difference. So the general rule is this: *When you want your communicating to move toward the left-hand end of the continuum, it can help to make identity-construction responses that are closer to option 1, closed stereotyping. When you want your communicating to move toward the right-hand end of the continuum, try to make identity-construction responses that are closer to option 4, open sensitivity.*

Notice how all this talk about "responses" can be tricky when you're dealing with something as subtle as identity construction. This is because, by the time each person reaches adulthood, he or she has learned several habits or patterns, and as long as they're just habits or patterns, *they feel more like reactions than responses.* For example, one of your patterns may be that you just about always respond with closed stereotyping when first meeting someone who has power over you—an employer, professor, or leader. Or, you may be relatively comfortable with the habit of practicing closed sensitivity with your friends—always being the one who listens to their troubles but never having someone to listen to yours. Or, you may have learned that one of your parents or a special friend will just about always respond to your open sensitivity with more of the same. In all these situations, it may not seem like you have much of a "choice" about what you do. But one of the main purposes of this book and the course you're taking is to *reacquaint you with your ability to respond rather than simply react.* Regardless of the patterns or habits that you've learned, you can make some changes, a little bit at a time if necessary. Constructing selves is a living process, one that's continually ongoing and continually changing. So you can experiment with new choices, ones that move your communicating in either direction along the impersonal◄──────►interpersonal scale.

Chapter Summary

This chapter describes one important process that's going on in *every communication situation you experience.* Whenever you contact anyone, in a letter or report, over the computer or telephone, face-to-face in a meeting, in a store, or on a date, you are involved in identity construction.

This process is collaborative, which means that it always involves more than one person, and it stays collaborative in this sense even when the people involved disagree. The process includes reactions and responses, produces emergent rather than predictable outcomes, includes two basic moves that we're calling *inhaling* and *exhaling,* and happens intentionally and unintentionally. The selves that emerge from this process are relational rather than individual, fluid rather than static. In addition, your identities or selves are multidimensional and changing, shaped and influenced in past and present relationships. This process affects people's identities throughout their lives, and it continues to affect who we are. All this means that you have the opportunity to continue making the same identity construction you always have, or to change the ways you define yourself in relation to others. These changes, if you decide to make them, can affect the quality of the communication you experience—and thus the quality of your life.

This chapter outlines the four identity construction responses people make as they communicate. When someone expresses social features and pays attention only to the other's social features—his gender, demographic characteristics, or role identity—the person is responding with *closed stereotyping.* If someone ignores the other person or denies his existence, she's responding with the extreme form of closed stereotyping called *disconfirmation*. When someone expresses only social features while noticing some of the other's personal characteristics—his uniqueness, feelings, choices, and so forth—she's responding with *closed sensitivity*. When someone makes available some of her uniqueness, feelings, choices, and such while noticing only the other person's social roles, she is responding with *open stereotyping*. And when someone expresses some of who he is as a person and receives some of who the other is as a person, he's responding with *open sensitivity*.

Many of your self-construction responses are likely pretty well-established habits and patterns. But you can still change them, if you want. Family patterns, cultural forces, professional expectations, and other peoples' assumptions can make it difficult to make changes, but not impossible. If the pressures are intense, make changes a little at a time. And as we said, the general rule is, when you want your communicating to move toward the left-hand end of the continuum, it can help to make responses that are closer to closed stereotyping, and when you want your communicating to move toward the right-hand end of the continuum, try to respond with communicating that is closer to open sensitivity.

In Other Words

We said in this chapter that identity is something that we *do* and not something that we *have*. The following selection can help you to better understand what we mean. Wood and Reich show that identity is not related to genes but to socialization at home and by peers. In this piece, they show that cultures and individuals perform their gender identities in their interactions with other people. They note that every society and culture makes up norms and rules for how men and women should behave and talk and that individuals can choose to follow, bend, or reject those rules.

After reading the article you should be able to respond to the following questions:

1. What does it mean when someone says, "She talks like a man" or "He talks like a woman"? Give examples from the text and your own experience.

2. In what contexts are you more likely to use feminine or masculine communication styles?

3. To what extent are you comfortable with those labels (masculine versus feminine)? What aspects of your cultural identity are linked to your comfort level?

4. Who are the people in your life who have had the most influence on your gender identity? What did they do or say that shaped or shapes your sense of self as a gendered person?

***

Gendered Speech Communities

Julia T. Wood and Nina M. Reich

BECOMING GENDERED

Let's now look more closely at how people become gendered. Many factors influence our gender development. Two of the most important are (1) the continuous communication of social expectations for males and females, and (2) interaction in sex-segregated children's play groups.

Communication of Social Expectations and Development of Gender

Cultural constructions of gender are communicated to individuals through a range of structures and practices that make up our everyday world. From birth on, individuals are besieged with communication that presents cultural prescriptions for gender as natural and right. Beginning with the pink and blue blankets wrapped around newborns, gender socialization continues in interactions with parents, teachers, peers, and media. In magazines and on television, we are more likely to see women in the home and men in the boardroom; girls in soft colors and frilly fashions and boys in stronger, darker colors and rugged clothes; women needing help and men performing daring rescues; men driving cars and women riding in them. In cartoons and prime-time programming we see male characters being more active (bold, dominant, aggressive) than female characters (more subdued, subordinate, and gentle). In kindergarten and elementary school, children are more likely to see women as teachers and men as principals, a difference that sends a clear message about the status society prescribes to each sex. In offices, virtually all secretaries and receptionists are female, sending the message that assisting others is part of feminine identity. When children visit toy stores, they see pink bicycles with delicate baskets for girls and blue or black bicycles with sturdy baskets for boys. As children participate in the many spheres of society, they receive continuous messages that reinforce social views of gender.

The pervasive messages about how boys and girls are "supposed to be" make gender roles seem natural, normal, and right. Because cultures systematically normalize arbitrary definitions of gender, we seldom reflect on how *unnatural* it is that half of humans are assumed to be deferential, emotional, and interested in building relationships whereas the other half are assumed to be ambitious, assertive, and self-sufficient (Janeway, 1971; Miller, 1986). If we do reflect on social definitions of masculinity and femininity, they don't make a great deal of sense!

The intensity and pervasiveness of social prescriptions for gender ensure that most females will become predominantly feminine (nurturing, cooperative, sensitive to others) and most males will become predominantly masculine (assertive, competitive, independent). Notice that we stated most females and males will become *predominantly* feminine or masculine. Very few, if any, people are exclusively one gender. You can be masculine, feminine, or—like most of us—a combination of genders that allows you to be effective in diverse situations.

Peer Interaction's Impact on Development of Gender

A second significant influence on the development of gender is peer interaction among children. As children play together, they teach each other how to be boys and girls. Insight into the significance of play was pioneered by Daniel Maltz and Ruth Borker (1982), who studied children at play. The researchers noticed recreation was usually sex-segregated, and boys and girls tended to favor discrete kinds of games—the ones that are socially prescribed for each sex through media, advertising, toy manufacturers, parents, and so forth. Whereas girls were more likely to play house, school, or jump rope, boys tended to play competitive team sports like football and baseball. Because different goals, strategies, and relationships characterize some girls' and boys' games, the children learned divergent rules for interaction. Engaging in play, Maltz and Borker concluded, contributes to socializing children into predominantly masculine and feminine identities (again, notice the word, *predominantly*).

Maltz and Borker's classic study has been replicated by other researchers, who have shown that their findings continue to hold up in the present time. Psychologist Campbell Leaper reports that children still tend to prefer sex-segregated play groups, a finding that is reinforced by other researchers (Clark, 1998; Harris, 1998; Moller & Serbin, 1998). Leaper and the other researchers also report that the sex-segregated play groups engage in different kinds of games that, in turn, socialize them into different ways of communicating.

Girls' Games. Many games that girls typically play, such as house and school, require just two or three people so they promote personal relationships. Further, these games don't have preset or fixed rules, roles, and objectives. Whereas touchdowns and home runs are goals in boys' games and roles such as pitcher, forward, and blocker are clearly defined, how to play house is open to negotiation. To make their games work, girls talk with each other and agree on rules, roles, and goals: "You be the mommy and I'll be the daddy, and we'll clean house." From unstructured, cooperative play, girls learn three basis rules for how to communicate:

1. Be cooperative, collaborative, inclusive. It's important that everyone feels involved and has a chance to play.

2. Don't criticize or outdo others. Cultivate egalitarian relationships so the group is cohesive and gratifying to all.

3. Pay attention to others' feelings and needs and be sensitive in interpreting and responding to them.

In sum, games that are more likely to be played by girls emphasize relationships more than outcomes, sensitivity to others, and cooperative, inclusive interpersonal orientations.

Boys' Games. Unlike girls' games, some of the games that boys are most likely to play involve fairly large groups (for instance, baseball requires nine players plus extras to fill in) and proceed by rules and goals that are externally established and constant (there are nine innings, three strikes and you're out). Also, boys' games allow for individual stars—MVP, for instance—and, in fact a boy's status depends on his rank relative to others. The more structured, large, and individualized character of boys' games teaches them three rules of interaction:

1. Assert yourself. Use talk and action to highlight your ideas and to establish both your status and leadership.
2. Focus on outcomes. Use your talk and actions to make things happen, to solve problems, and to achieve goals.
3. Be competitive. Vie for the talk stage Keep attention focused on you, outdo others, and make yourself stand out.

Some of the games more likely to be played by boys emphasize achievement—both for the team and the individual members. The goals are to win for the team and to be the top player on it. Interaction is more an area for negotiating power and status than for building relationships with others, and competitiveness is customary in masculine communities.

The nature of interaction in the games that society encourages girls and boys to play teaches children society's prescriptions for males and females. It's not surprising, then, that most girls and boys learn some different ways of communicating. We use the qualifying word "most" to remind you that we are discussing general differences, not absolute ones. Some women sometimes act in ways that are considered masculine and some women have a primarily masculine style. Some men sometimes act in ways that are considered feminine and some men have a primarily feminine style. In most situations, however, most females adopt a primarily feminine style of communicating and most males adopt a predominantly masculine one.

In combination, messages woven into the fabric of society and peer interaction among children clarify how people become gendered.

FEMININE AND MASCULINE COMMUNICATION COMMUNITIES

Beginning in the 1970s, scholars noticed that some groups of people share communication practice not common to, or understood by, people outside of the groups. This led to the realization that there are distinctive speech communities, or communication communities. William Labov (1972) defined a speech community as existing when a set of norms regarding how to communicate is shared by a group of people. Within a communication community, members embrace similar understandings of how to use talk and what purposes it serves.

Once scholars realized that distinctive speech communities exist, they identified many, some of which are discussed in this book: African Americans, Native Americans, gay men, lesbians, and people with disabilities. Members in each of these groups share perspectives that outsiders seldom have. By extension, the values, viewpoints, and experiences that are distinct to a particular group influence how members of that group communicate. That's why there are some gender differences in why, when, and how we communicate.

Feminine and masculine speech communities have been explored by many scholars (Aries, 1987; Beck, 1988; Coates & Cameron, 1989; Johnson, 1989; Kramarae, 1981; Spender, 1984; Tannen, 1990a, b; Treichler & Kramarae, 1983; Wood, 1993a, b, c, 2001; Wood & Inman, 1993). Their research reveals that most girls and women operate from assumptions about communication and use rules for communicating that differ in some ways from those endorsed by most boys and men.

At the heart of the process by which we become gendered is human communication. It is through interaction with others that we learn what masculine and feminine mean in our society and how we are expected to think, talk, feel, and act. Communication is also the primary means by which we embody gender personally. When we conform to social prescriptions for gender, we reinforce prevailing social views of masculinity and femininity. Table 1 summarizes how these differences in gender communities may affect communication. . . .

Table 1. Differences Between Feminine and Masculine Communication Culture

Feminine Talk	Masculine Talk
1. Use talk to build and sustain rapport with others.	1. Use talk to assert yourself and your ideas.
2. Share yourself and disclose to others.	2. Personal disclosures can make you vulnerable.
3. Use talk to create symmetry or equality between people.	3. Use talk to establish your status and power.
4. Matching experiences with others shows understanding and empathy ("I know how you feel").	4. Matching experiences is a competitive strategy to command attention. ("I can top that.")
5. To support others, express understanding of their feelings.	5. To support others, do something helpful—give advice or tell them how to solve a problem.
6. Include others in conversation by asking their opinions and encouraging them to elaborate. Wait your turn to speak so others can participate.	6. Don't share the talk stage with others; wrest it from them with communication. Interrupt others to make your own points.
7. Keep the conversation going by asking questions and showing interest in others' ideas.	7. Each person is on her or his own; it's not your job to help others join in.
8. Be responsive. Let others know you hear and care about what they say.	8. Use responses to make your own points and to outshine others.
9. Be tentative so that others feel free to add their ideas.	9. Be assertive so others perceive you as confident and in command.
10. Talking is a human relationship in which details and interesting side comments enhance depth of connection.	10. Talking is a linear sequence that should convey information and accomplish goals. Extraneous details get in the way and achieve nothing.

References

Aries, E. (1987). Gender and communication. In P. Shaver (Ed.), *Sex and gender* (pp. 149–176). Newbury Park, CA: Sage.

Beck, A. (1988). *Love is never enough.* New York: Harper & Row.

Clark, R. (1998). A comparison of topics and objectives in a cross section of young men's and women's everyday conversations. In D. Canary and K. Dindia (Eds.), *Sex differences and similarities in communication* (pp. 303–319). Mahwah, NJ: Lawrence Erlbaum.

Coates, J., and Cameron, D. (1989). *Women in their speech communities: New perspectives in language and sex.* London: Longman.

Harris, J. (1998). *The nurture assumption.* New York: Simon & Schuster/Free Press.

Janeway, E. (1971). *Man's world, woman's place: A study in social mythology.* New York: Dell.

Johnson, F. L. (1989). Women's culture and communication: An analytic perspective. in C. M. Lont and S. A. Friedley (Eds.), *Beyond boundaries: Sex and gender diversity in communication.* Fairfax, VA: George Mason University Press.

Kramarae, C. (1981). *Women and men speaking: Frameworks for analysis.* Rowley, MA: Newbury House.

Labov, W. (1972). *Sociolinguistic patterns.* Philadelphia: University of Pennsylvania Press.

Leaper, C. (1994). *Childhood gender segregation: Causes and consequences.* San Francisco: Jossey-Bass.

Maltz, D. N., and Borker, R. (1982). A cultural approach to male-female communication. In J. J. Gumpertz (Ed.), *Language and social identity* (pp. 196–216). Cambridge, England: Cambridge University Press.

Miller, J. B. (1986). *Toward a new psychology of women.* Boston: Beacon Press.

Moller, L., and Serbin, L. (1998). Antecedents of toddler gender segregation: Cognitive consonance, gender-typed toy preferences and behavioral compatibility. *Sex Roles, 35,* 445–460.

Spender, D. (1984). *Man made language.* London: Routledge and Kegan Paul.

Tannen, D. (1986). *That's now what I meant! How conversational style makes or breaks relationships.* New York: Ballantine.

——. (1990a). Gender differences in conversational coherence: Physical alignment and topical cohesion. In B. Dorval (Ed.), *Conversational organization and its development: XXXVIII* (pp. 167–206). Norwood, NJ: Ablex.

——. (1990b). *You just don't understand: Women and men in conversation.* New York: William Morrow.

Treichler, P. A., and Kramarae, C. (1983). Women's talk in the ivory tower. *Communication Quarterly, 31,* 118–132.

Wood, J. T. (1993a). Engendered relationships: Interaction, caring, power, and responsibility in close relationships. In S. Duck (Ed.), *Processes in close relationships: Contexts of close relationships* (Vol. 3). Beverly Hills, CA: Sage.

——. (1993b). Engendered identities: Shaping voice and mind through gender. In D. Vocate (Ed.), *Intrapersonal communication: Different voices, different minds.* Hillsdale, NJ: Lawrence Erlbaum.

——. (1993c). *Who cares? Women, care, and culture.* Carbondale: Southern Illinois University Press.

——. (2001). *Gendered lives: Communication, gender, and culture* (4th ed.). Belmont, CA: Wadsworth.

Wood, J. T., and Inman, C. C. (1993). In a different mode: Masculine styles of communicating closeness. *Journal of Applied Communication Research, 21,* 279–295.

From *Intercultural Communication: A Reader,* 10th Edition, by Samovar/Porter. © 2003. Reprinted with permission of Wadsworth, a division of Thomson Learning: www.thomsonrights.com. Fax 800-730-2215.

References

Bach, G. R., and Wyden, P. 1968. *The Intimate Enemy: How to Fight Fair in Love and Marriage.* New York: Avon Books.

Bailey, B. 2000. "Language and Negotiation of Ethnic/Racial Identity Among Dominican Americans." *Language in Society,* 29: 555–582.

Bakhtin, M. M. 1986. *Speech Genres and Other Late Essays.* (Translated by V. W. McGee). Austin: University of Texas Press. (Originally published 1953.)

Beatty, M. 1989. *Beyond Codependency.* New York: Harper/Hazelden.

Black, C. 1982. *'It Will Never Happen to Me!' Children of Alcoholics as Youngsters—Adolescents—Adults.* Denver: M.A.C.

Cissna, K. N. L., and Sieburg, E. 1981. "Patterns of Interactional Confirmation and Disconfirmation." In C. Wilder-Mott and J. H. Weakland (eds.), *Rigor and Imagination: Essays from the Legacy of Gregory Bateson.* New York: Praeger. Pages 230–239.

Collier, M. J., and Thomas, M. 1988. "Cultural Identity: An Interpretive Perspective." In Y. Y. Kim and W. B. Gudykunst (eds.), *Theories of Intercultural Communication.* Newbury Park, CA: Sage. Pages 99–120.

Fuller, B. E., Chermack, S. T., Cruise, K. A., Kirsch, E., Fitzgerald, H. E., and Zucker, R. A. 2003. "Predictors of Aggression Across Three Generations Among Sons of Alcoholics: Relationships Involving Grandparental and Parental Alcoholism, Child Aggression, Marital Aggression and Parenting Practices." *Journal of Studies on Alcohol,* 64: 472–484.

Geertz, C. 1979. "From the Native's Point of View: On the Nature of Anthropological Understanding." In P. Rabinow and W. M. Sullivan (eds.), *Interpretive Social Science.* Berkeley: University of California Press. Pages 225–246.

Hall, B. J. 2002. *Among Cultures: The Challenge of Communication.* New York: Harcourt College Publishers.

Hecht, M. L., Jackson II, R. L., and Ribeau, S. A. 2003. *African American Communication: Exploring Identity and Culture.* 2nd ed. Mahwah, NJ: Erlbaum.

Hegde, R. S. 1998. "A View From Elsewhere: Locating Difference and the Politics of Representation From a Transnational Feminist Perspective." *Communication Theory,* 8: 271–297.

Hofstede, G. 1980. *Culture's Consequences: International Differences in Work-Related Values.* Beverly Hills, CA: Sage.

Kojima, H. 1984. "A Significant Stride Toward the Comparative Study of Control." *American Psychologist,* 39: 972–973.

Laing, R. D. 1961. *The Self and Others.* New York: Pantheon.

——. 1969. *The Self and Others.* Baltimore: Penguin Books.

Lakoff, G. 1987. *Women, Fire, and Dangerous Things.* Chicago: University of Chicago Press.

Miller, J. G. 1984. *The Development of Women's Sense of Self.* Work in Progress, No. 12. Wellesley, MA: Stone Center Working Paper Series.

Ochs, E. 1988. *Culture and Language Development: Language Acquisition and Language Socialization in a Samoan Village.* Cambridge: Cambridge University Press.

Rogers, C. R. 1965. "Dialogue Between Martin Buber and Carl R. Rogers." In M. Friedman and R. G. Smith (eds.), *The Knowledge of Man.* London: Allen and Unwin.

Sampson, E. E. 1993. *Celebrating the Other: A Dialogic Account of Human Nature.* Boulder, CO: Westview.

Scotton, C. M. 1983. "The Negotiation of Identities in Conversation: A Theory of Markedness and Code Choice." *International Journal of Sociological Linguistics,* 44: 119–125. ✦

Part II

Inhaling and Exhaling

Chapter Five

Inhaling: Perception

Chapter Objectives

After reading this chapter, you should be able to do the following:

- Understand how all perception involves the interpretation of sensory cues.
- Identify the three sub-processes of perception as selecting, organizing, and inferring.
- Explain person prototypes and scripts and give examples.
- Recognize three kinds of inferences people make when perceiving persons: stereotypes, attributions, and impressions.
- Give examples of five difficulties that people encounter when they interpret sensory cues.

Chapter Preview

Remember that we're using the metaphor of inhaling and exhaling to explain the receptive and expressive parts of communication. This chapter and the next one focus on inhaling. The first point to remember is that there's much more to inhaling than the passive reception of incoming messages. Inhaling combines the two active, interpretive processes of perceiving and listening. In this chapter we will talk about perception; listening will be discussed in Chapter Six.

People make sense out of the world through their perceptual experience, and experience is affected by culture, membership in various social groups, and, in fact, by every relationship a person has. Your perceptions influence and contribute to the inhaling process in profound ways. You select sensory cues, organize them mentally, and make inferences about them. One of the reasons why people select, organize, and make inferences is that each of us lives in a complex world that we have to make sense of. Three kinds of inference-making processes that people use to make sense of the world and the people in it are stereotyping, attribution, and impression formation.

Perception: An Interpretive Process

Perception can be defined as a social and cognitive process in which people assign meaning to sensory cues. People often assume that the "truth" of things exists out there somewhere in what they are seeing, hearing, touching, tasting, and smelling. For example, you know the old saying "Seeing is believing." It is tempting to think that your eyes give you a perfect picture of what is happening in your own portion of "reality." But perception takes a picture through a lens, not through a window.

Perception is shaped by the perceiving person's experience and understanding of his or her place in the world. If perception were simply a matter of accurately processing sensory cues, you would expect everybody to perceive in a fairly similar way. However, this is not how perception works; as we said, it's an active process. When we make this point, we also mean that perception is, to a considerable extent, self-initiated and voluntary, a function of each person's response choices. You are not forced to interpret cues in a certain way; you have consid-

Up Periscope! How might the direction of the periscope and its viewer's experience in the maze influence the selection, organization, and inference making about what is 'outside' of this maze?

erable control over your perceptual processes, especially as you become more aware of them.

Perception occurs through three basic sub-processes: selection, organization, and inference-making. But before these three can begin, a person has to receive information through the senses—touch, taste, smell, hearing, and sight. This information is received in the form of sensory data, or cues. A cue is the smallest perceivable "bit" of information. As soon as your outermost sensory neurons receive a cue, you begin selecting, organizing, and inferring from this information. It isn't possible to perceive anything without selecting, organizing, and inferring. So, from the start, perception is an *interpretive process*. The following brief exercise will show you that interpretation is a large part of perceiving things in the environment.

Selecting, Organizing, and Inferring

The three sub-processes of perception do not occur in any distinct, step-by-step sequence. They happen simultaneously as three inseparable events. Selection generally refers to how you pay attention to sensory cues. Organization describes the ways you construct and impose patterns or structure onto the stream of sensory cues you receive. Inferring is a label for the way you "go beyond" or interpret the cues that your senses select and organize.

Selecting. You first decide at some level of consciousness which cues to pay attention to. Sometimes it seems that you don't have a choice about whether or not to attend to certain cues—for example, a siren, a sudden bright light out of the dark, a loud scream, or a sharp pain. But most of the time people exercise a fair amount of choice about the cues they perceive.

Selection is operating when you're rushed for time in an airport looking for the ticket counter of your airline and you don't notice many details about the people around you. Your attention is focused on signs identifying airlines and listing arrivals or departures. Or, when looking for new shoes in a shopping mall, you selectively pay attention to store signs and window displays that relate to your task and typically ignore the bed and bath shop and the espresso stand. But if you suddenly become hungry, you shift your attention to anything that smells or looks like food. You can be at a noisy party and have trouble hearing another person standing less than two feet away, but magically overhear your name mentioned by two people gossiping at some distance. And if you are concentrating on reading this book right now, you are probably not aware of the pressure of the chair against your body or noises from the next room until reading this sentence shifts your attention to these cues.

When communicating with others, people also perceive selectively. Some research indicates that people tend to focus on whatever or whomever is easiest to attend to—the closest person, the person with the loudest voice, the person we can see most easily. For example, in a series of studies, two researchers asked subjects to observe conversations between two people and varied the seating positions of the observers (see Figure 5.1). Some observers looked directly at one of the two conversation partners but could see only the back and side of the other. When these observers were asked to rate the conversational partners on a number of scales, they found they rated the person they faced as more responsible for the topic and tone of the conversation. The observers who could see both participants equally well rated them during the same period of time as equally responsible for the tone and topics of conversation. The researchers concluded that where your attention is directed influences what you perceive. Your selective perceptions affect your judgments about the people involved (Maltz and Borker 1982).

But the process of selection is not this simple. What you attend to is not just a response to a property of some cue—the loudest, brightest, or most visually direct. You also select cues about people based on your past judgments of them. So, if you are angry with your partner, you are far more likely to perceive all sorts of little irritating habits, just as you overlook or don't see negative characteristics in someone you love. The bottom line is that you cannot perceive all the sensory cues that are available to you. Perception is selective, and what we choose to notice affects how we respond to both things and people.

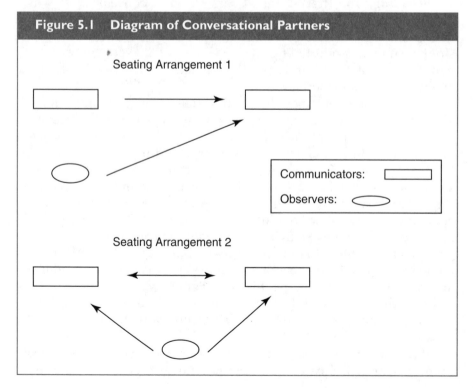

Figure 5.1   Diagram of Conversational Partners

Seating Arrangement 1

Communicators:

Observers:

Seating Arrangement 2

Organizing. Another way people actively participate in perception is by organizing the cues they select. You literally cannot help applying structure and stability to your world of sensations. Whenever you look at something that is vague or ambiguous in shape or size or color, for example, you continue to focus on it until you recognize what it is. What you are doing is arranging and rearranging the information you have according to a series of possible patterns or forms until the information finally makes sense to you, and you have an "Oh, so that's what it is!" experience.

You can have this experience of perceiving patterns or structures whenever you listen to music, too. How do you recognize your favorite songs? Research shows that people hear something much more than note-to-note; they tend to focus on the organized *pattern* of the sounds—the melody (Fiske and Shelley 1984). If you've ever played the game Name That Tune, you have had the experience of suddenly recognizing not individual notes but the pattern that exists among the notes.

Once you apply a particular structure to your experience, you stabilize this perceptual version. For example, if you've been humming a particular tune for days, it's hard to think of how other songs sound, especially if they have somewhat similar patterns. The organization of perceptions helps you to make sense out of whatever is occurring. You can apply the patterns or structures to very small sensory events. Or you can develop patterns that characterize people you know. Later on in this chapter, we'll talk about how these more complex patterns are formed through stereotyping, the process of attribution, and impression formation. But for now, we just want to emphasize how important the way people organize cues is to the entire process of perception and the unavoidable effects this step has on your communication.

Inferring. To infer is to conclude, judge, or go beyond evidence. So in the perception process, inferring means going beyond sensory cues to your own interpretations. The inferences or judgments you make depend on the cues you select and the ways you organize them in relation to your own assumptions, expectations, and goals.

It might sound like inference making is a risky or even foolish process because it means that you go beyond the "hard facts." In some ways it is dangerous, but it's also impossible not to do it. Just like selecting and organizing, inferring is hard-wired into human sense making. This is part of what we meant when we said in Chapter Two that humans live in worlds of *meaning*, not worlds of pure objective reality. *Meaning* is a label for the outcome of selecting, organizing, and inferring.

Our interpretations of other people and events depend on our worldviews, past experiences, goals in life, and expectations, all of which differ from culture to culture. Cultures are marked by the ways they answer such basic questions as the following:

- What is the value of the individual versus the value of the group?

- How do people advance in life, by heritage or by achievement?

- How should society be organized?

- Is the nature of a human being good or evil?

- How do humans relate to each other?

- Where does meaning lie, explicitly in the language or hidden in the context? (Hall 2002; Kluckhorn and Strodtbeck 1961)

Many more elements can constitute a worldview of a culture, and the answers to each question lie on a continuum. In other words, world-views are not simple; they are complex. You can value individualism, for example, when you want to make your own decisions about going to college. But you can value collectivism and the group when it comes to supporting your parents in their old age.

Worldviews influence responses to these questions and affect how people interpret cues. Saskia, for instance, was confused when she arrived on the West Coast of the United States and people smiled at her, greeted her in the streets, and talked with her on the bus. She was raised to be respectful and friendly to strangers but at the same time maintains her privacy and does not impose herself on people she does not know. It made her a little uncomfortable at first because she didn't know how to interpret certain cues she got from strangers. Was the man in the supermarket hitting on her when he smiled and asked how her day was going? Or was it just friendliness? When Saskia's parents came from Germany to visit her, her dad was impressed with "how many people she knew." He interpreted the greetings in the streets and the small talk of the checkers in the supermarket as meaning "They must know her, otherwise they wouldn't be talking to her." He was very surprised when he found out that they were strangers to Saskia. This example shows the impact of Saskia's family's worldview on their interpretations of communicative interactions.

But perceptual differences don't occur just between different ethnic or national groups—they are also gender specific. According to Malz and Borker (1982), women and men in North America interpret the same actions in conversation very differently. For example, men appear to perceive head nodding while listening as a way of indicating *agreement* with the speaker, whereas women tend to perceive head nodding as a way of signaling *that they are listening* to the speaker. For women, this is another way of indicating "I'm with you. Keep going." This difference may be at the root of a common complaint some women have about some men: "He never listens to me" (because he doesn't signal listening with head nodding) or "He's always so rational. Sometimes I just want emotional support." At the same time, frequent use of head nodding reinforces the stereotype some men have of women as unreliable because "You're always agreeing with me no matter what I say."

Socialization and biology play a role in how men and women communicate, especially when it comes to communicating emotions (Konner 2002). Researchers say that male and female brains differ in terms of sex differences in a frontal-lobe region that is responsible for emotional reasoning. They also found that the corpus callosum, which is a mass of fibers connecting the two halves of the brain, may be larger in women's than in men's brains. If this is so, then the larger fiber mass in women's brains might help integrate the language and emotional centers better in female brains, which means that women can verbalize feelings more than men. This does not mean that they automatically do. Socialization plays another major role in how people communicate. We'll say more about this in Chapter Seven when we talk about language.

'But . . .' A Student Responds

If perception is such an active process, then is the "real world" only in our heads? Is there no objective reality out there? This sounds kind of weird.

No, we're not saying that people imagine what they perceive. Obviously, the reality people encounter is filled with concrete objects that we sometimes bump into painfully. But humans can't have simple, "pure" perceptions of these concrete objects. We perceive them selectively, and we make interpretations based on our selections. The result is that we live, as we've said in Chapter Two, in worlds of meanings.

For example, think about the inferences you almost automatically make about something as relatively stable as a landscape. You look out your window, notice what the view tells you about the weather, and make inferences that help you decide how to dress for going outside. Or you infer from the color of the leaves that autumn is coming or that it's the height of summer. And, as we'll explain in just a minute, the inferring process is even more pronounced when we're perceiving people than when we're perceiving landscapes, other objects, or nonhuman animals.

'But . . .' A Student Responds

What happened to objectivity? All this talk about selecting, organizing, and inferring makes it sound like it's impossible to be objective. I know that some grades are more objective than others and that disinterested third parties are always more objective than people directly involved in a dispute. Why don't you teach people how to perceive objectively?

Because we believe that the term *objective* makes it sound like people can do or be something that we're convinced they can't. You're absolutely right that some grades are less biased than those influenced by the personalities of the teacher and students, and that arbitrators and judges can often make better decisions than the people caught up in an argument or lawsuit. But it's not because the decision-makers are being more objective, but because they're being more *balanced* and fair. Judges, for example, are usually very biased against any social contact with the plaintiffs, defendants, or lawyers in their courtrooms. They're also biased against lying, exaggerating damages, and name-calling. These biases help make the process more fair, but they're still biases, and in that sense judges definitely aren't simply being objective.

Our main point throughout this book is that the human world is just exactly that: *human* rather than mechanical, and a *world*, not simply an objective reality. Humans naturally and constantly select, organize, and interpret the sensory cues they receive. These processes are hard-wired into peoples' minds and bodies. Absolute objectivity is an impossibility, which means that it makes the most sense to look for some other standard. In the place of an impossible standard of objectivity, we prefer three other standards: *reflectiveness*—people staying critically aware of their perceptual processes so they can understand how they work; *humility*—people remembering that their view of the world is not the only possible one; and *engagement*—people being willing to check their perceptions against others' perceptions and to work through the differences they discover.

The points that we're making about perception in this chapter are designed to help you adopt these standards. When you know how human perception works, you can be more *reflective* about your own perceptual processes. When you remember how culture affects everyone's perceptions, it's easier to remember that your ways of understanding are not the only ways that can make sense. And studying these processes in a classroom should encourage you to engage, compare, and contrast your ways of perceiving with those of your classmates.

Now that we have explained the basic sub-processes of perception, we want to talk more about mental guidelines, or *cognitive schemata*, that help us to organize incoming information. Then we'll talk about the processes that you engage in when you make interpretations of people or things around you.

Cognitive Schemata

In order to recognize persons and objects around us, we need mental guidelines that help us process incoming cues. These mental guidelines are called *cognitive schemata* (in the singular it's *cognitive schema*). Schemata help us to organize incoming cues about people, animals, behaviors, and objects.

Almost 80 years ago, the originator of schema theory made the point that all remembering is constructive. Rather than storing all stimuli in memory, the brain uses schemata to provide an impression of the whole. In his experiments, Bartlett (1932) used a version of the child's game Telephone, in which a message is passed along a chain of people and the story changes with each retelling. In some experiments he asked British college students to read a story from another culture, put it aside, reproduce it, and pass it on to other students. Bartlett noticed that the stories changed in systematic ways as they were passed along. This led him to suggest that in acquiring new information, humans must assimilate the new material to existing concepts or schemas. People change new information to fit their existing concepts by organizing it into previously existing mental structures. In this process, details are lost, and the knowledge fits the interpretive frames of the individual (Mayer 1992, 230).

This explanation about how people organize new information makes sense. Saskia participated in a class where the professor played the telephone game. The students had to remember a story that included a variety of blue dragons, monks, and story characters from Asian cultures. In the end, the monks became "the dudes," the princess became a cheerleader, and the head monk a pharmacist. This does not mean that the students were careless or stupid. It means that they adapted the information to stories they had heard before. The students also ended their version of the story with "and they lived happily ever after," which did not occur in the original story but which is an ending that's very common in fairy tales that are written or translated into English.

Overall, people have schemata for people, relationships, actions, and even emotions. Let's talk a little bit more about two types of these schemata: person prototypes and scripts.

Person Prototypes

A person prototype is a generalized representation of certain types of persons. It is usually based on experience and repeated personal interactions with people. Just pause and think for a moment about what *mental image* comes to your mind when you think of student, professor, lawyer, gamer, or car salesperson. Person prototypes contain information about traits and verbal and nonverbal behaviors that you believe characterize a certain type of person. What are the traits and behaviors that you associate with a professor? How about a lawyer? How about a cheerleader? And how about a homeless person? Overall, prototypes help us to orient ourselves in the world. They can help us to meet people who we think we might feel comfortable with and can also help us to avoid dangerous situations. But they can also be misleading and can make us stereotype people. Why? Because they omit specific features. If you communicate based only on your person schemata, you will stay on the impersonal side of the communication scale described in Chapter Three.

Scripts

Scripts, which are structures dealing with certain sequences of action, are another type of cognitive schema. We all have a repertoire of scripts in our heads. They are usually based on experience and help us to know what happens next. Examples of scripts are riding the bus, greeting another person, attending a wedding, or going to a restaurant. Consider the "restaurant script" (Abelson 1981). When people enter a restaurant, they know the different steps to go through to accomplish the goal of satisfying their hunger, having good conversation over a good meal, or both. This knowledge of the different steps helps us go into an almost automatic action mode so that we don't have to make decisions every single moment. So, imagine you go to a restaurant. What do you do? We guess that you would do the following in the following order: enter, be seated, order, eat, pay, tip 10 to 20 percent of the bill, and exit.

In addition, person prototypes help you to orient yourself in your restaurant environment. Near the entrance, there will usually be a person who says, "How many?" You know that this must be a host or manager. When a person comes to your table and asks "Are you ready to order?" wearing a certain outfit—for instance, a T-shirt with the name of the restaurant on it—you know that he or she is your server (person prototype). You also know what to expect from a server and how you are supposed to behave. You know, for instance, that the server is not supposed to yell at you, sit at your table, or spill your soda on you. The server also knows that the customer (you) is not supposed to come into the kitchen or sit on the floor when eating.

Also remember that scripts can differ in different cultures. One reason that people sometimes feel insecure when they travel is that they are not familiar with certain scripts. When Saskia is in Germany, her restaurant script looks like the following: enter the restaurant, sit down, order food and drink, eat, sit for a while after eating, call the waiter to bring the check, pay the check, leave a tip that is fair, and exit. You see that there are many similarities between the U.S. and German restaurant scripts. However, there are also differences: calling the waiter to bring the check, not leaving the money on the table, and tipping conventions. In Germany, the server will usually leave you alone for a while after you have dined, and it is considered rude to take away your

What are your initial impressions of the two men in this photograph? What specifically do you observe that leads you to your interpretations?

plates immediately. In many European countries, clearing the table right after people have eaten and putting the check on the table is interpreted as rushing the customer. So, often you have to call the waiter or waitress to bring the check. Usually you pay directly and don't leave money on the table.

Tipping conventions in U.S. and German restaurant scripts also differ. In Germany, you round up a small bill to the next dollar or, when the bill is over 10 euros, you give 10 percent or so. In the United States the standard expectation is that the tip will be around 15 percent of the bill. Knowledge about different cultural scripts for certain situations makes you a more competent communicator and can also help you to avoid embarrassment or confusion.

Person prototypes and *scripts* influence how people *organize* sensory cues. In addition, there are three processes that influence how people make *interpretations*. These processes are *impression formation, attribution,* and *stereotyping*.

Cognitive Processes

Impression Formation

Impression formation is the complex process of integrating or synthesizing a variety of sometimes contradictory observations into a coherent overall "picture" of a person. The impression that you form is basically a combination of traits that are similar or fit together for you. When you connect a series of related interpretations about someone's behavior, you begin to develop what's called an *implicit personality theory* about the person doing the behavior. This is simply your picture (theory) of what the person's personality "must be," based on qualities or characteristics that are implied by their behavior.

In a widely cited book about person perception, three psychologists give an excellent example of how impressions form themselves into an implicit personality theory:

> Suppose you have been watching a woman at a party. A lot of other people are congregated around her and you discover that she has just had a novel published. You observe her long enough to draw some tentative conclusions about her. Some of these result from attribution work; she is smart, ambitious, but particularly hard-working—conclusions you are able to draw because few people write novels and because you discover that this is her second novel and fourth published book. . . . You note that she is in her early 40s and reasonably attractive; her hair is a rather unnatural shade of yellow. Furthermore, she is wearing an expensive long dress. Your snap judgment is that artificial blondes who wear expensive dresses are on the frivolous side. You note that the woman is witty, and that she giggles a great deal. . . . Finally, you note she is consuming drinks at a rapid pace and that she has smoked several cigarettes.
>
> What have you decided? Our novelist is intelligent, ambitious, hard-working, frivolous, witty, "giggly," and nervous. Now your work really begins. How, you might ask yourself, can a person be both hard-working and frivolous? Or perhaps she is trying to create a really good impression for someone so that her hairstyle does not so much indicate frivolousness as a concern to create a good impression . . . But why would she be nervous? She's a hit, the star of the party. Maybe she is insecure (all those giggles); nervous people and people who try to create a good impression are nervous—or so you believe. Why is she insecure? (Schneider, Hastorf, and Ellsworth 1979)

And so on. In order to give some consistency to all these observations and inferences, people work to organize the data they perceive into some coherent, stable impression. Although this impression is continually revised, it remains a global characterization of another person in which much of the original and inconsistent details get lost. So, depending on your past experience, you may conclude, for example, that the woman is very admirable but unusually nervous, a phony who's afraid of being discovered, or book smart but socially awkward.

There is now a considerable amount of communication research showing that people differ in how effectively they perceive others. For instance, researchers have discovered that stereotyping depends upon a person's mental state. If someone has high anxiety and tries to suppress stereotypic thinking, stereotyping may actually increase (Hall

With the addition of two young boys to the mix, how are your initial perceptions of these two men reinforced? Challenged? Revised?

and Crisp 2003). You probably have experienced this yourself. If you are traveling in a foreign country and people told you before you left to "never leave anything unattended because people steal there all the time," you may become tense and see every person around you as a potential thief.

Some people generalize and categorize more than others, and thus tend to contribute more to impersonal rather than interpersonal communication events. Their talk is *position centered* because it focuses on social roles and norms rather than the unique characteristics of individuals.

Other communicators seem better able to use the discriminatory power of perception and to note fine distinctions between one type of behavior and another. They appear to be more flexible in the perceptions they construct of others, using a higher number and more types of categories. These more sophisticated social perceivers are more likely to engage in more communication toward the right-hand end of the impersonal⟷interpersonal scale. These communicators are sensitive to perceptual features across a variety of different types of social situations, which makes their communication much more *person-centered*. In other words, position-centered communication is nearer the left end of the continuum, and person-centered communication is nearer the right end.

Attribution

A second process of person perception is called *attribution*. When people form attributions, they devise theories or explanations about other people's behavior that provide a way of making sense out of whatever is occurring (Heider 1958; Kelley 1973). Often, this means assigning a cause or intention to the behavior (Kelley 1972). For instance, a student might come late to class and the instructor might think, "That student is lazy." In the same situation a different instructor might think, "Must have been a lot of traffic today." Each of these attributions is a way for the instructor to explain or make sense of the student's behavior. The attributions also provide the instructor with some sense that he or she can predict how the student will behave in the future. When you can devise explanations for how people behave and predictions of their future behavior, you can operate with much more certainty about what is happening in a particular situation.

Notice how one of the two causes or reasons the instructor assigned to the student's behavior is anchored in the student's personality ("lazy") and the other is anchored in external factors ("traffic"). These are the response options people commonly select from: You attribute the cause of the behavior either to a character trait, mood, or disposition *(internal factors)* or to the situation *(external factors),* or to both (Heider 1958; Rotter 1966). When your attributions emphasize internal factors, you're more likely to interpret what happened as the person's fault or responsibility. When someone else makes mistakes, people tend to attribute the behavior to internal causes. So, for instance, imagine you're giving a presentation. You have worked hard for weeks and are very nervous. A friend has promised to come and give you mental and emotional support during the presentation. You start your presentation and realize that your friend is not there. He walks in 10 minutes late, which makes you think, "I'm not worth his time. My buddy let me down." You attribute his behavior to internal causes instead of wondering whether he got stuck in traffic.

By contrast, when people make mistakes themselves, they tend to attribute their behavior to external causes. So, when you come late to class, you might automatically offer an excuse that attributes your being late to external causes, such as "The bus didn't show up" or "My roommate had a panic attack this morning and I had to drive him to the hospital." The reason why people attribute personal mistakes to external causes is to save face and keep themselves from becoming vulnerable.

If you remember what we said about fault and blame, you'll probably get a sense of why attributions can be dangerous. Although attributions about others can help guide understanding, they also often interfere with your ability to see alternative reasons for why people behave the way they do. For instance, one researcher (Manusov 1990) studied what happens when couples playing the game Trivial Pursuit have to make sense of their partner's obviously positive or negative nonverbal behavior. One member of each couple was recruited to act positively at one point in the game and to act negatively at another point. The study showed that couples who were happy with their relationship and each other tended to attribute positive behavior to internal causes in their partners. In contrast, unhappy couples made more external attributions. So, in this study, a person's overall attitude toward his or her partner significantly affected the attributions made about the partner's nonverbal behavior.

Applying What You Know

Think about someone you know (friend, classmate, teacher). Describe two of the person's attitudes, beliefs, or goals and two of his or her personality characteristics. Then identify the perceptual cues that led you to infer each of those characteristics. See if you can tell how a cue led you to an attributed inference. You can use the following example:

Inferred Characteristic: **Observed Cues:**

She is extremely impatient.   I was 10 minutes late for a date; she left before I got there. She constantly plays with objects in her hands. She once knocked the phone to the floor when her parents didn't call her at the scheduled time.

Inferred Characteristic of a Friend: Observed Cues:

Stereotyping

A stereotype is defined in the *Oxford English Dictionary* (2003) as a "preconceived and oversimplified idea of the characteristics which typify a person, situation, etc.; an attitude based on such a preconception. Also, a person who appears to conform closely to the idea of a type." In other words, a stereotype is a category that people apply to other people, often based on their group membership. These categories can include gender, ethnic or national, religious, and vocational groups. Overall, stereotypes are a way that people make sense of the world and orient themselves to the people around them.

Two important dimensions of stereotypes are the following: (1) They can be positive or negative and (2) they can vary in intensity. Positive stereotypes are categorizations that evoke favorable associations, such as "Asians are good at math," "Chinese are polite," "African women are beautiful," or "African-Americans are athletic." Negative stereotypes are unfavorable categorizations of a whole group of people—for example, "East Coasters are rude," "Arabs are terrorists," or "football players are lazy students." In addition to direction, stereotypes can also vary in intensity—the strength with which the stereotype is maintained. Families and peer groups affect the intensity of most people's stereotypes (Tan et al. 2001). If you continually heard when you were growing up that "foreigners" are bad because they take jobs away from native-born citizens, you are likely to believe it and may even be suspicious of foreigners.

You've undoubtedly been told many times that stereotyping is dangerous and stereotypes are bad. In many ways, this is true. Racism and sexism continue, to a considerable degree, because of stereotypes. Communication based on stereotyped perceptions of people will fall on the impersonal side of the impersonal⟷interpersonal continuum.

On the other hand, some stereotyping is unavoidable, and in some cases it can be helpful. When you're walking alone at night in a city, it can be legitimate and helpful to stereotype the person matching your route and your pace as a threat. The natural human tendency to categorize influences all perceptions, so it is impossible to stop stereotyping completely. You just have to be careful not to let your stereotypes become too rigid. You can do that by being aware that people sometimes put other people into boxes and by trying to see the person with his or her individual characteristics behind the stereotype.

In addition, researchers have found that communication is not always influenced by stereotypes as much as it is affected by the interaction itself (Manusov and Hegde 1993; Manusov, Winchatz, and Manning 1997). For instance, researchers asked how neutral, positive, and negative stereotypes about people from other cultures affect the ways in which people communicate and the judgments they make about their conversation partners. So far, they've found that stereotyped-

Reflect for a moment on this picture of a student athlete. What do you see? What is in this picture and in your experience that lead you to your interpretations? How might this person be stereotyped?

based expectancies do affect people's evaluations of their conversation partners from other cultures, but they also found that what happens during the actual conversation is more important than the stereotype. People base their judgments of others more on facial pleasantness, fluency in conversation, relaxed posture, and similar vocal cues than on the stereotypes that they bring to the interaction (Manusov, Winchatz, and Manning 1997). This evidence indicates that even in cross-cultural conversations, where you'd think stereotypes would be most influential, these generalizations don't completely control how people respond.

'But . . .' A Student Responds

Why do some people make such strange inferences? Sometimes I hear people talking about a film, program, or other message and I can't believe they interpret it as they do.

It sounds like in this case that by "strange," you mainly mean "different from mine." Inference-making is a complex process, and we only scratched its surface in this chapter. Inferences reflect people's cultures, value systems, expectations, beliefs, opinions, attitudes, preferences, and even moment-to-moment moods. You've heard the expression "You are what you eat." Some people also say, "Perception is projection," that is, what I perceive is a projection of who I am—my gender, age, culture, social class, occupation, family situation, disabilities, and so on. If this is as true for everybody around you as it is for you, and if some of the people around you are really different from you, then it's no wonder that, to you, some of their inferences seem really strange.

Start by remembering that what's strange to one person can be ordinary to somebody else. You can either just accept the fact that your world is diverse, or you can take strangeness as a signal that it's going to take work for you to understand what you're hearing. When you respond in the second way, you can figure that it's time to do some analytic listening (or maybe, as we'll note in the next chapter, some empathic or dialogic listening).

Practical Perception Problems

As part of our continuing effort to blend theory and practice, we want to end this chapter with a description of five specific difficulties that you might encounter in your perception processes. Each grows out of the complexity and culture dependence of the perception process. Each can also affect where your communication is on the impersonal⟷interpersonal scale.

Fast Thinking

One problem people have with the selection part of perception is that, when listening to someone, we have a great deal of spare time. In a normal conversation, native English speakers tend to speak from 115 to 130 words per minute. But normal thinking speed—if it can be quantified this way—exceeds 500 words per minute. This means that people listening to speech have a lot of extra time to get perceptually sidetracked by other cues or by their own thoughts. You might think of this perception problem as the challenge of what to do with this free time. Since it's harder to concentrate on another person's ideas than it is to focus on our own, we often take the easy way out and spend our free time thinking about our own concerns. The listening skills we describe in the next chapter clarify what else might be done with this free time.

Avoiding Overload

A second reason people sometimes tune out is to preserve some control over their environment. We are constantly bombarded with countless messages from family members, supervisors, teachers, friends, acquaintances, strangers, and the media, and if we tried to pay attention to it all, we would quickly go crazy. We can't turn off the perceptual process entirely, so we have to make decisions about the things we will attend to and the things we will let go. So sometimes we tune out to preserve our physical and emotional health. The trick is not to let the real potential of information overload force you into the habit of tuning out.

The Entertainment Factor

A third reason people sometimes fail to pay attention is that they're used to getting information in entertaining packages. Adults who grew up spending a great deal of time watching television are especially prone to expect ideas and information to come in attractive, lively, and stimulating packages with economical sound bites. If you doubt the influence of this factor, notice the way television packages the news and the way advertisers on radio, television, and in magazines present their products. Awareness of this expectation can go a long way toward reducing its impact on your perception.

In addition to these three selection problems, there are at least two types of problems that can interfere with the kind of person perception that promotes interpersonal communicating.

Snap Judgments

Snap judgments are inferences that are "usually rather immediate and do not involve complex cognitive processes" (Schneider, Hastorf, and Ellsworth 1979, 20). They are the most limited kind of stereotype people make about others. Snap judgments are usually based on the physical characteristics of the other person and a very limited set of observations of their behavior. In the earlier description of the novelist at the cocktail party, the snap judgment is that "artificial blondes who wear expensive dresses are on the frivolous side." Snap judgments result when people evaluate whether the person they're perceiving is old or young, male or female, physically able or disabled, richly or poorly dressed, from a particular culture, and under- or overweight. Occasionally a snap judgment can be useful, such as when you're aggressively approached by a telemarketer as you're sitting down for dinner. But most of the time snap judgments are liable to distort your understanding of what the person is saying.

Attributional Errors

Earlier we explained that people make attributions to help make sense out of someone else's behavior by assigning a cause or intention to their actions. These causes or reasons for behavior get associated with the other's personality (internal factors) or something in the situation (external factors). These often lead to oversimplified conclusions about fault and blame, which, as we explained in Chapter Two, interfere with our ability to see communication as a collaborative process. One form of distortion happens when people unequally balance internal and external factors and commit what's called the *fundamental attribution error* and the *ultimate attribution error.*

The fundamental attribution error is the mistaken tendency people have to attribute others' behaviors to internal, rather than external, causes. The ultimate attribution error assumes that, as we mentioned, people's negative behavior is caused by internal factors and that their positive behavior is caused by external factors. This means that there is a tendency to underestimate the impact of situational factors in producing another's behavior and to overestimate the role of personality factors (Kelley 1972).

For instance, the person evaluating her *own* tendency to drive over the speed limit or be late for an appointment would be likely to attribute her actions to the situation—she is just "keeping up with traffic" or "unavoidably delayed by traffic signals and detours." But the fundamental attribution error happens when she fails to give others the benefit of this explanation and instead accounts for *their* speeding and lateness as "irresponsibility" or "carelessness."

One example of the ultimate attribution error concerns perceptions of obesity. Researchers have concluded that many people attribute obesity in other people to internal, controllable causes. Thus, those who are significantly overweight are often regarded as having no self-control and are therefore subject to blame and ridicule (Rush 1998). Obese people are also usually viewed as unattractive, sad, depressed, and unlikable (Hiller 1981; Triplett 2003). Many people who think that obesity is the fault of the individual fall into the trap of the ultimate attribution error: They assign what is perceived to be negative behavior to internal personality characteristics. They also commit this error when they conclude that weight loss is caused by a good diet and the help of other people instead of asking themselves whether the weight loss also has something to do with the strong will of the person. It can help to avoid the fundamental attribution error by remembering that others' actions—just like our own—are responses to both internal and external factors.

Chapter Summary

Our main point about perception is that the ways people select, organize, and make inferences about others affect the ways people communicate. Person perception by its very nature forms the basis of the "reality" you share with others every time you make contact with them. By becoming aware of the ways you perceive others, you can learn to generalize less, that is, to be more sensitive to the unique and distinctive features others make available to you as you communicate with them. Increasing your perceptual sensitivity is a major step in making the inhaling part of your communicating more effective.

Up until now, though, we've been treating the parts of perception that are considered cognitive or mental processes as occurring largely in your head. If we stayed with just this simple a picture, we would be seriously misrepresenting the way perception works. Why? Because, as we said before, listening is where the rubber of perception meets the road of communication. Listening is the concrete manifestation-in-communication of all the perceptual processes we have discussed in this chapter. When you communicate, your listening enables you to interpret (select, organize, and make inferences about) what your conversation partners are saying and doing. These perceptions change as you collaboratively build meaning. Listening is the inhaling part of communicating, which includes your perception and your response to others. This is why we focus on listening in the next chapter.

In Other Words

So—now you have some theoretical background about stereotypes and you probably already know from your life experience that stereotypes can be problematic. In this reading an African American woman tells you an all-too-common story about stereotypes. As you reflect on the reading, consider the following questions:

1. What is the secretary's stereotype about black people?
2. How does the professor respond when she hears that she's accused of being a thief?
3. Think about the last time that you inadvertently stereotyped someone. In what ways did your act of stereotyping influence how you communicated with the person?
4. Now, think about the last time that someone else stereotyped you. How did you respond?
5. What can you do to break down stereotypes?

*** * ***

A Whole Lot of Milk With a Drop of Chocolate: An African American Woman's Story

Veronica J. Duncan

This essay shares two stories about my experiences as an African American woman. I do not presume to speak for ALL African American women, but I know that there are many whose experiences are similar to mine.

Before we begin, let me tell you a little bit about myself. I am a first generation African American female college graduate and a professor of communication. I am a mother, wife, daughter, sister, teacher, mentor, protege, friend, colleague, and healer. You may wonder why all of this information is necessary. In other words, why am I telling you "all of my business"? This information is important because you are reading MY STORY. Throughout this essay you will hear MY VOICE, which I hope will help you to undertake a critical examination of your own beliefs, attitudes, values, and roles in the oppression of an "Other."

I chose the title "A Whole Lot of Milk with a Drop of Chocolate" because drinking milk with chocolate is a different experience from drinking milk alone. The chocolate gives the milk a little more flava'. Now, let's begin by examining individual racism.

Individual racism occurs when people of color, as a group, are regarded as inferior because of their physical characteristics. These physical traits, the individual racist believes, cause all who have them to be antisocial, morally decadent, and intellectually mediocre, which justifies and legitimates inferior social treatment directed against those individuals.

I will describe an incident that, for me, identifies how deeply ingrained individual racism is. As a new faculty member at a predominantly white university, I was leery of the kind of environment I would find. However, being the optimistic person that I am, I like to give people an opportunity to show me where they are coming from in terms of dealing with African Americans. Yes, I still believe that there is hope for humanity. The first week I was at this institution as a FACULTY member, the secretaries had money stolen from their purses. The structure of the department was such that we had a department secretary, whom I will call Susan, and an assistant to the chair, whom I will call Betty. I am changing the names of these individuals not to protect the innocent but because, in talking to other African American and female faculty members,

I know that the names may change but the behaviors are often similar. Anyway, I had noticed that Susan was acting rather strangely toward me, but I attributed it to her personality. She did not seem to be the happiest person in the world, for whatever reason. Then *it* happened.

I was trying to help Betty by getting some computer assistance from a technician. I had been told that the computer support people did not respond quickly to the secretary's calls, so I called to help her speed up the process. During the course of our attempts to take care of the computer issues, we needed some disks to complete the task. I asked Susan if she knew where the disks were kept. She told me that she didn't, so I went to look for them so that we could finish. When I went into the other secretary's office, which was also the department office, Susan followed me and stood in the doorway, watching me. By this time I was rather perturbed but chose not to dignify her behavior with a reaction. I went on "about my business," as we would say in the African American community. Once the task was completed, I had to go to the office to get something; the door was shut, but I heard whispering. By this time I was really feeling like something was wrong, but I couldn't believe that they might think that I STOLE THEIR MONEY! So I listened at the door. Talk about being "the spook by the door"; well, that was me. I wanted to know what was going on, and no one would tell me. I overheard Susan telling someone that "she just walked in the office like she owned the place. And I didn't know if your purse was out or not." I was LIVID. Who did they think they were? I was a PROFESSOR. I even had nearly finished my Ph.D. Me? A thief? I banged on the door. It opened and when people realized it was me, they scattered. Everyone got extremely quiet. Everyone, that is, except me. I let them have it. I told Betty, who was Susan's direct supervisor, that I was offended at the way Susan had been treating me. I proceeded to let her know that I didn't appreciate Susan talking about me behind my back. If she had anything to say about me, then she needed to say it TO me. You may be wondering why I didn't just say these things to Susan, since she was in the next room and I was speaking loud enough for her to hear me. If I had said anything to Susan at that moment, I would have lost it. I knew I needed to cool down. I will tell you that all the "street" in me would have come out. I actually wanted to hit her. That may seem stereotypically "black", but I am being honest here. I'm not a fighter, but I can be if I need to be.

Betty was terrified. Susan was gone, and the others had scattered. I said to Betty that Susan and I needed to have a meeting, turned on my heels, and went back to my office. I'm sure that people could almost see the steam coming from my ears as I walked down the hall. If someone had placed a piece of ice on me, it would have melted so quickly and completely that by the time I reached my office there would have been no trace that it had ever existed. That is how HOT I was as I walked to my office.

Once I shut my office door, all of the hardness on the outside melted. I sat there and I cried. I cried for me because even though I was a PROFESSOR, they still thought I was a thief. I cried for my people because it seems that no matter how much we advance, we're still just NIGGERS to some white people. And I cried for them, because they obviously had missed out on the opportunity to learn some wonderful things about African American people and had only gotten the negative. One thing was certain: I cried out of anger, frustration, and hurt. But they wouldn't see me cry. . . .

Excerpts pp. 172–174 from *Among Us: Essays on Identity, Belonging and Intercultural Competence,* edited by M. W. Lustig and J. Koester. Copyright © 2000 by Addison Wesley Longman, Inc. Reprinted by permission of Pearson Education, Inc.

References

Abelson, R. P. 1981. "Psychological Status of the Script Concept." *American Psychologist* 36: 715–729.

Bartlett, F. C. 1932. *Remembering: A Study in Experimental and Social Psychology.* London: Cambridge University Press.

Casson, R. W. 1983. "Schemata in Cognitive Anthropology." *Annual Review of Anthropology,* 12: 429–462.

Fiske, S. T., and Shelley, E. T. 1984. *Social Cognition.* New York: Random House.

Hall, B. J. 2002. *Among Cultures: The Challenge of Communication.* New York: Wadsworth.

Hall, N., and Crisp, R. 2003. "Anxiety-Induced Response Perseverance and Stereotype Change." *Current Research in Social Psychology,* 8: 242–253.

Heider, F. 1958. *The Psychology of Interpersonal Relations.* New York: Wiley.

Hiller, D. V. 1981. "The Salience of Overweight in Personality Characterization." *Journal of Psychology,* 108: 233–240.

Hudson, J. A., and Shapiro, L. R. 1991. "From Knowing to Telling: The Development of Children's Scripts, Stories, and Personal Narratives." In A. McCabe and C. Peterson (eds.), *Developing Narrative Structure.* Hillsdale, NJ: Erlbaum. Pages 89–136.

Kelley, H. H. 1972. "Causal Schemata and the Attribution Process." In E. E. Jones and D. E. Kanouse, H. H. Kelley, R. E. Nisbett, S. Valins, and B. Weiner (eds.), *Attribution: Perceiving the Causes of Behavior.* Morristown, NJ: General Learning Press.

Kelley, H. H. 1973. "The Process of Causal Attribution." *American Psychologist,* 28: 107–128.

Kluckhorn, F. R., and Strodtbeck, F. L. 1961. *Variations in Value Orientations.* Evanston, IL: Row Peterson.

Konner, M. 2002. *The Tangled Wing: Biological Constraints on the Human Spirit.* 2nd ed. New York: Holt, Rinehart and Winston.

Maltz, D. N., and Borker, R. A. 1982. "A Cultural Approach to Male-Female Miscommunication." In J. J. Gumperz (ed.), *Language and Social Identity.* Cambridge: Cambridge University Press. Pages 196–216.

Manusov, V. 1990. "An Application of Attribution Principles to Nonverbal Behavior in Romantic Dyads." *Communication Monographs,* 57: 104–118.

Manusov, V., and Hegde, R. 1993. "Communicative Outcomes of Stereotype-Based Expectancies: An Observational Study of Cross-Cultural Dyads." *Communication Quarterly,* 41: 338–354.

Manusov, M., Winchatz, M., and Manning, L. M. 1997. "Acting Out Our Minds: Incorporating Behavior Into Models of Stereotype-Based Expectancies for Cross-Cultural Interactions." *Communication Monographs,* 64: 119–139.

Mayer, R. E. 1992. *Thinking, Problem-Solving, Cognition.* 2nd ed. San Francisco: Freeman.

Oxford English Dictionary. 3rd ed. 2003. *Stereotype* [online version]. Retrieved July 25, 2003, from http://dictionary.oed.com/cgi/findword?query_type= word&queryword=stereotype.

Rotter, J. B. 1966. "Generalized Expectancies for Internal vs. External Control of Reinforcement." *Psychological Monographs,* 80: 609.

Rush, L. L. 1998. "Affective Reactions to Multiple Social Stigmas." *Journal of Social Psychology,* 138: 421–430.

Schneider, D. J., Hastorf, A. H., and Ellsworth, P. C. 1979. *Person Perception.* 2nd ed. Reading, MA: Addison-Wesley. Pages 20–26.

Tan, A., Tan, G., Avdeyeva, T., Crandall, H., Fukushi, Y., Nyandwi, A., Chin, H., Wu, C., Fujioka, Y. 2001. "Changing Negative Racial Stereotypes: The Influence of Normative Peer Information." *Howard Journal of Communications,* 12: 171–180.

Triplett, L. 2003. "Blame It on the Baby: The Use of External Causal Attributions to Justify Female Obesity." Paper presented at the Doctoral Honors Seminar at Bowling Green State University, Ohio, August. ✦

Chapter Six

Inhaling: Listening

<table>
<tr><th colspan="1">Chapter Objectives</th></tr>
</table>

After reading this chapter, you should be able to do the following:

- Identify four factors that inhibit effective listening.
- Explain the similarities and differences among analytic, empathic, and dialogic listening.
- Describe some situations where empathic listening is appropriate.
- Explain and give examples of four empathic focusing skills.
- Explain and give examples of six empathic encouraging skills.
- Explain and give examples of three reflecting skills.
- Identify the primary attitude or mind-set behind dialogic listening.
- Explain why we call dialogic listening "sculpting mutual meanings."
- Describe the difference between empathic focusing and dialogic focusing.
- Describe the difference between empathic encouraging and dialogic encouraging.
- Explain and give examples of three dialogic listening skills.
- Contrast the Western cultural assumptions behind analytic listening with the Eastern cultural assumptions behind dialogic listening.

Chapter Preview

"He never listens to me!" "She doesn't understand what I'm trying to say!" These are just a couple of the ways that relational partners frustrated with the state of their relationships express their concerns. In fact, one of the biggest complaints family and relational therapists hear from their clients is that others just don't listen. When people ask how to build better relationships, they often expect to learn what they should say. This way of thinking overlooks the fact that *most of the time you don't talk your way into good relationships—you listen your way into them.* In this chapter, we continue with the theme of inhaling and talk about some of the challenges or barriers to listening, some coping strategies to deal with these challenges, and three different forms of listening you can practice to enhance your relationships.

The three forms of listening we introduce are analytic, empathic, and dialogic listening. Analytic listening provides you the opportunity to focus on *your* ability to critically evaluate what you hear. Empathic listening concentrates on the *other's* meaning; its goal is not to analyze or criticize what the other person is saying, but rather to fully understand his or her thinking and feeling. Dialogic listening moves the listener's awareness one more step—from *me* (analytic listening) and *you* (empathic listening) to *us*, to the meanings that listener and speaker construct together. As a result, dialogic listening is our label for a kind of involvement in the communication process that applies almost this entire book's approach to co-constructing meaning in interpersonal contact.

In his book *The Lost Art of Listening*, family therapist Michael Nichols describes many instances where friends, spouses, coworkers, parents and children, bosses, and acquaintances fail to listen to each other. He reminds his readers that when we don't listen to people, they come to feel that their ideas and emotions are not taken seriously and that what they say doesn't matter. Learning how to be an effective listener means becoming aware of the ways ethical standards and cultural norms both help and hinder interpersonal connections between people. And what's at stake, as Nichols puts it, is that "our lives are coauthored in dialogue" (1995, 6).

Challenges to Effective Listening

In the previous chapter, we described how perception works and introduced the idea that listening skills can help you overcome problems like attribution errors and stereotyping. But listening isn't easy. The perception process itself generates some barriers to listening that effective communicators need to learn to overcome. To get a sense of how significant these barriers are, consider the results of one study of an introductory college lecture course that found that, at any given moment during a lecture, only 12 percent of the students in the room were actively listening. About 20 percent were pursuing erotic thoughts; another 20 percent were reminiscing about something; about 40 percent were worrying, daydreaming, or thinking about such topics as lunch or religion; 20 percent were paying general attention to the lecture; and only 12 percent of this 20 percent were summarizing, organizing, silently paraphrasing, and in other ways actively and responsively listening (Weaver 1987).

Most of us can identify with these college students, whether in lecture halls, in meetings at work, at club functions, or around the dinner table. At every point in the perceptual process, people can be easily distracted. Perhaps you realize that you often have only one ear trained on the speaker, television newscaster, coworker, or family member you're supposedly "listening to." It's likely you've also experienced this same half interest from others in your circle of friends, living group, or company.

We regularly ask our students to reflect on their abilities as listeners. Are they superlisteners or do they have lots of room to develop their listening skills? Most place themselves somewhere between the two extremes, but all believe they can be better listeners to their friends, family, teachers, and coworkers. We then ask what keeps them or others they know from being the best listeners they can be. Over the years, Karen has noted that students' long lists of reasons for not listening can consistently be categorized into four sets of barriers: content, context, characteristics of the speaker, and issues that are connected to them as listeners.

Content

Students identify the content of conversations and lectures as one significant barrier to their listening. If they consider the topic to be boring, for example, they find it difficult to listen carefully. Also, when the presentation of an issue is too simple or too complex, people tend not to listen. Attributions about the appropriateness of the subject of conversation can also inhibit people's willingness and ability to listen. If you don't find the information presented to be relevant, credible, or consistent with your ethical standards, you may find yourself tuning out on a regular basis. Or if the topic is taboo, based on your cultural norms or upbringing, it is safe to say that your listening will be affected.

Context

The context in which a communication event is taking place also affects students' listening. If you and a friend are talking together in the comfort of your home, you may be a better listener than if you are trying to have an important conversation in the midst of many other people at a basketball, football, or baseball game. For some people it is easier to listen when they feel anonymous (as in a large lecture hall) and difficult to listen in a one-on-one situation. For others it is just the opposite. Many dimensions of your world of meaning (e.g., physical environment, time, relationships, technology) influence the contexts in which you are called to listen, and most students report that context matters.

Characteristics of the Speaker

Qualities of the speaker are the most frequently reported barriers to students' listening. Perhaps because many still follow fault-and-blame thinking, they generate long lists of speaker characteristics that "keep me from listening." Monotone speakers, overenthusiastic speakers, communication partners who just want to hear themselves speak, physical appearance, accents and dialects, cultural differences, value systems, and even body odor are identified as characteristics of communicative partners that inhibit effective listening. "If only the speaker were _____ (and you can fill in the blank), I would be a better listener."

Issues Connected to the Listener

Many students also describe things about themselves that make it difficult to listen effectively. Fatigue, mental distraction, inability to see or hear the person speaking, and feeling sick or hungry are some of the issues they list. Many also admit that they are busy developing a rebuttal to what the other is saying. In a sense, they are too busy preparing to speak to listen well. Of course, even when students recognize that they aren't really listening, they often attribute their distraction to others or to the context rather than identifying it as a choice they are making. If you remember what we said in Chapter Five about the fundamental attribution error, you shouldn't be surprised to learn that most people are more likely to identify the things about themselves that inhibit their listening as situational factors and the things about the speaker as personal traits that are relatively stable.

But what difference can it make to know these reasons for not listening well? Students report later in the term that, in order to improve their listening, it is important to reflect for a while on what's going on so you can make informed choices about what you are going to do next. If your biggest barrier to listening is content (for example, you don't have a clue what the other person is talking about), you can do something about that. You can choose to learn something new, ask a question, or do some additional research on your own about the topic so that the next time you are listening to that topic, you'll be more informed. If context is an issue for you, you can choose to change it. If you want to talk with your boyfriend about the state of your relationship, and you want him to be able to listen, don't start the conversation in the midst of a play-off party for his favorite sports team—especially when his buddies are present. Choose a context for the conversation where it is more likely that he can focus on what you have to say. Realize that, although no listener is likely to change a speaker's accent or value system, you can choose to assess and alter your perceptions of the speaker as a person. You can choose to spend your energy focusing on what you might gain from listening to someone, rather than complaining about who you think that person is. And, of course, you can have the most control over issues associated with yourself. If you know that you don't listen well when you are hungry, eat something first. If you are tired and cannot focus on your relational partner, get more sleep or tell him that you will be a better listener once you are rested. Once you take a moment to reflect that barriers that are most significant to you as a listener, you can choose to do something to cope with the challenges of listening.

When you make the choice to improve your listening, a reasonable next step is to learn about some of the different ways you can listen. We emphasize three here: analytic, empathic, and dialogic listening. All three require you to engage actively in the communication process, and each form of listening can help you move your communication from one end of the impersonal←——→interpersonal continuum to the other.

Analytic Listening

You can practice this kind of listening most appropriately when you're in the audience at a lecture, a political speech, or a committee report; when you view a television or film documentary, news broadcast, or TV magazine show like *Dateline* or *60 Minutes*; or when you conduct an interview. You're in the same situation when you are a consumer of advertising, whether from the radio, over television, or face-to-face. Analytic listening pursues three goals: becoming more aware of your own beliefs and inferences, developing an understanding of the other person's beliefs and inferences, and analyzing or testing what you hear. Remember that the point of understanding is *not* necessarily to agree. In fact, one of the features of analytic listening is that you listen from your own point of view. Your purpose is to hear the other person out, to get a clear sense of what they're saying and why, but as a critical thinker rather than a puppet. This type of listening helps you to clarify your own perspective as distinct from that of the speaker and to respond to what you hear critically, rather than simply to react to it.

Analytic comes from the word analyze, and to analyze something means to break it down into its parts and to examine each part. So, one of the goals of analytic listening is to figure out what parts make up the whole message that you're listening to. Another is to get information about your own assumptions and the assumptions others are making. A person listening analytically is trying to uncover the premises used in reasoning about whatever issues are being discussed. One danger of analytic listening is that this stance can be confused with being judgmental. Remember, the point of analytic listening is to examine ideas carefully, not to be closed minded. Your goal should be to clarify what's behind the message and what's implied by it, rather than jumping to

Analytic listening is usually most appropriate in this kind of setting. How can you tell which students are engaged analytically with the speaker?

judgmental conclusions—"What is the question we are trying to answer?" rather than "Why can't you see that your point of view is stupid?"

You can improve your ability to listen analytically if you follow these six guidelines: (1) physically and mentally prepare to listen; (2) organize what you hear; (3) get the whole picture before you respond; (4) silently restate main points to yourself; (5) pay attention to the supporting material; and (6) ask yourself the "So what?" question.

Get Ready to Listen

By now you recognize that every kind of listening is an active, not a passive, process. It's easy to believe that all you have to be is a "cognitive sponge," just a passive receptacle for other people's messages. But this is not how effective listening works. People who listen for a living—counselors, therapists, doctors—will tell you that it takes real effort.

As a result, don't expect yourself to listen well when you are distracted or physically uncomfortable. Instead, plan to spend time focused on whatever or whomever you're listening to. When listening analytically, sit or stand where you can see and hear comfortably. Postpone as many as you can of your own concerns about whether you turned off the stove before you left home, when your friend is going to call, and how you're going to afford the next trip you're planning. Concentrate on the presenter or program. In short, look on the listening event as one that deserves some initial planning and preparation, and begin listening by getting ready for it.

Organize What You Hear

We say we understand something not necessarily when we agree with it, but when we can fit all its parts together, and when we can hook it up with something else we know. This is why understanding requires internal and external organization—relating the parts of a message to one another and linking the whole to other relevant information. When you're listening, you can apply this insight by consciously organizing what you hear into "chunks," or wholes.

It's easy to see how this process works. Try giving someone this string of numbers—0015635893202—and asking the person to repeat it. Then chunk, or organize, the string as telephone numbers are organized: 001 (563) 589-3202. Notice how much easier it is to understand and remember. You can do the same thing with ideas. To organize the ideas you hear, you don't have to be a genius at logic or outlining. Just try these suggestions:

(1) Organize by Key Ideas. All you have to do is remember that some parts of what you hear are going to be main points and some are going to be supporting or subordinate points. Listen first for the main points, and link the subpoints to the ideas they support. You can also compare the speaker's main points with your main ideas about this topic. The most important ideas to you may be subpoints in his or her message. If you notice this and even make note of it, you'll be developing a strong sense of the structure of what's being said.

(2) Organize by Overall Pattern. Listen for the pattern of ideas the speaker is following. Often it's a problem-solution pattern. "This is what's wrong, and this is what I think we should do about it." Other times speakers organize their ideas in time sequence—first this happened, then this, and now we need to do this. Descriptions of objects, institutions, systems, or processes will often move from bottom to top, front to back, inside to outside, management to workers, faculty to students to administrators to staff, or something similar. Some of the easiest-to-understand messages are in story form. Then you just need to listen for the main characters, the chronology, and the key events that give the story its point. But however the message is organized, if you can identify the overall pattern, you'll have a framework for understanding everything you hear.

(3) Organize by Noticing Transitions. Listen for links between ideas. Examples include "On the one hand . . . on the other hand"; "First, second, third . . . ," "But this isn't the only problem we have . . . ," "Not only . . . but also . . . "; and "Before we begin . . . after that . . . after that . . . ." Often speakers use questions to connect ideas, as in "So what can we do about this threat?" or "How does this all relate to you?" Many listeners don't pay much attention to transitions, but they are particularly important because they are the points at which the

speaker signals how one idea relates to the others. So, if you learn to spot them both in speech and writing, you can tell what whole (pattern) the speaker or writer is making out of the parts of his or her message. This will put you well on your way toward being able to understand the structure of what you're hearing or reading.

(4) Organize With Notes Whenever You Can. Analytic listening requires a thought-through response, and notes can help you do this well. You don't need an elaborate system, just a small piece of paper will do. Jot down key ideas and, where important, your first responses to them. Use the spacing on the page to show how the ideas connect in, for example, some rough outline form, a tree diagram, or maybe just a simple list. In a one-on-one situation you'll probably want to keep note-taking to a minimum, but speakers are often flattered to see listeners making notes.

(5) Organize With a Mnemonic. Especially where you can't or don't want to take notes, consider using a mnemonic device. This is a pattern of letters or words that helps you remember ideas. For example, your music teacher in grade school might have helped you remember the notes of the treble clef lines (EGBDF) with the mnemonic "Every Good Boy Does Fine." The treble clef spaces are even easier; they spell FACE. We do not recommend that you spend a large chunk of your listening time trying to come up with a clever acronym or other mnemonic, but if one strikes you quickly, use it to help remember what you have heard. KOLNOM is a mnemonic for the five ways of organizing we just discussed (*K*ey ideas, *O*verall pattern, *L*inks, *N*otes, *M*nemonics).

'But . . .' A Student Responds

When I use critical evaluation as part of my analytic listening, in my efforts to organize the speaker's comment, I turn his or her ideas into versions of my own. I am reflecting and responding, yet the result seems more impersonal than interpersonal. I'm trying to have someone's ideas make sense to me rather than trying to understand things from his or her unique point of view.

You're on to something when you notice that effective analytic listening may shift your communication more to the impersonal end of the continuum, or be most appropriate in contexts that are already more impersonal than interpersonal. Remember that the perception part of inhaling requires you to select some information, organize it in ways that make sense to you, and interpret it. Analytic listening gives you a structure to do just this—and to help you recall what the other is saying. It is true that in the process you may categorize or stereotype the speaker; you are likely to focus more on your cognitive schemata and less on the specific details and complex interplay of verbal and nonverbal cues from the speaker. The set of strategies we've just outlined offers a kind of compromise, an effort to enable you to fully and clearly understand what you hear *in a situation where conversational give-and-take is limited or impossible.* If your goal is to help your communication move further toward the interpersonal end of the continuum, then you are better off choosing to develop your empathic and dialogic listening skills.

Get the Whole Picture

Far too often people hear a few words or sentences, decide they know exactly what the speaker's point is going to be, and stop listening. In terms we introduced earlier, this is a type of snap judgment, or stereotype. Sometimes the results can even be embarrassing. You can ask a question that's already been answered or raise an objection that's already been covered. But even when it's not embarrassing, this kind of partial listening is at least discourteous and usually unwise. It interferes with your ability to remain flexible. Always try to respond to the whole; hear the person out before you decide how to respond.

The other part of getting the whole picture is becoming aware of your own and the other's assumptions. Assumptions are the fundamental beliefs that ground or lie behind interpretations people make. If you assume that it's a dog-eat-dog world, for example, you're likely to listen differently from the person who assumes that almost everybody does his or her best almost all the time. Culture provides a great many assumptions. When people learn what it means to be Latino, African American, working class, gay, or even male or female, they're learning a set of assumptions—basic beliefs about the way things are and about what's important.

Especially when you have a strong reaction to something you hear—anger, disgust, fear, ridicule—it's a good idea to ask yourself how your assumptions might be different from those of the person you're listening to. Remember again that the point is *not* necessarily to agree with the other person's message, but just to *understand* it. It can often be helpful to remember that other people have as good a set of reasons for believing and saying what they do as you have. When listening analytically, one of your jobs is to try to figure out what these reasons are.

For example, a person who is pro-choice might be incensed to hear someone hoping out loud that a new Supreme Court appointment will push the Court to overturn the *Roe vs. Wade* decision. She might get even more upset as she hears the speaker condemning doctors who perform abortions as "murderers." Nobody would expect the pro-choice person to agree with the pro-life comments she's hearing. But it can help her understand them if she thinks about the assumptions they're based on. For example, *if* one believes that human life begins at conception, and *if* he or she believes that there is a higher moral law that all laws made by humans should be subject to, and *if* one further believes that this higher moral law forbids the taking of any innocent human life, *then*, since abortion does terminate a human life, and since murder is defined as "the unlawful killing of a human being," it would be appropriate to call abortion "murder." These assumptions, in other words, can be understood as supporting this communicative response. Of course, if you begin with different assumptions, the label *murderer* is not at all appropriate. *If* one prioritizes the sanctity of the life of the mother, and *if* one believes that no government has the right to govern a woman's body, and *if* you believe that women have historically been prevented from having choices about matters that affect them most closely, and *if* you want to help equalize an unequal power relationship between women and men, *then* these assumptions can be understood as supporting a pro-choice position.

The point is if you want to understand another message or point of view, even while not necessarily agreeing with it, it helps to examine the assumptions it's based on. This kind of reflection can also lead you to reflect on your own assumptions, and this is another important part of critical thinking.

Silently Restate the Ideas You Hear

After you've been listening for a minute or two, you can say to yourself: "In other words, she's worried that news reports have completely distorted her actual position." The idea here is not just to *repeat* what the speaker said, but to *restate* it, to express it in your own words. In other words, offer yourself a paraphrase of what you hear. This technique can be helpful for two reasons. First, in order to restate rather than just repeat, what you hear has to "go through your brain cells." Second, if you have trouble restating what you've heard, this is a good indicator of where your listening is breaking down. Your efforts can tell you what question you might need to ask the speaker, or what additional information you need to seek out.

Pay Attention to How the Person Supports Her or His Ideas

When it's time to make a critical assessment, try to explore how the person supports her or his argument. Supporting material might include examples of the main ideas, analogies or comparisons to other similar situations, statistics that provide evidence for an argument, stories of actual events, or expert testimony. As a listener, you should consider whether *enough* support is present, whether it is reported *accurately*, and whether the information is *relevant*. These criteria will help you to make careful judgments. If, for instance, a television exposé shows only interviews with people on one side of an issue, or if a pro-nuclear energy speaker uses statistics and expert testimony from studies conducted only by the nuclear industry, it would be wise to consider what information is being left out of these messages. This can help you assess both the accuracy and the relevance of what you're hearing.

Ask the 'So What?' Question

This is the culmination of the analytical process because it prepares you to respond critically. Remember that "critical" doesn't necessarily mean "negative." It just means that you have identified the message, developed an understanding of it, tested it against some criteria, and arrived at a conclusion. Your critical response can be positive or negative.

Asking yourself the "So what?" question is the most direct way to connect with what you're hearing. We don't mean the question to be cynical or even skeptical; you don't have to sneer when you ask it. Instead, the point is to figure out how *you* fit into what you're hearing. Asking this question can enable you to identify the relevance of the content, the parts of your life that the information touches on. This question can also help you clarify where you agree and disagree with what you're hearing. When you use the question to help identify the assumptions you and the other person make, you can respond thoughtfully and critically. Analytic listening can help protect the listener from weak arguments and faulty reasoning, and it can help you think through your own reasons for holding important beliefs and opinions.

Sometimes a listener will *start* with this question rather than end with it. If you ask, "So what does this have to do with me?" or "So what does this add to my current understanding of this topic?" you may find that your response motivates you to listen more carefully.

To summarize, if you want to improve your own analytic listening, it can help to follow the suggestions or guidelines we have identified in this section: (1) physically and mentally prepare to listen; (2) organize what you hear; (3) get the whole picture before you respond; (4) silently restate main points to yourself; (5) pay attention to the supporting material; and (6) ask yourself the "so what?" question.

Empathic Listening

Empathic listening is most closely associated with the closed sensitivity response we described in Chapter Four. Here the listener is receptive or sensitive to the full range of characteristics shared by the other person, but responds only with his or her own impersonal characteristics. Carl Rogers, a famous counselor who pioneered the technique of empathic listening, describes it as "entering the private perceptual world of the other and becoming thoroughly at home in it." He continued:

It involves being sensitive, moment by moment, to the changing felt meanings which flow in this other person. . . . To be with another in this way means that for the time being, you lay aside your own views and values in order to enter another's world without prejudice. In some sense it means that you lay aside yourself. (Rogers 1980, 142–143)

This kind of listening is important, for example, when you are aware that your friend needs to vent and you are willing to listen without adding anything beyond your friend's point of view. In fact, if you respond in these situations by saying, "Well, if I were you . . . " your friend may insist, "I don't need your advice. I want you to just *listen* to me." It can also be important to listen empathically if you've been asked to mediate a dispute. You can't function very well as a mediator until you fully understand each person's point of view, and empathic listening can help you build this understanding.

Empathic listening is also an important skill for parents, teachers, and managers. Family communication research indicates, for example, that toddlers, children, and adolescents often feel that their parents listen only from their own point of view, rather than taking the time and effort to fully understand the young person's thinking and feeling. Books such as *How to Talk so Kids Will Listen and Listen so Kids*

Empathic listeners develop appropriate focusing skills. Note how the men in this picture aim their posture toward the speaker and are making natural and appropriate eye contact. How might their behaviors encourage the speaker?

Will Talk (Faber and Mazlish 1982) also emphasize how pity and advice can leave one feeling worse than before.

> But let someone really listen [empathically], let someone acknowledge my inner pain and give me a chance to talk more about what's troubling me and I begin to feel less upset, less confused, more able to cope with my feelings and my problem. (Faber and Mazlish 1982, 9)

Managers and teachers often need to listen empathically in order to understand how to help their subordinates or students, and, as we said in Chapter Four, counselors and doctors also routinely respond this way to their clients.

In order to listen empathically, it's important to develop three sets of competencies: focusing, encouraging, and reflecting skills (Bolton 1990). As with any complex process, it works best to select from among the various ways to focus, encourage, and reflect. Think of the specific skills like a salad bar—put on your plate the ones that you're comfortable with and that fit the situation you're in.

Focusing Skills

As with analytic listening, the first step is to orient your attention to the person you're listening to. This begins with an internal decision about how you are going to invest your time and energy. Here it helps to recall the distinction between *spending* time and *investing* it and to realize that empathic listening can often pay the dividends of any good investment. Then you remember that listening takes effort, and you put aside the other things you're doing to concentrate on the other person. At this point, focusing surfaces in four skills.

The first is *aiming your posture.* Turn your body so you're facing or nearly facing the person you're listening to, and if you're seated, lean toward your conversation partner. This is a simple thing to do, and yet a variety of studies have underscored its importance. One textbook for counselors puts it this way: "Usually, the interested helper leans toward the helpee in a relaxed manner. Relaxation is important because tenseness tends to shift the focus from the helpee to the helper . . . ." (Brammer 1979, 70). It's been demonstrated that when listeners focus their bodies this way, the people they're talking with perceive them as more "warm" and accessible and consequently they find it's easier to volunteer more information (Reece and Whiteman 1962).

A second part of focusing is making *natural and appropriate eye contact.* In Western cultures, when you look the other person in the eye, you are not only acutely aware of him or her, but you are also directly available to that person. Studies of nonverbal listening behavior in these cultures typically identify eye contact and forward body lean or movement toward the other as two of the most important indicators of attraction and contact (Clore, Wiggins, and Itkin, 1975). So, if you cannot easily make eye contact with the other person, move to a position where you can. If you're talking with children, get down on the same level by kneeling or sitting, so that they can see you looking at them.

As we've already noted, the amount and kind of eye contact that are "appropriate" depend partly on the cultural identities of the people involved. If you're talking with a person from a culture that proscribes eye contact except between intimates or from a superior to an inferior, it's important to try to honor these guidelines. If you're from one of these cultures, and your conversation partner is not, it can help to alter your own behavior in the direction of the other person's expectations as far as you comfortably can. But so long as you are operating in a generally Western communication context, it's important to work toward making eye contact 50 percent to 70 percent of the time.

In cultures that value direct eye contact, breaking it while listening can create real problems. As one of our students put it, "Based on my own experience, and that of a few others I've talked with, when a listening partner suddenly breaks eye contact to focus on something else (say, a friend who's walking by and waving), it can have an almost disconfirming effect on those of us who want to express ourselves" (Adams 1996).

The third and fourth ways to focus are to *move responsively* and to *make responsive sounds*. We've known people who believed they're listening intently when they sat staring at the other person, completely immobile, and with an unchanging, deadpan expression on their faces. There are two problems with this habit. The most obvious one is that, even though you may think you're listening well, it doesn't look like you are. Unless I see some response in your body and on your face, I'm not convinced that you're really being affected by what I'm saying. The second problem is more subtle: Actually you are not fully involved in what you're hearing until your body begins to register your involvement. So even though you might think you're focused when you're immobile and silent, you are not as focused as you will be when you start moving responsively and making responsive sounds. Since everybody's mind and body are intimately connected, the kinesthetic sensations of your body's responsiveness will actually help your mind stay focused.

By moving responsively, we mean smiling, nodding or shaking your head, moving your eyebrows, shrugging your shoulders, frowning, and so on. These actions should be prompted by, in response to, and linked up with what the other person says and does. So an effective listener isn't nodding or smiling all the time; she nods or smiles when that is responsive to what the other person is saying, and she frowns or shakes her head when that's responsive.

Responsive sounds include the "Mnnhuh," "Oh?" "Yeah . . ." "Ahh?" "Sure!" "Really?" and "Awww" utterances that audibly tell the other person you're tuned in to what he or she is saying. If you doubt the importance of responsive sounds, try being completely silent the next time you're listening over the phone. After a very short time the other person will ask something like "Are you still there?" We need sounds like these to reassure us that our hearer is actually listening.

These four skills may seem overly obvious or simplistic, but it is quite clear from a number of communication studies that people differ greatly in their ability to apply these behaviors.

Encouraging Skills

The second set of empathic listening skills is designed to "pull" more talk from the other person. More talk is obviously not always a good thing. But when you want to understand as completely as possible where another person is coming from, you need to have enough verbal and nonverbal talk to make the picture clear. As a result, we want to make six specific suggestions about how to encourage.

The first is the most direct one: As a listener, respond when appropriate with "Say more," "Keep talking," "Could you elaborate on that?" or "For example?" One situation where this response can help is when someone makes a comment that sounds fuzzy or incomplete. Frequently the listener's inclination is to try to paraphrase what's been said or to act on the information even though it's uncertain whether he or she has the materials to do so. Of course, it would be pretty ridiculous to respond to "I wonder what time it is" with "Could you say more about that?" But each time you hear a new idea, a new topic, or an important point being made, we suggest you begin your empathic listening effort at that moment not by guessing what the other person means but by asking her or him to tell you. "Say more," "Keep talking," or some similar encouragement can help.

A second encouraging skill is called *mirroring*. Mirroring means repeating a key word or phrase of the other person's with a question on your face and in your voice. "Repeating?" Yes, you just pick up on one term, for example, and feed it back with a questioning inflection and raised eyebrows, and the other person will elaborate on what he has just said. "Elaborate?" Yeah—you know, he will give an example, or restate what he said in other terms, or make some such effort to clarify the point he is making. Just as we have been doing here.

A third encouraging response is the *clarifying question*. Often this takes the form "Do you mean. . . ?" or "When you say _____, do you mean _____?" You might ask the person to explain how he or she is defining a word or phrase, or you might ask for the implications of what is being said. In a job interview, for example, the interviewer might comment, "Our company is interested only in assertive people. . . ." and the candidate could ask, "When you say 'assertive,' what do you mean?" Tone of voice is an important part of clarifying questions. Remember, your questions are motivated by a need to understand more clearly; they are not meant to force the other person into a corner with a demand to "define your terms!"

Open questions are a fourth way to encourage. *Closed* questions call for a yes or no, single-word, or simple-sentence answer. *Open* questions just identify a topic area and encourage the other person to talk about it. So, "Who was that person I saw you with last night?" is a closed question, and "How's your love life going?" is a more open one. Open questions often begin with "What do you think about . . . ?" or "How do you feel about . . . ?" while a closed version of a similar question might begin "Do you think . . . ?" "Do you like this chapter?" is a closed question; "Which parts of this chapter do you like best?" is more open. Both types of questions can be useful, but when you want to encourage, use open ones.

A fifth way to encourage is by using *attentive silence*. As we've said before, the point of empathic listening is to develop and understand the perspective of the speaker. So stay focused and give the other person plenty of room to talk. This is frequently all a person needs to be encouraged to contribute more.

Our two final suggestions about encouraging highlight what *not* to do. Encouraging obviously involves asking questions, but not just any question. We have already explained why using open questions is generally more effective than using closed questions. But there are also two types of questions that it helps to avoid. The first are what we call *pseudoquestions*. *Pseudo* means pretend, unreal, or fake, and a pseudoquestion is a judgment or opinion pretending to be a question. "Where

How is this woman demonstrating encouraging skills?

do you think you're going?" is not really a question, it's a pseudo-question. In other words, if you think about how this question functions in actual conversation, you can hear how it's almost always a complaint or a judgment one person is making about the other. "Where do you think you're going?" usually says something like "Get back here!" or "I don't want you to leave." "Is it safe to drive this fast?" is another pseudoquestion; here, the hidden statement is something like "I'm scared by your driving," or "I wish you'd slow down." At times, we may use pseudoquestions to soften a more directly negative evaluation of the other person (Goodman and Esterly 1990, 760). But often such softening attempts are confusing and add more frustration than they're worth. Our point here is that if you use them in your efforts to encourage, they can backfire. Instead of pseudoquestions, try to ask only real ones, genuine requests for information or elaboration.

A second kind of question to avoid is the one that begins with the word "why," because these questions tend to promote defensiveness. When people hear "Why?" questions, they often believe the questioner is asking them for a rationale or an excuse. "Why did you decide to bring him to this meeting?" "Why are you turning that in now?" "Why didn't you call me?" "Why did you decide to do it that way?" Do you hear the implicit demand in these questions? The problem is that "Why?" questions often put the questioned person on the spot. They seem to call for a moral or value justification. As a result, they don't work as encouragers. In their place, try asking exactly the same question but begin it with different words. For example, try "How did you decide to . . . ?" or "What are your reasons for . . . ?" We believe that you will find it works better.

Reflecting Skills

This third set of skills will help you directly reflect the other person's perspective in the communication process. This is the central goal of empathic listening. There are three skills in this final set. The first is called *paraphrasing. A paraphrase is a restatement of the other's meaning in your own words, followed by a verification check.* This means there are four important parts to a paraphrase: (1) It's a restatement, not a question. A paraphrase doesn't start out by asking; it starts out by telling the other what you have heard. The first words of a paraphrase might be "So you believe that . . . " or "In other words, you're saying that . . . " (2) It's a restatement of the other's *meaning*, not a repeat of the other's words. Meanings include both ideas and feelings, and the fullest paraphrase captures some of both. Sometimes the feeling content is very important, and sometimes it is less so. But your paraphrase ought at least to suggest the emotion that's included in what the other person said. "So you're worried that . . . " or "It sounds like you are really upset because you believe that . . . " are two examples of restating feelings—"worry" and "upset." (3) A paraphrase has to be in your own words. We have already mentioned why when we talked about restatement in the section on analytic listening. Translating the other's meaning into your words demonstrates that you've thought about it, that it's gone through your brain cells. (4) After the restatement, you finish a paraphrase with an opportunity for the other person to verify your understanding. You can do this very simply—just by pausing and raising your eyebrows, or asking "Right?" or "Is that it?" Paraphrasing is such a powerful communication move that, if you follow these four steps periodically in your conversations, your empathic listening effectiveness will improve significantly.

The second reflective skill is *adding an example.* You can contribute to the listening process by asking the other person to respond to an example from your own experience that you believe illustrates his or her point. Remember that this is an effort to listen empathically, not to turn the conversation away from the other person's concerns and toward yours. So the example needs clearly to be one that makes his or her main point. Here is part of a conversation that illustrates what we mean.

	Laura	I've had my share of problems with this TA position, but in some ways this job is actually rewarding.
(clarifying question)	*Habib:*	Since it's payday, are you talking about your check?
	Laura:	No, one of my students just wrote this note on her copy of the exam we were going over in class: "I liked the way you were willing to listen to our side and to consider giving back some points. I think it takes real confidence as a teacher to do that."
(adds example)	*Habib:*	That's really great. But I got a comment like that from a student once, and it turned out that he was being sarcastic. He was really ticked off about the way I graded his exam, and he even complained to the department chair. Do you think she could be setting you up?
(clarifies)	*Laura:*	I never thought about that. No, I don't think so. This is a returning student, and I think she appreciates it when she feels like she's being treated as an adult.

Remember that understanding is very different from agreement, and that neither the paraphrase nor adding an example requires you to agree with the other person. These listening responses are designed to promote the empathic listening process, to simply help you understand the other person's perspective.

The third and final reflecting skill also takes some finesse. The skill consists of *gently pursuing verbal and nonverbal inconsistencies*. The first step is to identify when you think they've occurred. You have to be sensitive enough to recognize when the words a person is speaking don't match the way she or he is saying them. As we noted earlier, a shouted, scowling "I'm not mad!!" is an obvious example of an inconsistency between verbal and nonverbal cues. Most of the time, though, it's much more subtle. John had a friend who declared she was not going to waste any more time being angry at her boss, and then spent the next half hour complaining about the boss's most recent actions. In other situations, facial expression and tone of voice accompanying a person's "Sure," "I don't care," "Go ahead with it," or "It doesn't make any difference to me" can reveal that the words are thin masks for disappointment, concern, or hurt feelings.

As a listener you can help move beyond surface-level meanings by gently pursuing the verbal/nonverbal inconsistencies you notice. We stress the word *gently*. When you notice an inconsistency, remember that it's your interpretation of what's going on; be willing to own it as your own. Remember, too, that if the other person also sees an inconsistency, there's a reason for its being there. He or she may not be ready or willing to admit the difference between cues at one level and cues at another. So don't use this skill as a license to clobber someone with a club made out of sidewalk psychoanalysis. Instead, just describe the inconsistency you think is there and open the door for the other person to talk about it.

For example, one group of professionals John worked with were experiencing some conflict over a proposal made by their new manager. The manager decided that the group needed to be more cohesive, so she proposed that each Friday afternoon the office close down an hour early so the workers could spend some time together informally chatting over wine and cheese. Most of the people welcomed the idea, but two resisted it. They didn't like what they saw as "forced socializing," and they resented the fact that only alcoholic drinks were being served. They didn't think it was appropriate to "drink on the job." John asked the group to discuss this issue as part of their listening training. Ann, the manager, turned to Gene, one of the two persons resisting the plan, and asked what he thought about these Friday afternoon get-togethers. Gene turned slightly away in his chair, folded his arms in front of him, looked down at the floor, and said, "Well . . . it's a pretty . . . good idea . . . . " Ann smiled and softly said, "Gene, your words tell me one thing and your body says something else." Then she was silent. After a couple of seconds, Gene relaxed his body posture, smiled, and admitted that he actually didn't like the plan very much. This began a conversation that ended up redesigning the get-togethers to respond to Gene's concerns.

The primary reason this listening response works is that nonverbal cues can "leak" implicit or hidden messages. Thus, a person's tone of voice, posture, eye behavior, and even facial expression often reveal levels of meaning that are obscured by his or her choice of words. Sensitive listeners try to respond to such inconsistencies and, as we suggest, gently pursue them.

Summary So Far

A student named Mandy Lam provided the following example of empathic listening in a brief conversation she had with a friend:

Mandy: Oh, Lily! Haven't seen you around for a while. How's it going?

Lily: Hi, Mandy. Yeah, I know. I've been so stressed out these last few weeks working on my medical school applications. As you probably know, I haven't been to biochem lectures lately.

Mandy: Yeah, I noticed. Medical school applications, huh? Have they been a pain in the butt?

Lily: Well, I'm finding that I have to juggle trying to put together 15 applications with schoolwork. It's stressing me big time! What's worse is that they often require a couple of pages of essay-type responses, and that just takes me awhile.

Mandy: It sounds like you have your plate full this quarter with classes and your med school apps. So that's why I've missed you in class lately, huh?

Lily: Yup. Wish things could get back to some sense of normalcy.

As this example shows, empathic listening is the kind that's generated by the closed sensitivity response we described in Chapter Four. Empathic listening happens when the listener focuses closely on the perspective of the speaker. The listener tries to "get inside" the other person's thoughts or to "walk a mile in his moccasins." This is often the goal of a counselor or therapist, but it's also an important thing for friends, parents, and managers. But if you want to make the most of each person's contributions to the conversation, it's more effective to shift the focus from the speaker to both participants. Then you move to what we call dialogic listening.

Dialogic Listening

There is no simple recipe for dialogic listening—no "six easy steps" or "five surefire techniques." This is something that anybody who wants to can definitely do, but it requires an overall approach to communicating that's different from the stance most people ordinarily take when they listen or talk. You also need to maintain a sometimes-difficult tension or balance (remember the idea of tension in Chapter Two) between holding your own ground and being open to the person(s) you're communicating with. The best way to get a sense of this approach and this tension is to understand a little bit about the idea of *dialogue.*

Ordinarily, dialogue means just conversation between two or more people, or between the characters in a novel or play. But in two periods of recent history the term has taken on some special meanings. First, between about 1925 and the early 1960s, the philosopher and teacher Martin Buber and some other writers used the term to talk about a special kind of communication. In his famous book *I and Thou* and in many other books and articles, Buber tried to point toward a way of communicating that he had noticed in some factories, family homes, schools, political organizations, churches, and even buses and planes, a way of communicating that accomplished genuine inter*personal* contact. Buber readily admitted that people can't and don't communicate dialogically all the time, but he maintained that we could do more of it, and if we did, we'd be better off.

For Buber, dialogue basically meant communication characterized by what in Chapter Four we call open sensitivity. As we've noted, this definitely doesn't require agreement, but it does require alignment. It can and does sometimes happen in committee meetings, family discussions, telephone calls between friends, doctor-patient exchanges, lovers' quarrels, and even occasionally between labor-management negotiators and political enemies.

Buber's view of dialogue lost credibility in the United States when it became associated with the hippie movement of the 1960s and 1970s. But since the early 1990s, the term and the ideas surrounding it have become prominent again. Today, though, the main writer everybody's quoting is another early-twentieth-century author with the initials MB, the Russian theorist Mikhail Bakhtin (Holquist 1981).

If you're going into business, it is very likely that you will run across Bakhtin's name in discussions about the importance of dialogue in what are called "learning organizations" (Senge 1990). Management theorists from the Sloane School at M.I.T., Harvard, and other prominent business schools argue that in this age of globalization and constant rapid change, the only way a company can keep up is to be constantly learning from its successes and mistakes. And the only way to become a learning organization is to replace traditional hierarchical communication with dialogue. Beginning in the late 1990s, large organizations like Ford Motor Company and Boeing started investing thousands of hours and dollars in training designed to help their employees learn to open spaces in their organizations for dialogue.

Dialogue is also being promoted as the best way to improve the quality of public discourse in the United States (Roth, Chasin, Chasin, Becker, and Herzig 1992) and Great Britain (in 1995 and 1996, British Telecommunications was engaged in a nationwide project to enhance the quality of interpersonal communication; several U.S. interpersonal communication scholars contributed to this effort). And some psychologists are arguing that the focus of the entire discipline of psychology needs to shift from the individual psyche to the dialogic person-in-relation (Sampson 1993). The concept is also being used more and more by communication researchers and teachers (Baxter and Montgomery 1996). In short, increasing numbers of influential people are recognizing that dialogue is a seriously beneficial phenomenon. The three of us believe that dialogic listening is the most direct way to promote dialogue. By "promote" we mean that dialogue can't be guaranteed, but it can be encouraged. And dialogic listening will help open up a space for the kind of person-to-person contact that Buber, Bakhtin, and all these other theorists and teachers call dialogue.

Dia-logos as Meaning-Through

One good way to open up this space is to focus on the term *dialogue* itself. This term consists of two Greek words, *dia* and *logos*. The *logos* in dia-logos is the Greek word for *meaning or understanding.* (The Greek term logos has other meanings, too. Sometimes it is translated as "logic," and at other times it comes into English as "language." But its most fundamental meaning is "meaning.") The *dia* in dia-logos means not "two" but *"through"* (Bohm 1990). So dialogue is not restricted to two-person communicating, and it is an event where meaning emerges *through* all the participants. This is another way of saying that, in dialogue, meaning or understanding is *collaboratively co-constructed.* The important implication of this idea for each participant is that, when you're listening and talking dialogically, *you are not in control of what comes out of the communicating.* This is a point we've made in various ways before, and it's stated clearly by Abraham Kaplan:

> When people are in [dialogue] . . . the content of what is being communicated does not exist prior to and independently of that particular context. There is no message, except in a post hoc reconstruction, which is fixed and complete beforehand. If I am really talking with you, I have nothing to say; what I say arises as you and I genuinely relate to one another. I do not know beforehand who I will be, because I am open to you just as you are open to me. (Anderson, Cissna, and Arnett 1994)

As communication teacher Bruce Hyde points out, the main obstacle to dialogic listening is the kind of self or identity that replaces this openness to collaboration with the conviction that the ideas I utter are tightly connected with who I am. There's a big difference, Bruce notes, "between being right about something and being committed to something. Being right makes somebody else wrong; being committed has room to engage productively with other points of view." In other words, if you're committed, you might even welcome the chance to talk with someone who believes differently from the way you believe, but if you're committed to being right, there's not much room for people who don't share your position to be anything but wrong. The key difference has to do with identity. The person who's caught up in being right identifies him- or herself first as an advocate for a certain position. The person who's committed, on the other hand, identifies him- or herself first as a listener who's collaborating on, but not in control of, what comes out of the conversation. If you're going to listen dialogically, you have to be more interested in building-meaning-through than in being right. And this, Bruce writes, "in my experience is the hardest single thing you can ask of anyone." (We got this from an e-mail contribution by Hyde on August 29, 1996, to Redwood Forest Dialogue. Kimberly Pearce was crucial in sharpening what Bruce wrote.)

Communication theorist and teacher Barnett Pearce expresses basically this same idea but with a cultural slant, when he contrasts an *ethnocentric* with a *cosmopolitan* approach to communication. Recall that the term *ethnocentric* means viewing other cultures from the perspective of one's own. When I communicate from an ethnocentric attitude, I begin with the assumption that my culture's way is "normal," "natural," "preferred," and, in these important senses, "right." Barnett argues that "ethnocentric communication is the norm in contemporary American society. It is, of course, the stuff of racism, sexism, and the like. It also structures domestic political discourse" (Pearce 1989, 120). Another feature of ethnocentric communication is that it privileges *coherence*—the kind of sense that emerges when other ideas fit into a comfortable whole, in part by matching or echoing what's "already there" and hence what is "normal and natural." So a person who approaches communication with an ethnocentric attitude assumes that his or her ways of thinking and doing are normal and natural and that conversations ought to make the kind of sense that you get when feelings and ideas fit together into familiar patterns.

A cosmopolitan attitude, on the other hand, is one that embraces all the "politics" in the "cosmos." It is inclusive rather than exclusive. A person with a cosmopolitan attitude may be *committed* to an idea or position, but he or she does not assume that it is absolutely "right." As a result, cosmopolitan communication privileges *coordination* rather than *coherence*. There's no assumption that the only way to put ideas or people together is the "logical" way, or the way based on "what we've always believed and done." People with a cosmopolitan attitude are open to all kinds of creative syntheses of ideas, procedures, and past experiences. The main goal is to work toward alignment, even when there is little or no agreement. As psychologist Gordon Allport is reported to have said, this kind of communicator is "half-sure yet wholehearted." *Dialogic listening begins with a cosmopolitan rather than an ethnocentric attitude.* The first step toward dialogic listening is to recognize that each communication event is a ride on a tandem bicycle, and you may or may not be in the front seat.

Sculpting Mutual Meanings

To shift from the bicycle metaphor, we've found that it helps to think and talk about the nuts and bolts of dialogic listening with the help of the image of a potter's wheel (Stewart and Thomas 1995). The sculpting mutual meanings metaphor was created by communication teacher Milt Thomas, and he uses it to suggest a concrete, graphic image of what it means to listen dialogically.

Picture yourself sitting on one side of a potter's wheel with your conversation partner across from you. As you participate (talk) together, each of you adds clay to the form on the wheel, and each uses wet fingers, thumbs, and palms to shape the finished product. Like clay, verbal and nonverbal talk are tangible and malleable; they're out there between people to hear, to record, and to shape. If I am unclear or uncertain about what I am thinking about or what I want to say, I can put something out there and you can modify its shape, ask me to add more clay, or add some of your own. Your specific shaping, which you could only have done in response to the shape I formed, may move in a direction that I would never have envisioned. The clay you add may be

This is mutual sculpting. Imagine that the clay is meaning, and you have a picture of how dialogic listening works.

an idea I've thought about before—-although not here or in this form—
or it may be completely new to me. Sometimes these "co-sculpting"
sessions will be mostly playful, with general notions tossed on the
wheel and the result looking like a vaguely shaped mass. At other
times, the basic shape is well defined and conversation partners spend
their time on detail and refinement. Peoples' efforts, though, always
produce some kind of result, and frequently it can be very gratifying.
Sometimes I feel that our talk helps me understand myself better than I
could have alone. At other times, we produce something that tran-
scends anything either of us could have conceived of separately. This is
because the figure we sculpt is not mine or yours but *ours*, the outcome
of both of our active shapings.

So in order to enter into the sculpting process effectively, you need
to remember, as we have said many times before, that the meanings
that count between people are not just the ones inside somebody's head
but also the ones that are constructed in conversations. With this understanding you will be willing to sit down at the potter's wheel, throw
your clay on the wheel, and encourage the other person to add clay,
too. Then you need to be willing to get your hands dirty, to participate
in the collaborative process of molding meanings together.

As you might have guessed, in order to put this basic attitude into
action, you need to practice some special kinds of focusing and encouraging.

Focus on 'Ours.' We mentioned before that dialogic listening involves a crucial change from a focus on *me* or the *other* to a focus on
ours, on what's *between* speaker(s) and listener(s). Contrast this with
empathic listening, which requires you to try to experience what is "behind" another's outward communication. When you focus on ours, you
don't look behind the verbal and nonverbal cues. You don't try to de-
duce or guess what internal state the other is experiencing. Instead,
you concentrate on the meanings you and the other person are mutually creating between yourselves. Empathic listening can be helpful, as
we said, but dialogic listening requires a move beyond empathy to a
focus on ours.

It can make a big difference whether you are trying to identify
what's going on inside the other person or whether you're focusing on
building-meaning-between. When your focus is on the other's thoughts
and feelings "behind" their words, you spend your time and mental energy searching for possible links between what you're seeing and hearing and what the other "must be" meaning. "Look at those crossed
arms. She must be feeling angry and defensive." Or, "He said he'd
'never' pay all the money back. That means it's hopeless to try to change
his mind." When you think this way, your attention is moving back and
forth between what's outside, in the verbal and nonverbal talk, and
what's inside the person's head. From this position it's easy to believe

that what's inside is more reliable, more important, more true, and hence more interesting than the talk on the surface.

But when you're focusing on ours, you concentrate on what's outside, not what's supposedly inside. We don't mean that you should be insensitive to the other person's feelings. In fact, you will be even more sensitive when you are focused on what's between you here and now. You concentrate on the verbal and nonverbal talk that the two (or more) of you are building together. In a sense, you take the conversation at face value; you never stop attending to *it* instead of focusing mainly on something you infer is behind it. This doesn't mean you uncritically accept everything that's said as "the whole truth and nothing but the truth." But you do realize that meaning is not just what's inside one person's head. Focusing on ours prepares you to respond and inquire in ways that make it clear that "getting to the meaning" is a mutual process.

Encouraging as Nexting. Dialogic listening also requires a special form of encouraging. Basically, instead of encouraging the other person(s) to "say more," you're encouraging him or her to respond to something you've just put on the potter's wheel in response to something he or she has just said. So your encouraging is a "nexting" move; it actively and relevantly keeps the collaborative co-construction process going.

One specific way to do this is with a *paraphrase-plus*. We've already said that a paraphrase consists of (1) a restatement, (2) of the other's meaning, (3) in your own verbal and nonverbal talk, (4) concluded with an opportunity for the other person to verify your understanding. The paraphrase-plus includes all of these elements *plus* a small but important addition.

The plus is your own response to the question "What's next?" or "Now what?" You start by remembering that the meanings you are developing are created between the two of you, and individual perspectives are only a part of that. If you stopped with just the paraphrase, you would be focusing on the *other* person exclusively instead of keeping the focus on what is happening *between* you. So, you follow your verifying or perception-checking paraphrase with whatever your good judgment tells you is your response to what the person said, and you conclude your paraphrase-plus with an invitation for the person to respond to your synthesis of his or her meaning and yours. The spirit of the paraphrase-plus is that each individual perspective is a building block for the team effort. For example, notice the three possible responses to Rita's comments.

> *Rita:* I like having an "exclusive" relationship, and I want you to be committed to me. But I still sometimes want to go out with other people.

1. *Muneo:* So even though part of you agrees with me about our plan not to date others, you're still a little uncertain about it. Right? (Paraphrase)

2. *Tim:* Oh, so you want me to hang around like an idiot while you go out and play social butterfly! Talk about a double standard! (Attack)

3. *Scott:* It sounds like you think there are some pluses and minuses in the kind of relationship we have now. I like it the way it is, but I don't like knowing that you aren't sure. I guess I want you to tell me some more about why you're questioning it. (Paraphrase-plus)

Muneo responds to Rita's comment with a paraphrase. This tells us that Muneo listened to Rita, but not much more. Tim makes a caricature of Rita's comment; his interpretation reflects his own uncertainty, anger, and fear. His comment is more a condemnation than a paraphrase. Scott offers a paraphrase-plus. He explains his interpretation of what Rita was saying, then he says briefly how he *responds* to her point, and then he moves the focus back between the two of them, to the middle, where both persons are present in the conversation and can work on the problem together. He does this by putting some of his own clay onto the potter's wheel. He paraphrases, but he also addresses the "What's next?" question as he interprets and responds to her comments. Then he concludes the paraphrase-plus with encouraging rather than simply verifying the accuracy of his paraphrase. When all this happens, both the paraphrase and the plus keep understanding growing between the individuals.

Another way to think about the paraphrase-plus is that you're broadening your goal beyond listening for "fidelity" or "correspondence." If you're paraphrasing for fidelity or correspondence, you're satisfied and "finished" with the task as soon as you've successfully *reproduced* "what she means." Your paraphrase is a success if it corresponds accurately to the other person's intent. We're suggesting that you go beyond correspondence to creativity, beyond reproducing to producing, to mutually constructing meanings or understandings between you.

Because paraphrasing is so potentially helpful, another sculpting skill is to *ask for a paraphrase*. Whenever you're uncertain about the extent of the other person's involvement or whether the two of you share an understanding, you can ask the person for his or her version of the point you're making. It is difficult to do this well. Often a request for a paraphrase sounds like an accusation: "Okay, stupid, why don't you try telling me what I just said?" This is obviously not going to contribute much to the co-sculpting process. The idea is to ask for a paraphrase without demanding a response and without setting up the person so you can play "Gotcha!" if she or he doesn't get it right. You can try putting it this way: "Just to make sure we're going in the same direction, could you tell me what you think we've agreed to so far?" Or you might say "I'm not sure I've been clear—what do you hear me saying?" The point is, if it's done with an eye toward nexting, a paraphrase can promote collaborating whether it comes from your side or the other's. You can sometimes help that happen by asking for one.

Another skill you can use in the sculpting process is to *run with the metaphor.* You can build meaning into the conversation by extending whatever metaphors the other person has used to express her or his ideas, developing your own metaphors, and encouraging the other person to extend yours. As you probably know, metaphors are figures of speech that link two dissimilar objects or ideas in order to make a point. Besides "Communication is made up of inhaling and exhaling," "Conversation is a ride on a tandem bicycle," and "Dialogic listening is sculpting mutual meanings," "This place is a zoo," "My vacation was a circus," and "She's as nervous as a flea on a griddle" all contain metaphors. As these examples illustrate, metaphors don't appear only in poetry or other literature; they are a major part of most everyday conversation. In fact, it's becoming increasingly clear that virtually all language is metaphoric (Lakoff and Johnson 1980; Ricoeur 1978). In our label for this skill, "run with the metaphor," for example, the term *run* itself is metaphoric.

This skill consists of listening for both subtle and obvious metaphors and then weaving them into your responses. We have found that when other people hear their metaphor coming back to them, they can get a very quick and clear sense of how they're being heard, and they typically can develop the thought along the lines sketched by the metaphor. For example, in a workshop he was leading, John was listening to an engineer describe part of his job, which involved going before regulatory boards and municipal committees to answer questions and make arguments for various construction projects. Part of what Phil said about his job was that it was a "game." John tried to run with the metaphor by asking "What's the name of the game?" "Winning," Phil responded. John recognized that his question had been ambiguous, so he continued: "Okay, but what kind of game is it—is it baseball, football, soccer, chess, or what?" "It's football," Phil replied. "What position do you play?" "Fullback." "And who's the offensive line?" "All the people in the office who give me the information I take to the meetings." "Who's the coach?" "We don't have one. That's the major problem." This was a telling response. In fact, from that point on, the workshop was focused on one of the major management problems that engineering firm was having.

Here's another example of how running with the metaphor can work in conversation:

Tanya: You look a lot less happy than when I saw you this morning. What's happening?

Ann: I just got out of my second two-hour class today, and I can't believe how much I have to do. I'm really feeling squashed.

Tanya: Squashed like you can't come up for air, or *squashed* as in you have to do what everybody else wants and you can't pursue your own ideas?

Ann: More like I can't come up for air. Every professor seems to think his or her class is the only one I'm taking.

Again, the purpose of running with the metaphor is to encourage nexting, to build the conversation between the two of you in order to produce as full as possible a response to the issues you're talking about. In addition, the metaphors themselves reframe or give a new perspective on the topic of your conversation. A project manager who sees her- or himself as a "fullback" is going to think and behave differently from one who thinks in other metaphorical terms, like "general," "Joan of Arc," "guide," or "mother hen." And the work stress that "squashes" you is different from the pressure that "keeps you jumping like a flea on a griddle." Listen for metaphors and take advantage of their power to shape and extend ideas. (You might also want to compare this skill with circular questioning, which we describe in Chapter Eleven.)

Remember our point that all these specific listening skills are like dishes in a salad bar: You don't eat everything, and at different times you select different dishes. Let's look at an extended example of a conversation that illustrates some of the listening attitudes and skills we've discussed. Sally and Julio start out at opposite sides in their opinions about the class. But first Julio and then both he and Sally dialogically listen to each other. As a result, their interpretations of the class and the teacher change; together they build a meaning that neither of them had at the beginning of the conversation. At the left

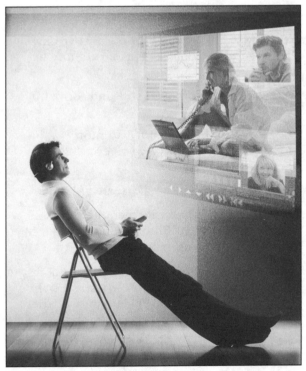

Is dialogic listening possible in this teleconferencing situation?

margins we've labeled some of the specific empathic and dialogic listening skills they're using.

Sally: That class drives me up a wall.

(open question) **Julio:** I thought it was going pretty well. What happened?

Sally: She's so strict! We can't miss more than five hours of class, everything has to be submitted electronically, she won't take late papers, I'll bet she wouldn't even allow a makeup exam if I was in the hospital!

(say more) **Julio:** I didn't know she wouldn't take late papers. Where did you hear that?

Sally: Alaysha told me that on Tuesday she tried to hand in the article analysis that was due Monday and Dr. Clinton wouldn't accept it.

(clarifying question) **Julio:** Was there anything else going on? Hilary and I both turned in our journals late and she took them. I also thought the five-hour restriction and the e-mail requirement were pretty standard at this school.

(say more) **Sally:** Do you have them in other classes?

Julio: Yeah. My geology prof allows only two days' absence and won't accept hardly any excuses.

(say more) **Sally:** Are your other profs so stiff and formal in class?

Julio: Some are and some aren't. Clinton is a lot looser in her office. Have you ever talked to her there?

Sally: No, I don't like the way she treated Alaysha.

(paraphrase) **Julio:** So Alaysha did the assignment like she was supposed to and Clinton wouldn't take it even though it was only one day late?

Sally: Well, it wasn't e-mailed, but I still think it's pretty unreasonable. I haven't started the paper that's due this Friday, and I'll bet there's no way she'd accept it Monday.

(paraphrase-plus) **Julio:** I know how that feels. But if you've got a good reason, I'll bet she would. She told me last term that most of her rules come from

what other profs tell her are the standards here. This school is really into developing responsibility and treating everybody like an adult. That's why I thought they required attendance and e-mailed papers. But I think Clinton is willing to listen, and she's bent the rules for me a couple of times. You've been doing great in class, and I'd really be surprised if she turned you down.

Sally: I didn't know that about this school; this is my first term here.

Julio: Well, I didn't know about Alaysha, but she probably should have printed it out.

Sally: Yeah. Well, thanks for listening—and for the information.

Remember that we do not mean to present these skills as a guaranteed step-by-step way to instant success. They are suggestions, guidelines, examples of ways you can behaviorally work the focusing, encouraging, and sculpting processes of dialogic listening. They won't work if you apply them woodenly or mechanically; you have to use them with sensitivity to the relationship and the situation.

As you begin using these skills—and this also applies to all the skills we have discussed—you may feel awkward and even phony. This is natural. It is part of learning any new skill, whether it's skiing, tennis, aerobics, or listening. Remember that the better you get with practice, the less awkward you will feel. Try not to let any initial feelings of discomfort distract you from working on specific ways to improve.

'But . . .' A Student Responds

So far you've said in this book that the highest level of listening is dialogic, the best kind of response is open sensitivity, and the healthiest quality of communication is interpersonal. You've also said that all of these involve accepting the concept that meaning is collaborative and selves are co-constructed. Are you saying that those are good and that analytic or empathic listening and responding with closed stereotyping are bad?

You ask an important question here, and our response may or may not be satisfying to you, but here goes. We do believe that your choice to engage in dialogic listening, to select open sensitivity responses, and in other ways to move toward the interpersonal end of the continuum will enhance the quality of your relationships and your life. And we recognize that other choices are functional in a variety of contexts and relationships. Our definition of good goes beyond functionality, however, and if you want full and rich interpersonal rela-

> tionships, we believe that you are more likely to help create them when your choices include more dialogic listening and open sensitivity.

One final point: Just as analytic listening is consistent with what many people would call Western, white, and male ways of thinking, dialogic and even empathic listening represents perspectives that are more Eastern, diverse, and androgynous (combined male-female) or female. Many popular (Gray 1992; Tannen 1995) and scholarly discussions of gender and communication (Harding 1991; Rakow 1992), for example, emphasize that in the Western world, linear logic and the goals of closure, certainty, and control are often associated with male thinkers and male-dominated activities. Androgynous and female approaches tend to be more inclusive of differing points of view and of the importance of both logic and emotion, mind and body, yin and yang (Chapter Two). People thinking and writing from these perspectives

> have advocated integration: wholism by which each pole of a dualism is seen as necessary to constitute a whole entity—institution or individual. . . . Both the feminine and masculine components must be accepted and valued in order to be complete. (Cirksena and Cuklanz 1992, 370)

As we (John, Karen, and Saskia) discuss communication and interpersonal communication, inhaling and exhaling, and communication contexts, problems, and solutions, we try to approach our topics holistically, which means that our perspective is more Eastern, androgynous, and female than narrowly Western and male. If you are female and/or a person of color, we hope this feature increases the accessibility of these concepts and skills. If you are Western, white, and male, we hope you will recognize some of the benefits of broadening your perspective beyond the one you might have uncritically inherited. Speaking as a Western white male, I (John) have become convinced that a narrowly and rigidly Western, white, and male perspective often works against effective interpersonal communicating.

Chapter Summary

In this chapter, we explored the listening parts of the inhaling processes. We introduced analytic listening as a way to use your perceptions to enhance your critical thinking and responding. If you practice the skills we identify in this section of the chapter, they will help you learn to pay attention better, to organize what you are hearing, and to get past the typical problems of making inferences we all frequently experience.

At the same time, remember that analytic listening is culturally rather narrow. It assumes that understandability happens because of clear organization, logical connections among ideas, and adequate factual support. But contemporary anthropologists, psychologists, and philosophers point out that this view of rationality is prominent in Western, white, and male cultures, but not in many other cultures. So this is the sense in which it's narrow. Analytic listening will help you to discern your own point of view and will increase your general flexibility as a communicator by enabling you to respond critically to what you hear. But it still constitutes only a partial approach to inhaling and is a kind of listening that is only appropriate in some situations. Analytic listening needs to be balanced with empathic and dialogic listening.

Empathic listening is designed to develop and verify a full understanding of the other person's meaning—his or her thinking and feeling—without adding your own. Friends, parents, managers, and many professionals can often use empathic listening very profitably. This kind of listening emerges when you *focus* on the other with such skills as aiming your posture, making natural and appropriate eye contact, moving responsively, and making responsive sounds. It also helps to *encourage* the other with "Say more," mirror responses, clarifying questions, open questions, and attentive silence. We suggest that you avoid pseudoquestions and "Why?" questions. The third part of empathic listening involves *reflecting* what the other is saying with a paraphrase, by adding an example, and by gently pursuing verbal-nonverbal inconsistencies.

Dialogic listening is the best way, we believe, to make a space for dialogue that is fully collaborative meaning-making. Since it is so dependent on the other's responses and on the context in which it happens, there is no recipe for "doing it perfectly." But when you want to listen dialogically, you need to begin with a commitment to co-constructing that is captured in the distinction between an ethnocentric (monologic) and cosmopolitan (dialogic) attitude and that is reflected in this section of the chapter's main metaphor, *sculpting mutual meanings.*

As this metaphor suggests, dialogic listening requires a shift in *focus* from the me-orientation of analytic listening and the you-orientation of empathic listening to a concentration on what listener and speaker(s) are constructing together, between them. It also requires a different kind of *encouraging,* one that motivates your conversation partner to add clay to the potter's wheel next to and on top of your clay, and to join his or her hands with your in an active shaping of your collaborative meanings. We also suggest three specific sculpting skills:

paraphrase-plus, asking for a paraphrase, and running with the metaphor.

In Other Words

In this reading, the author describes six different types of listening problems he has encountered in his role as a teacher. You have probably experienced many of them in your role as students. These habits are not limited to the classroom, however. Many of you will be able to identify their use and abuse in a variety of different relational contexts. When you finish this reading you should be able to respond to the following questions:

1. What are the six different listening "pathologies" that Leonard describes?
2. What are his suggestions for responding to them?
3. In the past few days, which challenging listening habit has been the most frustrating for you? How did you respond to it?
4. Which of the strategies you have been introduced to in this chapter might influence your response to the same annoying listening behavior in the future?
5. How does your own listening behavior differ in different relationships? Are you more likely to fall into particular listening habits in different relationships or do you have the same habits in all relationships?

* * *

With Open Ears: Listening and the Art of Discussion Leading

Herman B. Leonard

Diagnosis and Treatment of Listening Pathologies

Our capacity for critical listening is often undermined in the class by particular habits of bad listening. There are many ways to poorly and often it is difficult to tell why someone failed to hear. Sometimes the group as a whole is confused, perhaps because of ambiguity or confusion in what the speaker said. But often poor listening is due to a recognizable pathology. You probably already have your own list of classroom problems. I would not be surprised if you encountered a few of my favorites.

1. *The Mortar Lob.* This student has prepared a single point he found in the materials for the day's discussion and is ready to discuss it in detail. The mortar is loaded with one round, to be fired when the discussion moves within range. Throughout the session, the student is trying to decide when the conversation has moved as close to the point of impact as it is likely to get. Whenever the cue arrives, he will fire off the prepared set of comments.

Obviously, this behavior does not often build on the contributions of others. As an instructor, you want to reward preparation for class, but you don't want to encourage unconnected observations. At a minimum, each speaker should be expected to provide a link between the new observation and the preceding discussion. "That's an interesting analysis, Rick," you might comment. "But I'm not sure how it relates to what Sharon was just saying. Can you help us to see the connection?" Such a response will at least convey the requirement that "contributions" fit into the flow of the overall conversation.

2. *The Mongoose's Strike.* The mongoose survives by striking swiftly when it sees an opening in its opponent's defenses. Much of what passes for listening is really only (barely polite) attention as students wait for the speaker to finish so that they can make their own point. Often the pounce will be highly selective, concentrating on a minor weakness in some part of the last speaker's statement rather than engaging her whole set of ideas. When hands go up while a student is still talking, suspect a mongoose problem. One of my colleagues stops the class whenever someone starts waving a hand before the speaker has finished. "Put your hand down," he says, "you can't be listening if you already know what you are going to say.

Simply waiting for someone to stop talking is not true listening, of course, and this behavior pattern can result in a disjointed series of comments. A good remedy is to require the speaker to relate his or her comments to those of the last speaker. "Well, Cheryl, I guess you disagreed with John about one small piece of what he was saying—how do you respond to the rest of his statement?"

3. *The Spartan's Shield.* Warriors in ancient times believed that Spartans carried shields that could not be penetrated by ordinary arrows or swords Though untrue, the story was useful to the Spartans, and they may have started it themselves. Some students seem to have similar armor. When asked a question, they turn it aside with a deft parry, and go on to make whatever observation they had in mind. A good poke will reveal that the shield is not really impervious. Ask the student to return to your question and answer it; this reinforces the necessity to keep comments in context.

4. *The Pit Bull.* Pit bulls have a reputation for always pursuing the same line of attack and for hanging on tenaciously once engaged. Some students evidently believe that this kind of single-mindedness is a great virtue They seize on a particular issue and pursue it relentlessly; often, they will pick similar issues in every discussion. One will always emphasize goals and another tactics. One will always serve up the libertarian perspective, another the Marxist view, and yet another the feminist approach. Of course, it is often useful to have a variety of different views represented in the classroom, but when a particular perspective becomes identified with a given student, the class (and the leader) may stop listening because the points seem automated. This pathology leads to two disagreeable syndromes: first, the pit bull listens only for the right opening in which to raise his or her familiar issue; second, the rest of the class stops listening to the pit bull at all. One possible solution is systematically to require nonbulldogs to present different points of view. Encourage other

members of the class to explore the issues presented from a perspective different from their own. This may lead to a more original and less predictable presentation.

These four pathologies are variations on the same theme: students often want to make independent observations rather than relate them to what others have said. It is harder to comment on the ongoing conversation than to introduce wholly independent thought; because it does not require careful attention or listening, the latter procedure is considerably less taxing. For many, it is also more comfortable; many students need to feel well prepared before they speak in a group, and are not comfortable thinking on their feet in the midst of a fast-moving conversation. These pathologies, which threaten the integrity of the discussion structure, come in many forms. Fortunately, most of them can be cleared away by exposure. Discussing these problems explicitly when they occur is a good way to redirect energy toward the productive parts of class discussion.

5. *The Tune-Out, Type A: I Don't Need to Know This.* Students' attention often wavers during a conversation, frustrating the instructor who senses that they do not recognize the relevance and importance of the points being made. Discussion-based teaching provides an opportunity for motivated learning spurred by an understanding of relevance—but it doesn't guarantee success. I find this pathology is best addressed by a frontal assault. Rather than pontificate about why I think the material is important, I ask the class to identify why the points under discussion are relevant. When they have focused on the issue and persuaded themselves, we can move on.

A particularly pernicious form of the Type A tune-out is active disrespect for other students' contributions. Some members of the group sit waiting in sullen boredom while another student is talking, ready to rejoin the discussion only when the instructor starts speaking again. I try to ask students who are having this problem (the nonlisteners, not the speaker!) to think out loud about what their classmate has just said and why it may be important.

6. *The Tune-Out, Type B: I Already Know This.* Nothing shuts students' ears more surely than the feeling that they have already learned this material. Sometimes they are right. More frequently, they have overestimated their command of these ideas, and the instructor is deliberately encouraging the class to dwell on them. Often, though, the students do not pick up the difference between what they already know and what is being discussed now. This failure comes from bad listening, but the listening it generates is even worse. All learning will cease until this veil is pierced. Here again, I usually attempt a frontal attack by posing a problem designed to highlight the limit of their existing knowledge. . . .

Excerpted with permission from "With Open Ears: Listening and the Art of Discussion Leading" by Herman B. Leonard, in C. R. Christensen, D. A. Garvin, and A. Sweet (eds.), *The Artistry of Discussion Leadership.* Copyright © 1991 from Harvard Business School Publishing Division.

References

Adams, J. 1996. *Journal entry in SpCmu 103, Autumn 2001.* University of Washington. Used by permission.

Anderson, R., Cissna, K. N., and Arnett, R. C. (eds.) 1994. *The Reach of Dialogue: Confirmation, Voice, and Community.* Cresskill, NJ: Hampton Press.

Baxter, L. A., and Montgomery, B. M. 1996. *Relating: Dialogue and Dialectics.* New York: Guilford.

Bohm, D. 1990. *On Dialogue.* Ojai, CA: David Bohm Seminars.

Bolton, R. 1990. "Listening Is More than Merely Hearing." In J. Stewart (ed.), *Bridges Not Walls.* 5th ed. New York: McGraw-Hill. Pages 175–191.

Brammer, L. M. 1979. *The Helping Relationship: Process and Skills.* 2nd ed. Englewood Cliffs, NJ: Prentice Hall.

Buber, Martin. 1970. *I and Thou.* Trans. W. Kaufmann. New York: Scribner.

Cirksena, K. and Cuklanz, L. 1992. "Male Is to Female as ___ is to ___: A Guided Tour of Five Feminist Frameworks for Communication Studies." In L. F. Rakow (ed.), *Women Making Meaning.* New York: Routledge. Page 370.

Clore, G. L., Wiggins, N. H., and Itkin, S. 1975. "Judging Attraction from Nonverbal Behavior: The Gait Phenomenon." *Journal of Counseling and Clinical Psychology,* 43: 491–497.

Faber, A., and Mazlish, E. 1982. *How to Talk so Kids Will Listen and Listen so Kids Will Talk.* New York: Avon.

Goodman, G., and Esterly, G. 1990. "Questions—The Most Popular Piece of Language." In J. Stewart (ed.), *Bridges Not Walls.* 5th ed. New York: McGraw-Hill. Page 760.

Gray, J. 1992. *Men Are From Mars, Women Are From Venus.* New York: HarperCollins.

Harding, S. 1991. *Whose Science? Whose Knowledge: Thinking from Women's Lives.* Ithaca, NY: Cornell University Press.

Holquist, M. (ed.) 1981. *Mikhail M. Bakhtin. The Dialogic Imagination.* Translated by C. Emerson and M. Holquist. Austin: University of Texas Press.

Lakoff, G. and Johnson, M. 1980. *Metaphors We Live By.* Chicago: University of Chicago Press.

Nichols, M. 1995. *The Lost Art of Listening.* New York: Guilford.

Pearce, B. 1989. *Communication and the Human Condition.* Carbondale: Southern Illinois University Press.

Rakow, L. F. 1992. *Women Making Meaning.* New York: Routledge.

Reece, M., and Whiteman, R. 1962. "Expressive Movements, Warmth and Nonverbal Reinforcement." *Journal of Abnormal and Social Psychology,* 64: 234–236.

Ricoeur, P. 1978. *The Rule of Metaphor.* Translated by R. Czerny, K. McLaughlin, and J. Costello. London: Routledge & Kegan Paul.

Rogers. C. R. 1980. *A Way of Being.* Boston: Houghton Mifflin.

Roth, S., Chasin, L., Chason, R., Becker, C., and Herzig, M. 1992. "From Debate to Dialogue: A Facilitating Role for Family Therapists in the Public Forum." *Dulwich Centre Newsletter,* 2: 41–48.

Sampson, E. E. 1993. *Celebrating the Other: A Dialogic Account of Human Nature.* Boulder, CO: Westview.

Senge, P. 1990. *The Fifth Discipline: The Art and Practice of the Learning Organization.* New York: Doubleday.

Shotter, J. 1993. *Conversational Realities: Constructing Life Through Language*. London: Sage.

Stewart, J., and Thomas, M. 1990. "Dialogic Listening: Sculpting Mutual Meanings." In J. Stewart (ed.), *Bridges Not Walls*. 6th ed. New York: McGraw-Hill. Pages 184–202.

Tannen, D. 1995. *Talking From 9 to 5*. New York: William Morrow.

Weaver, R. L. II 1987. *Understanding Interpersonal Communication*. 4th ed. New York: Scott-Foresman. ✦

Chapter Seven

Verbal Dimensions of Talk

After reading this chapter, you should be able to do the following:
- Distinguish among verbal, oral, nonverbal, and non-oral communicating.
- Identify and describe what it means to say that language is a way of being.
- Connect this idea to the discussion of worlds of meaning in Chapter Two.
- Explain and give examples of how language affects perception.
- Explain differences between "political correctness" and the effects of language on perception.
- Explain how the performance of gender illustrates the effects of language on perception.
- Be able to apply the six guidelines for language use to your own communication life.

Chapter Preview

For hundreds of years, explorers, politicians, philosophers, linguists, poets, psychologists, and communication scholars have analyzed human language and languages. Why? Because language sets humans apart from other animals, distinguishes particular cultural groups, empowers humans to transmit knowledge and manipulate each other, and enriches music and art. Throughout history, most of this analysis has focused on words and their contributions. Until recently, little systematic attention has been paid to the nonverbal elements that are also parts of language—the tone of voice, facial expression, timing, and posture that accompany all speech, or the white space, font type and size, and graphic design that are parts of all written language.

Then, in the late 1960s, communication scholars and psychologists started seriously studying nonverbal cues, and textbooks like this one began a tradition of treating the verbal and nonverbal elements of language separately. Although it was definitely good to learn more about nonverbal cues, two problems emerged from this separate treatment. The first was that, as an academic newcomer, the study of nonverbal communicating often was treated as secondary. People believed that serious scholars focused on the verbal parts, as they had for centuries, and nonverbal research was done by "touchy-feely types." The second problem with this separation was that it didn't fit human experience. People generally experience verbal and nonverbal elements together. Spoken words (verbal) are always uttered in some tone of voice (nonverbal), and written words (verbal) are always surrounded by more or less white space (nonverbal).

We want to emphasize that verbal and nonverbal communication cues are interdependent. As we said in Chapter Two, the verbal affects the nonverbal, the nonverbal affects the verbal, and neither determines the meaning of the other. In order to make this point, we considered treating verbal and nonverbal communicating together, in the same chapter. But students complained legitimately that the chapter was too long. So we decided to follow current tradition and have a chapter on each. We will reemphasize the interrelatedness of verbal and nonverbal communication when we discuss the concept of supportive communication at the end of the nonverbal chapter.

This chapter on the verbal dimensions of talk selects from among many treatments of language the one that fits best with our descriptions of communication and interpersonal communication in Chapters Two and Three. We start by giving you a simple way to think about how the verbal and nonverbal parts of language interrelate, and then we explain how language is what we call a "way of being." We clarify the importance of understanding language this way and then we use the last part of the chapter to describe six practical language guidelines that can help you move your communicating along the impersonal ←——→interpersonal continuum.

Four Elements of Language

English speakers and writers often treat the verbal and oral parts of language synonymously. This happens, for example, when a businessperson refers to a spoken agreement with a customer as a "verbal contract" rather than an "oral" one, even though written agreements are exactly as "verbal" as spoken ones. This is because *verbal* comes from the Latin word for *word*, so both written and spoken words are forms of "verbal" communicating. *Oral* comes from the Latin word for

	Oral	**Non-Oral**
Verbal	spoken words	written words
Nonverbal	tone of voice, sigh, scream, vocal quality, pitch, loudness, etc.	gestures, movement, appearance, facial expression, touch, etc.

Table 7.1 Elements of Language

mouth, so not only spoken words but also intonation, vocal quality, and nervous coughing are all oral parts of communicating. *Language* is the general term used for the verbal parts of communicating. But, as we said, language actually includes both verbal and nonverbal aspects. Table 7.1 shows how the verbal, nonverbal, oral, and non-oral parts of communicating are interrelated. All four boxes together make up language. That's why the lines separating the four boxes are dotted. When it comes to something as complex as language, the categories are not quite as simple as Table 7.1 suggests.

The point of Table 7.1 is not just to make an academic distinction. When you remember these differences, you'll be more aware of all the ways the nonverbal parts of your speech affect how other people understand and interpret what you say and write. For example, you might be sounding tired, hyper, sarcastic, or scared when you don't mean to. This matrix can also help you see how many ways you communicate without speaking (nonverbal-oral). And it can remind you of the dangers of writing out the text of a speech word for word. Because verbal-oral and verbal–non-oral language are so different, most written speech sounds artificial and disconnected from its listeners.

Language Is a Way of Being

Although the distinctions in Table 7.1 might be new to you, you've already studied language in elementary and secondary school when you learned the differences between nouns and verbs, adjectives and adverbs, active and passive voice, and taboo or obscene words in your culture. As we said, most of what you've learned has focused on written language (verbal non-oral), and most has also emphasized two characteristics of language.

The first characteristic that's been emphasized in what you've already studied is that language is a *system* of symbols. Language is a system in that it consists of units and rules for their combination and use. The units are not only words but also phrases (" . . . in the kitchen"), clauses (". . . she said hopefully"), sentences, and paragraphs. Units of language that are smaller than words include morphemes—the smallest units of meaning, like the "s" that turns a word plural—and phonemes, the smallest units of sound, like "th."

Language is *symbolic* in that its units—especially words—can sometimes be thought of as "standing for" or symbolizing a concept, idea, or meaning. This symbolic feature enables language users to talk about things that are not present, like history and the future, and about abstract things like love and faith. It is also one of the important reasons why people often misunderstand each other. One person thinks some words or phrases symbolize one thing and another thinks they symbolize something else.

The second characteristic of language that you have already studied is that language is an activity. It does not just symbolize or stand for concepts or meanings, but language often performs actions. When the bride and groom say "I do" or "I will" during a marriage ceremony, for example, these language actions perform the event of marrying. In many cultures the person who is officiating—the priest, pastor, judge, or government official—blesses or sanctions the marriage. But the bride and groom make it happen with their talk. As each of us grows up in our family and culture, we learn how to do things with words (Austin 1962). We learn, for example, how to greet others, give an excuse, make a commitment, give an order, and make a threat. Lawyers study language very carefully to determine if someone has made a contract, advised an accused person of his or her rights, or committed perjury or slander.

As we hope you can tell from our examples, both of these characteristics of language are important. You can't work with language effectively if you don't understand that it is a system of symbols and that it performs important actions. In addition, there is a third important characteristic of language that is important to understand if you are going to apply the approach to interpersonal communication that is in this book: Language is a way of being.

Especially in the last 40 years, many people who study language have recognized how both the system and action characteristics of language are incomplete. Both of these treat language as a tool humans manipulate, either to stand for some referent or to perform an action. As we have explained, these analyses can teach us some important things about language. But language is more than a tool. If it were just a tool, we could lay language aside when we didn't need it and pick up some other tool, just as we can lay aside a screwdriver and pick up a hammer. But we can't do that. As humans, we're immersed in language, like a fish in water. As one writer puts it:

> In all our knowledge of ourselves and in all knowledge of the world, we are always already encompassed by the language that is our own. We grow up, and we become acquainted with [people] and in the last analysis with ourselves when we learn to speak. Learning to speak does not mean learning to use a preexistent tool for designating a world already somehow familiar to us; it means

acquiring a familiarity and acquaintance with the world itself and how it confronts us. (Gadamer 1976, 62–63)

This is what it means to say language is a way of being. We're immersed in language from birth to death, just like a fish is immersed in the water in which it lives. Language is actually "languaging," and it's the way humans "bring forth a world." This is a "continuous" process that keeps "bringing forth" worlds "with others." Do you get the sense how, for this approach, language is like the water in which a fish lives?

This approach is reinforced by the fact that, for humans, language experience may begin even before birth. As little as 20 weeks after conception, the human fetus has functioning ears and is beginning to respond to sounds (Chamberlain 1987). Its mother's voice is clearly one sound the fetus learns to identify (Tomatis 1987). Some pregnant couples talk to and play music for their unborn child. When an infant is born, it typically enters an environment of exclamations and greetings. Then verbal and nonverbal communication experiences fill the infant's life. Touch, eye contact, smiles, and a great deal of talk are directed to him or her. As infants develop, parents and other caregivers invite them into conversations or exclude them from conversations by providing a context for talk, by encouraging them with positive attitudes toward talk or discouraging them with negative attitudes, and by interpreting, modeling, and extending talk (Haslett 1984). This process continues right up to the last tearful good-byes we hear at death. In fact, the theorists and researchers who treat language as a way of being have begun to mean by *language* what used to be called *communication*—all the verbal and nonverbal, oral and non-oral ways humans make meaning together. As you might notice, this view of language fits closely with the approach to communication we outlined in Chapter Two.

Adults can promote communication development in children by inviting them into conversations.

Language and Perception

If the notion of language as a way of being sounds a little abstract, consider one important practical implication of the fact that language is this all encompassing: Because we are immersed in language all our lives, language and perception are thoroughly interrelated. This means that everything we perceive, all the things that make up our worlds, are affected by the language we live in.

In the early twentieth century one version of this insight about language and perception was called the *Sapir-Whorf hypothesis,* which was named after the two people who originally wrote about it, Edward Sapir and Benjamin Lee Whorf. The strong version of the hypothesis says that our language determines how we perceive the world. In other words, it claims that we dissect nature along lines laid down by our native language (Carroll 1956). So, if you have spent enough time on boats and around the water to learn a dozen different words for water conditions, you will perceive more differences in the water than will the person who was born and raised in Cheyenne, Oklahoma City, or Calgary. That person might distinguish between *waves* and *smooth water,* but you will see and feel differences between *cats' paws, ripples, chop,* and *swells* that he or she probably won't even notice.[1]

As the three of us try in this book to write about communication as a continuous, complex, collaborative meaning-making process, we especially notice two particular ways our native language limits our perceptions. The first has to do with the ways the English language affects how people understand ongoing processes. Unlike some languages, English maintains clear distinctions between noun subjects and verb predicates, causes, and effects, and beginnings and ends, and this affects how native English speakers perceive communication. A surprising number of other language systems do not do this. According to one researcher, for example, Navajo speakers characteristically talk in terms of processes—uncaused, ongoing, incomplete, dynamic happenings. The word Navajos use for wagon, for example, translates roughly as "wood rolls about hooplike" (Hoijer 1951). The Navajo words that we would translate "He begins to carry a stone" mean not that the actor produces an action but that the person is simply linked with a given round object and with an already existing, continuous movement of all round objects in the universe. The English language, by contrast, requires its users to talk in terms of present, past, future; cause and effect; beginning and end. Problems arise when some things that English speakers would like to discuss just can't be expressed in these terms. So to continue our example, we would like to be able to talk more clearly about the emergent, ongoing nature of communication and about the collaborative quality we have labeled "interpersonal" in Chapter Three. But especially since communication doesn't always obey the rules of cause and effect, the noun + verb + object structure of the English language makes it difficult to do this. For this topic, Navajo would probably work better than English.

Another example comes from the German language and the concept of *Gemütlichkeit*. This word is not directly translatable into English because there is no English word for it. *Gemütlichkeit* means coziness, relaxedness, feeling easygoing, feeling at home, being hospitable. German speakers would use it in the context of "Let's go home and have a cozy evening together." This means that you would go home, have something good to eat, perhaps light some candles, and sit together and talk, or watch your favorite TV program or listen to your favorite music. You will find that many Germans use this word not only for situations at home but also for social gatherings. You will often hear the phrase *gemütliches Beisammensein,* which means "cozy togetherness." This is associated with being together with a group of friends, eating, and talking. If you've grown up speaking German, you're likely to notice and value this kind of cozy togetherness more than someone who is born into and grows up speaking English.

Consider one additional example. How does the phrase *third world countries* affect people's perceptions of the countries the term is used to describe? On the surface, it might sound like a pretty neutral way to talk about places like Algeria, Bolivia, Somalia, Guyana, Nepal, or Afghanistan. But if you think about it even a little, you recognize that "third" implies that there is a "first" and a "second" world, and that these are better civilized, more educated, and more highly valued than what comes "third." This is also a general term, so it lumps together countries with very different histories, economies, and cultures. The term *developing countries,* on the other hand, implies that the countries are changing, rather than that the one you're talking about is stuck in third-place status. Since change is foregrounded, this label also makes it harder to lump different countries into one stereotype. So the different label is not just superficial political correctness. Language used to talk about others can affect people's perceptions—which is why the term *developing countries* is now preferred.

This strong version of the Sapir-Whorf hypothesis has been criticized for being too deterministic. Researchers have come to believe that although language and thought are closely connected, people are still able to perceive differences, even if they don't have the words for them (Eastman 1985). But without getting into that scholarly debate, these examples illustrate that you can begin to notice how your language affects what you perceive. And you can understand why it's important to keep learning new words—because that will help you learn new concepts!

Language Is a Way of Being: Examples From Ethnic and Gender Communication

One of the clearest examples of how language can influence perception and relationships with others comes from the work of Richard Rodriguez (1982), a Latino teacher and writer. Rodriguez is the author of the "In Other Words" reading at the end of this chapter. He describes the two language worlds he grew up in: the private Spanish world at home, where he and his parents spoke only in Spanish with each other when he was small, and the public world of school and commerce, where he had to speak and was addressed only in English. When he was a child, he associated Spanish with the warm feelings of family, protection, and love. English, on the other hand, meant the world "out there" because it was the language of instruction and survival.

> A family member would say something to me and I would feel myself specially recognized. My parents would say something to me and I would feel embraced by the sounds of their words. Those sounds said: *I am speaking with ease in Spanish. I am addressing you in words I never use with los gringos. I recognize you as someone special, close, like no one outside. You belong with us. In the family* . . .

> Walking down the sidewalk, under the canopy of tall trees, I'd warily notice the—suddenly—silent neighborhood kids who stood warily watching me. Nervously, I'd arrive at the grocery store to hear the sounds of the *gringo*—foreign to me—reminding me that in this world so big, I was a foreigner. But then I'd return. Walking back toward our house, climbing the steps from the sidewalk, when the front door was open in summer, I'd hear voices beyond the screen door talking in Spanish. For a second or two, I'd stay, linger there, listening. Smiling, I'd hear my mother call out, saying in Spanish (words): "Is that you, Richard?" All the while her sounds would assure me: *You are home now; come closer; inside. With us.* (Rodriguez 1982, 16–17)

Rodriguez's story poignantly illustrates that, although there's definitely some truth to the ideas that "language is a system of symbols," and "people use language to perform actions," there is much more to language than these descriptions include. Language is an all-encompassing way of being that we are born into and that constantly affects our thinking and way of interacting with others.

As the three of us work on this book, another place where we notice how English affects perception has to do with the ways English speakers perceive gender differences. One accomplishment of research encouraged by the feminist movement of the 1960s and 1970s is that people now recognize how the male bias of Standard American English has contributed to the ways English-speaking cultures perceive women and men. The fact that, until recently, there were no female firefighters was not caused merely by the existence of the word fire*man*. It's not that simple. But research indicates that gender-biased words affect perceptions in at least three ways: They shape people's attitudes about careers that are "appropriate" for one sex but not the other, they lead some women to believe that certain jobs and roles aren't attainable, and they contribute to the belief that men deserve higher status in society than women do (Biriere and Lanktree 1984). This is why changes in job titles have helped open several occupations to more equal male-female participation. Consider, for example, *parking checker* instead of *meter maid, chair* or *chairperson* instead of *chairman, salesperson* instead of *salesman,* and *server* instead of *waiter* or *waitress.* We have also just about stopped referring to female physicians as "woman doctors" and female attorneys as "lady lawyers," and it is more than a coincidence that these changes have been accompanied by significant increases in the numbers of women in these two professions.

Some men and women disagree with this talk about gender bias in English. They argue that there are not that many offending terms, and that it sounds awkward and silly to put "person" in the place of "man" or its female equivalent. One joker asked whether the post office employee delivering the mail is now going to be called a "person person." But it's pretty difficult to make this argument today. For example, the authors of a recent book on gender communication easily came up with over a hundred common gendered terms and alternatives that don't sound awkward (Ivy and Backlund 1994, 78–80).

Gendered Term	Gender-Neutral Alternatives
adman	advertising executive, ad executive
anchorman	anchor, newscaster
bachelorette	single person
bellman/bellboy	attendant, luggage handler
cameraman	camera operator
chairman	chair, chairperson
congressman	senator, representative, legislator
con man	con artist
foreman	supervisor
freshman	first-year student
gunman	killer, assassin, sniper
layman	layperson
manhole	sewer, utility hole
man of the world	sophisticate
marksman/rifleman	sharpshooter
murderess	murderer
patrolman	patrol officer, trooper
spaceman	astronaut
stewardess	flight attendant
watchman	security guard, guard

Since the mid-1990s both scholarly and popular books have emphasized this point about gender, language, and perception by highlighting the differences between the language worlds that men and women are socialized into in North America. Books like sociolinguist Deborah Tannen's *You Just Don't Understand: Women and Men in Communication* describe the ways women's communication differs from men's and explain how many problems between genders are influenced by these differences. Some people complain that the books reinforce the very stereotypes they are trying to reduce by generalizing about "women's communication" and "men's communication."

In order to avoid these overgeneralizations, researchers distinguish more and more between sex and gender. Sex is determined by the genetic codes that program biological features (Wood and Reich 2003). When people talk about sex, they mainly refer to men or women, males or females. Gender is the social construction of what it means to be a man or a woman. So, when researchers talk about gender, they will usually talk about masculine or feminine styles. It is true that many men have a masculine communication style and many women a feminine style. But you should understand that being a man does not always correspond to communicating in a masculine style. And vice versa.

Recognizing this important qualifier, Julia Wood and Nina Reich highlight the differences between masculine and feminine talk. Feminine talk is used to build and maintain rapport with others, share personal information or opinions, express empathy, ask for opinions from others, keep the conversation going, and be responsive. You probably know some people with a feminine style of communicating who nod their heads, smile, and in other ways encourage you to keep talking (Wood and Reich 2003).

Masculine talk, on the other hand, functions to assert one's self, to establish status and power, and to solve problems. Details are not so important because they can get in the way of problem solving or asserting power. Again, you might have experienced this difference. You come home after a bad day and are tired. You are silent when you enter the apartment, grunt a "Hi" to your roommate, and go to your room. Immediately, you are confronted with the response "What's up, why are you so grumpy? What happened? Come on, tell me." The speaker with the feminine style wants to connect with you and show sympathy for the obviously bad day you had. The masculine speaker, in contrast, does not want to self-disclose and believes that being alone will help him get over the day better than talking about it.

People adopt a masculine or feminine style of communicating primarily because of the ways they are socialized. Girls often are encouraged to play more "harmonious" games that emphasize solidarity and sharing. Boys are encouraged to be assertive and competitive, to express their point of view, and to find ways to solve problems on their own. In addition, the media encourage specific images of what it means to be a man or a woman. Women are supposed to be feminine, wear clothes and shoes that encourage little, ladylike steps, and not use swearwords. Men are supposed to be masculine, not show emotions in public, and act courageously.

A great deal of a person's gender identity is expressed in his or her language, which means not just the words or phrases they utter but all the verbal and nonverbal ways they communicate. The gendered cues you are socialized into also affect your perception of what it means to be masculine or feminine. In order to cope with the limitations of each communication style, the authors of most books on gender and communication believe that both women and men should become, in effect, bilingual—able to speak both their own language and the language or communication style of the other gender to avoid misunderstandings and improve the quality of their relationships.

You might be feeling some of this challenge as you work to understand and apply the approach to interpersonal communication laid out in this book, especially if you're male. As we say in Chapter Two, we believe that you *can* look at communication as a process of idea-transmission-and-reception, but if you do, you're likely to have problems. We are convinced that you'll experience fewer problems and be able to manage the impersonal◄──────►interpersonal quality of your communicating more effectively if you look at communication as a collaborative process. But even though this way of looking at communication was originally developed by the male member of this writing team, it's considered culturally to be more a "feminine" than a "masculine" approach to communication. It might be helpful for you to keep this in mind as you work to understand and apply the ideas and skills in this textbook. In effect, this book asks its male readers to become more bilingual in their understanding of communication, and it challenges its female readers to also become more bilingual by adapting their culturally preferred style to male conversation partners.

So, what can you take away from this perspective? When we say that "language is a way of being," we are saying that it is more than a *system* we use or an *activity* we perform. Language is larger than any of us; it happens to us and we are subject to it as much as we manipulate or "use" it. People are not "taught" their native language in the sense that our parents don't develop even informal lesson plans or a sequence of concepts to develop. From birth, we are immersed in living language. It's going on all around us. Rather than being taught, we *learn* how to cope with, to make sense of what confronts us, whether it's supportive and responsive comfort or threatening and disconfirming abuse. We inhabit language, live inside it. In fact, at least until we become fluent in a second language, we can't get outside the language that is our original human home. (And even then, a fluent speaker of Japanese or French whose first language is English has different expe-

Gender identities are also negotiated nonverbally. What typically male postures, gestures, and facial expressions are these women using?

riences from the speaker whose first language is Japanese or French.) To say it in another way, language shapes the *world* we inhabit—just as we discussed in Chapter Two. Our model of a world of meaning could be called a "language world." The language world we inhabit strongly affects how we can successfully "make sense," "be polite," "act mature," and even "be a man" or "be feminine." All that is what it means to say that language is a way of being.

So What? Some Language Guidelines

You might be feeling that all this "way of being" stuff is pretty abstract. But we don't want to leave it at that level. There are at least six practical suggestions that emerge from the point that language is the human way of being:

- Develop inclusive and respectful language.
- Use metaphors.
- Limit ambiguity.
- Use jargon carefully.
- Illustrate your ideas.
- Use examples.

Develop Inclusive and Respectful Language

Since the talk people engage in helps shape the worlds they inhabit, language can help make worlds narrow, rigid, and closed or their opposites. Inclusive language is talk that acknowledges the legitimacy of diverse identities and perspectives. It is talk that shows awareness that perspectives differ, so it does not pretend to be completely correct or always "True" (with a capital T). Whenever you want to promote interpersonal rather than impersonal communicating, it is important to acknowledge both differences and commonalities among people. How can you do this? In part by thinking inclusively and using inclusive language.

For instance, be careful with words such as *normal*. This is a term that establishes boundaries and that evaluates what's inside the boundaries as "good" and what's outside as "not as good." What have you heard people assume is "normal" height, for example, or "normal" weight, intelligence, skin color, wealth, or age? Often the term functions as an ethnocentric marker, a label for features or qualities that are like the speaker or that the speaker prefers. "Why doesn't she act normal?" often means something like, "Why doesn't she act more like I would?" What is normal for one person is often different for someone else. In these ways, normal is often used as an exclusive rather than an inclusive word.

Sometimes the problem is more blatant and what is needed is respectful language. You have probably heard people use derogatory or offensive words that demean people different from themselves. You might have heard of "Jewing down the price" or "shylocks," of "chinks" or "towelheads," of "queens" or "dykes," of "doughboy," "gimp," or "munchkin." There are people who would tell those offended by labels like these to "relax" or "stop being so sensitive." They might insist that "They're just words," so the other person shouldn't take them personally. But language that includes words like these is not just a neutral tool. Because language is the way humans be who we are, words can hurt. Words help build worlds between people, and negative labels help build toxic worlds. So both the label user and the label hearer have responsibility for what happens between them.

Your language can reflect the mature awareness that people differ in important ways but that we also hold many beliefs and hopes in common, one of which is the legitimate expectation to be treated with respect. In other words, your language can demonstrate that you pay attention to what we called in Chapter Three the personal rather than the impersonal features of those you talk with and about: how they are unique, the choices they make, their unmeasurable parts, their reflectiveness, and their addressability.

We are not suggesting that you try to eliminate evaluations or that you treat everything as "just fine" and everyone as "perfectly acceptable." Values are consequential, individual values differ, and it is important to live by the values you believe in. But you can affirm your own values without excluding or disrespecting others. That's the key. The goal is not to be wishy-washy or two-faced, but to be inclusive and respectful.

We are also not suggesting that you manage your language only when you believe that someone within earshot might be a member of a potentially offended group. We don't advocate covering up your stereotypes of others with the "right" words. That is what some shortsighted people mean by being "politically correct." We are suggesting that you work to make *all* your language inclusive and respectful. Because language affects perception, this might eventually also change your attitudes toward certain people and groups. But if you selectively use respectful language as just a technique or communication strategy, you are definitely not following the suggestions we are making here.

Our point is that you adopt this perspective as a part of your communicating all the time. For example, if you are not sure whether to use what you believe is a respectful term, such as *Latina* or *African American*, ask the person which label he or she would prefer. Latino or Latina, for example, are more associated with cultural pride and political empowerment, whereas *Hispanic* is more associated with European heritage. So if someone is proud to have native ancestors and is critical of the Spanish conquistadores, she might prefer to be called Latina rather than Hispanic. Similarly, when you think and talk about someone who is disabled, the most important thing you can do is to acknowledge that his or her disability is only part of who he or she is, so it isn't that "there's a handicap in the group" but that "there's a person who won't be able to do what we're planning." Treat the individuals first as persons and only secondarily as persons with disabilities. That's what it means to be inclusive and respectful.

Use Metaphors

As we've said before, metaphors can help communicators to develop a common understanding of each other and the world. A metaphor is a way of talking that links two things that are not actually related in order to explain one of them. For example, you could say that chemistry is like learning how to cook, except that in chemistry the danger of an explosion is greater, and you cannot usually eat the results.

Metaphors can add both interest and life to your communicating and can do great things for understandability. A heart surgeon told a friend of ours about a problem he was having trying to get a patient to understand his upcoming heart bypass surgery. The patient was frightened—naturally—and couldn't understand what the doctor was actually going to do between the time he cut him open and the time he sewed him up again. After several fruitless attempts to explain, the doctor said, "You're a mechanic, right?" When the patient said, "Yes," the doctor asked, "What do you do with a truck that has a clogged fuel line?" "I try to clean it out" was the reply. "And what if you can't clean it out?" "I make another one—get some copper tubing and run a new line from the tank to the fuel injector pump." "That's exactly what I'm going to do—get a vein from your leg and run a new line from one side of your heart to the other." "Oh!" the mechanic said. "Why didn't you say so in the first place? Let's get on with it!" A metaphor was all it took to clarify the procedure.

As this example and many others in this book indicate, metaphors don't just appear in poems, novels, and plays. They are a part of each person's everyday communicating. They have been a central part of every chapter so far in this book—think of "world of meaning," "inhaling and exhaling," and "sculpting mutual meanings," for example. And they are present in your everyday communicating, too.

A first step toward enhancing your use of metaphor is to listen for the ones you already use. What do you have in mind, for example, when someone calls something "awesome"? There are many possible mental pictures, but one could be the look and feeling someone has as they watch the finale of a fireworks display—head back, eyes wide open, mouth open, totally focused attention, maybe even clapping. When you call a party, film, or someone's performance in sports awesome, you are connecting some of your mental picture of the term to the party, film, or performance. That's what metaphor can do.

It can help to use metaphors to talk about a wide range of ideas, from everyday, mundane topics to exotic ones. Metaphors can both increase the interest level of your talk and enhance its clarity. Others will often understand you when you explain how your topic or point is "like" something else.

Limit Ambiguity

A statement is ambiguous when it can be interpreted in more than one way and the context does not make clear which is appropriate. Some of the most fun examples of ambiguity come from newspaper and magazine headlines:

Dog Judging Course Offered at College

Hundreds Vaccinated After Death

Smuggler of Beer Loses Case

Pentagon Urged to Keep Personnel Exposed to AIDS

U's Food Service Feeds Thousands, Grosses Millions

The headline writers would probably prefer that their readers *didn't* interpret these headlines to say that a dog is judging the course offered at the college, that dead people were vaccinated, that the beer smuggler lost 24 cans of brew, or that the U's food service is grossing out millions of its patrons. But their language permitted all these interpretations.

As we noted earlier, language is inherently ambiguous because it reflects individual perceptions, and some people use vague language strategically. But the heading of this section, "Limit Ambiguity," suggests that effective and flexible communicators keep ambiguity to a minimum. When you recognize that your speech can be interpreted in more than one way, you can provide cues to help reduce the ambiguity as much as possible.

The following example illustrates how an ambiguous label can lead to all kinds of misunderstanding:

> A woman from the United Kingdom who was visiting Switzerland looked at several rooms in an apartment house. She told the schoolmaster who owned the house that she'd let him know about renting one of the rooms later. However, after she arrived back at her hotel, the thought occurred to her that she had not asked about the water closet (bathroom). She immediately wrote a note to the schoolmaster asking about the "W.C.," being too bashful to write out the words "water closet." The schoolmaster, who was far from being an expert in English, did not know what the initials "W.C." meant. He asked the parish priest, and together they decided that it must mean wayside chapel. The schoolmaster then wrote the following letter to the very surprised woman.

> Dear Madame,

> I take great pleasure in informing you that the W.C. is located seven miles from the house in the center of a beautiful grove of pine trees. It is capable of holding 229 people and is open on Sunday and Thursday only. I recommend that you come early, although there is plenty of standing room. This is an unfortunate situation, especially if you are in the habit of going regularly. You will no doubt be glad to hear that a good number bring their lunch and make a day of it, while others who can afford it go by car and arrive just in time. It may interest you to know that my daughter was married in the W.C. and that it was there she met her husband. A bazaar is held to provide plush seats for all, since the people think it is a long-felt need. My wife is rather delicate and does not go regularly. Naturally, it pains her very much not to attend more often. If you wish, I shall be glad to reserve the best seat for you where you will be seen by all. Hoping I have been of service to you, I remain

> [the schoolmaster]

One effective way to prevent misleading ambiguity is to listen to what you say as if you were the person you are talking with. Develop a first-time orientation toward what you say to parallel the fact that your listener(s) are in fact hearing it for the first time—even though you might have run through it several times in your head. There is no guaranteed formula for "disambiguating" everything you say. But you can reduce the ambiguity of your talk by thinking from the point of view of your listener.

Use Jargon Carefully

One way social, professional, cultural, and political groups define themselves is by creating their own *jargon,* or in-group vocabulary. You might be frightened to hear your physician tell you that you have "prolapse of the mitral valve," even though these words label a usually harmless heart murmur. Auto mechanics talk about "detent springs" and "socket ratchets," and have special uses for many common words like "come-along," "stand," "drift," and "mike." Interpersonal communication teachers also create their own jargon—the term *disambiguating* in the previous paragraph is an example. We also talk about "relationship cues," "nexting," and "co-constructing selves."

You probably use some jargon terms, too, and they can be useful and helpful. For one thing, special terms can help develop cohesiveness or a sense of connection. When you hear other people speaking "your language," it's easy to feel connected to them. In addition, jargon can help you notice some feature or characteristic that you didn't notice before you knew the special term. Students in our introductory lectures to communication remember learning the label *idiosyncrasy credits,* for example. This is a jargon term for the "bank account" of goodwill that a group member earns by doing what the group wants and helping the group function. After a group member has built up an account of idiosyncrasy credits, he or she can make mistakes or even go against the group without being punished or labeled a deviant. But if you haven't banked enough idiosyncrasy credits to "pay for" your negative actions, you will be criticized or even asked to leave the group. Only after learning this piece of jargon did the students begin to see how this phenomenon actually operated in the groups they worked with.

But jargon can also create problems, because it can confuse and frustrate someone who is not a member of the in-group but who still wants to understand. A serious basketball player, for example, could confuse a person in a pickup game by telling her, "Defensively you need to shut the baseline and stay tight on them." Or a lawyer can puzzle a first-time client with talk about the "inadvisability of proceeding *pro se*" and the hassles of "interrogatories." So it is best to explain or define unusual terms before you use them to develop your ideas. "All I mean by 'relationship cues' are the messages we communicate that define our relationship—how much we touch, the tone of voice we use, things like that." Or " 'Nexting' means the willingness and ability to focus on what to do next in the communication, regardless of what's happening right then." One communication teacher we know expresses this guideline as a "Key to the Kingdom of Clarity." He calls it "the principle of prior definition," and it states: "Define before you develop; explain before you amplify." It is a useful principle.

When you get right down to it, taking your listener's perspective means never forgetting that although what you say makes sense to you, it may not make sense to your listeners. Understandability often suffers most when people act as if they were talking to themselves.

Illustrate Your Ideas

Notice the differences between the following two examples of *written* communication.

Example 1

In the short term any point in phase space can stand for a possible behavior of the dynamical system. In the long term the only possible behaviors are the attractors themselves. Other kinds of motion are transient. By definition, attractors had the important property of stability—in a real system, where moving parts are subject to bumps and jiggles from real-world noise, motion tends to return to the attractor. A bump may shove a trajectory away for a brief time, but the resulting transient motions die out. . . . Turbulence is like white noise, or static. Could such a thing arise from a simple, deterministic system of equations?

Example 2

The nurse is at the door of the glass station, issuing nighttime pills to the men that shuffle past her in a line, and she's having a hard time keeping straight who gets poisoned with what tonight. She's not even watching where she pours the water. What has distracted her attention this way is that big red-headed man with the dreadful cap and the horrible-looking scar coming her way. She's watching McMurphy walk away from the card table in the dark day room, his one horny hand twisting the red tuft of hair that sticks out of the little cup at the throat of his work-farm shirt, and I figure by the way she rears back when he reaches the door of the station that she's probably been warned by the Big Nurse. ("Oh, one more thing before I leave it in your hands tonight, Miss Pilbow, that new man sitting over there, the one with the garish red sideburns and facial lacerations—I've reason to believe he is a sex maniac.")

Example 2 is full of concrete words—"pills," "water," "big red-headed man," "dreadful cap," "horrible-looking scar," "card table," "dark day room," "one horny hand," "red tuft of hair," "work-farm shirt," and so on. The passage moves in a narrative or storylike way, just as you might see it and describe it if you were there. Its structure links together concrete and tangible things, people, and movements. As you read the passage you can't help imagining the looks of the places and persons described. You think of it in terms of *pictures*.

By contrast, Example 1 is full of abstract words—"possible behavior," "dynamical system," "attractors," "property of stability," "transient," "turbulence," "deterministic system of equations." The text moves in a kind of logical order, but you need to have some special knowledge in order to understand the logic. Even the most familiar words—such as "bumps and jiggles"—appear in a sentence with no links to visible things. As you read and think about the passage, it's pretty difficult to imagine a picture of what's being discussed.

The main difference between the two examples is that Example 2 is filled with words that *illustrate* what's being said and Example 1 isn't. The same thing happens in spoken communication. Look at and listen to the differences in concreteness and movement between these two excerpts from student-teacher conferences:

Example 1

Teacher: How would you evaluate your involvement in the class? Remember that "involvement" means more than just contributing to class discussions. How involved do you think you have been?

Anita: Pretty much.

Teacher: How so? Were there some times you remember especially?

Anita: Oh, yeah. I'm a good listener and I paid attention all the time. I can see the relevance of the course to other parts of my life. I think about it, and talk about it, and stuff. People are always telling me that my communication is improving.

Example 2

Teacher: How would you evaluate your involvement in the class? Remember that "involvement" means more than just contributing to class discussions. How involved do you think you have been?

Miyako: A lot, I think. Angela and I have spent a lot of time talking about how the course applies to our living situations—we're both living with our boyfriends. We're both trying to change how we communicate when we first get home at night, and also what we do when there's a conflict.

Teacher: Good idea.

210 Part II ◆ *Inhaling and Exhaling*

Miyako: I also used the paper assignment as an excuse to talk with my dad about communication in our family. He told me what I'd guessed before—that my folks' culture often values silence more than talk. There's a strong belief among Japanese that intimacy comes from being silent with each other rather than always talking things through. I've noticed that at home before, when Mom and Dad got away from us kids just to sit quietly next to each other, but I never understood it. Usually, I'm more comfortable talking things out with my boyfriend, but I think he often prefers silence, too. So right now we're pretty "involved" in these class concepts.

One main difference between Anita's and Miyako's responses is that Miyako talks about specifics and Anita doesn't. Miyako illustrates her belief about her level of involvement by describing specific situations and events. She doesn't use as many vivid adjectives as the novelist does in writing about the sex maniac, but her speech is still concrete and evocative. On the other hand, Anita only talks in generalities— "pretty much," "parts of my life," "people are always telling me. . ." As a result, Miyako's responses make it easier for the teacher to connect with her than do Anita's.

Use Examples

A major way to illustrate what you say is to use examples, specific instances or concrete cases of what you're discussing. Sometimes people confuse examples with lists of characteristics. When asked to give an example of a difficult class, they might reply, "Well, it'd be one with several hundred pages of reading and three or four major assignments or papers." This is not an example. It is a list of characteristics rather than a specific case, and although it adds information and does respond directly to the question, it doesn't do much to help the person *picture* what's being discussed. Here are some examples of examples:

1. "You know, adults sometimes over-analyze things to the point where the fun goes out of them. Children can often just appreciate them for what they are." (Not clear yet; too many possible ways to interpret what's being said. But notice what happens.) "For example, I remember when we took our kids to the Moscow Circus. Lisa was only five at the time. There was a magician with some really amazing tricks. At one point he seemed to change two performers into completely different persons while they were suspended ten feet off the ground in steel cages. 'Wow!' I said to Lisa. 'That was really something! I wonder how he did that!' Lisa turned to me with a quizzical face and said, 'What do you mean? It's magic, Daddy.' "

(Now the general statement is clarified by this specific instance.)

2. "I've come to the conclusion that major holidays are probably the occasion for more frustration and sadness than joy."

(Sounds important, but I wonder if she means what I'd mean if I said this.)

"For example, I can still remember how hard it was when I was little for Hanukkah to compete with Christmas. My friends got excited about Santa Claus, sang lots of traditional carols, and celebrated for most of December. Our family had some special times and a few gifts, but nothing as big as the Christian holiday. Now that I'm older, I hear all the time from both Christian and Jewish friends whose holiday expectations are never matched by the realities. Real people just don't live the holiday fantasies presented in books and on TV."

Chapter Summary

Our main goal in this chapter has been to build on the extensive knowledge of language that you have already developed. As you've grown up—if English is your first language—and as you've gone through school, you have learned that language is a system of symbols and that it also performs specific actions. You may not have heard it put in exactly those terms, but you have learned about the power of language that comes from it being symbolic and the importance of knowing how to perform certain actions correctly. On that foundation, we want to build a third insight about language: It is a human way of being.

This idea is admittedly a little abstract, but it can be made both concrete and significant. Your language is something that you don't just "use." You inhabit it, like a fish lives in water. It surrounds you and influences *everything* you think and do. People who grow up in different languages inhabit different *worlds*—just as we said in Chapter Two. In that chapter we described seven dimensions of each person's world of meaning: physical environment, time, relationship, spirituality, vocation, language(s), and technology. In this chapter we focus on the sixth one. You could say that, along with physical environment, time, vocation, and so on, language is one primary dimension of each person's world of meaning. Or you could say that, because language affects *all* perception and understanding—including our perception and understanding of the physical world, time, technology, etc.—language is the most fundamental and primary dimension of each person's world of meaning. But whichever view you take, the point is that language is more than a tool or a way to perform actions, because it is the "water" that surrounds all humans all the time, like the water in which a fish swims.

The main application of this idea comes as you understand how language affects perception. We made this general point and then described specifically how English affects people's perceptions of complex processes—like communicating. Then we described how English and other languages affect gender perception. We asked you to think about how your language affects your perceptions and your performance of yours and others' gender identities.

The final part of the chapter moved from this basic idea and its application to six language guidelines. We suggest that you develop inclusive and respectful language, use metaphors to help others understand you, limit the ambiguity of your talk, use jargon carefully, illustrate your ideas, and especially use examples as illustrations.

As the learning objectives at the beginning of the chapter indicate, our overall goal here is to have you develop one important general understanding about language—that it is a way of being—and some specific ideas about how you can *apply* that idea to your communicating.

In Other Words

In Chapter Seven you learned that language can be described as a way of being. Language is not a tool that you can pick up and lay down and that exists separately from you. You are entrenched in it like a fish in water, with your mind and your emotions. Perhaps you've had the experience when you traveled in a foreign country and no one spoke English. You might remember the feeling of being lost and the joy when you heard the sound of the English language, which you could understand and which made you feel at home.

This text introduces you to Richard Rodriguez, who grew up with two languages: Spanish and English. Living in and between these two languages has very specific and different meanings for the boy Richard. Pay attention to these meanings when you read the text.

You should be able to respond to the following questions:

1. What does it *mean* to Richard to speak Spanish?

2. What does it mean for him to speak English?

3. Think about how *language* as one dimension of worlds of meanings influences the other dimensions. For instances, how does language influence Richard's relationships?

* * *

Aria

Richard Rodriguez

I grew up in a house where the only regular guests were my relations. For ... one day, enormous families of relatives would visit and there would be so many people that the noise and the bodies would spill out to the backyard and front porch. Then for weeks, no one came by. (It was usually a salesman who rang the doorbell.) Our house stood apart. A gaudy yellow in a row of white bungalows. We were the people with the noisy dog. The people who raised pigeons and chickens. We were the foreigners on the block. A few neighbors smiled and waved. We waved back. But no one in the family knew the names of the old couple who lived next door; until I was seven years old, I did not know the names of the kids who lived across the street.

In public, my father and mother spoke a hesitant, accented, not always grammatical English. And they would have to strain—their bodies tense—to catch the sense of what was rapidly said by *los gringos*. At home they spoke Spanish. The language of their Mexican past sounded in counterpoint to the English of public society. The words would come quickly, with ease. Conveyed through those sounds was the pleasing, soothing, consoling reminder of being at home.

During those years when I was first conscious of hearing, my mother and father addressed me only in Spanish, in Spanish I learned to reply. By contrast, English (*inglés*), rarely heard in the house, was the language I came to associate with *gringos*. I learned my first words of English overhearing my parents speak to strangers. At five years of age, I knew just enough English for my mother to trust me on errands to stores one block away. No more.

I was a listening child, careful to hear the very different sounds of Spanish and English. Wide-eyed with hearing, I'd listen to sounds more than words. First there were English (gringo) sounds. So many words were still unknown that when the butcher or the lady at the drugstore said something to me, exotic polysyllabic sounds would bloom in the midst of the sentences. Often, the speech of people in public seemed to me very loud, booming with confidence. The man behind the counter would literally ask, "What can I do for you?" But by being so firm and so clear, the sound of his voice said that he was a *gringo*; he belonged in public society.

I would also hear then the high nasal notes of middle-class American speech. The air stirred with sound. Sometimes, even now, when I have been traveling abroad for several weeks, I will hear what I heard as a boy. In hotel lobbies or airports, in Turkey or Brazil, some Americans will pass, and suddenly I will hear it again—the high sound of American voices. For a few seconds I will hear it with pleasure, for it is now the sound of *my* society—a reminder of home. But inevitably—already on the flight headed for home—the sound fades with repetition. I will be unable to hear it anymore.

When I was a boy, things were different. The accent of *los gringos* was never pleasing nor was it hard to hear. Crowds at Safeway or at bus stops would be noisy with sound. And I would be forced to edge away from the chirping chatter above me.

I was unable to hear my own sounds, but I knew very well that I spoke English poorly. My words could not stretch far enough to form complete thoughts. And the words I did speak I didn't know well enough to make into distinct sounds. (Listeners would usually lower their heads, better to hear what I was trying to say.) But it was one thing for *me* to speak English with difficulty. It was more troubling for me to hear my parents speak in public: their high-whining vowels and guttural consonants; their sentences that got stuck with "eh" and "ah" sounds; the confused syntax; the hesitant rhythm of sounds so different from the way *gringos* spoke. I'd notice, moreover, that my parents' voices were softer than those of *gringos* we'd meet.

I am tempted now to say that none of this mattered. In adulthood I am embarrassed by childhood fears. And, in a way, it didn't matter very much that my parents could not speak English with ease. Their linguistic difficulties had no serious consequences. My mother and father made themselves understood at the county hospital clinic and at government offices. And yet, in another way, it mattered very much—it was unsettling to hear my parents struggle with English. Hearing them, I'd grow nervous, my clutching trust in their protection and power weakened.

There were many times like the night at a brightly lit gasoline station (a blaring white memory) when I stood uneasily, hearing my father. He was talking to a teenaged attendant. I do not recall what they were saying, but I cannot forget the sounds my father made as he spoke. At one point his words slid together to form one word—sounds as confused as the threads of blue and green oil in the puddle next to my shoes. His voice rushed through what he had left to say. And, toward the end, reached falsetto notes, appealing to his listener's understanding. I looked away to the lights of passing automobiles. I tried not to hear anymore. But I heard only too well the calm, easy tones in the attendant's reply. Shortly afterward, walking toward home with my father, I shivered when he put his hand on my shoulder. The very first chance that I got, I evaded his grasp and ran on ahead into the dark, skipping with feigned boyish exuberance.

But then there was Spanish. *Español*: my family's language. *Español*: the language that seemed to me a private language. I'd hear strangers on the radio and in the Mexican Catholic church across town speaking in Spanish, but I couldn't really believe that Spanish was a public language, like English. Spanish speakers, rather, seemed related to me, for I sensed that we shared through our language the experience of feeling apart from *los gringos*. It was thus a ghetto Spanish that I heard and I spoke. Like those whose lives are bound by a barrio, I was reminded by Spanish of my separateness from *los otros, los gringos* in power. But more intensely than for most barrio children—because I did not live in a barrio—Spanish seemed to me the language of home. (Most days it was only at home that I'd hear it.) It became the language of joyful return.

A family member would say something to me and I would feel myself specially recognized. My parents would say something to me and I would feel embraced by the sounds of their words. Those sounds said: *I am speaking with ease in Spanish. I am addressing you in words I never use with* los gringos. *I recognize you as someone special, close, like no one outside. You belong with us. In the family.*

(*Ricardo.*)

At the age of five, six, well past the time when most other children no longer easily notice the difference between sounds uttered at home and words spoken in public, I had a different experience. I lived in a world magically compounded of sounds. I remained a child longer than most; I lingered too long, poised at the edge of language—often frightened by the sounds of *los gringos*, delighted by the sounds of Spanish at home. I shared with my family a language that was startlingly different from that used in the great city around us.

For me there were none of the gradations between public and private society so normal to a maturing child. Outside the house was public society; inside the house was private. Just opening or closing the screen door behind me was an important experience. I'd rarely leave home all alone or without reluctance. Walking down the sidewalk, under the canopy of tall trees, I'd warily notice the—suddenly—silent neighborhood kids who stood warily watching me. Nervously, I'd arrive at the grocery store to hear there the sounds of the *gringo*—foreign to me—reminding me that in this world so big, I was a foreigner. But then I'd return. Walking back toward our house, climbing the steps from the sidewalk, when the front door was open in summer, I'd hear voices beyond the screen door talking in Spanish. For a second or two, I'd stay, linger there, listening. Smiling, I'd hear my mother call out, saying in Spanish (words): "Is that you, Richard?" All the while her sounds would assure me: *You are home now; come closer; inside. With us.*

"*Si*," I'd reply.

Once more inside the house I would resume (assume) my place in the family. The sounds would dim, grow harder to hear. Once more at home, I would grow less aware of that fact. It required, however, no more than the blurt of the doorbell to alert me to listen to sounds all over again. The house would turn instantly still while my mother went to the door. I'd hear her hard English sounds. I'd wait to hear her voice return to soft-sounding Spanish, which assured me, as surely as did the clicking tongue of the lock on the door, that the stranger was gone. . . .

From *Hunger of Memory* by Richard Rodriguez. Reprinted by permission of David R. Godine, Publisher, Inc. Copyright © 1982 by Richard Rodriguez.

Endnote

1. For over 50 years, linguistics, anthropology, and communication textbooks have used the example of Eskimo words for snow to illustrate how language and perception are interrelated. You may have seen it before. According to this account, the importance of snow in Eskimo culture is reflected in the many terms it has for "falling snow," "drifting snow," "snow on the ground," "slushy snow," and so on. Earlier editions of this text repeated this myth. But we now know it isn't true. The myth began in 1911 when an anthropologist working in Alaska compared the different Eskimo root words for "snow on the ground," "falling snow," "drifting snow," and "a snow drift" with different English root words for a variety of forms of water (liquid, lake, river, brook, rain, dew, wave, foam, and so on). The anthropologist's comment was popularized in a 1940 article and then found its way into literally hundreds of publications which confidently asserted that Eskimos had "nine," "twenty-three," "fifty," and even "one hundred" words for "snow." But they don't. The best available source, *A Dictionary of the*

West Greenlandic Eskimo Language, gives just two: quanik, meaning "snow in the air" and aput, meaning "snow on the ground." So if you hear or read of the Eskimo-words-for-snow example, feel free to correct it. Or at least don't repeat it. Pullum, G. 1997. "The Great Eskimo Vocabulary Hoax." In Peschholz, A. Rosa, and V. Clark (eds.), *Language Awareness* (Seventh ed.). Pages 128–139. New York: St. Martin's Press.

References

Aristotle, *De Interpretatione,* Translated by E. M. Edgehill, McKeon, Richard (ed.). 1941. *The Basic Works of Aristotle.* New York: Random House. Page 20.

Austin, J. L. 1962. *How to Do Things With Words.* New York: Oxford.

Biriere, J., and Lanktree, C. "Sex-Role Related Effects of Sex Bias in Language," *Sex Roles,* 9: 635–632.

Carroll, John B. (ed.). 1956. *Language, Thought and Reality: Selected Writings of Benjamin Lee Whorf.* New York: Wiley. Pages 212–213.

Chamberlain, D. B. 1987. "Consciousness at Birth: The Range of Empirical Evidence." In T. R. Verney (ed.), *Pre- and Perinatal Psychology: An Introduction.* New York: Human Sciences. Pages 70–86.

Eastman, C. M. 1985. *Aspects of Language and Culture.* Novato, CA: Chandler and Sharp.

Gadamer, H. G. 1976. *Philosophical Hermeneutics.* Trans. D. Lunge. Berkeley: University of California Press.

Haslett, B. 1984. "Acquiring Conversational Competence." *Western Journal of Speech Communication,* 48: 120.

Hoijer, H. 1951. "Cultural Implications of Some Navajo Linguistic Categories." *Language,* 27: 117.

Ivy, D. K. 1986. "Who's the Boss?: He, He/She, or They?" Unpublished paper, cited in D. K. Ivy and Phil Backlund, *Exploring Gender Speak: Personal Effectiveness in Gender Communication.* New York: McGraw-Hill 1994. Page 75.

Ivy, D. K., and Backlund, P. C. 1994. *Exploring Genderspeak.* New York: McGraw-Hill. Pages 78-80.

Rodriguez, R. 1981. *Hunger of Memory: The Education of Richard Rodriguez.* New York: Bantam.

Swift, J. 1906. *Gulliver's Travels and Other Works.* London: Routledge.

Tannen, D. 1990. *You Just Don't Understand: Women and Men in Communication* New York: William Morrow.

Tomatis, A. "Ontogenesis of the Faculty of Listening." In Verney (ed.), Pages 23–35.

Wood, J. T. , and Reich, N. 2002. "Gendered Speech Communities." In L. Samovar and R. E. Porter (eds.), *Intercultural Communication: A Reader.* Belmont, CA: Wadsworth. Page 214. ✦

Chapter Eight

Nonverbal Communicating

Chapter Objectives

After reading this chapter, you should be able to do the following:
- Define nonverbal communicating and fit it into the verbal/nonverbal–oral/non-oral table in Chapter Seven.
- Explain why nonverbal communicating is important.
- List six different types of nonverbal cues or codes.
- Give examples from your own experience of each of the six.
- Identify how each of the six codes can work in face-to-face and mediated communication situations.
- Distinguish among intimate, personal, social, and public distance.
- Define paralinguistics and explain how pause can affect meaning.
- Describe some cultural differences among the six nonverbal codes.
- Explain the three primary functions of nonverbal cues.

Chapter Preview

You probably already know that you communicate as much with your facial expression, tone of voice, eye contact, and even silence as you do with words. That's why this chapter talks about the ways people communicate nonverbally. Those who study and teach about nonverbal communicating have identified dozens of different kinds of cues, including aroma, dress, and the use of badges, insignia, and logos. But rather than try to "cover the universe" in this chapter, we will focus on the nonverbal cues that most directly affect where your communication is on the impersonal⟷interpersonal continuum we discussed in Chapter Three. These include kinesics (gesture, posture, facial expression, and eye contact), proxemics (or space), haptics

217

(or touch), voice, silence, and chronemics, which is the communicative use of time.

Remember that a cue is the smallest identifiable unit of communication. The basic verbal cue, as we said in Chapter Seven, is usually a single word or phrase (but it can also be a morpheme). The basic nonverbal cue is the smallest nonword unit that the people communicating notice or respond to. What counts as a nonverbal cue varies with the sensitivity, interest, and levels of awareness of the people involved. Most people notice the tone of voice that distinguishes a sincere comment from a sarcastic one and the differences in intensity, duration, and location of a touch that says, "Hi, friend" versus one that says, "I'm sexually attracted to you." So in these cases, the distinctive tone of voice or the kind of touch would be a nonverbal cue. On the other hand, most people will not notice subtle changes in breathing or the small differences in the dilation of a person's pupils that often accompany feelings of pleasure or displeasure. So these wouldn't be cues unless the people noticed and responded to them.

Importance of Nonverbal Communicating

Three communication writers and teachers say that nonverbal communication includes "all the messages other than words that people exchange in interactive contexts . . . the final goal of nonverbal communication usually is to create shared meaning" (Hecht, DeVito, and Guerrero 1999, 5). This definition reinforces the point we made at the start of Chapter Seven that nonverbal cues can be expressed orally—for instance, when you raise the volume of your voice as you speak. Many other nonverbal cues, such as obscene gestures or shoulder shrugs, are not only nonverbal but also non-oral. Usually, as we've said, nonverbal cues accompany words. Sometimes people just nod, wave, shrug, slouch, scowl, or walk away without speaking. But most of the time verbal and nonverbal cues occur together.

Why should you care about nonverbal communicating? First of all, when people engage in interactions, we pay a lot of attention to nonverbal cues. Burgoon (1994) says that 60–65 percent of social meaning is connected to nonverbal behavior. This means that, oftentimes, *people pay more attention to nonverbal than verbal cues.* For instance, consider what could happen when you ask your professor whether you can have an extension on your assignment. The professor says, "Yes, you can have two more days, but that's it." The professor says this sentence with a sharp twist in her voice and with an angry facial expression. Although you might be thankful to learn that you can have two more days, you will probably interpret the tone of voice and facial expression as impatience or anger, and you will be careful not to ask for another extension. In this case, the nonverbal cues told you more about the professor's attitude toward late assignments than the verbal cues.

Another reason to learn more about nonverbal cues is the common *misconception that nonverbal cues cannot be controlled* and that nonverbal behavior spontaneously expresses a person's true thoughts and feelings. Although there is definitely some truth to the idea that nonverbal cues can spontaneously express feelings and thoughts, nonverbal cues can also be manipulated. For example, many film stars and other public figures constantly smile whenever they sense a camera, no matter how bad they feel. Or someone who is lying might strategically try to look you in the eyes because they know that one way people believe they can spot a liar is by the lack of eye contact. As we said earlier, nonverbal cues become especially important when they contradict what is being said verbally. Have you ever heard someone loudly shout, *"I'm not mad!"*? When cues contradict each other, people usually pay more attention to the nonverbal—in this case, the tone of voice (Hecht, DeVito, and Guerrero 1999).

A third reason to learn about nonverbal cues is that they *help to create and maintain group identities.* In one of John's classes, several African American male students tried to teach the "white guys" the subtle head nod the African Americans used to greet each other on campus. The "black guys" laughed at how hard it was for their trainees to get the head nod exactly right. Or you might have noticed that people from France or Latin and South America kiss each other on both cheeks, twice or three times, when they greet each other. When you are a member of one of these cultures, you may try to use the head nod or the kiss on the cheeks to show the other members that you're comfortable in their culture. And by doing this over and over again, you and the other members of the group affirm that you have your own sense of identity. In fact, as you may have already learned, the primary way you join a cultural group is to become familiar with and take on its ways of communicating nonverbally. Cultures are defined, to a considerable degree, by their nonverbal cues, and a given pattern of nonverbal cues reflects the person's cultural identity.

Nonverbal cues are also very important in *initial encounters and first judgments* about people. For instance, we might look how someone walks in public and conclude, "She might be an athlete." Or someone might make an impression of being "fidgety" because he uses many gestures at the same time and talks very fast with few pauses. People also use facial expressions to express emotions and space and touch to express perceptions of their relationships with another person. For all these reasons, it would be useful for you to be as aware of, and skilled at, nonverbal communicating as you can.

Six Nonverbal Codes

Because there are so many ways of communicating nonverbally, this behavior is usually chunked into different codes, such as gestures, eye contact, touch, or voice (Knapp and Hall 1992). So a code of gestures, for example, is made up of various movements of hands, arms, or the head, along with the socially agreed-upon interpretation and meanings for each movement in context. All humans employ basically the same gestures, eye behavior, movement, and so forth, but the rules for their meaning and use can vary widely from culture to culture. As we already said, these six codes affect interpersonal communicating the most:

- Kinesics (gestures, posture, facial expression, and eye contact).
- Proxemics (space).
- Haptics (touch).
- Voice.
- Silence.
- Time.

When you understand something about these six codes, you will be able to use them to help move your communicating along the impersonal←——→interpersonal continuum.

Kinesics

The technical term for the study of body posture, gestures, and facial expressions is *kinesics,* from the Greek word for motion. These cues are far more important than people sometimes think. When someone walks into a job interview erectly and confidently, he or she is likely to make a more positive impression on the interviewer than someone who walks in with bent shoulders and shuffling feet. You may sit rather rigidly when you meet your in-laws for the first time, because you are more nervous and on guard, and you will have a more relaxed posture when sitting with friends over coffee or a beer. Let's have a closer look at gestures before we move on to talk more about posture and facial expressions.

Gestures

Overall, gestures can be categorized into four main types: emblems, illustrators, regulators, and adaptors.

This gesture is an emblem, because it has a specific meaning. The meaning changes, however, from subculture to subculture.

Emblems. Emblems are gestures that have a concrete meaning attached to them. They can be interpreted *independently* from verbal cues and usually have a *direct translation*. In other words, they can substitute, in a given culture, for a verbal cue. Examples in U.S. and Western cultures would be waving of your hand to say "good-bye" or thumbs-up for saying "o.k." Emblems are culture specific, but some have become almost universal through travel and the media. For instance, the emblem "thumbs-up" apparently originated in the Roman Empire and was used by the emperor to signal whether a slave could live (thumbs-up) or had to die after a fight (thumbs-down). This gesture is understood in many cultures today. However, there are other emblems that are culture specific. For instance, when Saskia points her index finger at her temples, what does that mean to you? In Germany, it means that the person to whom this emblem is addressed is stupid. People use this emblem especially in the streets to give their opinion of a bad driver. But if you don't know how and when to use this emblem properly, you might get into trouble, because it is also an insult. The same is true for the "V" sign. If you do it with your thumb pointing outward, it means victory. But with your thumb pointed toward you, it has a sexual meaning in England and Australia.

Illustrators. Illustrators are gestures that *accompany* a verbal message and function to clarify or emphasize it. An example would be the use of your arms and hands to describe how to get to a certain restaurant. Verbally, you would say, for instance, "You go right, then take a left, and then a left again." Usually you would use your hands and arms to point into the direction. Other illustrators indicate how tall someone is, the size of fish a person caught, or the diameter of the tree that fell in the park.

Regulators. Regulators help people to coordinate turn-taking in conversations. Usually, people don't think about these cues because, like much of nonverbal communicating, they happen so quickly and routinely. You can directly say "It's your turn to talk" by pointing to someone with your hand, and you can do the same thing more subtly by nodding your head, slightly leaning forward, or looking at someone expectantly.

Adaptors. Adaptors are hand or arm movements that occur below a person's level of awareness and that are a source of information about how a person is feeling. A person who is playing with an object, such as a pen, or using her fingers to play with her hair is often signaling nervousness or impatience. Adaptors are examples of unintentional nonverbal communicating.

Posture

People can communicate dominance and submission with their postures. A male may hook his thumbs in his belt, and both females and males may stand with hands on hips in the akimbo position. When a seated person leans back with hands clasped behind her or his head, this is often another dominance posture. When a conversational group of three is approached by a fourth person, they typically rotate their bodies out to encourage the fourth to join them or in to discourage him or her.

Forward lean is a posture that is commonly interpreted as more involved and usually more positive, whereas "seated male and female communicators both perceived a person leaning backward and away from them as having a more negative attitude than one who was leaning forward" (Knapp 1980, 224). A posture that faces the other directly, movement toward the other, affirmative head nods, expressive hand gestures, and stretching are all rated as "warm" behaviors, while moving away, picking teeth, shaking the head, and playing with hair are rated as "cold" (Clore, Wiggins, and Itkin 1975). All of these descriptions illustrate how body movement and gesture can promote impersonal or interpersonal communicating.

Facial Expression

Your face is probably the most expressive part of your body and one of the more important focal points for nonverbal communicating. Most of the time people are unaware of how much they are relying on faces to give and get information. But a little reflection—or reading some of the research—can change your level of awareness. Consider, for example, how important the face is to expressing emotion. An extensive program of research has demonstrated that certain basic emo-

Figure 8.1   Common Facial Expressions

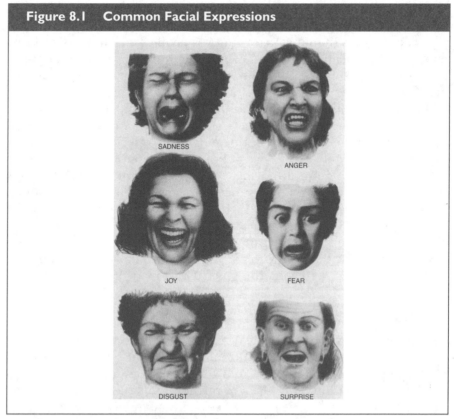

From *Gary Faigin*, The Artists's Complete Guide to Facial Expression, *Watson-Guptil Publications, New York, 1990. Reproduced by permission.*

tions appear to be facially expressed in similar ways across cultures (Ekman 1972). Every culture studied so far has been found to include some conventional facial expressions that people use to communicate joy or happiness, sadness, surprise, fear, anger, and disgust. There are some culture-specific rules for the display of these emotions, but they are expressed in very similar ways across cultures. The six are pictured in Figure 8.1.

Researchers have discovered these similarities by showing photographs of North American faces to Japanese or preliterate New Guinean observers and then showing photographs of Japanese and New Guineans to North Americans. In most cases, members of one culture were able to accurately identify the emotions being expressed by the faces of persons from the other cultures (Ekman, Friesen, and Ancoli 1980). They recognized, for example, that surprise is consistently communicated by a face with widened eyes, head tilted up, raised brow, and open mouth. Disgust is communicated with brows pulled down, wrinkled nose, and a mouth with raised upper lip and downturned corners.

Although the facial expression of emotions is similar across cultures, there are important differences in cultural norms for the expression of emotions. In many Asian cultures people learn not to be too expressive. Historically, members of Asian cultures have been taught to mask negative facial expressions with smiles and laughter and to display less facial emotion overall (Miller 1982). The researchers Chen and Starosta (1998) say that an athlete in Japan who loses a competition must cover his disappointment or anger with a smile. In contrast, in many Southern European, Latin, and South American cultures, people learn to be highly expressive at home and in public.

In addition to cultural norms, the expression of emotions always depends on the context. For instance, you can laugh out loud about a joke when you're with friends in the streets or in your room, but it probably would be inappropriate to do so during your graduation ceremony. A flight attendant is trained to smile while on duty, no matter what happens. At home, the same flight attendant will probably not smile all the time when something is frustrating or irritating.

Eye Contact and Gaze

Although eyes are obviously a part of facial expression and therefore kinesics, eye contact and gaze are important enough to discuss separately. Eye contact appears to be one of the first behaviors that infants develop. Within a few days of birth, infants seem to concentrate on their caregiver's eyes. In the weeks immediately after birth, researchers have observed that simply seeing the eyes of the caregiver is enough to produce a smiling reaction (Argyle and Cook 1976). Eye contact also significantly affects development. Infants who lack mutual gaze do not appear to mature perceptually and socially as rapidly as those who experience regular eye contact (Andersen, Andersen, and Landgraf 1985).

If you doubt the importance of eye contact, consider the inferences you make about someone who doesn't look you in the eye "enough." What enough means varies from person to person, and certainly from culture to culture. Most white Anglo Americans infer that the person with too little eye contact is insincere, disinterested, lacks confidence, is trying to avoid contact, or is lying. Generally in these cultures, there are *no* positive interpretations of too little eye contact.

Problems can also be created by cultural differences regarding how much is enough eye contact. For example, some white Anglo Americans mistakenly consider their African American conversation partners to be inattentive and uninterested when they aren't. This can happen because many—though not all—white Americans tend to use a combination of head nods, vocal sounds, *and* eye gaze to maintain contact, while some African Americans use *one* of the three to do the same thing. So in this case the African American's silent, head-down nodding can express as much attention as do the white's eye contact, "uh-huh," and head movement. But whites unaware of these differences can perceive the African American responses as insufficient. These African Americans may also perceive their white conversation partners to be hostile or overbearing because they use continuous eye contact when listening and less when speaking (Erickson 1979). Overall, eye behavior serves several functions.

One important function of eye gaze is *to enhance the intimacy of the relationship.* Especially when it is accompanied by forward lean, direct body orientation, and more gesturing, eye contact can help promote closeness (Burgoon, Buller, and Woodall 1989). Some researchers have studied the kind of intimacy that increases the desire to help another person. Gaze has been found to increase the probability that a bystander will help a person with a medical problem or someone who has fallen (Shotland and Johnson 1978). But this phenomenon seems to characterize female-female contacts more than those involving males. As Judee Burgoon and her colleagues (1989, 438) summarize, "Under some circumstances, prolonged gaze may serve as an affiliative cue in the form of a plea for help, while in other cases it may be seen as overly forward or aggressive behavior."

A second important function of eye contact is *to recognize members of the same group.* For instance, a study found that for lesbians and gay men eye contact is very important for identifying one another (Carrol and Gilroy 2002). Especially for people who face prejudice and violence in some cases, recognizing each other through brief eye contact is one way to promote self-protection.

A third function of eye behavior is *to express emotions.* Some of the same people who studied facial expressions have also researched how people use eyes and eyebrows to interpret the six common emotions shown in Figure 8.1. People looking at pictures noticed eyes more than the eyebrow-forehead region or the lower face for the accurate perception of fear, but eyes helped less for the accurate perception of anger and disgust (Ekman and Friesen 1975).

A fourth function of eye behavior is *to communicate feelings about others.* For example, if you perceive a person as of significantly lower status than you are, the tendency will be for you to maintain considerable eye contact. On the other hand, many people tend to look much less at high-status people. Generally, we also look more at people we like and at those who we believe like us. The obvious reason, as Albert Mehrabian (1981) explains, is that eye contact is a kind of approach behavior, and approach behaviors are connected with liking. So one response to someone who appeals to us is to approach by looking, and one way to avoid a person we dislike is to look away.

Finally, people also use gaze and eye behavior *to make and influence credibility judgments.* Several studies on persuasive effectiveness and willingness to hire a job applicant have underscored the importance of nearly continuous gaze. It appears that gaze avoidance is interpreted negatively, as we mentioned above, and that it can significantly affect your chances of being perceived as credible (Burgoon, Manusov, Mineo, and Hale 1985). This is why those who teach or coach people for public speaking or interview situations emphasize that speakers and interviewees should generally try to maintain eye contact 50–70 percent of the time. As we mentioned earlier, cultural identities affect this formula, but it is a reliable basic guideline for most Caucasian North American communication situations.

The bottom line is that people give considerable weight to eye behavior and eye contact because we apparently believe that the eyes are indeed the "windows of the soul." Especially in Western cultures, people are confident that we can spot even the most practiced liar if we can just "look the person in the eye" (Bavelas, Black, Chovil, and Mullet 1990), even though deception-detection is considerably more complicated than this. People are also generally impressed by the confidence and overall effectiveness of a speaker with "good" eye contact. But, especially since different cultures have varying estimates of what "good" means in this context, it's important not to oversimplify gaze and eye behavior and to remember that, since this category of nonverbal cues is given so much credence, it's important to become aware of and to learn to manage your own eye behavior.

Proxemics

You have probably noticed that you often feel possessive about some spaces—perhaps your room, yard, or car—and that you sometimes sit or stand very close to people you're talking with and at other times feel more comfortable several feet away. These feelings are related to what is known as *proxemics,* the study of the communicative use of space or distance. Proxemics can be divided into the study of *territory* and the study of *personal space.*

All humans have basic human needs for both contact (nearness) and independence (distance), and one way we manage this tension is by defining and defending a *territory.* A territory is an identifiable geographic area that is occupied, controlled, and often defended by a person or group as their exclusive domain (Burgoon, Buller, and Woodall 1989). For example, for a considerable part of the lives of many North Americans, the person's bedroom, or a particular space in a shared room, is his or hers whether they're in it or not, and one of the reasons people guard their right to keep it in a preferred state of neatness or disorder is to underscore the point that it's their territory. In a library, cafeteria, or other public space, people use overcoats, briefcases, newspapers, food trays, dishes, and utensils to establish a claim over "their" space, even though it's temporary.

A number of studies have identified differences between ways women and men use territory. For example, in most cultures, women are allowed to have less territory than men. As Judy Pearson noted,

> . . . [F]ew women have a particular and unviolated room in their homes while many men have dens, studies, or work areas which are off limits to others. Similarly, it appears that more men than women have particular chairs reserved for their use. (Pearson 1989, 78)

The defense of territory is also culture-specific. Just think of the many fences and "no trespassing" signs that exist in the United States. Fences and no trespassing signs are indicators of the importance of private property in a culture. You will find very few fences on the land making up a Navajo reservation. Why? Because in Navajo culture, land is regarded as public rather than private.

In addition to territory, each of us also lives in our own personal space, a smaller, invisible, portable, and adjustable "bubble" that we maintain to protect ourselves from physical and emotional threats. The size of this bubble varies; how far away we sit or stand depends on our family and cultural memberships, the relationship we have with the other person, the situation or the context, and how we are feeling toward the other person at the time. As anthropologist Edward Hall puts it,

> Some individuals never develop the public phase of their personalities and, therefore, cannot fill public spaces; they make very poor speakers or moderators. As many psychiatrists know, other people have trouble with the intimate and personal zones and cannot endure closeness to others. (Hall 1966, 115)

Within these limitations, Hall identifies four distances he observed among middle-class adults in the northeastern United States. Although the limits of each zone differ from culture to culture, something like these four types of space exist in many cultures.

Intimate Distance (Contact to 18 Inches). This zone begins with skin contact and ranges to about a foot and a half. People usually reserve this distance for those they are emotionally close to and for comforting, protecting, caressing, or lovemaking. When forced into intimate distance with strangers—as on an elevator, for example—we tend to use other nonverbal cues to reestablish our separateness. So we avoid eye contact, fold our arms, or perhaps hold a briefcase or purse in front of our body. Allowing someone to enter this zone is a sign of trust; it says we have willingly lowered our defenses. At this distance not only touch but also smells, body temperature, and the feel and smell of breath can all be parts of what we experience. Voices are usually kept at a low level to emphasize the "closed circle" established by intimates.

Personal Distance (1.5 to 4 Feet). This is the distance preferred by most conversation partners in a public setting. Typically, subjects of personal interest and moderate involvement can be discussed at this distance. Touch is still possible, but it is limited to brief pats of emphasis and reassurance. Finer details of the other's skin, hair, eyes, and teeth are visible, but not body temperature or feel of the breath.

The far range of this distance is just beyond where conversation partners can comfortably touch each other. Hall calls it the distance we can use to keep someone "at arm's length." John sometimes works as a communication consultant

Intimate distance is contact to 18 inches.

training people to do information-gathering interviews. In that context, he encourages the people he's training to try to work within this zone. It appears that three to four feet is far enough away not to

Notice how personal distance does not always result in personal contact.

In the courtroom, attorneys use personal, social, and public distance strategically.

threaten the other and still close enough to encourage the kind of relatively candid responses that make the interviews most successful.

Social Distance (4 to 12 Feet). More impersonal business generally occurs at this distance. People who work together or who are attending a social gathering tend to use the closer ranges of social distance. Salespeople and customers typically are comfortable within the four- to seven-foot zone. Most people feel uncomfortable if a salesperson approaches within three feet, but five or six feet nonverbally says "I'm here to help, but I don't want to be pushy."

At the farther ranges of this distance, eye contact becomes especially important. When a person is 10 or 11 feet away, it's easy to be uncertain about whom the person is talking with until you can determine where the person is looking. This is also the distance people often use with someone of significantly higher or lower status. Sitting at this distance from a superior will tend to create a much more formal conversation than might occur if one or both persons moved their chairs significantly closer. As a result, it can be more effective to reprimand using social distance and less effective to give praise in this zone.

Public Distance (12 to 25 Feet). The closer range of this distance is the one commonly used by instructors and managers addressing work groups. The farthest end of this zone is usually reserved for public speeches. When communicating at this distance, your voice needs to be loud or electronically amplified. At the farther ranges of this distance, facial expression, movements, and gestures also need to be exaggerated in order to be meaningful.

Like many other general observations about human communication, these four distances need to be taken with a grain of salt. Several studies have shown, for example, that females sit and stand closer together than males and that mixed-sex pairs consistently adopt closer distances than male-male pairs (Sussman and Rosenfeld 1982). Interpersonal distance also generally increases with age from preschool and grade school through teen years to adulthood, but this tendency is mitigated some by the fact that people also tend to adopt closer distances with age peers than with those who are younger or older (Burgoon, Buller, and Woodall 1989). So people's interpretations of distance and closeness will depend not only on their cultural identity but also on their sex and age and on the sex and age of the person they're conversing with.

In addition, space has different meanings in different cultures. For example, a Chinese American student reported that her Chinese grandfather

A second glance at this picture suggests that these public displays of affection are part of a staged experiment. What elements of nonverbal communication can you identify to support this conclusion? What elements might refute it?

> commands his presence with silence, limited facial expressions and lots of space between himself and others. I have never thought of jumping into his lap like Ol' St. Nick or even felt comfortable talking to him at any great length. When I do scrounge up the courage to speak to him, it is almost always to greet him or ask him to come to dinner. The speech used would have to be laden with respectful words. (Lam 1996)

As you can see, space can indicate respect. However, in other cultures too much space between you and others can be interpreted as you not liking the other person. Most Latinos in the United States, for instance, use closer personal distances than most Anglo Americans. One researcher says that in Latino culture the body is public, which means that one's personal bubble is very small and that close contact and touch are not regarded as trespassing into an individual's territory (Lozano 2000). In the United States when you come too close to a person and inadvertently touch him or her, you will probably say, "Excuse me" or "I'm sorry." In Mexico, inadvertently touching a stranger on the arm or shoulder is not necessarily accompanied by an excuse because it is not regarded as an insult. However, even in cultures that are characterized by close personal distances, there is a fine line between touching inadvertently and sexual harassment. In Mexico City, for instance, there are separate subway compartments for men and women during rush hour, which are designed to reduce the number of complaints by women about men touching them inappropriately.

Haptics

Haptics is the study of the communicative use of touch. As the example from Mexico suggests, touch can be the most direct way that humans establish the contacts that define our identity. "It is well documented that touch is essential to the physical, emotional, and psychological well-being of human infants and to their intellectual, social, and communication development" (Burgoon, Buller, and Woodall 1989, 75). Two communication researchers named Stan Jones and Elaine Yarbrough (1985) found that people in the United States touch to indicate positive feelings, to play, to control, as part of a greeting or departure ritual, to help accomplish a task, to combine greeting or departure with affection, and accidentally. In their studies, control touches—touches that were primarily interpreted to mean a request for compliance or attention getting—occurred most frequently. A "spot touch with the hand" to a "nonvulnerable body part"—hands, arms, shoulders, or upper back—frequently accompanies and emphasizes statements like "Move over," "Hurry up," "Stay here," "Be serious," and "Do it." A similar touch reinforces messages like "Listen to this, " "Look at that," and "I want your attention." These touches are almost always accompanied by verbalization, and both genders initiate these touches with almost equal frequency.

"Positive affect touches" were the second most frequent kind Jones and Yarbrough observed. The highest number of these touches were expressions of affection. As you would expect, these occur predominantly in close relationships and include hugs, kisses, and often contacts with "vulnerable body parts"—head, neck, torso, lower back, buttocks, legs, or feet. But affection can also be communicated by touch in some business settings. Long-term work teams sometimes engage in spontaneous brief touches among team members that are interpreted as positive and supportive. On the other hand, as we note in Chapter Ten, sexual harassment in the workplace often consists in part of inappropriate or manipulative positive affect touching.

One of the most interesting types of touches Jones and Yarbrough identified were what they call "playful affection" and "playful aggression" touches. These communicate a double message, something like "I like/love you and I'm not serious" or "I want to hurt you but not really." They are often quasi-sexual. For example, playful affection was communicated when a woman said to her partner, "Hello, sweetheart" while grabbing his nose. Most instances of playful affection that Jones and Yarbrough observed were cross-sex, though the authors report an example where "a male puts his arm around the shoulders of his close

---

'But . . .' A Student Responds

What is the difference between nonverbal communication and American Sign Language? Is ASL only one form of nonverbal communication? And how do ASL speakers use gestures to express grammar? I am confused.

American Sign Language is a non-oral language learned by many deaf persons and taught alongside Spanish, German, and French.

Remember the chart at the beginning of Chapter Seven? American Sign Language, commonly abbreviated as ASL, is a specific type of verbal, primarily non-oral communication. ASL is verbal because it is a language that has its own words, phrases, and grammatical rules. But it relies on sight rather than hearing or speech, because its users are typically Deaf. This is the sense that it is non-oral. On the other hand, as you learn ASL, you will discover how this language also integrates such "nonverbal" elements as tone of voice. The signing person's facial expression and the ways he or she makes the signs indicate emphasis, volume, and emotional tone like excitement or sadness. So like every other complete language, ASL has verbal and nonverbal elements—even though it is non-oral.

male friend and roommate who is finishing the dishes and in the presence of several other people in the kitchen says, "You would make a good wife" (1985, 40). Playful aggression involved "mock strangling, mock wrestling, a 'pulled' punch, pinching, grabbing, tickling, pushing, slapping, and standing on another's toes" (1985, 40–41). These touches occur frequently in relationships that are not close as well as in those that are and include a large proportion of male-male touches. Research like Jones and Yarbrough's is important because it helps us comprehend a poorly understood and sometimes even feared aspect of our communicating. As Mark Knapp points out:

> Some people grow up learning "not to touch" a multitude of animate and inanimate objects; they are told not to touch their own body and later not to touch the body of their dating partner; care is taken so children do not see their parents "touch" one another intimately; some parents demonstrate a noncontact norm through the use of twin beds; touching is associated with admonitions of "not nice" or "bad" and is punished accordingly—and frequent touching between father and son is thought to be something less than masculine. (Knapp 1980, 108–109)

We know that touch is an enormously powerful kind of nonverbal communication; a very small amount of it can say a great deal. We can harness this power by becoming aware of how touch affects where our communication is on the impersonal⟷interpersonal scale.

Voice

Sometimes people overlook the fact that spoken language includes many different nonverbal vocal elements. The technical term for these cues is *paralinguistics,* and they include rate of speech, pitch variation, volume, and vocal quality. If you think about your perceptions of someone who speaks really rapidly or v-e-r-r-r-y s-l-o-o-o-w-l-y, you have a sense of how rate affects communicating. Listeners and conversation partners also make inferences about how monotone or melodic speech is, how softly or loudly someone talks, and whether a speaker's vocal quality is resonant, squeaky, nasal, or breathy. Sometimes people manipulate these four dimensions of their voice (rate, pitch, volume, and quality) to assist listeners in interpreting what they're saying, whether they're giving emphasis to various words or phrases, expressing feelings, or indicating when they're serious and when they're sarcastic or joking. In other cases speakers don't mean to manipulate any of the four; they're "just talking normally" when people hear them as too fast, too soft, monotone, or too loud.

As these examples suggest, one of the ways people interpret another's vocal cues is to make stereotyped judgments about the speaker's personality. It's not a good idea, but we do it nonetheless. For example, a male with a breathy voice is likely to be stereotyped as gay, or at least young and artistic, whereas a female with the same vocal quality is usually thought of as "more feminine, prettier, more petite, more effervescent, more high-strung, and shallower" (Addington 1968). Nasal voices are heard as undesirable for both males and females, and low, deep voices are perceived as being more sophisticated, appealing, and sexy than higher-pitched voices. We also use vocal cues to draw conclusions about the age, gender, and ethnicity of speakers we hear.

In addition, in high-contact cultures, speakers tend to use louder voices in public places like a crowded bus. If you don't know this, you might think of the people who speak so loud in public settings as rude.

Communication researcher and teacher Mark Knapp emphasizes the importance of vocal cues when he writes,

> You should be quick to challenge the cliché that vocal cues only concern how something is said—frequently they are what is said. What is said might be an attitude ("I like you" or "I'm superior to you"), it might be an emotion . . . or it might be the presentation of some aspect of your personality, background, or physical features. Vocal cues will, depending on the situation and the communicators, carry a great deal of information. (Knapp 1980, 361)

Vocal pitch changes and pauses work in some special ways to organize people's talk. If you're reading words on a page, you get a sense of the text's organization from the way it's divided into sentences, paragraphs, and pages. But conversation is not organized this way. The basic unit of conversation is not the sentence or paragraph but the *utterance* or *turn*. An utterance is roughly one stream of talk spoken by one speaker, such as "Uh huh" or "You can go ahead and call her, but I'm telling you she's not gonna want to talk to you." The phrase "Well, I think . . ." interrupted by another speaker is the first speaker's turn even though the utterance wasn't finished.

Researchers who analyze everyday talk have found that it's very useful to treat conversations in terms of utterances or turns, and that brief pauses help define both turns and the meaning of any given turn. Think about the following utterance: "If we're going to party this weekend, we've got to do some work on Thursday and Friday." This statement is usually made in two parts: (1) If we're going to party this weekend, (2) we've got to do some work on Thursday or Friday. The speaker inserts a brief, almost indistinguishable pause in the middle, and the resulting rhythm helps clarify what the speaker is saying. By moving these pauses around, and changing the pitch and volume for certain words, the meaning of the utterance is likely to change. For example, vocally stressing Thursday and Friday might suggest that the speaker doesn't usually work on these days but will to compensate for partying on the weekend. Or it might mean that the activity of "partying" is preferred and more of a time commitment than "relaxing" and "spending time with friends." Or the speaker might even mean that "we won't work *too* much—just Thursday and Friday."

This simple example illustrates how everyday conversation is produced in "chunks" that are determined not just by verbal (i.e., semantic or grammatical) features but also by the nonverbal ones—rhythm, loudness, and pitch. Researchers call these chunks *phonemic clauses* (Boomer 1986). The production of phonemic clauses is important for both speakers and listeners. Speakers can subtly or indirectly alter what they say by changing phonemic clause units like the above example illustrates, or the more familiar "Don't!" "Stop!" versus "Don't stop!" The presence and prevalence of phonemic clauses is one piece of evidence that, as we experience it, spoken language or conversation consists of a subtle and complex combination of verbal and nonverbal messages.

Silence

An Italian author writes:

> With silence we express the most varied and conflicting states, sentiments, thoughts and desires. Silence is meaningful. There is the silence of fear and terror, of wonder and stupor, of pain and joy. . . . "Dumb silence" is a contradictory expression. Instead of describing the same thing, the two terms exclude each other; silence is not dumb and whatever is dumb is not silent. Silence is a form of communication . . . dumbness, on the other hand, isolates and excludes us from all communication. (Sciacca 1963, 129)

The same writer says that "a discourse without pauses [is] incomprehensible. Silence is not an interval . . . but the bridge that unites sounds" (Sciacca 1963, 26). In other words, silence is significant because of the way it relates to speaking. Examples include the failure or refusal to respond to a question and the "pregnant pause." Even the silence of the forest, prairie, mountain, lake, or bayou is most meaningful because of the way it contrasts with the noises of city crowds.

Silence is one of the least understood nonverbal behaviors, partly because people use and interpret it in so many different ways. Silence can be interpreted to mean apathy, patience, boredom, fear, sadness, love, intimacy, anger, or intimidation. We have talked with married couples who use silence as a weapon. One husband who knew his wife hated it when he didn't talk out a problem would sometimes refuse to talk to her for two or three days. His wife said she found this "devastating." When there are prolonged silences in group meetings, people start shifting nervously and making inferences like "Nobody is interested," "People don't like this group," and "Nobody really cares what we're doing."

But silence also works in positive ways. Beginning teachers, for example, have to learn that the silence that sometimes comes after they ask their students a question can be very fruitful. A group's silence can mean that there's considerable thinking going on. Two close friends may also say nothing to each other just so they can share the experience of the moment. Or in an interview, silence can be a welcome opportunity for the interviewee to elaborate, return to a topic discussed earlier, or simply reorganize her or his thoughts. A friend of ours also reported that the long silences he and his mother shared during the last two days of her life were some of the richest times they had spent together. Love, warmth, and sympathy are sometimes best expressed through silent facial and body movements and touch.

The use of silence is also very culture specific. In some Western cultures, like the United States, silence is often regarded as a sign of conversational failure. You have probably experienced conversations where the silence almost hurt and you tried to make up something to keep the conversation going. In most Asian cultures and Native American cultures as well as in Finland, silence is regarded as an important part of the conversation and as a sign of maturity and reflection. For instance, communication researcher Donal Carbaugh (Carbaugh and Poutiainen 2000) was surprised at the high amount of silence used even in initial interactions in Finland. People would introduce each other and then just stand there in silence for one or two minutes before asking another question. Small talk and asking too many questions are regarded as a sign of superficiality and intrusion into the private space of another individual. How might you feel if you met someone new only to stand or sit in silence for more than 30 seconds? Unless you are familiar with one of these cultures, you would probably hurry to ask another question or make a comment about the weather to keep the conversation going and not to feel awkward.

One team of researchers distinguished among three kinds of silence that occur in conversations: the *lapse*, the *gap*, and the *pause* (Sacks, Schegloff, and Jefferson 1978). A *lapse* is a silence created when one speaker decides not to continue and nobody else in the conversation is willing or able to take the speaker's place. In many cultures, lapses can often be uncomfortable. A *gap* is a silence created when one speaker finishes and it's clear who the next speaker will be, but that person has not yet started. If it extends too long, a gap can begin to feel like a lapse. A *pause* is a silence built into someone's conversational turn. The example we gave in the previous section about partying and working illustrates the significance of pauses. It's important to remember that verbal messages would be a jumble of sounds without short silences, and that language is a combination of talk and quiet.

Now that you know more about nonverbal codes, such as kinesics, proxemics, haptics, eye contact, voice, and silence, let's talk about a final nonverbal code that you might not necessarily connect to nonverbal communication. This final code is called chronemics.

Chronemics

Chronemics is the study of the communicative use of *time*. Time affects many aspects of our lives and influences how we communicate with each other. It may surprise you, but there are many kinds of time. Sometimes we tend to think of minutes, hours, and seconds as time that is "just there." Then, we have to remind ourselves that it is not just there but that we as human beings have invented the time we know today to make our societies function. For example, we have created distinctions among biological, institutional, and cultural time.

Biological time means the division between day and night, the division between ebb and flow, and the changing of the seasons. These processes influence humans and what we do. For instance, when it is day, we usually busy ourselves with some kind of task. When it gets dark, we get tired and sleep, unless we have to work a night shift. Human bodies have a biological clock that tells us when to eat and sleep, which are two of the most important needs for humans. You can especially feel how biological time influences your biorhythm when you are jet-lagged. Your body is used to being awake and sleeping at a certain time, and unless you reprogram your body with sleeping medication, it may take one day for each hour of time difference to adjust to the new time.

In addition to biological time, people also experience *institutional* time. This is made up of the times of day and night, day and period names, and time blocks that people have invented to make their societies function. Most urban cultures can function only when paying attention to this institutionalized time. There is a clock in almost every classroom because education operates in a rather rigid time frame. Students—and teachers—can be penalized if they are late for class. You probably plan your day according to what you have to do at certain hours, and you probably don't like it when someone is half an hour late. There are schedules for buses, subways, planes, and trains, and people get nervous when these schedules are not met. However, in more agrarian societies, the clock is not as important. In these societies, daylight dictates what to do: when to work in the fields, feed the cattle, or milk the cows.

Finally, there are important differences in how different cultures *value* time. The major difference is between monochronic and polychronic cultures (Hall 1976). Cultures with polychronic perspectives toward time value relationships over time, are usually more present and past oriented, and allow for multiple things ("poly") to be done at once. Clock time is less important than the biological time it takes to complete an activity. In this perspective, it would be rude and inappropriate to cut off a conversation in the middle because one has to catch a bus or go to another meeting. Monochronic cultures have a more limited and rigid sense of time.

Saskia experienced a polychronic perspective when traveling from San Francisco to Quito, Ecuador. The plane departed three hours late from San Francisco. Almost all the passengers were Latin and South Americans, and showed no sign of impatience. The flight attendants distributed hot coffee and muffins, and everyone was chatting together happily. Only Saskia paced up and down and asked when the plane would finally leave. When it was time to depart, Saskia got a special greeting from the flight deck that went like this: "We greet our German passenger on board and apologize for the delay." What does this indicate about the crew's perception of "Germans"? Traditionally, German trains and planes are supposed to be on time by the minute, and many people think of Germans as almost religiously punctual. However, the story is not finished. The flight to Ecuador was supposed to take eight hours, but it took 12. Why? Because the crew decided to make a four-hour stop in Costa Rica, where all the passengers had the opportunity to take a city tour and enjoy lunch at a fine hotel. It was again a time of bonding among the passengers, and Saskia finally was able to adapt. The two additional landings in Nicaragua and El Salvador didn't matter that much anymore. One passenger even told Saskia that until 10 years ago the Ecuadorian crew would ask the passengers during the flight whether someone needed to land in Panama and would do so if necessary.

The United States tends to be a monochronic culture where compliance with schedules and planning for the future are important. This does not mean that every person in the United States adopts this monochronic perspective. However, work organizations, transportation, and schools enforce compliance with this perspective. As a result, when you work within this system, you are better off to think monochronically.

What Are Functions of Nonverbal Cues?

So far we've devoted the lion's share of this chapter to a discussion of "the big six," those sets of nonverbal cues that most influence where your communication will be on the impersonal ←——→ interpersonal scale. We want to finish the chapter with an explanation of the three main ways nonverbal cues generally work: to express emotions, to express cultural identity, and to define relationships.

Express Emotions

It is probably obvious to you that such emotions as anger, sadness, pity, envy, passion, and pain are hardly ever communicated primarily by words. Instead, people behave or act angrily, sadly, or passionately, and we "read" these emotions in others' facial expressions, posture and gestures, tones of voice, and silence. Since we've already discussed how various cues communicate emotions, we won't repeat ourselves here. Remember that, among the cues we've discussed, facial expression and voice are the primary channels for expressing emotion, and that posture and touch play lesser, but still important, roles.

Express Cultural Identity

There are dozens of stereotypes about how Latinos, Japanese, African Americans, lesbians, and even New Yorkers supposedly communicate. These stereotypes are obviously dangerous because they overlook variations within large groups, they often exaggerate minor differences, and they frequently reflect prejudice and ignorance. No single cue or set of cues can or should be relied on to categorize an individual into a specific culture.

At the same time, each of us grows up in one or more identifiable cultures, and each culture is distinguished from others primarily by the ways people in the culture communicate. It is important to realize that nonverbal cues do function to help to express cultural identity *and* you have to be careful not to stereotype dress, gestures, forms of touch, tones of voice, or facial expressions. Earlier in the chapter we talked about this function of nonverbal cues. Here we'll offer a couple of additional examples from the research on this function of nonverbal cues and then encourage you to develop your understanding further by discussing this function with your classmates.

E. T. Hall (1966) points out that people regulate intimacy through the use of interpersonal space. Cultures in which the people prefer close interpersonal spaces and frequent touch are called *high-contact cultures*. Those where people prefer to have more space in between them and do not touch frequently are called *low-contact cultures*. There are individual differences in both, and there are people who like to touch and be close to others although they've been socialized in a low-contact culture and vice versa. But this distinction can help you understand how nonverbal space, eye contact, and touch define cultural identity differently for someone socialized in an Arab or Polynesian culture.

With regard to eye contact, members of low-contact cultures (for example, Japan and China) tend to avoid eye contact when speaking and listening. Members of moderate-contact cultures like Australia tend to engage in more eye contact than low-contact cultures. And members of many high-contact cultures in the Mediterranean engage in even more eye contact. Specifically, Hall (1963) found that Greeks,

South Americans, and many people from the Arab world (high contact) emphasize intense eye contact as evidence of sincerity and interest, whereas many Asians and Native Americans are taught not to make direct eye contact when talking with someone who is older or higher in status (low contact). Members of high-contact cultures also tend to speak more loudly than members of low-contact cultures (Hall 1959). You might remember situations when you were in a public place with your parents and you started to scream or to laugh loudly, and one of your parents looked at you in embarrassment and told you to keep quiet. People from Northern Europe and in the United States also tend to keep their voices low in buses, trains, or planes. In contrast, if you take a bus in a city in Latin America or South America, you will realize the difference in the noise level. People engage with each other in animated conversation. Finally, although touching in public places occurs much more frequently in Mediterranean and South American cultures than in the United States or in Germany, remember that touching is very gender specific. In many Muslim societies, men and women do not generally hug, hold hands, or kiss in public. But same-sex touching, like holding hands or putting one's arm over the shoulder of a friend, is very common. The opposite is true for central and northern Europeans as well as Anglo Americans.

There are also some differences in how men and women express emotions and present themselves in terms of posture. In many Western cultures, men have been observed to use different postures from women—less direct body orientation and more backward lean compared to women's vis-à-vis posture with more forward lean. Women have been found to be generally more expressive facially than men; they smile more and often engage in more positive head-nodding. One researcher found that when men are around other men and they look at something cute, such as a baby, they suppress smiling. In contrast, when they are alone or with women, they do smile. In other words, the presence of same-sex people affected how males expressed their gender identity (Pothier 1999).

Recall and Application

Ethnic/Cultural Identity and Nonverbal Cues

Survey some persons who are culturally different from you to identify which nonverbal cues function to help define their cultural identity. Choose three persons from your class, or from among your other acquaintances, whose race, ethnicity, age, religion, economic class, sexual orientation, or disability is different from yours. At least one of the three should also be of a different gender. Interview each of these persons for five to 15 minutes. Use the interviews to identify how they, and others in their group, use nonverbal cues to establish their identity as members of their group. Be prepared to give them the same kind of information about you and your group identities.

Define Relationships

A third primary function of nonverbal cues is to define relationships. Think for a minute about some of your own relationships at school or work. At work, when you have a meeting for the first time with a new group of people, how do you tell who the leader is? If you're not told, you probably use such nonverbal cues as dress, the kinds of materials the person is carrying, tone of voice, or where he or she sits or stands. Students also usually get a pretty good idea of what kind of relationship they'll have with their teacher by observing such things as the facial expression, eye contact, and tone of voice he or she displays when talking with them; whether the teacher avoids them or goes out of the way to converse with them; and how the teacher's office is arranged or decorated. What is a person saying about your relationship, for example, if the office is arranged in such a way that a desk is always kept between the two of you? Similarly, how do you determine that someone is a close personal friend of yours? It's hardly ever because the person says the words, "I am your close personal friend." You pay more attention to how closely the two of you sit or stand together, tone of voice, eye contact, and touch.

Many nonverbal cues say, in effect, "This is what I think of myself," "This is how I perceive you," and "This is what I think you think of me." For example, when talking with little children, adults often use a smile and a gentle, singsong tone of voice to say something like "Bring your boots right over here by the door so you can get them when you go out-

How would you define the relationship between the two people in this picture? What nonverbal cues help you develop your definition? How might you put words to their interaction?

side again." The nonverbal parts of this utterance indirectly say, "I see myself as older, smarter, and more experienced than you" (This is what I think of myself in this relationship), "I see you as my follower" (This is what I think of you), and "I believe you see me as your superior or leader, too" (This is what I think you think of me). All three of these messages are implicit in the tone of voice, posture, and facial expression. And even though a person may not be consciously aware of these relational messages, they are nonverbally pretty obvious. If you doubt this, try talking to your boss or your teacher with the same melodic tone of voice, posture, and smile you'd use with a 6-year-old. Not only will you feel foolish, but the adult will believe you're either joking with or insulting them. Why? Because the relationship your nonverbal cues define is not the relationship they believe exists between the two of you.

This same function of nonverbal cues also surfaces in elevator communication. Notice how in North American cultures the first four people on the elevator usually stand in the corners, and then the fifth one stands right in the middle, just like the dots on the "5" side of dice. In addition, everybody intently watches the numbers over the door. People know that there is virtually no information in these numbers—they're going to go up or down in increments of one, and that's the only option. Yet we watch them. Why? Because the space we're forced into on the elevator defines the relationship among us as "close friends," but that's usually not true, so we avoid eye contact in order to redefine the relationship accurately.

'But . . .' A Student Responds

If nonverbal messages are important when expressing emotion and communicating relational messages, such as intimacy, then are women better at using and reading nonverbal messages than men?

Generally, yes. In the United States, female children still tend to be socialized into roles that emphasize nurturance and support. Male children tend to be socialized into roles that emphasize task accomplishment, problem solving, and proactivity. In order to perform typically female roles effectively, girls and women need to learn to read and respond to nonverbal cues. Many men can get by without developing those skills. Of course, there are many exceptions to this general rule, and this pattern clearly does not hold in all cultures. But if you're asking your question from the perspective of membership in a majority U.S. culture, the general answer is yes, women are better at using and reading nonverbal messages than men.

Chapter Summary

You can do the most to manage your nonverbal communicating by learning about the six kinds of nonverbal cues we have discussed in this chapter and by remembering the four main ways that nonverbal cues function. It is important to remember that, if you want to move your communicating along the impersonal⟷interpersonal continuum, you will need to pay attention to cultural and personal identity negotiations, and these centrally involve nonverbal cues. People communicating interpersonally experience a fairly high level of trust, and trust can be undercut by scowls, shouting, and threatening gestures. Interpersonal communication requires contact between unique persons, and this kind of contact does not happen in many cultures without considerable eye contact. A sarcastic or superior tone of voice will discourage interpersonal connection. And so on. Use what you've

---

In Other Words

By now you should have a pretty good understanding about the characteristics and functions of nonverbal cues. We want you to think a little bit more about one specific nonverbal cue and how its meaning can differ in different cultures. The nonverbal cue is space. Remember our discussion about proximity and personal, social, and public distance? Space is one important nonverbal cue that people use consciously or unconsciously all the time. The examples in the text will tell you more about what space means for Anglo-Americans and people with a Latin American background who live in the United States. It will also give you a better understanding about some characteristics of interpersonal communication that might not be that familiar to you, such as street flirting. After reading the text, you should be able to respond to the following questions:

1. What are the meanings of public space for people with a Latin American cultural background?

2. What are the meanings for Anglo Americans?

3. What is your comfort zone with social and public distances?

4. Do you have examples for the use of space from other cultural groups?

5. Do you ever flirt in public? If so, does flirting influence how you use space?

* * *

The Cultural Experience of Space and Body: A Reading of Latin American and Anglo American Comportment in Public

Elizabeth Lozano

The U.S. Public Space

It is 6:00 p.m. The Bayfront, a shopping mall near the Miami marina, reverberates with the noise and movement of people coming and going, contemplating the lights of the bay, sampling exotic juice blends, savoring the not-so-exotic foods from Cuba, Nicaragua, or Mexico, and listening to the bands that here and there intone rock songs, blues, ballads, and, once in a while, something with a Hispanic flavor—"La Bamba," most likely, or "Guantanamera." The Bayfront is at once an outdoor and indoor space. It is a mall of homogenous halls, predictable stores, and casual window-shopping. It extends into a plaza that faces the sea and sky and invites one to contemplate the spectacle of people, sunsets, and boats.

The Bayfront provides an environment for the exercise of two different rituals: the Anglo American visit to the mall and the Latin American *paseo*, the visit to the outdoor spaces of the city—the plaza, the streets of the barrio, and the open cafes. The Bayfront is simultaneously a place for window shoppers and a place to see and be seen, where display and consumption include the display of oneself and the consumption of others. It is a place where one goes if one wants the company of Latinos and the sight of others.

Some of the people sitting in the plaza look insistently at me, making comments, laughing, whispering. Instead of feeling uneasy or surprised, I find myself looking back at them, entering this inquisitive game and asking myself some of the same questions they might be asking. Who are they, where are they from, what are they up to? I follow their gaze and I see it extend to other groups, the couples holding hands and kissing, the young women who have started dancing to the band, the children playing on the stairs. The gaze is returned by some in the crowd, so that a play of silent dialogue seems to grow amidst the anonymity of the crowd.

The crowd that participates in this complicity of wandering looks is not Anglo American. English is the language spoken; Anglo American, the architecture, the bands, the dress code, and the social rules. But the play of looks described above has a different "accent," a Hispanic accent, which reveals a different understanding of the plaza and its public space.

The Bicultural Dialogue

The Miami Bayfront is a place in which two cultural styles of body expressivity can be seen enacted simultaneously, interacting and overlapping. Although the Hispanic passers-by are strangers to one another, there is a sense of interaction among them. If I were to be addressed by anyone in this crowd, I would not be surprised, nor would I feel threatened. It would be no different from being addressed by someone in a crowded room. When I am walking by myself along the halls of a "Hispanic" mall, I am not *alone*. I do not expect, therefore, to be treated by others as if they were suddenly confronting me in a dark alley. I am in a crowd, with the crowd, and anyone there has access to my attention.

The Anglo American passers-by understand their vital space, their relationship with strangers, and their public interaction in a different manner. If I address them in the street, I better assume that I am confronting them in an alley. Pragmatically speaking, Anglo Americans are alone (even in the middle of the crowd) if they choose to be, for they have a guaranteed cultural right to be "left alone" on their private way to and from anywhere.

To approach or touch someone without that person's consent is a violation of a fundamental right within the Anglo-Saxon, Protestant cultural tradition. This is the right to one's own body as private property. Within this tradition, touching is understood as an excursion into someone else's territory. It requires, as such, an explicit permission to "trespass" the spatial barriers that protect the perimeter of that physical property. The American remains in a private niche, the personal bubble, even when being in a public space.

It is understandable that, to the surprise of the Latin American newcomer, Anglo Americans excuse themselves not only when they accidentally touch someone, but even when there is the imminence of a touch. To accidentally penetrate someone else's boundary (especially if that person is a stranger) demands an apology and a willingness to repair the damage—by stepping back from the violated territory. This supposes an allegiance to the fundamental principles that the law dictates and protects (i.e., private property, autonomy, equality), as well as acceptance of the law as a universal mediator that guarantees the exercise of basic social rights. To excuse oneself, therefore, is to assure the other person that one recognizes and believes in the law and that no harm is intended.[1]

One can see how rude a Latin American might appear to an Anglo American when the former distractingly touches another person without apologizing or showing concern. Within the Latino and Mediterranean traditions (which are predominantly Catholic), the body is not understood as property. There is no formal distance between self and body, so that it is not possible to say "*I* own my body," as if it were something "I" have acquired somewhere. That is, the body is not understood as *belonging* to its owner. It does not belong to me or anyone else; it is, in principle, *public*. It is an expressive and sensual region open to the scrutiny, discipline, and sanction of the community; not to be regulated by universal law as property, but by the contextual rules of interaction.

It is, therefore, quite impossible to be "left alone" on the Latin American street. As long as one is there, one is a visible and accessible cipher, an enigma subject to interrogation. This implies that it is not possible to be neutral in the public space; it is sensually and erotically charged, a territory of mutual flirting and *seducción* that is expressed bodily in the ways of walking, moving, looking, smiling and—in the case of men—direct interpellation.[2]

In the United States, street flirting is understood basically as a form of harassment. In Latin America, street flirting has more ambiguous significations. Public forms of flirting (such as the *piropo*) are not only socially sanctioned but also welcomed—and expected—as expressions of a man's gallantry or *caballerosidad* regarding a woman's appeal or charm.[3] Piropos are *frases galantes*, courtly phrases that are meant to be celebrating, flattering, and appreciative of a woman's "graces." Piropos range from exclamations such as "adiós mamita," (hi/bye, mama), "*qué buena que está*" (how good/delicious you look), or "*adiós cuñado*" (hi/bye, brother-in-law, said to the man who accompanies a woman), to statements such as "*si cocina como camina, me como hasta el pegado*" (if you cook like you walk, I'll eat the left-overs), "*bendita la madre que la trajo al mundo*" (blessed be the mother who brought you to the world), or "*benditos los ojos que la ven*" (blessed be the eyes that can see you). But the distance between flattery and abuse grows very thin when a piropo progresses from "gallant" salutation to an appraisal of beauty to an explicit comment about somebody's anatomy. It may be that the only one flattered by the flattery is the one who volunteers it. Street flirting in Latin America can be play or provocation, cordiality or aggression, salutation or harassment.

While interrogating and examining others within the Latino public space are not gender-exclusive privileges (i.e., both men and women participate), such activity is, nonetheless, *gendered*. That is, the forms of such public interpellation are defined along gender lines, their direct and most explicit forms being the male prerogative. Although women might use *piropos* with men, men will "celebrate" women in the street, regardless of the latter's acknowledgement or approval. Both the Latin American and the Anglo American public spaces demand different attitudes by men and women—although this is more openly and clearly the case in Latin America.

Civility and Politeness

The U.S. public space is a homogeneous territory in which there is little ambiguity and options are clear and well-articulated. The struggle for non-ambiguity can be seen in the very architectural logic of the mall, a space in which everything is clearly identified, named, and defined in terms of purpose and function. It can also be seen in the logic of the fast-food purchase. When buying a hamburger at McDonald's, one knows precisely how the food is going to taste, how much it is going to cost, how long it is going to take before the order is ready, and how many options are offered. Every number corresponds to a different option, every name to a mass-produced, identical item. The space has been designed so that no time or energy is wasted, and no extra gestures, conversation, or interactions are required.

Walking the street in the United States is very much an anonymous activity to be performed in a field of unobstructive and invisible bodies. Since one is essentially carrying one's own space into the public sphere, no one is actually ever *in public*, exposed to the simultaneous and pervasive accessibility of others—unless that is one's specific function, as in the case of a public performer. Given that the public is private, no intimacy is granted in the public space, for its compartmentalization prevents any contact that lacks a specific and sanctioned function. Thus, while the Latin American public look is round, inquisitive, and wandering, the Anglo American is straight, non-obstructive, and neutral.

For Latin Americans, the access to others in a public space is not restricted by the "privacy" of their bodies. Thus, the Latin American does not find casual contact a form of property trespassing or a violation of rights. Civility requires the Anglo American to restrict looks, de-limit gestures, and orient movement; civility requires the Latin American to acknowledge looks, gestures, and movement and actively engage with them. For example, the Anglo American will respect the sorrow of another by remaining distant. He or she will likely intervene only if the other explicitly asks for help or consolation. On the other hand, the Latin American will approach the sorrowed one and offer consolation, even if it is not requested. For the Latin American, the unavoidable nature of a shared space is always a demand for attention and a request to participate.

An Anglo American considers "mind your own business" to be fair and civil. A Latin American might find this an ungranted restriction. What takes place in the public space is everybody's business by the very fact that it is taking place *in public*.

One can understand, in light of the above, the possible cultural misunderstandings between Anglo Americans and Latin Americans. If Anglo Americans protest the "impertinence" of Latin Americans as nosy and curious, Latin Americans protest the indifference and lack of concern of Anglo Americans. Anglo Americans would defend their privacy above all, and Latin Americans would take for granted their right to access in a communal space.

Endnotes

1. A gender difference still pervades what is supposed to be a gender-blind right to privacy. Although nobody has access to a man's or a woman's body without their consent in the Anglo American tradition, women find this right often violated in subtle (and not so subtle) ways. In spite of an equal right to privacy, the culture still assigns a higher value to the respect of "his" right. "No trespassing" penalties are much higher for the violation of a man's territory. Historically speaking, "her" rights are not as clearly defined or socially grounded as are "his."

2. I am using the Spanish word, *seducción,* instead of its English translation, *seduction;* although they might appear to mean the same thing, they have very different implications. Indeed, the meaning here is closer to the French *seduisant* than to the English *seduction.* It does not imply a malicious abuse of an innocent, but a mix of personal attractiveness, sensuous appeal, and coquettish behavior.

3. This does not mean, though, that women like *piropos,* but that it is very gentlemanly to speak in courteous and embellishing ways to women. Most forms of gallantry and deference to women are well accepted and indeed expected from men.

＊ ＊ ＊

Excerpted from Elizabeth Lozano, "The Cultural Experience of Space and Body: A Reading of Latin American and Anglo American Comportment in Public." In A. Gonzalez, M. Houston, and V. Chen (eds.), *Our Voices: Essays in Culture, Ethnicity, and Communication,* Fourth Edition. Copyright © 2004 by Roxbury Publishing. All rights reserved.

learned in this chapter to adapt to the intercultural situations you experience and to encourage the quality of contact you prefer.

References

Addington, D. W. 1968. "The Relationship of Selected Vocal Characteristics to Personality Perception." *Speech Monographs,* 35: 492–503.

Andersen, J., Andersen, P., and Landgraf, J. 1985. "The Development of Nonverbal Communication Competence in Childhood." Paper presented at the annual meeting of the International Communication Association, Honolulu, HI.

Argyle, M., and Cook, M. 1976. *Gaze and Mutual Gaze.* Cambridge: Cambridge University Press.

Bavelas, J. B., Black, A., Chovil, N., and Mullet, J. 1990. "Truths, Lies, and Equivocation." In J. B. Bavelas, A. Black, N. Chovil, and J. Mullet (series eds.), *Sage Series in Interpersonal Communication,* Volume 11: *Equivocal Communication.* Newbury Park, CA: Sage. Pages 170–207.

Boomer, D. S. 1986. "The Phonemic Clause: Speech Unit in Human Communication." In A. W. Siegman and S. Felstein (eds.), *Nonverbal Behavior and Communication.* Hillsdale, NJ: Lawrence Erlbaum. Pages 245–262.

Burgoon, J. K. 1994. "Nonverbal Signals." In M. L. Knapp and G. R. Miller (eds.), *Handbook of Interpersonal Communication.* 2nd ed. Thousand Oaks, CA: Sage. Pages 229–285.

Burgoon, J. K., Buller, D. B., and Woodall, W. G. 1989. *Nonverbal Communication: The Unspoken Dialogue.* New York: Harper & Row.

Burgoon, J. K., Manusov, V., Mineo, P., and Hale, J. L. 1985. "Effects of Eye Gaze on Hiring Credibility, Attraction, and Relational Message Interpretation." *Journal of Nonverbal Behavior,* 9: 133–146.

Carbaugh, D., and Poutiainen, S. 2000. "By Way of Introduction: An American and Finnish Dialogue." In M. W. Lustig and J. Koester (eds.), *Among Us: Essays on Identity, Belonging, and Intercultural Competence* New York: Longman. Pages 203–212.

Carrol, L., and Gilroy, P. J. 2002. "Role of Appearance and Nonverbal Behaviors in the Perception of Sexual Orientation Among Lesbians and Gay Men." *Psychological Reports,* 91: 115–122.

Chen, G. M., and Starosta, W. J. 1998. *Foundations of Intercultural Communication.* Boston: Allyn & Bacon.

Clore, G. L., Wiggins, N. H., and Itkin, S. 1975. "Judging Attraction From Nonverbal Behavior: The Gain Phenomenon." *Journal of Consulting and Clinical Psychology,* 43: 491–497.

Ekman, P. 1972. "Universal and Cultural Differences in Facial Expression of Emotions." In J. K. Cole (ed.), *Nebraska Symposium on Motivation* (vol. 19). Lincoln: University of Nebraska Press. Pages 207–283.

Ekman, P., and Friesen, W. V. 1975. *Unmasking the Face.* Englewood Cliffs, NJ: Prentice-Hall.

Ekman, P., Friesen, W. V., and Ancoli, S. 1980. "Facial Signs of Emotional Experience." *Journal of Personality and Social Psychology,* 39: 1125–1134.

Erickson, F. 1979. "Talking Down: Some Cultural Sources of Miscommunication in Interracial Interviews." In A. Wolfgang (ed.), *Nonverbal Behavior: Applications and Cultural Implications.* New York: Academic Press. Pages 99–126.

Fitzpatrick, M. A. 1988. *Between Husbands and Wives.* Newbury Park, CA: Sage.

Hall, E. T. 1959. *The Silent Language.* Garden City, NY: Doubleday.

——. 1963. "A System for the Notation of Proxemic Behavior." *American Anthropologist,* 65: 1003–1026.

——. 1966. *The Hidden Dimension.* Garden City, NY: Doubleday.

——. 1976. *Beyond Culture.* Garden City, NY: Doubleday.

Hecht, M. L., De Vito, J. A., and Guerrero, L. K. 1999. "Perspectives on Nonverbal Communication: Codes, Functions, and Contexts." In L. K. Guerrero, H. A. De Vito, and M. L. Hecht (eds.), *The Nonverbal Communication Reader: Classic and Contemporary Readings.* 2nd ed. Prospect Heights, IL: Waveland. Pages 3–18.

Jones, S. E., and Yarbrough, A. E. 1985. "A Naturalistic Study of the Meanings of Touch." *Communication Monographs,* 52: 19–56.

Knapp, M. L. 1980. *Essentials of Nonverbal Communication.* New York: Holt.

Knapp, M. L., and Hall, J. A. 1992. *Nonverbal Communication in Human Interaction* (Third Ed.). Fort Worth, TX: Holt, Rinehart & Winston.

Lam, M. 1996. *Interpersonal Communication Journal*. Used with permission.

Lozano, E. 2000. "The Cultural Experience of Space and Body: A Reading of Latin American and Anglo American Comportment in Public." In A. Gonzalez, M. Houston, and V. Chen (eds.), *Our Voices: Essays in Culture, Ethnicity, and Communication*. 4th ed. Los Angeles, CA: Roxbury. Pages 274–280.

Mehrabian, A. 1981. *Silent Messages: Implicit Communication of Emotion and Attitudes* (Second Ed.). New York: Random House.

Miller, R. A. 1982. *Japan's Modern Myth: The Language and Beyond*. Tokyo: Weatherhill.

Pearson, J. C. 1989. *Communication in the Family*. New York: Harper & Row.

Pothier, D. 1999. "Who Can Resist Smiling at a Baby?" In L. K. Guerrero, H. A. De Vito, and M. L. Hecht (eds.), *The Nonverbal Communication Reader: Classic and Contemporary Readings*. 2nd ed. Prospect Heights, IL: Waveland. Pages 79–81.

Sacks, H., Schegloff, E. A., and Jefferson, G. 1978. "A Simplest Systematics for the Organization of Turn-Taking in Conversation." In J. Schenkein (ed.), *Studies in the Organization of Conversational Interaction*. New York: Academic Press. Pages 7–55.

Sciacca, M. F. 1963. *Come Si Vinci a Waterloo*. Milano: Marzorati.

Shotland, R. L., and Johnson, M. P. 1978. "Bystander Behavior and Kinesics: The Interaction Between the Helper and Victim." *Environmental Psychology and Nonverbal Behavior*, 2: 181–190.

Sussman, N. M., and Rosenfeld, H. M. 1982. "Influence of Culture, Language, and Sex on Conversational Distance." *Journal of Personality and Social Psychology*, 42: 66–74. ✦

Part III

Relating Together

Chapter Nine

Constructing Relational Systems: Friends, Partners, and Families

Chapter Objectives

After reading this chapter, you should be able to do the following:

- Define relationship and draw a basic model of one.
- Describe how relationships change over time in three different ways by using stage models, dialectical tensions and turning points, and a helical model.
- Describe three general types of relationships: friendship, romantic relationships, and family relationships.
- Identify the three motives for friendship.
- Describe the importance of six different types of love in understanding romantic partnerships.
- Describe three basic couple types in romantic relationships.
- Identify four dysfunctional extremes in family patterns of communication.

Chapter Preview

The word *Together* in this book's title is meant to focus attention on what occurs between people, and in most cases the relationship is exactly what is continually being collaboratively constructed there. Just as human beings are unique, reflective, addressable, unmeasurable, and responsive, relationships are best characterized by their uniqueness and unmeasurable qualities, and by the responses people make as they address one another in the daily active construction of their relationships. Virtually all the other aspects of communication we have discussed—nonverbal and verbal parts, listening, expressing, and so on—also culminate in relationships.

We begin this chapter by defining a relationship as a special kind of identity that links two individuals or the people in a group. Next we talk about three ways people understand and explain their relationships and make sense of how they change over time. The first uses a stage model, the second applies the dialectical tension idea introduced in Chapter Two, and the third combines these basic notions into a helical model of relationship change. Last, we focus on three of the most important kinds of relationships—friendships, romantic partners, and families. We show how communication is absolutely fundamental to all three, and that successful or effective communication differs from one kind of relationship to another. Our goals are to help develop your awareness of where your relationships are on the impersonal⟷interpersonal continuum and to help you move them along this continuum by increasing your communication flexibility and effectiveness.

What Is a Relationship?

Defining the term *relationship* is more difficult than you might think. Relationships are very fluid, just like people's selves. Who you are changes constantly, and because a relationship is based on the identities of you and at least one other person, the relationship undergoes just as much change. This can be a difficult idea to remember, because it's easier to think of a relationship as a "thing." Even the English language helps to make this a very static concept. People talk, for example, about *having* or *not having* a relationship, like it's a possession or an object. But relationships are best described not as things but as continuously changing systems. The title of this chapter mentions relational "systems" because systems are characterized not only by constant growth and development but also by coherent patterns. *Relationships are coherent patterns of communicating between people* (Baxter and Montgomery 1996). The patterns form a unique fabric so that no two are ever alike. In this way, relationships have their own "identities" just as much as your "self."

Communication teacher and researcher Bill Wilmot applies this basic idea when he describes a relationship as a "miniculture" with its own rules and customs (Wilmot 1995). Like the term *system*, his term *miniculture* suggests the richness of the communicating that goes on between people in a relationship. You could also say that a relationship is like an unfinished story. It certainly has a beginning, a plot with a supporting cast of characters that develops in the conversations of daily life, and, in some cases, you could even say that relationships end (B. A. Fisher 1987). But technically speaking, no relationship ever completely ceases to exist until the people who constructed it do. Anyone who has been through a divorce with children knows that although the marriage relationship ends, the mom and dad continue to share the parenting role throughout their lives, even if one or both parents neglect this role. This is also true after children are grown, and when families with divorced spouses gather for births, baptisms, graduations, and marriages of grandchildren. Even when two people do not have children, the relationship does not completely end when they stop seeing each other. Their memories of the relationship and the patterns developed in it continue to affect their interactions with other people. But as we mention when we talk about breakup in the next chapter, the important difference between an active relationship and one that exists only in memory is that two people contribute to the development of the relational "story" while it is ongoing, and only one person authors the narrative as it changes in memory.

The best way to begin to understand relationships as living entities (systems, minicultures, or stories) is to recognize that the substance of any relationship is the day-to-day communicating between its participants. Each time they communicate, relational partners construct and modify patterns that define who they are for and with each other. Another way to put this is to say that a couple's conversations don't just "build" or "modify" their relationship. The conversations *are* the relationship. The same is true of a superior and a subordinate in a work situation. As one author puts it, "Each of us accumulates or loses emotional capital, building relationships we enjoy or endure with colleagues, bosses, customers and vendors one conversation at a time. . . . The conversation is the relationship" (Scott 2003, C1).

Countless conversations make up the relationship of this couple celebrating their 40th wedding anniversary. What would you infer are some of the features of this "miniculture" and in what ways do you think this story is unfinished?

There are three ways to understand the conversational process that makes up every relationship. One assumes that there is some endpoint and that the relationship evolves or develops by steps or stages toward this endpoint. From this point of view, relationships that are increasing in intimacy have as an endpoint some sort of definitive bond that marks an ultimate state of intimacy, like marriage. And when relationships are in decline, the ultimate phase is the final dissolution of the relationship. This is the picture that's presented by *stage models*. A second way to view relationships is to look at the movement or tension between dialectical opposites. For example, each person has the need to be an individual in his or her relationships, but each also has the need to be connected to others. These two needs create a rubber band pull or *tension* that creates movement in the daily communicating between relational partners. A third approach to relationships considers how the first two can be combined in a *helical* model.

Changing Relational Patterns of Communicating

Each of these three models of relational change can contribute to your understanding, and each leaves out some features. We discuss all three in order to clarify what effective interpersonal communication means within the context of changing relationships.

Stage Models of Relational Change

A number of researchers and teachers explain how relationships begin, grow, and deteriorate as movement through a series of stages or phases. Perhaps the best-known description of these phases is the *Staircase Model of Interaction Stages*. As shown in Table 9.1, Knapp and Vangelisti synthesize and expand other scholars' work to arrive at a 10-stage model of the processes of "coming together" and "coming apart" (Knapp and Vangelisti 1996).

As these authors explain, the model is descriptive, not prescriptive; it shows "what seems to happen—not what should happen." They are not suggesting that "coming together" is good and "coming apart" is bad. They also note that this model simplifies a very complex process. There are overlaps between adjacent stages, so it is difficult in practice to identify what stage a relationship is in. For example, small talk occurs during both the initiating and experimenting stages of relationship development, but the emphasis on and goals for small talk are different for each stage. Small talk in the initiating phase is used primarily for establishing contact with the other person. During the experimenting stage, people use small talk as a way of reducing uncertainty about the other person by searching for commonalities and discovering differences. The model is based on research with mixed-sex pairs and may not apply to relationships between family members or friends; nor will it necessarily apply to gay and lesbian relationships,

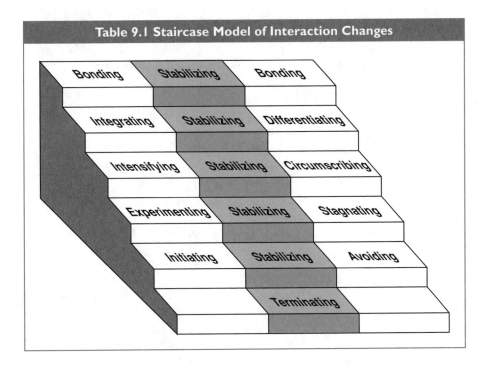

Table 9.1 Staircase Model of Interaction Changes

or to arranged marriages, prison cellmates, or other nonvoluntary associations.

The definition of each stage is fairly clear from the "representative dialogue" column of Table 9.2. When *initiating*, people are trying to display themselves as someone who is likable, understanding, and socially adept, and they are also observing the other's orientation toward them. Each culture includes various rituals or standardized patterns for initiating relationships. Among many Japanese people, for example, there are restrictions on who may initiate a relationship with whom, depending on such factors as status and "in-group" versus "out-group" membership. There are more sanctions imposed on those who violate these norms than there are in more individualistic cultures like those in the United States.

During the *experimenting* phase, people use small talk to reduce the uncertainty they have about each other, as we mentioned earlier. But even this function seems to vary by culture. Some cultures seem to have a high need to reduce uncertainty while others have a relatively low need. These differences may also be related to cultural norms for primarily nonverbal contact (touching, proximity, and so on). High-contact cultures appear also to have greater needs to reduce uncertainty (Gudykunst 2004). So you could expect, for example, that people in Spain, Italy, and Greece would spend more time and have more norms regulating the experimenting phase of relationships.

		Table 9.2 A Model of Interaction Stages	
Process	**Stage**	**Representative Dialogue**	
Coming Together	Initiating	"Hi, how ya doin'?" "Fine. You?"	
	Experimenting	"Oh, so you like to ski . . . so do I." "You do? Great. Where do you go?"	
	Intensifying	"I—I think I love you." "I love you too."	
	Integrating	"I feel so much a part of you." "Yeah, we are like one person. What happens to you happens to me."	
	Bonding	"I want to be with you always." "Let's get married."	
Coming Apart	Differentiating	"I just don't like big social gatherings." "Sometimes I don't understand you. This is one area where I'm certainly not like you at all."	
	Circumscribing	"Did you have a good time on your trip?" "What time will dinner be ready?"	
	Stagnating	"What's there to talk about?" "Right. I know what you're going to say and you know what I'm going to say."	
	Avoiding	"I'm so busy, I just don't know when I'll be able to see you." "If I'm not around when you try, you'll understand."	
	Terminating	"I'm leaving you . . . and don't bother trying to contact me." "Don't worry."	

From Mark L. Knapp, *Interpersonal Communication and Human Relationships* (Boston: Allyn & Bacon, 1984), p. 33. Copyright © 1984 by Allyn & Bacon, Inc. Reprinted by permission.

Intensifying communication is often hesitant, tentative, and probing. Verbally it may be characterized by more informal forms of address, uses of *we* and *our* instead of *I* and *you,* and increasingly direct expressions of commitment. *Integrating,* the next phase, develops togetherness to the point where attitudes, interests, and tastes become similar. Social circles merge and "intimacy trophies" such as rings or pins may be exchanged. *Bonding* names the performance of a public ritual that announces a formally contracted commitment. Clear examples of bonding are the marriage ceremony or adoption of a child. These rituals also vary by culture from the specific rite of marriage and the accompanying familial obligations to "moving in together."

In this model, the stages of coming apart are mirror images of the stages of coming together. Basically, relational partners move apart from each other in steps that begin with *differentiating* and end in the *terminating* stage (see Figure 9.2). Knapp and Vangelisti (1996) make the point about their staircase model that movement through the stages "is generally systematic and sequential." Typically, when coming together, people follow a process of moving up the left side of the staircase; when coming apart, they commonly move down the right side. This, however, does not suggest that the process is linear or that there is a fixed, unchangeable sequence. Relationships can move backward or forward and can stabilize at one stage in particular, but generally the movement is recognized as sequential.

Clearly the stage model approach to understanding relationships captures part of most people's experience. Each of us has lived through almost every stage of relationship development identified in this model, and the sequence of stages seems reasonable. And yet people have also noticed weaknesses in this analysis. John vividly remembers a painful discussion he had with a woman who was studying Knapp and Vangelisti's model at the same time her marriage was failing. Judy described through tears of frustration the chasm between her lived experience and the categories of the "staircase model." Her life told her that things were much more complicated and much less ordered than the model pictured, and, even considering these authors' comments about oversimplification, she felt that the people whose work the model summarizes were distorting human experience by trying to reduce it to static categories.

What stage do you think this relationship is in? Initiating? Experimenting? Intensifying? Integrating?

Some research leads to the same conclusion. For example, B. Aubrey Fisher criticized stage models in his discussion of the roller-coaster dimension of relationships. As he put it,

> We typically think of evolution or developmental change as constant and steady, like walking up a flight of stairs . . . But a natural process of evolutionary change doesn't happen in a consistent manner. Rather, evolutionary change is a start-and-stop process of progress and regress, of spurts of change and lulls of no change. (Fisher 1987)

The changes in a relationship often resemble the unpredictable careening and noisy jostling of a roller coaster more than they resemble a stroll up and down a set of stairs. Another assumption of stage models is that the coming-together phases are the mirror opposites of the coming-apart phases. This type of linear progression is called the reversal hypothesis. Communication researchers and teachers Leslie Baxter and Barbara Montgomery think this type of hypothesis comes from believing that relationships are always progressing logically toward some endpoint. From this point of view, one stage replaces the other as relationships change. But Baxter and Montgomery believe that relationships are better characterized by a model that assumes that relational patterns of communicating are both cyclical and linear (Baxter and Montgomery 1996). That is, relationships repeat patterns many times, but the repetition is never identically the same each time it occurs. To understand this idea more fully, we need to explain what Baxter and Montgomery mean by "relational dialectics," and how spiraling change might signal both cyclical and progressive change.

Applying What You Know

Relationship Stages

Test the model of relationship stages by applying it to your own experience.

1. Pick a relationship you have established in the past six months, and describe how it moved through the stages of initiating, experimenting, intensifying, integrating, and bonding. Did the stages occur in this order? Did the relationship skip any stages? Were there any stages added to these?

2. Choose a relationship you have been in that has been "terminated" within the last six months. Describe whether it moved through Knapp and Vangelisti's stages of differentiating, circumscribing, stagnating, avoiding, and terminating, and how. Did the relationship skip any of these stages? Did they occur in this order? Does your experience confirm or disconfirm the "reversal hypothesis" (that is, the hypothesis that stages of deterioration are the mirror image of stages of growth)?

Relational Dialectics

In order to understand what Baxter and Montgomery mean by the term relational dialectics, consider their four basic assumptions: (1) communication is the means or method of personal and social definition; (2) the quality of relation between yourself and another is constructed from the patterns of stability and change between contradictory opposites in interpersonal needs; (3) relationships exist in time and space, though we tend to treat relationships as unchanging things; and (4) communication requires the presence of two distinct voices that change as each becomes the reference point for the other (Baxter and Montgomery 1996, 41–47).

Their first assumption closely fits the view of communication developed in this text. Baxter and Montgomery emphasize, as Chapter Two does, that communication is the way people construct definitions of themselves, of their cultures, and ultimately, of society itself. The term relationship labels an ongoing systematic pattern of communication between two people.

Baxter and Montgomery identify a pattern of opposing forces at the center of the second assumption. These theorists describe relational life as a complex interplay of contradictions at many levels reminiscent of the seven-dimensional model of communication worlds that we explain in Chapter One. But Baxter and Montgomery identify three main dimensions or tensional pairs: separateness–connectedness, certainty–uncertainty, and openness (disclosure)–closedness (privacy).

The first dimension makes the point that people need to be separate, which is to say that they need to experience themselves as an individual, to be autonomous and distinctive. At the same time, people also need connectedness, the experience that we exist in relation with other people. One way relationships change is that partners express and experience more or less separateness and more or less connectedness at any given time. One pole of the second basic need is for certainty. This is the inclination people feel to increase predictability and security in the events they experience. This need exists in tension with the desire for uncertainty that surfaces in the inherent tendency to become bored when life becomes too controlled and predictable. Third, people have a need to share emotional, physical, mental, and spiritual intimacy through disclosure. This tendency is balanced or held in check by a privacy need that surfaces in the desire for silence and solitude, and the need to maintain or keep some information about ourselves hidden

The three tensional needs can be pictured as in Figure 9.1 (next page).

People individually fluctuate between these poles all of the time, like the way you steer your car between the center line and the shoulder. Sometimes you might feel pulled toward the right-hand side by the need to just be with the other person; at other times, you might feel

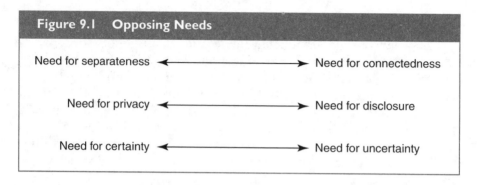

Figure 9.1   Opposing Needs

Need for separateness ←——————————→ Need for connectedness

Need for privacy ←——————————→ Need for disclosure

Need for certainty ←——————————→ Need for uncertainty

pulled to the left by your preference to be independent, regarded not as a couple but as your own person. Sometimes you're pulled toward privacy, and other times you want to disclose some of your deepest feelings. This dynamic movement back and forth is what Baxter and Montgomery call relational dialectics. How relational partners deal together with these contradictory or tensional forces provides them with definitions of who they are and what kind of relationship they have together.

Specific events that lead to changes in the way people define their relationships are called *turning points*. Baxter and Montgomery define turning points as "moments in a relationship's history when the pressures of dialogic interplay are of sufficient intensity that a major quantitative or qualitative change occurs for the pair" (Baxter and Montgomery 1996, 72). Examples in a romantic relationship include the first kiss and the first "I love you." In one study, Baxter and Bullis interviewed 80 college students about the turning points in their romantic relationships (Baxter and Bullis 1986). The students made up 40 couples who had been dating for at least six months; the average length of their relationship was almost two years. Over 750 turning points were mentioned in the interviews, and the researchers were able to classify them into 26 types of events. Those were further grouped into 14 "supratypes" to make the data easier to handle. We'll note several of the most familiar ones.

Three types of turning points were especially important early in the relationship: "getting-to-know time," "quality time," and "physical separation." Not surprisingly, the first meeting was mentioned as a turning point 80 times. The first date was also important, but more significant was "activity time," periods early in the relationship when the couple spent time at various activities, such as studying together. "Quality time" consisted of opportunities for the couple to spend time away from others without the necessity of being engaged in some activity. "Meeting the family" and "getting-away time" labeled opportunities for the people in the relationships to break the routine of school and work to go away together. For this group of people, "physical separation" refers to separation caused by vacations, breaks, or overseas trips; this was mentioned 76 times as a turning point in the relationship.

Events labeled "external competition" were also mentioned as important turning points. They included the appearance of a "new rival" competing for one of the partner's affections, the reemergence of an "old rival," and the threat from "competing demands" in the form of school, work, or sports on one or both of the parties' time.

"Passion" was mentioned as a turning point, but interestingly, only 48 out of 759 turning-point events fell into this category. "First kiss," "first sex," and the first utterance of "I love you" were the most frequently mentioned occurrences in this category.

In another study, Bullis, Clark, and Sline (1993) identified four new categories of turning points: "positive evaluation," "negative evaluation," "commitment tension," and "relational talk." Positive and negative evaluations occurred when respondents observed their partners and reached a significant conclusion regarding their observation. For example, the authors cite one woman who explained observing her partner enjoy her children, which helped her positively evaluate her partner's suitability or desirability. Commitment tension refers to the realization by one or both partners that commitment levels are different for each of the people involved. Relational talk is a turning point when some aspect of the relationship is identified, discussed, and redefined in some way.

Turning points involve different construction of selves' choices, and they lead relational partners to look at their relationship in a new light or from a new perspective. The partners reassess the nature of the relationship and their participation in it. Two people in a relationship can go through this reassessment phase either alone or together. The process may not even be conscious. In a number of cases where these turning points were reported, explicit verbal metacommunication about them did not occur, which shows that these relational partners did not necessarily feel that they had to talk to each other about the significance of the turning-point event. In some types of turning points, however, explicit talk about the relationship was important. For example, metacommunication was vital to "exclusivity," "making up," "disengagement," and "serious commitment." So, after the partners had made their move toward exclusivity, they tended to talk about it—"I'm glad we agreed we aren't going to date other people. I feel really close to you." But in this study, metacommunication did not appear to be a significant part of "get-to-know time," "physical separation," or helping with an external crisis (Baxter and Bullis 1986, 481).

Baxter and Bullis note that more research needs to be done on turning points. It is not yet clear how turning points specifically affect various relationships. But you can see from even this brief review that romantic relationships do appear to move through a number of different types of positive and negative critical events, and the ways the partners cope with these events significantly affect the trajectory of their relationship. For this reason, Baxter and Montgomery identify turning points as the central units of change in the history of a relationship. Rather than mark change as a transition from one stage to another, they believe that relational change is characterized by significant events.

Applying What You Know

Turning Points

Think about a romantic relationship you have experienced that lasted at least three months. It may be a relationship you're currently in. Graph the relationship on a horizontal scale that represents time and a vertical scale representing commitment. The graph should look like Figure 9.2 (below).

Circle each sharp rise or fall in the line on the graph. These are the relationship's turning points. Label each one. You might use Baxter and Bullis' labels—"quality time," "first kiss," "first sex," "physical separation," "new rival," and so on. Or you might devise your own labels.

What do you learn about the nature of your relationship by looking at its turning points?

When we combine an understanding of the general trajectories of relational change provided by the stage models with a recognition of the dialectics people often experience between competing needs, it is possible to develop a third approach to understanding the change pro-

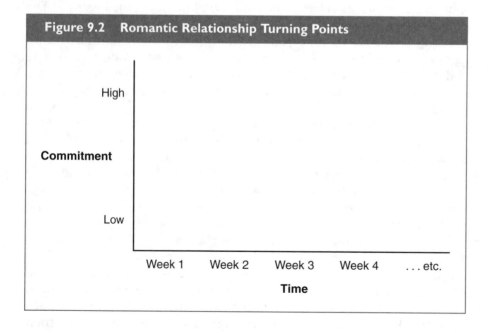

Figure 9.2   Romantic Relationship Turning Points

cess in relationships. This approach highlights a helical model of relationship change.

A Helical Model of Relationship Development

A helix is basically a series of spirals connected together, as shown in Figure 9.3.

The helical model describes relational change as movement along this kind of curve. The model begins with the recognition that change is an inevitable part of all relationships, whether the people involved accept it or not. This does not mean that there aren't periods of stabilization. In fact, the helical model can make concepts of change and stabilization more clear.

When relationships are described as helical, this approach emphasizes how they are characterized by spirals, or repetitive patterns. Communication researcher Bill Wilmot identifies two kinds of spirals (Wilmot 1995). *Generative spirals* are repetitive patterns that lead to positive attitudes, feelings, and beliefs about the relationship. So, for example, Dan believes that Laurie manages her money very well, Laurie responds in part by carefully managing her money, and Dan is increasingly impressed. This part of their relationship is characterized by a repetitive pattern of movement in increasingly satisfying directions—Dan feels like his opinion of Laurie is accurate and he likes how she lives up to his opinion; Laurie likes Dan's respect and she feels good about her money management success.

Degenerative spirals are repetitive patterns that lead to more and more negative attitudes, feelings, and beliefs about one's self and the other person. In the same relationship, Laurie might believe that Dan is verbally abusive when they argue, but Dan believes he's just being "open and honest" and "sharing his feelings." When they argue, she accuses him of being abusive, he gets defensive, and the result is more of

Figure 9.3   A Basic Helix

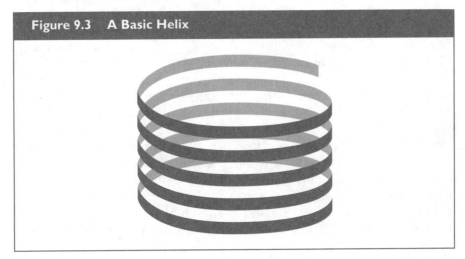

what sounds to Laurie like abuse. Negative inferences and feelings lead to more and more of the same, which creates damage to the relationship. We discuss degenerative spirals in Chapter Eleven.

Richard Conville takes this image one step further by combining the spiral model with what he calls "cycles." The combination results in a circular repetition that cycles from one stage to another, a pattern Conville describes as a helix. The primary relational cycle Conville traces on a helical curve is made up of five moves:

Figure 9.4   Conville's Primary Relational Cycle

Security 1 ⟶ Disintegration ⟶ Alienation ⟶ Resynthesis ⟶ Security 2

One of Conville's main points is that the security people enjoy in a relationship is bound to change. When couples experience this security, they "feel comfortable, share complementary [interdependent] roles, and act in coordinated fashion" (Conville 1991, 80). For example, two people who define themselves as "friends" may be in the "experimenting" stage of Knapp and Vangelisti's model. But then, as time passes, change occurs from differences in competing personal needs, or events within the relationship (such as turning points), or social events within a larger network. The "just friends" in the experimenting phase enjoy some unusually rich "quality time" together, they experience their "first kiss," or one turns to the other and says "I love you" for the first time. These events signal that a change has occurred that puts the relationship "out of kilter." Ordinary routines are replaced with uncertainty and the relationship begins the first phase of change, which Conville calls *disintegration*.

Disintegration literally means that the old relationship has ceased to work in some way. The sense of security has been disrupted and replaced with a new "noticing and questioning" of the relationship. The next phase of change Conville calls *alienation*. At this point, it is recognized that the old relationship is gone, but there is nothing to replace it with yet. It is a period of maximum uncertainty characterized by "withdrawal, separation, nonmutuality" and problems with coordinating roles (Conville 1991, 39). For example, after the first kiss or "I love you," each partner is no longer sure how the other feels or is interpreting the relationship. Both partners are often tentative with each other and may withdraw temporarily. But it's important to note that the separation or disconnection suggested by the term alienation is from the relationship, not necessarily from each other. Conville's point is that the old security of the relationship is somehow dissolved and the result of this is a sense of strangeness (alienation) from the way things used to be.

Since people generally do not like extended periods of uncertainty, relational partners at this point on the helix then concentrate their efforts on reducing the alienation. This period of the cycle is called *resynthesis*, because the relationship is redefined and rediscovered by "seeking confirmation from the other" and "coping with dialectical tensions" such as the need for separateness balanced by the need for connectedness (Conville 1991, 39). In our example, the first quality time, kiss, or "I love you" is a turning point that shifts the relationship from the experimenting phase to the intensifying phase of the staircase model. Resynthesis means putting things together again, so during the resynthesis period the relationship will be redefined in a way that acknowledges this transition to a new stage. There is also the strong sense that the relationship cannot return to the same condition before the change occurred.

When resynthesis is complete, the couple returns to a state of *security*. But here Conville stresses that it is not the same security as before; there is a new level of intimacy, new events have happened, things will never be as they were, and the relationship has irrevocably changed (Conville 1991, 131).

Sometimes the change is profound—for example, from friends to lovers or from married to divorced. Other changes are much more subtle—for example, from unconditional trust to the recognition that the other person is human after all. But in each case the cycle has moved

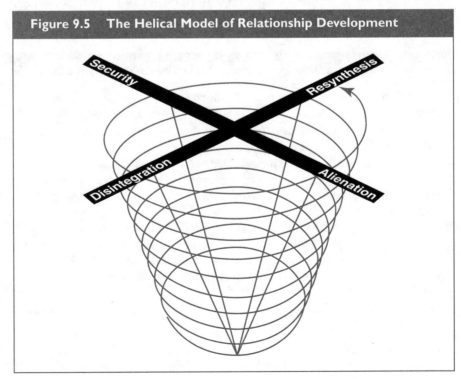

Figure 9.5   The Helical Model of Relationship Development

the relationship to a new and different security point. Security 2 is different in some important way from Security 1. It is either one turn of the circle "above" or one turn "below" where it was before. This is why the model is helical rather than simply circular.

The helical model emphasizes how cycles occur in successive layers. Events, issues, and problems do recur in relationships, but each time a change occurs (whether the issue is old or new), the couple will go through a new Security 1—Disintegration—Alienation—Resynthesis—Security 2 cycle as they move with the relationship through stabilization and change.

Conville's helical model can be used to explain part of John's experience with family relationships. Now that John's son Lincoln is 12, he is steadily expressing a greater need for autonomy. He still likes to have his parents around much of the time—this will change when he's a teenager—but he wants more control over which video games he can play and purchase and how often he's required to check in at home. There are "security" periods in the family and these are disrupted by "bids for autonomy." Each time he is allowed to play a more mature video game, the relationship between Lincoln and his parents goes through elements of the destabilization that Conville describes. Parts of the relationship and the definitions of each other get renegotiated. Then there is a new stability, and after a time, Lincoln makes another move toward autonomy that destabilizes the relationship again, and the helical cycle continues. We have a hunch that most parents experience something similar.

'But . . .' A Student Responds

This helical model is way too complicated. Why do you try to give such a complex explanation for things as simple as getting mad, getting even, breaking up, or fighting?

Your experience sounds different from ours. When we get mad or fight with somebody in one of our relationships, things don't seem simple *at all.* It helps for us to recognize that changes like these are part of all relationships, and that we're either going to be moving in a positive direction—a generative spiral—or a negative one—a degenerative spiral. It also helps us to recognize that, even if the spiral is negative, we can still do something different *next,* because the cycle of change is continuous. So these are some of the benefits we get from Conville's model. If the helical model doesn't work for you, then stick with the phase or dialectical approaches. But we encourage you to develop some way to think about relationship change, because it's going on all the time and will certainly continue throughout your life.

Not all relationships successfully make it through the cycle Conville describes. When relationships are in trouble, they may "get stuck" in the alienation phase of the cycle. The old relationship gets destabilized, but the partners are unable or unwilling to renegotiate the definitions of who they are and how the relationship can change to be mutually satisfying to them both. When it becomes clear that redefinition is impossible, then the relationship is usually dissolved (Conville 1991, 115). As we mentioned, relational termination and the types of significant events that lead to them are discussed in Chapter Eleven.

Conville's helical model can help clarify that relationships will inevitably change and that change can signal a generative spiraling toward growth and development or a degenerative spiraling toward deterioration and dissolution. We believe that the skills discussed in previous chapters will help you with each change that happens in your relationships, and those described in Chapter Ten will help when conflicts occur. We don't guarantee that all your relationships will always have the outcomes you hope for, but by increasing your interpersonal communication skills, you will be able to cope more effectively with changes and challenges.

Applying What You Know

Helical Model of Relationships

First individually and then with one other person, test Conville's cycle of relationships. Pick an ongoing relationship that you have. Think about the last period of change, upheaval, or a turning point you went through together. Did you go through the Security 1—Disintegration—Alienation—Resynthesis—Security 2 cycle described by Conville? How did your relationship change as a result? Did you go through a stage transition? In what ways did you redefine your relationship?

The bulk of research on relationships and relationship change has focused on romantic partnerships. But there is now enough known about other types of relationships to describe the types of effective and ineffective communication patterns that characterize not only romantic partners but also friendships and families. In the next section, we explore each of the three types.

Types of Relationships

Friendships

Friendships are very interesting and complicated relationships to study. In part, this is because it is difficult to define what a friend is. The terms *relative* and *neighbor* are much easier to describe. But friends can be both relatives and neighbors, from different or similar social groups, and this term can also refer to one's spouse, someone known from childhood, or someone you just recently met. Moreover, what it means to have and be a friend changes, depending on your gender, age, culture, religion, social status, and history of past friendships (Blieszner and Adams 1992). Your friendships provide you with a rich source of communication, companionship, affection, and support. But they can also be sources of conflict and betrayal. Like all types of relationships, friendships are initiated, maintained, and in some cases, terminated. And work by communication researcher and teacher Bill Rawlins indicates that friendships are just as easily characterized by the dialectical pairs we discussed in the last section as any other type of relationship (Rawlins 1992).

Rawlins' studies of nonsexual friendships explore how these relationships change across the lifespan. Relational change from this perspective is both progressive and cyclical; that is, there is a natural progression of stages through childhood, adolescence, young adulthood, middle adulthood, and later adulthood, and across work, marriage, family, retirement, and death. Change is also cyclical, as friendships move back and forth on various dialectical scales. The three primary dialectics or tensions that Rawlins' research identifies are independent/dependent, disclosing/private, and instrumental/affectionate. The first two are the same that Baxter and her colleagues have described, and the third one—instrumental/affectionate—is the tension between having a friend because he or she can do something for you and having a friend just for the companionship. Rawlins also notes that dialectical change in friendships moves between social and private definitions of friendship and real versus ideal conceptions of friendship.

The close link between friendship and interpersonal communicating suggests why friendships are more important than we sometimes think. Even 2,500 years ago they were seen as significant enough for the Greek philosopher Aristotle to dedicate two chapters of one of his major works, *Nicomachean Ethics,* to the topic of friendship. One point Aristotle made is that there are three motives for friendship: usefulness, pleasure, and a common commitment to the good. The first two are partial or "incidental." For example, pleasure, or the enjoyment of each other's company, is the primary focus of many friendships among young people. This is because, according to Aristotle, the lives of young people "are guided by emotion, and they pursue most intensely what they find pleasant and what the moment brings" (Aristotle 1962, 32). Sometimes this pleasure component of friendship gets overemphasized. People overlook the highest form of the relationship where, wrote Aristotle, "[F]riends wish alike for one another's good . . . Those who wish for their friends' good for their friends' sake are friends in the truest sense, since their attitude is determined by what their friends are and not by incidental considerations" (Aristotle 1962, 7). Although, Aristotle admitted, this kind of friendship is rare, it is worth pursuing not only for what it does for the individuals involved but also for what it contributes to the community and culture.

Aristotle also noted that friendship is the fundamental human relationship, the one that provides a reference point for all other relationships. We recognize the truth of what he said when we talk today about the friendship stage in the development of an intimate relationship and the importance of partners or spouses being each other's "best friend." And Aristotle noted—as social scientists have since confirmed—that you can only have a very few "best friends." Close friendships are possible with only a small number of people. It is possible, he admitted, "to please many people on the basis of usefulness and pleasantness, but not to be true friends with many" (Aristotle 1962, 16).

Today, many people in the United States are guided more by what Aristotle called the "using" motive for friendship. Self-help teacher Dale Carnegie's classic advice about "how to win friends and influence people" has had much more impact than Aristotle's lofty ideal. You can get a sense of the difference between this modern view and the idea of "helping one another to be better persons" by scanning the titles of the major sections of Carnegie's book: *Six Ways to Make People Like You, Twelve Ways to Win People to Your Way of Thinking,* and *Nine Ways to Change People Without Giving Offense or Arousing Resentment* (Carnegie 1964). As one author put it, "For Carnegie, friendship was an occupational tool for entrepreneurs, an instrument of the will in an inherently competitive society" (Bellah 1985, 134). To the degree that people have adopted Carnegie's perspective, people in U.S. culture have let one dimension of friendship become our primary or exclusive goal.

What can be done about this distorted focus? Well, the primary point we want to make about friendship is that the status of your friendship relations can be one of the clearest indicators of the quality of your communication and hence the quality of your life. This is partly because, as one researcher of friendships, Paul H. Wright, has noted, a friendship is the one kind of relationship that is both voluntary and personal (Wright 1978, 196). The fact that it's voluntary means that you choose your friends. You may be forced to associate with some people, but, by definition, friends become friends by choice. As a result, you can tell just by looking at your friends how frequently you are exercising your right to choose and the criteria you're applying. The second point is especially revealing. Are you friends only with people whom you can use? Or do you have a friend who tells you more than just what he or she thinks you want to hear? Do you choose friends who help you become all you can be, or do you stick with people whose standards are lower and easier to meet?

Friendships are also important because friends are chosen for their personal characteristics—their uniqueness, unmeasurable aspects, choices that they make, reflectiveness, and addressability. As a result, friend relationships offer a window into a person's constructing-selves

Friendship relations can contribute significantly to the quality of your life.

choices. By becoming aware of those characteristics and responding with communication choices that confirm the other person, we can often see more clearly the patterns we favor (Wright 1989). It's impossible to have a large number of really close friends. But the presence of a few real friends in your life is concrete evidence of your willingness and ability to choose negotiation options that encourage interpersonal communicating. If you're dissatisfied with the current status of your friendships, think back over what you have read in this book. Do you view your situation as somebody else's "fault"? How responsive a listener are you? How do you present yourself to others? Do you prefer ambiguity, or do you work to be understandable? What communication choices do you most often choose? Closed stereotyping? Closed sensitivity? Or open sensitivity? If, when you reflect on the status of your friendships, you find some things you want to change, the chapters on inhaling and exhaling all make some specific suggestions about the kinds of changes you can make.

This process can be guided by the results of several multicultural studies of friendships that have identified dimensions of behavior that seem to appear to some degree across all friendships. One research team calls these the six "universal rules of relationships," which were derived from interviews with over 800 United Kingdom and North American respondents and then checked with groups in Japan, Hong Kong, and Italy. The universal rules are these:

1. Respect the other's privacy.

2. Look the other person in the eye during conversation.

3. Do not discuss that which is said in confidence with the other person.

4. Do not indulge in sexual activity with the other person.

5. Do not criticize the other person publicly.

6. Seek to repay debts, favors, or compliments, no matter how small.

But there are also cultural differences in friendship values and behaviors. For example, studies of friendship in India show an emphasis on self-restraint, obedience, and lack of covetousness as key values that are very different from the emphasis in the United States on developing friendships to increase power, prestige, and material wealth. The collectivistic culture of Taiwan stresses harmony, self-control, and endurance in friendships, which contrasts with the emphases on autonomy, competition, and democracy associated with friendships in the United States (Gareis 1995; Gudykunst 2004). Because relationships vary so widely by culture, we believe it is especially important that you hone the skills we identify in the chapters on expressing yourself and listening to others. These skills will help you develop the type of flexibility you will need to communicate competently across cultures.

'But . . .' A Student Responds

Do you mean that it's always wrong to develop friendships for pleasure or for personal gain?

No, we don't mean friendships should never be formed for these reasons. It can be wonderful to just enjoy another person's company and satisfying to make friends with someone who can help you. However, if "seeking pleasure" or using them for your own purposes is your primary or only reason for developing friendships, or if these motives get in the way of helping yourself and others to grow, then perhaps it's time to reevaluate your friendships. Remember that the status of your friendships is one clear indicator of the quality of your overall communication life.

To summarize, friendships are some of the most important human relationships. Especially in the United States, the current preoccupation with material success has probably distorted our view of what friendships can and should be. Many people do not fully realize the great potential this kind of relationship offers. Because friendships are both voluntary and personal, a self-inventory of your friendship relations can tell you how effectively you're applying the suggestions about communication made in the previous chapters of this book. These chapters and the six basic relationship rules can provide you with guidelines for improving your friendships.

Applying What You Know

Your Friendship Network

What does your friendship network look like? To begin describing it, try this:

1. Assume you have an extra ticket to a concert you have really been looking forward to. The friend who was going with you can't make it. List the four persons you would call, in the order in which you would call them.

2. Assume you are going to be out of town for a week and do not want to leave your home and pets unattended. Make a list of the four persons you would ask to house-sit, in the order in which you would call them. (Remember, family members can be friends, too.)

3. If you learned of the sudden, unexpected death of a family member, whom would you call? List three persons in the order in which you would contact them.

How would you describe the differences among the three "sets" of friends you have listed? How many fit in all three categories?

Romantic Relationships

Earlier John mentioned that he could still remember his first actual date. Shortly after Thanksgiving of his sixth-grade year, John took his girlfriend, Louise Spurling, to a Saturday afternoon movie. He can't remember what they saw, but he does vividly—and with some embarrassment—recall agonizing over what seemed at the time to be the two most important questions in the universe: "What will I talk about for all the time I'm with her?" and "Should I put my arm around her in the theater?"

For many of us, romantic relationships make up a primary topic of conversation and concern, and for the over 50 percent of us who experience divorce, the topic reemerges as one of those interpersonal challenges we continue to wrestle and grow with. Because scores of research reports, books, poems, and plays have been written about the topic, our comments here will have to be brief and incomplete. We will discuss the different kinds of love people experience and three types of relationship partners in marriages.

Love and Its Expression. If your main goal is not to be alone, a companion will give you that; if you're only interested in sexual gratification, you can provide it yourself or purchase it; and if what you're looking for is status, you can buy new clothes or a fancier car. But if you want love, you have to develop a relationship where it can exist.

The problem is that this necessary phenomenon—love—is a notoriously mysterious commodity. So it can help to understand some of its many dimensions.

A few years ago sociologist John Lee (1973) asked Americans, Canadians, and Britons to talk about love, and he discovered the term had six distinctive meanings. Lee describes them this way:

1. *Eros:* love of beauty. This is sexual love. Erotic lovers have an intense desire for sexual intimacy, are fascinated by physical aspects of their beloved, and want to know every detail about them.

2. *Ludus:* playful love. These lovers regard love as a game. They avoid long-range attachments and do not allow their partners to become too dependent on them.

3. *Storge:* compassionate love. This is love "without fever, tumult, or folly, a peaceful and enchanting affection." These feelings are similar to those one might have for a sister or brother.

4. *Mania:* obsessive love. Manic lovers are in a perpetual state of anxiety. They are consumed by thoughts of their beloved and have an insatiable need for their beloved's attention and affection. The manic lover alternates between ecstasy when the beloved is present and despair when the beloved is absent.

5. *Pragma:* realistic love. Pragmatic lovers seek a match with someone whose personality, background, values, interests, and so on will be compatible with their own.

6. *Agape:* altruistic love. This is the classical biblical form of love, which is patient and kind and demands nothing in return.

Twenty-five years later, Hendrick and Hendrick (1997) found that eros love is related to greater relational satisfaction, for both men and women in mainly Anglo American couples. Other studies showed that this is also true for Mexican American couples. In addition, researchers found that sometimes obsessive love (mania) and playful love (ludus) are related to lower relational satisfaction.

If you are aware of the different forms this goal of romantic relationships can take, you may be more able to understand why love relationships can sometimes be disappointing. Hendrick and Hendrick (1992, 1997) say that the six different types of love can be reconceptualized as distinct styles of loving. So from one person's point of view, love may be a combination of eros, ludus, and agape, while the other person experiences storge or pragma. In this case, the two agree with each other that they are "in love," *and* each is disappointed about what this means (Aron and Aron 1994). Disappointment also sometimes accompanies the inevitable change from erotic or romantic love to conjugal or "mature" love. As one book explains,

> Unlike romantic love, conjugal love is impossible for newly acquainted young people, since it takes time to form and grows from continuous association. Romantic love is greatest where each party knows least about the other—reality gets in the way of romance. This is the love that is blind. (Duvall and Hill 1960)

Teacher-counselors Gerald Corey and Marianne Schneider-Corey usefully contrast what they call "inauthentic" and "authentic" love. The former needs to be in charge, has rigid and unrealistic expectations of how the other person must act, depends on the other person to fill a void in the lover's life, and uses manipulation as a way of getting what the lover wants. Authentic love, on the other hand, is characterized by at least 17 features, including *knowing* not only the beautiful side but also the limitations and flaws in the person you love; having *respect* for the *dignity* of the person you love; making a *commitment* to stay with the other in times of pain, struggle, and despair as well as times of calm and enjoyment; being *trusting* and *vulnerable*; having a *want* for the other person without having a *need* for that person in order to be complete; and *seeing the potential* within the person you love (Corey and Schneider-Corey 1993).

You've probably discovered by now that no research report, textbook, novel, or poem is going to tell you once and for all "what love is" and that there's some truth in the patient advice of elders that "when it happens, you'll know it." In your romantic relationships it can help, though, to recognize that there are different kinds of love and different experiences and expressions of intimacy.

One researcher named R. J. Sternberg (1986) has proposed a "Triangular Theory of Love." The triangle is composed of passion, intimacy, and commitment. The fact that these make up a triangle indicates that all three dimensions rely on the other two. Whereas passion is important, it is usually identified as a quality that is heavily dependent on the other dimensions if the love is to last. Commitment is also critical but refers to the type of investment people put into a relationship rather than the experience or feeling of affection and closeness. Intimacy seems to constitute many of the attributes most people use to define love. Sternberg notes that the three dimensions of romantic love are expressed in different patterns across different types of couples.

Couple Types

As you might guess from our earlier discussions about gender and communication, communication patterns used to express love and intimacy are often different for women and men. For example, observational research indicates that women tend to look more directly at their partners than men and are more likely to provide direct and repeated expressions of feelings. Men tend to look at their partners much less frequently and are much more likely to use silence as a means of coping with relational differences. As we've noted, this type of difference in gender intimacy expression may lead to serious misunderstandings between partners (Tannen 1990; Wood 1996).

Several years ago, communication teacher and researcher Mary Anne Fitzpatrick developed a typology of marital couple types. She identified three basic kinds of couples whom she calls *traditionals, independents,* and *separates* (Fitzpatrick and Badzinski 1985). *Traditional* couples have conventional ideas about marriage and the roles each partner should play. Their relationship is characterized by interdependence, where high value is placed on sharing and conflicts are discussed rather than avoided. Couples sharing a traditional perspective emphasize stability rather than change, and disclose emotions and conflicts but with some degree of restraint.

Couples who are *independent* in their outlook hold many nonconventional views of marriage and family life. They are expressive with their spouses, openly and freely engaging in conflict. They value highly their ability to be frank and honest with each other, and emphasize novelty and change in their relationship. Partners with this orientation tend to see themselves as relatively autonomous, or able to make and act on their own decisions.

Separates in a marital relationship do not express much interdependence. They engage in many activities alone or without their partner and do not express much emotionally to each other. They tend to avoid conflict rather than openly express it and focus on autonomy and separate physical space as ways of regulating their relationship.

Instead of being "purely" traditional, independent, or separate, some couples are "mixed," with a traditional partner married to an independent, a separate married to a traditional, and so forth. Mixed couples usually express less stability and satisfaction with each other because they do not mutually share definitions of their relationship.

Mixed or pure, these relationship types are important ways of distinguishing how people perceive and interpret the state or condition of their long-term relationships. One way spouses can understand the disagreements and tensions in their relationship is by noting whether the two of them have different, and even conflicting, expectations. Mutually shared definitions are important for understanding how, for instance, separates are more satisfied with less frequent conflict and independents are more satisfied with more frequent conflict.

A great deal of research on romantic love has been done on heterosexual, Anglo American couples, but more recent research is beginning to examine the dynamics of gay and lesbian relationships and intercultural dating. A recent study found that the attitudes toward and frequency of intercultural dating have changed little in recent years (Martin, Bradford, Drzewiecka, and Chitgopekar 2003). The researchers show—not surprisingly—that people who grew up in culturally diverse environments and diverse friendship networks tend to engage more in intercultural dating than people who grew up in culturally homogeneous environments.

Another study found that Fitzpatrick's typology of heterosexual couples could also be applied to homosexual couples. Among gay couples, there were more separates than in the heterosexual population, fewer independents, and just about the same proportion of traditionals. In lesbian couples, there were fewer separates and independents, but more traditionals than in a heterosexual random sample (Fitzpatrick, Jandt, Myrick, and Edgar 1994). Michelle Huston and Pepper Schwartz (1996) have also identified some other differences between heterosexual and homosexual relationships. Many homosexual couples tend to feel freed from the gender stereotyping of roles dominant in the majority culture. Women, for instance, are traditionally assigned the role of housework (cooking, laundry, and cleaning). But gay couples divide the duties so that one of the partners often does all of the cooking *or* all of the laundry but not both, whereas lesbian couples tend to share the cooking, cleaning, and laundering responsibilities.

To supplement the research, we asked some of our gay and lesbian friends about their experiences of differences between heterosexual relationships and theirs. One significant difference that they reported is between "family of origin" and "family of choice." Especially when individuals have been rejected by some or all of their blood relatives, they develop families of choice with whom they share holidays, vacations, and other gathering times. Several differences also grow out of the absence, in the larger culture, of traditional rituals, symbolic markers, and terms for gay and lesbian relationships. Since most governments do not sanction legal marriage bonds between permanently committed gay and lesbian couples, there are no terms like *husband, wife,* or *spouse* to conveniently identify one's relationship to a romantic partner. It's also often necessary to invent and agree on "anniversary" dates so that the couple can commemorate important stages or turning points in the development of the relationship. One gay couple argued that the best way to respond to this ambiguity is to recognize that, since the culture doesn't provide much symbolic or ritualized help, you have to consciously and intentionally decide how to define your relationship and then take steps to make this definition a reality.

The gay and lesbian people we talked with also emphasized the diversity they experience. There is clearly not one single homosexual culture but a mixture of ethnicities, religions, social classes, gender roles, and value systems every bit as varied and changing as in straight society. There are cultural markers—for example, one joke is that among gay men there are four, not just three, levels of quality: good, better, best, and fabulous. But it is as difficult and dangerous to generalize about gay and lesbian people as about any other humans.

Gay and lesbian couples often create families of choice, because some blood-relation options are closed to them. The same communication issues arise in these families as in heterosexual ones.

'But . . .' A Student Responds

Is there one best way of communicating when problems come up in romantic relationships?

Research and everyday experience both emphasize that individuals approach relationships differently, especially depending on the kind of relationship they have developed. These differences lead to diverse ways of communicating. So no, there's not any one "best" way to handle the problems in romantic relationships. But we believe that if you try to follow the guidelines we have discussed in this book, understanding and growth can happen in your intimate relationships. And the attitudes and skills discussed in the two following chapters can be directly applied to conflicts in romantic relationships.

The topic of romantic relationships could fill several books this size, and if you're interested in reading more, several sources are listed in the references at the end of this chapter. But we hope our discussion of approaches and goals alerts you to the complexity of these relationships and their constantly changing qualities. Especially when you're in the midst of a confusing or frustrating romantic relationship, it can help to know that others have experienced something similar to what you're experiencing and that people have written books and articles about it. Approaching romantic relationships from a purely research or theoretical point of view will never capture the entire process. But we can get a sense of some of the differences in individuals, in relationships, and in the experience and expression of intimacy, and these help in coping with the challenges of a romantic relationship. As you think about how to troubleshoot your relationship or work toward improvement, we like the six suggestions made by Stuart and Jacobson (1985) in their book *Second Marriage*:

(1) Realize and expect that every long-term romantic relationship has good and bad times.

(2) Be willing to examine your role in every positive and negative exchange in the relationship [that is, they're *all* co-labor-ations].

(3) Be willing to consider everything as negotiable, with no demands that your partner accept your way of doing things without the fair consideration of alternatives.

(4) Be willing to consistently learn to understand your partner's point of view. (This gets decidedly more complex the longer the relationship lasts!)

(5) Be committed to try different ways of doing things long enough to see if the new way works.

(6) Have the maturity to forgive your partner for mistakes made in good-faith efforts to make your relationship better.

Applying What You Know

Romantic Relationship Metaphors

Some of the most interesting current research on love relationships focuses on analogies and metaphors. You can apply some of the insights of this research.

First identify two or three persons with whom you have a love relationship. You can include romantic partners, family members, or close friends. Then pick a metaphor that you believe captures the relationship. For example, is your relationship like a rocket ship ride? A soap opera? A chess game? A roller coaster? A symphony? What metaphor would you use?

Then get together with two other persons and discuss the metaphors all of you have chosen. Notice similarities and differences.

Finally, try deciding which of the six kinds of love are present in each relationship the group has discussed—eros, ludus, storge, mania, pragma, or agape. What is the relationship between the metaphors you chose and the kinds of love?

Family Relationships

Talk about a huge topic! It's going to be even more difficult in this section than in the last one to say something useful without letting this discussion balloon into a separate chapter or even a book of its own.

We will have to limit ourselves to some brief but important comments about the communication implications of family structure.

Changes in Family Structure. Twenty or 30 years ago, the norm was still a nuclear family: a mom, a dad, and two or three children living together, usually in one location for a long time. This picture still remains the stereotype of family for many, even though reality has changed. As you know, the incidence of divorce has gone from under 15 percent to over 50 percent, and the number of mothers who work has also increased sharply. As a result of these and other changes, today family can also mean "blended family," two adults and children who are not the biological offspring of these two adults; "single-parent family"; or "extended family," which includes relatives who live with or very close to one of the other family types; or a household containing a gay or lesbian couple and their natural or adopted children.

These changes in family type have significantly affected children, primarily because, as we have mentioned before, people learn their strongest communication patterns in their family of origin. Many children live with just one parent, and in families where both parents are present, each often works outside of the home. These changes have been accompanied by the growth of a whole new service industry providing preschooling and child care. You may well have experienced some of these changes, and you might be wondering how they have affected your communication development and what you can expect as you develop a family of your own.

Communication in Family Structures

Even without considering the impact of radical social change, families by themselves are already complex systems and subsystems of roles, rules, and communication patterns. The simplest nuclear family of parents and their children includes subsystems of parent-parent interaction, parent-child interaction, and child-child interaction, and their communication varies depending on the types of communication patterns the parents share (for example, traditionals, independents, and separates). All these variations have not yet been studied in detail. But, for example, if you're raised by two adults who prefer not to argue (separates who discourage conflict), you will be more likely to avoid conflict than the child raised by two parents who encourage open disagreement (as independents do).

Comparatively little is currently known about communication between siblings (sisters and brothers, or stepchildren). In the bestseller *Siblings Without Rivalry,* Adele Faber and Elaine Mazlish encourage parents to help children learn to fight their own battles by learning many of the skills we talk about in this book: being direct about and taking responsibility for one's own feelings, learning to become tolerant and appreciative of the differences between people, and encouraging children to manage their own conflicts effectively instead of always intervening as the controlling "third-party" parent (Faber and Mazlish 1987).

Communication scholars and teachers are also just beginning to understand the complexity of the parent-child relationship. We know it is primarily from the parent that the child learns the verbal and non-verbal codes of the surrounding culture. Intimate behaviors such as eye gaze and touching communicate the emotional depth of the bond between the parent and the child. Psychologist John Bowlby believes that children form different types of attachment bonds to their primary caregiver (1972). Some children are "overattached" in that their parents tend to be demanding and controlling of the children's behavior. The children in this type of relationship are called "anxious-ambivalent." Other children are "underattached" when their parents spend little time encouraging frequent or prolonged periods of interaction. Their children are termed "avoidant." Other parents seem to effectively balance periods of intense interaction without exerting too much control and by allowing adequate periods of "alone time," and Bowlby labels their children "secures." In recent studies, researchers show that attachment styles like these persist into adulthood. Anxious-ambivalent persons tend to report lower levels of satisfaction and income in their chosen work even when factors like gender, age, and education are held constant. And several factors related to relational adjustment like esteem, feelings of intimacy, and commitment are all affected by the person's early attachment style (Hazan and Shaver 1992).

Several communication researchers are also studying the types of responses that parents or other caregivers (like preschool and day care personnel) give children when comforting, requesting information, persuading the child, or requiring obedience to a specific rule. Generally, these researchers are finding that parents and caregivers who encourage flexibility, expressiveness, and reasoning about the situation are more effective than those who do not (Applegate 1986). For example, in comforting situations, parents or caregivers who confirm the feelings of the child and help the child reason about the discomforting situation by reframing it in a way where problems could be solved were more effective in their responses than any other type. Parental responses that did not work well were those that denied or dismissed the feelings of the child as unimportant, denied the importance of the situation, or demanded that the child see the problem from the parent's or caregiver's point of view.

Some clinicians and researchers have attempted to explore the whole family system. Boundaries in the system are important. Family therapist Salvador Minuchin (1974) believes that boundaries help to establish what's "mine" versus "yours," help children to balance the need for disclosure with the need for privacy, and generally serve as a foundation for learning to balance a series of relational contradictions arising in different roles and rules.

Some families have more fluid boundaries within the family system itself. As an example, scheduling or meal preparation may sometimes be the mother's responsibility and at other times may be up to one of the children. When families don't develop clear boundaries, Minuchin calls them "enmeshed." Other families emphasize autonomy and separateness in setting boundaries and resist any change within the family structure. This type of family is called "disengaged." Still other families develop fluid boundaries with the outside world, encouraging participation in many activities and relationships outside of the family. And some families restrict their social contact, preferring activities limited to family members.

Chapter Summary

When you are thinking about the various types of relationships you have, recall the interpersonal←——→impersonal continuum and the fact that the quality of your communication is directly related to the quality of your life.

Just as communication can best be viewed as a mutually constructed event between people and not as something one person does "to" another, each relationship you have also has an identity that emerges in patterns of stability and change created between you and the other(s) involved. This means that no feature of the relationship is ever entirely "caused" by any single person. Relationships are constructed, maintained, and changed *together*.

Stage models enable you to see the phases your relationships go through; dialectical models can help you identify significant, relationship-changing events; and Conville's helical model provides a relatively sophisticated picture of how relationships spiral up and down on various scales.

Each of these three ways of understanding relationships can contribute to your participation in your friend, romantic, and family relationships. Remember that there are many different kinds of friends, and that your friendship network is one clear indicator of your overall communication health. As you think about your romantic relationships, remember that there are many different kinds of love and different couple patterns for expressing it. There are also many different kinds of families. As we move into the next millennium, the so-called "nuclear" model is far from typical in most Western cultures. But step, extended, blended, and gay and lesbian families can appropriate their own versions of characteristics that have traditionally been found in effectively functioning families. The key, as you might expect, is as much quality interpersonal communicating as the partners can encourage.

In Other Words

In this article Dixson and Duck remind us that relationships are more than the individuals who constitute them. One of the "curiosities" of all relationships from impersonal to interpersonal is the fact that we cocreate them in the process of developing shared meanings. You might hear in their words something familiar—that "partners in relationships are using shared meaning systems or shared working models of the world to conduct the relational endeavor" (2001, 105)—to what we talk about as worlds of meaning. As you review this reading and reflect on this chapter, consider the following questions:

1. How has your world of meaning been shaped by individuals with whom you have been in, are, or may be in relationships?

2. In what ways have different dimensions of your own world of meaning been altered as you have come to know about aspects of another person's world of meaning?

3. What are some specific examples of how you have shared meaning with someone in your family through talk? How about someone you have dated? Your best friend?

4. What is different about the way(s) you talk with people in different types of relationships?

* * *

Understanding the Relationship Process: Uncovering the Human Search for Meaning

Marcia Dixson and Steve Duck

There is a curiosity about relationships: They are composed of individuals, yet are more than the sum of their parts. In understanding relationship processes, one therefore is faced with understanding not only what it is that individuals think, know, and do in relationships but also what they share and how they come to share it. Our analysis of this curiosity focuses on symbols and meaning because both of these entities can be "owned" by individuals themselves and also can be shared with others (Baxter, 1987b). Individuals can see symbolism and meaning in idiosyncratic ways that they have constructed for themselves. In relationships, partners also experience a commonality of meaning and symbolism between themselves on a variety of topics and concerns, and this experience "goes beyond" simple similarity in it effects.

We focus on this overlooked curiosity in a number of ways—sometimes looking at the ways two persons create, establish, and share meaning with one another as relaters, and sometimes looking at the ways researchers do exactly the same thing by developing terminologies and ways of experiencing the world that can be shared by colleagues. Threaded through this analysis is the notion that both examples are instances of a fundamental human tendency to use symbols, to seek, create, and develop meaning, and to analyze experience. Duck (1991) has developed the basis of this argument elsewhere, and here we go further and apply an analysis of this fundamental human tendency proposed by Kenneth Burke, a rhetorical theorist focused on the human use of symbols and the ways this use structures thought and explanation—whether at the level of relationships or at the level of scholarly discourse. We also see connections with the work of personality psychologist George Kelly (1955, but especially 1969), who also focused on the ways humans construct meanings as a way to deal with the "constantly unforeseen originality" (Shotter, 1987) of their lives.

It has been traditional to point to the fact that humans are able to live—actually cannot avoid living—simultaneously in reference to all three dimensions of time (past, present, and future). Thus our past, as we have accounted for it, echoes in the present and in the future; our present makes sense because of our images of the past and the future; and our anticipations of the future often recast the past and direct our behaviors of the moment. All three are always present, and all three are humanly, symbolically constructed. Use of symbols represents a parallel between social actors and researchers: All of us seek to describe (represent) and explain past and present happenings both for their own sake and to control and predict future events. Both Burke (1966) and Kelly (1955, 1969), however, retranslate these views into a future orientation; that is, they see humans as evaluating and interpreting the past in order to give it a meaning that helps one cope with it in the future if similar events happen again. Thus both theorists emphasize the importance, in understanding human behavior, of noting that humans are driven by a need to cope with the future that is unpredictable unless people develop categories of expectation ("constructs" for Kelly; "symbols" for Burke). Although meaning is often apparently retrospective, for Kelly constructs are personal creations developed and tested quasiscientifically to deal with the future (Duck & Condra, 1989). Burke wrote of symbols as human devices and schemes for comprehending life as a whole; they are not inherent in the phenomena that humans experience. Kelly wrote of the "anticipation of events by construing of their replications"; Burke (1966, p. 16) wrote, more opaquely, that humans are "rotten with perfection," meaning that humans place order on the phenomena they encounter, so as to organize their experience. Such activity inevitably provokes a restless hunt for the best way to do this organizing and creates a search for perfection or completeness (a tendency to continually revise, update, and regard as unfinished the business of their application and extension). In one sense, then, "rotten with perfection" is yet another way of saying that more research needs to be done!

The theme of dealing with change and the future has been a part of human thought about human behavior since at least the early Greek philosophers (e.g., Heraclitus) and takes its modern form in the emphasis on prediction and control that is found in many recent models of relationships (e.g., Kelley et al., 1983). We share the view that it is an important channeler of human thinking but feel that more can be said about its implications for the study and conduct of relationships. . . .

. . . *Symbols* and *meaning* are essentially motivating entities that exist in individual minds but about which two individual minds can (come to) agree.

They are examples of important forms of cognitive overlap in relationships, in culture, and indeed in the professional terminologies that researchers develop and use among themselves. One important question, then, is how people come to *develop* such meaning systems. . . . A second question is how such systems relate to cultural and social milieus. . . . a third question is how people come to share such symbols and meanings . . . and a fourth is how people use and can develop them once they are shared issues that we cover here. . . .

. . . We argue that partners in relationships are using shared meaning systems or shared working models of the world to conduct the relational endeavor, just as scholars use shared specialized symbol systems or working models to conduct the collegial research endeavor. Indeed there are striking parallels between the theoretical activities of scholars in different disciplines once one focuses on that activity as examples of human "effort after meaning" (Bartlett, 1932). . . .

. . . Just as two individuals bring their own individual systems of thinking into any relationship, so too researchers and scholars come to the study of relationships with their own patterns of thought, training, method, theory, perspective, and so on. Such patterns of thought, necessarily and ex hypothesi, influence the choice of phenomena selected for inquiry and inspection as the individual researchers take different perspectives on the phenomena. Sociologists will gravitate toward patterns of structure and power as issues to be explained. Social psychologists will focus on the individual or social cognitions that are evident to them in relationships and their participants. Communication scholars will look for the structures of messages or the construction of relationships that they imply. Developmentalists will ask how persons and their beliefs or skills change across time in relationships. In short, each discipline will take a perspective that focuses characteristically on those things that make most sense within its own frame of reference or terminological geography (agreed meaning systems). Although, for example, the differences between disciplines often are exaggerated at the expense of the similarities, such differences often are seen as little more than foibles caused by training, rather than as examples of human choices based on meaning systems. Nevertheless there is a deeper structural point about the human mind here, showing a common element that runs through most human action: that a fundamental structure of human minds is based on choice in the context of *meaning* and that this structure expresses itself in human behavior of all kinds, including the activities of scholars in various disciplines.

The reader already may be ahead of us in seeing that individuals who come to relationships are also examples of this same fact about the human mind. The anxious persons focus on likely evidence of rejection by others (Erickson, Sroufe, & Egeland, 1985; Raush, Barry, Hertel, & Swain, 1974); the extravert explores opportunities for social interaction, while the introvert seeks to avoid them in favor of quiet solitude; women typically notice the progress of intimate talk in relationships, while men are alerted to different aspects of social experience (Duck, Rutt et al., 1991).

The fundamental human commonality evident in all of these examples is that people choose to focus on things that make sense within their preexisting frames of reference, their system of meaning, about which deductions can be made on the basis of evident choices (Duck, 1991). Burke, a rhetorical theorist, put it thus:

> We can say that people interpret natural sequences in terms of cause and effect not because of something in the natural scene requiring this interpretation but because humans are the sort of agents that see things in terms of necessary relations. In this view we do not derive our ideas of cause and effect from experience; all that we can derive from experience is the observation that certain happenings seem likely to follow certain other happenings. But our ideas of cause and effect are derived from the nature of the mind. (Burke, 1945/1969, p. 187)

Natural phenomena do not scream out at us to be interpreted in a particular way; they make rather subliminal whispers that different people choose to hear in slightly different ways, as make sense to them within their frames of reference of meaning.

Meaning and Sharing of Meaning in Talk

We believe that such a view connects easily with several lines of thinking in psychology (e.g., personality psychology), as well as in communication studies (e.g., study of rhetoric and persuasion) and sociology (e.g., symbolic interaction). It also demonstrates the relevance of choice in the human endeavor. Choice of discipline, of structure for a series, of topics for a volume, of methodology, of research problem, friends, affiliative strategies, and many others are all expressions of a general human tendency to make choices within a framework of meanings accepted by the chooser (who also may be "a researcher," "a partner," "an author," "an editor," or "a person").

The notion of *meaning* has proven difficult in the history of ideas. By focusing . . . on what an individual knows about relating, we are emphasizing the way the person organizes, for him or herself, knowledge about relationships and partners; but his is only a part of the picture, even if it clearly ties in with work in this and other fields. . . . [S]everal authors adopt Bowlby's (1988) term *working models* to refer to a similar concept. For us, *meaning* is an organizational concept too and refers to the way a person organizes knowledge about relationships in the context of what else he or she knows about the world. We believe that . . . individuals represent that knowledge to other people by the language they use, as an invitation to those others to share and adopt that organization of knowledge. The formation of a dyadic relationship thus confronts the two partners with the organizational challenge of resolving any differences that exist between their respective working models or meaning systems. We follow Duck and Pond (1989) in seeing the formation, maintenance, and conduct of relationships as processes in which such organization and reconciliation of meaning systems is carried out, usually through talk—and everyday talk at that. But such talk is not to be dismissed as a trivial thing. One of our goals is to show that talk is not an idle medium in social (or scholarly) life: It represents, "constructs," and sustains (and perhaps helps develop and change) a person's system of meaning. It also represents the operation of cognition as choice, not just in the selection of terms and styles but also as reflected in the emphasis given to different terms in the presence of different audiences or for different purposes—or circumstances of human life not given the attention they truly deserve (cf. Billig, 1987). Finally it represents a *persuasive* activity with the effect of prodding other people into acceptance of the proffered organization of meaning.

References

Bartlet, F. (1932). *Remembering*. Cambridge, UK: Cambridge University Press.

Baxter, L. A. (1987). Symbols of relationship identity in relationship cultures. *Journal of Social and Personal Relationships, 4*, 261–279.

Billig, M. (1987). *Arguing and thinking: A rhetorical approach to social psychology*. Cambridge, UK: Cambridge University Press.

Bowlby, J. (1988). *A secure base: Parent-child attachment and healthy human development*. New York: Basic Books.

Burke, K. (1945/1969). *A grammar of motives*. Berkeley: University of California Press.

———. (1966). *Language as symbolic action: Essays on life, literature, and method*. Berkeley: University of California Press.

Duck, S. W. (1991, May). *New lamps for old: A new theory of relationships and a fresh look at some old research*. Paper presented at the Third Conference of the International Network on Personal Relationships, Normal/Bloomington, IL.

Duck, S. W., & Condrea, M. B. (1989). To be or not to be: Anticipation, persuasion, and retrospection in personal relationships. In R. Neimeyer & G. Neimeyer (Eds.), *Review of personal construct theory* (pp. 187–202). Greenwich, CT: JAI.

Duck, S. W., & Pond, K. (1989). Friends, Romans, countrymen, lend me your retrospections: Rhetoric and reality in personal relationships. In C. Hendrick (Ed.), *Close relationships* (pp. 17–38). Newbury Park, CA: Sage.

Duck, S. W., Rutt, D. J., Hurst, M. H., & Strejc, H. (1991). Some evident truths about conversations in everyday relationships: All communications are not created equal. *Human Communication Research, 18*, 228–267.

Erickson, M. F., Sroufle, L. A., & England, B. (1987). The relationship between quality of attachment and behavior problems in preschool in a high-risk sample. In I. Bretherton & E. Waters (Eds.), *Growing points for attachment theory and research* (Monographs of the Society for Research in Child Development, 50 [Serial No. 209]) (pp. 147–166). Chicago: University of Chicago Press.

Kelley, H. H., Berschied, E., Christensen, A., Harvey, J. H., Huston, T. L., Levinger, G., McClintock, E., Peplau, L. A., & Peterson, D. R. (1983). Analyzing close relationships. In H. H. Kelley, E. Berschied, A. Christensen, J. H. Harvey, T. L. Huston, G. Levinger, E. McClintock, L. A. Peplau, & D. R. Peterson (Eds.), *Close relationships* (pp. 20–67). San Francisco: Freeman.

Kelley, G. A. (1955). *The psychology of personal constructs*. New York: Norton.

———. (1969). Ontological acceleration. In B. Maher (Ed.), *Clinical psychology and personality: The collected papers of George Kelley* (pp. 7–45). New York: John Wiley.

Raush, H. L., Barry, W. A., Hertel, R. K., & Swain, M. A. (1974). *Communication, conflict, and marriage*. San Francisco: Jossey-Bass.

Shotter, J. (1987). The social construction of an "us": Problems of accountability and narratology. In R. Burnett, P. McGhee, and D. D. Clarke (Eds.), *Accounting for relationships* (pp. 225–247). New York: Methuen.

Excerpted from Dixson, M. and Duck, S., "Understanding the Relationship Process: Uncovering the Human Search for Meaning." In E. Englehardt (ed.), *Ethical Issues in Interpersonal Communication: Friends, Intimates, Sexuality, Marriage, & Family*, pp. 103–108, copyright © 2001 by Sage Publications. Reprinted by permission from Sage Publications, Inc.

References

Applegate, J. et al. 1986. "Reflection-Enhancing Parental Communication." In I. E. Sigel (ed.), *The Psychological Consequences for Children*. Hillsdale, NJ: Lawrence Erlbaum. Pages 107–142.

Aristotle. 1962. *Nicomachean Ethics*. Translated by M. Ostwald. New York: Bobbs-Merrill.

Aron, A., and Aron, E. 1994. *Love*. In A. Weber and J. Harvey (eds.), *Perspectives on Close Relationships*. Boston: Allyn and Bacon. Pages 131–152.

Baxter, L., and Bullis, C. 1986. "Turning Points in Developing Romantic Relationships." *Human Communication Research*, 12: 469–493.

Baxter, L., and Montgomery, B. 1996. *Relating: Dialogue and Dialectics*. New York: Guildford.

Bellah, R. 1985. *Habits of the Heart: Individualism and Commitment in American Life*. Berkeley: University of California Press.

Blieszner, R., and Adams, R. 1992. *Adult Friendship*. Newbury Park, CA: Sage.

Bowlby, J. 1972. *Attachment and Loss*. London: Hogarth.

Bullis, C., Clark, C., and Sline, R. 1993. "From Passion to Commitment: Turning Points in Romantic Relationships." In P. J. Kalbfleisch (ed.), *Interpersonal Communication: Evolving Interpersonal Relationships*. Hillsdale, NJ: Lawrence Erlbaum. Pages 213–236.

Carnegie, D. 1964. *How To Win Friends and Influence People*. New York: Simon and Schuster.

Conville, R. L. 1991. *The Evolution of Personal Relationships*. New York: Praeger.

Corey, G., and Schneider-Corey, M. 1993. *I Never Knew I Had a Choice*. 5th ed. Pacific Grove, CA: Wadsworth.

Duvall, E. M., and Hill, R. 1960. *Being Married*. New York: Associated Press.

Faber, A., and Mazlish, E. 1987. *Siblings Without Rivalry: How to Help Your Children Live Together So You Can Live Too*. New York: Avon.

Fisher, A. 1987. *Interpersonal Communication: Pragmatics of Human Relationships*. New York: Random House.

Fisher, W. 1987. *Human Communication as Narration: Toward a Philosophy of Reason, Value, and Action*. Columbia: University of South Carolina Press.

Fitzpatrick, M. A., and Badzinski, D. M. 1985. "All in the Family: Interpersonal Communication in Kin Relationships." In M. L. Knapp and G. R. Miller (eds.), *Handbook of Interpersonal Communication*. Beverly Hills, CA: Sage. Pages 687–736.

Fitzpatrick, M. A., Jandt, F., Myrick, F., and Edgar, T. 1994. "Gay and Lesbian Couple Relationships." In R. J. Ringer (ed.), *Queer Words, Queer Images*. New York: New York University Press. Pages 265–276.

Gareis, E. 1995. *Intercultural Friendships: A Qualitative Study*. New York: University Press of America.

Gudykunst, W. B. 2004. *Bridging Differences: Effective Intergroup Communication* (Fourth Ed.). Thousand Oaks, CA: Sage.

Hazan, C., and Shaver, P. 1992. "Broken Attachments: Relationship Loss From the Perspective of Attachment Theory." In T. E. Orbach (ed.), *Close Relationship Loss: Theoretical Approaches*. New York: Springer Verlag. Pages 90–108.

Hendrick, C., and Hendrick, S. S. 1997. "Love and Satisfaction." In R. J. Sternberg and M. Hojjat (eds.), *Satisfaction in Close Relationships*. New York: Guildford. Pages 56–78.

Hendrick, S., and Hendrick, C. 1992. *Romantic Love*. Newbury Park, CA: Sage.

Huston, M., and Schwartz, P. J. 1996. "Gendered Dynamics in the Romantic Relationships of Lesbians and Gay Men." In J. Wood (ed.), *Gendered Relationships*. Mountain View, CA: Mayfield. Pages 163–176.

Knapp, M. L., and Vangelisti, A. L. 1996. *Interpersonal Communication and Human Relationships*. Boston: Allyn and Bacon.

Lee, J. A. 1973. *The Colors of Love*. Toronto: New Press.

Martin, J. N., Bradford, L. J., Drzewiecka, J. A., and Chitgopekar, A. S. 2003. "Intercultural Dating Patterns Among Young White U.S. Americans: Have They Changed in the Past 20 Years?" *Howard Journal of Communications*, 14: 53–73.

Minuchin, S. 1974. *Families and Family Therapy*. Cambridge, MA: Harvard University Press.

Rawlins, W. 1992. *Friendship Matters: Communication, Dialectics, and the Life Course*. New York: De Gruyter.

Scott, S. 2003. "Everyday Explanations." *Seattle Post-Intelligencer*, October 6, C1–C2.

Sternberg, R. J. 1986. "A Triangular Theory of Love." *Psychological Review*, 93: 119–135.

Stuart, R., and Jacobson, B. 1985. *Second Marriage*. New York: Norton.

Tannen, D. 1990. *You Just Don't Understand: Women and Men in Conversation*. New York: Ballantine.

Wilmot, W. 1995. *Relational Communication*. New York: McGraw-Hill.

Wood, J. 1996. "Gender, Relationships, and Communication." In J. Wood (ed.), *Gendered Relationships*. Mountain View, CA: Mayfield. Pages 3–19.

Wright, P. H. 1978. "Toward a Theory of Friendship Based on a Conception of Self." *Human Communication Research*, 4: 196–207.

——. 1989. "The Essence of Personal Relationships and Their Value for the Individual." In G. Graham and H. Lafollette (eds.), *Person to Person*. Philadelphia: Temple University Press. Pages 15–31. ✦

Chapter Ten

Relating Through Problems

Chapter Objectives

After reading this chapter, you should be able to do the following:

- Explain how relationship problems are socially constructed.
- Describe how "fault" and "blame" are unproductive when responding to problems of deception, betrayal, and even violence in relationships.
- Identify and provide examples of the RICE power currencies negotiated in interpersonal relationships.
- Explain the similarities and differences between deception and betrayal.
- Describe the cycle of violence and identify at least one strategy for altering this communication pattern.
- Discuss the relationship between patterns of verbal and physical aggression.
- Explain why it is important to be able to identify communication patterns associated with relational problems.

Chapter Preview

This chapter discusses what the movie saga *Star Wars* called the "dark side" of interpersonal communication. Some researchers have also used that term to label studies of deception, betrayal, hurtful messages, harassment, and aggression. Other teachers and students have argued that using the terms "light" and "dark" to portray good and evil reinforces racial stereotypes. Whatever your position in that controversy, our goal here is to help you to understand some of the tensions and problems that inevitably occur in relationships without getting caught up in debate about what to label them. Like you, we know that positive relationships are not easy to maintain. And—again like you—even when one of us communicates in ways that we believe are helpful, we are sometimes confronted with the reality that, since relationships are collaboratively constructed, our effort to help can turn out to be useless or even hurtful.

This point is important: As we said in Chapter Nine, positive and negative communication spirals are made up of *repetitive patterns of interlocking behaviors*. This means that one of the greatest joys about interpersonal relationships is also one of the biggest frustrations—they take at least two people! In human relationships, the lowest common denominator is two. We rejoice when we know that a relational partner has our best interests at heart and when we have the comfort of companionship. *And,* as each of us has learned, relationships are painful when power imbalances are emphasized and patterns of deception, betrayal, and aggression form negative communication spirals.

One goal of this chapter is to clarify how power works in interpersonal relationships and to offer some realistic strategies for shifting the power balances that are changeable and coping with those that aren't. Another goal is to remind you that you always have choices about what to do next in a relationship and that your choices have consequences for which you are ethically accountable. Some of your choices will be influenced by the norms and practices of the cultures you inhabit. And *all* of your choices will be shaped by the choices made by your relational partner(s).

You might expect a chapter on relational problems to offer you a series of solutions or ways to "fix" what's broken in your relationships. You might also look for ways to justify walking—or running—away from relationships that are toxic rather than supportive. But our goal here is not to offer you naive solutions to complex problems, or to convince you to walk away from relationship difficulties. We can't know your situation well enough to offer that kind of advice. Instead, our goal in this chapter is to help you understand some of the problems in relationships for what they are and to give you a structure for evaluating your range of choices about what to do next.

We start by explaining that at the heart of each relational problem is the interdependent contact that brings people together in the first place. We explain how recurring difficulties in relationships don't simply happen but are the result of jointly constructed patterns of communicating. We review some of the research that's been done on these patterns in order to help you recognize what's happening when you experience them. We also discuss the important role of power dynamics in shaping and maintaining relational problems. We introduce you to theories of relational power and encourage you to understand that the ways you choose to use and abuse power contribute to the deception, betrayal, and aggression you experience in friendships, family, and romantic relationships. Finally, we offer some suggestions about how you can cope effectively with relational problems when they occur.

Constructing Relational Problems

Many students, teachers, and even scholars who understand communication to be collaboratively constructed find it difficult to set aside fault and blame when facing relational problems like deception, betrayal, and aggression. In theory, it may make sense that relationships are cocreated and even that people collaboratively construct degenerative as well as generative spirals. But it can seem foolish, if not impossible, to live this theory when betrayed by a best friend, deceived by a family member, or emotionally or physically abused by a life partner.

Students in our classes who have experienced physical violence in a relationship or who have witnessed it struggle with the contention that "victims" are part of the problem when hurtful communication—including verbal and physical abuse—occurs. Their experience tells them that when there is violence, abuse, and deception, someone is at fault, and that person is the violent, abusive, and deceptive relational partner. Some teachers and researchers also believe that whereas it sometimes makes sense to view communication as collaboratively constructed, it doesn't make sense to give up fault and blame when there is a clear power imbalance.

We agree that it is difficult to set aside beliefs about fault and blame, especially when a powerful relational partner is making choices that negatively affect the other person and the relationship. And despite this difficulty, we encourage you to look at relational problems as collaboratively constructed. It is true that in violent interactions, one relational partner may inflict significantly more physical damage than another. Sometimes individuals do choose to betray the trust of their partners by revealing private information. It's also true that family members lie to each other about where they have been and with whom. At the same time, violence clearly does not occur in a vacuum, and, as Dr. Phil McGraw reminds his viewing public, "We teach people how to treat us" (McGraw 2003). It's also true *that the actions of the "guilty" relational partner are nexting choices made in response to the patterns of communicating established prior to the breach in the relationship.* Every human action can be understood as a response to the contexts that frame it, including the actions of deception, betrayal, aggression, and violence.

Power is also central. Deception and betrayal, psychological and physical abuse, and sexual harassment are directly related to power imbalances. Like other dimensions of communication, power is negotiated relationally. Importantly, sometimes it is not possible to balance hurtful power imbalances. But the low-power person still has his or her own set of choices about what to do next. If you are in a relationship with skewed and toxic power dynamics, you *do* have choices, even though none of them may be "ideal."

We definitely are not saying in this chapter that you should try to maintain a relationship at the cost of your physical, emotional, or spiritual health, or for the sake of somebody else. We do not promise you a simplistic formula that can bridge cultures, gender, age, sexual orientation, or economic differences. But all three of us have life experiences with problematic relationships, and we have learned that the understandings and behaviors outlined in this text can help people make more informed choices about their communicative options. We encourage you to emphasize accountability and response-ability with respect to your own choices and to encourage others to be accountable and response-able for their choices, even as power imbalances and social pressures encourage each of you to rely on well-established patterns of fault and blame.

Power as Relational

Power is a word that has many meanings to many people. You know that there are many natural and mechanical forms of power, including hydroelectric, gas, wind, and nuclear power. In the human world, you've probably heard or even used the phrase "Absolute power corrupts absolutely." You could easily identify individuals who hold positions of power. However, you may not have taken much time to consider the role of power in relationships. In this section, we introduce a view of power that revises the common belief that power is something that *individuals* have.

We agree with scholars who contend that power is a *relational* phenomenon—and that relational partners negotiate the extent to which they wield it with one another (Wilmot and Hocker 2001). These scholars often cite an influential social psychologist named Morton Deutsch (1973), who argued that power does not reside within an individual and that it should be understood as a dynamic between an individual and others in his or her environment. Most of the time the negotiation of power between relational partners is implicit rather than explicit, which means that it happens more nonverbally than verbally. When relational partners are dissatisfied with the way power is being negotiated, the potential for problems increases. In fact, each of the relational problems we discuss in this chapter—deception, betrayal, aggression, harassment, and violence—emerges in the context of power struggles.

One useful way to understand the interdependent nature of power in interpersonal relationships was presented by psychologist Richard Emerson in 1962. He argued that one person (we'll call him Jay) has power over another (how about Jane?) only to the extent that Jane is dependent on Jay. As communication teachers Wilmot and Hocker (2001, 105) state, "Your dependence on another person is a function of (1) the importance of the goals the other can influence and (2) the availability of other avenues for you to accomplish what you want." In other words, one member of a relationship has power to the extent that he or she has resources or currencies that the other needs or desires and that cannot be procured elsewhere. For example, if your friend has a car and you hate to ride the bus, your friend has power in your relationship. However, even if you badly need transportation, you probably won't grant another acquaintance who rarely showers and is generally grumpy the same amount of power for the same car ride. The value of the second car ride is reduced by other factors. The same thing happens in relationships when more complex issues are at stake. If your self-esteem is boosted in the presence of another person, you are generally more accepting of others in his or her presence, and if you have fun hanging out together, you are likely to grant that person power to influence your life decisions. For example, the two of you might decide to attend the same college. You will probably grant much less power to someone who regularly puts you down, tells you that you're going nowhere fast, and with whom you only interact because social customs of politeness require it.

When you understand how power is relational, you'll be able to see how individuals use a variety of power currencies when they are negotiating power in relationships. Wilmot and Hocker (2001) summarize the research on individual power currencies in a set of four elements that consistently comes into play in interpersonal relationships. The acronym RICE helps to recall each of them: resource control, interpersonal linkages, communication skills, and expertise.

Resource control is a currency that often accompanies position or status. In the United Kingdom, for example, the prime minister has resources at his or her disposal that are not available to the average British citizen. In a fam-

Power imbalance can set the stage for sexual harassment. Notice how the lower-power woman in this picture is asserting some independence by disconnecting from the man in order to reduce the power imbalance.

ily, parents have resources available to them that are not generally available to their young children. In a group of young boys, the friend with the help codes for the latest Game Boy game has resources that give him power and status in the group, at least for as long as the codes are coveted by his peers. It is important to keep in mind, however, that what one person values as a resource may not be valued by another. Although it may be true that a parent has financial resources that are unavailable to her child, if the resource the child desires is time spent together, the value of the parent's resource decreases and so does the power that the resource provides.

Interpersonal linkages are a second power currency that people use in negotiating power in relationships. If you know that the mother of one of your friends is connected to a person you'd like to talk with about your career plans, your friend will have some relational power. You might agree to take a long road trip with him to visit his family rather than spend the weekend with other friends so that you can increase your chances of being introduced to the person you believe has the potential to influence your life. Interpersonal linkages are more than just knowing influential people, however. The power currency of interpersonal linkages increases when a person serves as a link between two groups. A person who can serve as a mediator between disgruntled coworkers also has this kind of power currency, as does a person who generally seems to attract others.

Communication skills are a third type of currency that affects the power dynamic in interpersonal relationships. Those individuals who are effective speakers, can persuade others, can lead people to make effective decisions, can listen in ways that make others feel understood as well as heard, and are able to express warmth and compassion are often attributed more power in relationships than those who cannot communicate effectively. Decisions are often made to support the position of a person who has articulated her ideas clearly, even if the ideas are not altogether consistent with the goals of others in the relationship. Having polished communication skills is not always a valued asset or power currency, however. In some contexts, if you are too competent, you may be perceived as insincere, "slick," or generally untrustworthy. This example reinforces the point that the value of any particular power currency is directly related to the context or the relationship in which it is used.

Expertise is the fourth power currency individuals can exchange in their relationships. People with knowledge, abilities, or skills that others value have the currency of expertise at their disposal. The friend who is a tech whiz is likely to have increased power when a worm or virus affects her friends' computers. Coaches have power with their athletes because of their knowledge of the sport. The member of the family who is the keeper of traditional recipes and who makes them without fail for family holiday dinners has an important power currency.

Even those who understand power currencies and the ways they can be exchanged still experience power imbalances. In fact, power imbalance seems to be the rule rather than the exception. Wilmot (1995) reports that most often when relational partners are asked about the power dynamics in their relationships, each reports that the other has more power. Perceived power differences are as important as actual ones, and when power dynamics are consistently imbalanced in a relationship, relational problems are more likely to occur.

In most circumstances, the value of power currencies is determined by the mutual needs and desires of the members of the relationship. There are times, however, when circumstances beyond the control of the people involved determine the relative value of power currencies. For example, when a family's primary breadwinner is laid off, the practical value of his or her resource control and even expertise may well diminish. When cultural norms and social expectations are in play, power balances negotiated by relational partners can also be challenged. For example, a couple who becomes romantically involved in college and negotiates an acceptable balance in their relationship at school may have to adapt to social and cultural pressures should they continue their relationship at home. This is exactly what happened with one of Karen's Muslim friends. He and his girlfriend met at college and shared experiences as international students from the same region of the world who negotiated differences in the tradition of their faith. However, they believed that if they were to return home the fact that one of their families was Sunni Muslim and the other was Shiite would be the first of many problems in their relationship. Other issues of power would also have come into play regarding their families' status in the community and the woman's independence and education. This couple decided to marry and negotiated the cultural and family concerns by remaining in the United States.

Control issues also affect relationships when one partner decides unilaterally to impose his or her power on the other. Not everyone is willing or able to negotiate in good faith, nor to seek balance in his or her relationships. Many people feel the need to have power over others rather than to share power with them. Sometimes this is understandable. You might not expect to have a balanced power relationship with your boss, but when power hierarchies are imposed or enforced in interpersonal relationships, typical relational problems are often amplified. When one member of an interpersonal relationship chooses to use manipulation, coercion, or intimidation to establish personal feelings of influence or control in a relationship, it is likely that deception, betrayal, or aggression may occur.

To summarize, power differences make up an important part of the context for deception, betrayal, harassment, aggression, and violence.

One important feature of power is that it is relational; like other aspects of communication, it happens between people. You can see how this works when you recognize some of the currencies people use to enhance their relational power. Resource control, interpersonal linkages, communication skills, and expertise all can increase or decrease power. And the actual impact of each currency depends on how it is valued by each person in the relationship.

Deception

I've been going out with my current boyfriend for several months now and we spend most of our time together. I went home for the weekend to visit my grandmother, and when I returned a friend of ours told me that Josh was out dancing with his ex-girlfriend while I was gone. Josh had told me that he didn't want to have anything to do with her anymore, so obviously I was hurt and confused. When I saw my boyfriend this morning I asked him about his weekend, and he didn't say anything about going out. I wonder if I should ask him if he was out with her, but I really don't want to hear it if he was. But I'm not sure I can trust him until I know the truth, and if it's truth I don't want to hear, I don't know how I can trust him any more in this relationship.

You've probably heard stories like this one. Perhaps you've even told a story like this, or had one told about you. The reality and even the perception of deception can profoundly affect interpersonal relationships. In the next several paragraphs, we explore the motives or reasons for deception in interpersonal communication and identify some of the potential consequences for the relationship.

Motives for Deception. Deception can vary from blatant lies to indirect actions such as exaggerations and false implications (Hopper and Bell 1984). Whereas most people believe that deception is intentional, it can also be unintentional, as when someone misremembers or mistakenly forgets or omits information. Like all other communication phenomena, deception is a joint action, the outcome of a collaboration between or among communicators. Some people make it relatively easy for others to lie to them when they make choices that are either gullible or overly demanding. It can be easy to lie to the person who believes almost everything he hears, for example. Authoritarian people also help create communication contexts in which lying is easier. If your parent is always on your case, demanding to know what you are doing all the time, you may be more inclined to lie in order to negotiate the tension between interdependence and autonomy we talked about in Chapter Nine. Some people decide whether or not to deceive others based on the threat of being caught. If the danger of being discovered is high, and discovery has undesirable consequences, then a person might choose not to lie.

In addition, sometimes you may know, or at least suspect, that you are not being told the truth but decide not to confront others about their deception. One of us has a friend who is a compulsive liar, and most people who know her well understand that this is part of her way of being with others. We know the verbal and nonverbal signs that accompany her deceptions, probably better than she does herself, and we choose not to "call her" on every one of her lies. Sometimes the choice to "let her lie" is made out of a desire to save time, because the issue of the lie is not central to the conversation or simply because holding her accountable for her lies would require more of an emotional investment than we'd like to make at the time. Occasionally, couples even collaborate on lies, and this is called collusion (Andersen 1998). One partner may routinely deceive the other about infidelities, for example, and although the other suspects the truth, he or she agrees, for whatever reasons, to look the other way. In short, like all other kinds of communication, deception is strongly influenced by its context.

Communication researchers Dan O'Hair and Michael Cody (1994) identify six motives or reasons people give for lying to their relational partners. Three of the motives—*egoism, benevolence,* and *utility*—are labeled positive because they generally have positive consequences for at least one individual and appear to O'Hair and Cody to do no harm to the relationship. The other three—*exploitation, malevolence,* and *regress*—are labeled negative because their consequences do include harm to at least one person in the relationship. Egoism and exploitation are positive and negative forms of *self-related* motives, benevolence and malevolence are related to the *other,* and utility and regress have to do with the *relationship.*

Self-related motives for deception highlight what an individual can gain or retain through deception. Egoism helps to protect or promote the deceiver's self-concept. Think about times when you have stretched the truth on a job application or told someone something about yourself that was not quite true in order to be viewed in a positive light or to avoid embarrassment. Exploitation is lying with a purely selfish motive. When you pretend to be interested in someone in order to get information or to achieve some other personal goal, you have exploited the deceived. You may believe that your decision to exploit another is no different from beefing up your resumé, but arguably there is a difference in degree regarding both the effect on the relationship and the potential damage to the other person.

Benevolence and malevolence are deceptive practices that are other-focused. Benevolent lies are motivated by the desire to protect the self-esteem, safety, or general well-being of the other person. Lies told by people who were hiding Jews from the Nazis in World War II, by members of the Underground Railroad facilitating travel of runaway slaves in the U.S. Civil War era, or by networks designed to help protect wives or husbands in physically abusive relationships are all deceptions motivated by benevolence. Distorted truths or blatant lies that parents tell their children in order to protect the child's sense of worth or well-being are another kind of benevolent deception. Malevolence, on the other hand, is motivated by the desire to hurt others and may include deception designed to sabotage others or to get revenge or retaliation. The motive for benevolence may be viewed as pure even though the consequences of the deception may not be altogether productive, but malevolence has at its core negativity, and the results of malevolent deception are almost always negative for both the people involved and the relationship.

The two final motivations for deception focus on outcomes for the relationship itself. When someone employs utility as a motive for deception, the goal is to improve, enhance, escalate, or repair the relationship. In the example at the beginning of this chapter, Josh could have been trying to protect the relationship when he avoided telling his girlfriend about running into his ex while his girlfriend was out of town. Since his girlfriend was already worried about her grandmother's health, Josh may have believed that is wasn't useful to bring up a casual contact, especially when the fact that they were at the same club at the same time didn't mean much to him. Utility can also be a motivation to ignore a friend's compulsive lying. Ignoring another's deception is one way to keep the peace in a relationship, even when that

In situations like this one, lies are often motivated by benevolence. What twenty-first-century contexts similarly motivate lies? Today, what conditions would lead you to feel comfortable lying?

stability is based on a lack of trust. Regress, on the other hand, means using a lie to damage or terminate a relationship. For instance, Jamal might tell his steady date Anna that they should go back to being "just friends" when the truth is that Jamal wants Anna to end the relationship. In this case, Jamal is manipulating Anna rather than being accountable for his own preference (O'Hair and Cody 1994, 196).

Consequences of Deception. Most acts of deception have unintended consequences. In fact, if people carefully considered the potential ramifications of deception, they would often find that, in the long run, it would be less trouble to tell the truth. One unintended consequence is that when deception is undetected, it becomes a burden for the deceiver. In some cases people who deceive others feel a sense of autonomy, privacy, or control, but often these feelings are compromised by feelings of shame or guilt for lying to others and perhaps even anger at or contempt for the person they are lying to. Frequently, in order to maintain a falsehood, additional lies must be told to additional people. Any deception requires the deceiver to remember the details of the lie for as long as it is maintained, coordinate subsequent supporting lies, and maintain a heightened awareness of both verbal and nonverbal cues. This increased attention to one's own communication usually generates stress, which is ironic, since stress avoidance may have been the reason for the deception in the first place.

Once a deception has been detected by or revealed to a relational partner, the consequences expand and are almost universally negative. Until people discover that someone has lied to them, they generally operate from a "truth bias," that is, a basic belief that the other communicator is telling the truth. This state quickly changes to a "lie bias" once deception is revealed (O'Hair and Cody 1994, 197). At this point, the deceived person is likely to assume that that communicator is always lying. This change in a relationship is one way that many people discover how trust is a precious commodity that, once lost, is difficult to fully regain.

The collaborative nature of deception becomes clearest when the deceived person decides to expose his or her relational partner's lies or to ignore or suppress them. Suppression may require increasingly monumental efforts, including lying to yourself about the fact that you are being lied to, accusing others of lying to you about a partner's indiscretions, and even lying to others about your relational partner's behaviors. Exposing the lie, however, means admitting to the deceiver and to others one's hurt, loss of esteem, anger, and increasing uncertainty about the future of the relationship. The deceiver who is caught and confronted by the deceived partner frequently also suffers embarrassment, guilt, and loss of credibility. Deception often increases tension, conflict, and even aggression in a relationship.

For these reasons and others, communication researcher and teacher Bill Wilmot argues that deception is *always* damaging to the other person and to the relationship. Wilmot contends that deception, by its very nature, is a self-centered act. Unlike O'Hair and Cody, Wilmot does not believe that any motives for deception are positive. Even when you convince yourself that your deception benefits the other or the relationship, Wilmot maintains that

> the recipient of the deception has no hand in deciding if it is "good" for the relationship or not—he or she is out of the loop. . . . Deception, even in its benign forms, is a form of information control that one exercises; you want to be the one determining the course of the relationship, so you withhold information from the partner. (Wilmot 1995, 107–108)

If indeed the lowest common denominator in a relationship is two, an individual's choice to deceive is also a choice to short circuit the relationship by leaving the other partner out.

'But . . .' A Student Responds

OK, wait a minute. Didn't you say earlier that lying to the Gestapo about hiding a Jew was an example of a benevolent lie? How can that be damaging and leaving the other relational partner out? The Jews knew their friends were lying to protect them and many of them lived, right? How can that be a problem?

This is a great question, and it gives us the opportunity to clarify something important. Benevolent deception is indeed motivated by the preservation of the other. In the case of the Jews hidden by their neighbors, the lies were told to someone else—the Nazis. In this case, the relationship with the Gestapo is what is at risk from Wilmot's perspective. If you lie to one person to protect another, you may argue that the lie was motivated by benevolence, but you are still damaging the relationship with the person you are deceiving. In the case of the lie to the Gestapo, the person who chooses to lie is in effect denying the power and authority of the police officer and undermining any relationship he or she may have with the officer. You may certainly decide that it is better to sacrifice a role-based relationship with a Gestapo officer for the good of a friendship or familial relationship with another, but that does not deny the fact that your deception affects the impersonal relationship negatively.

Importantly, though, most of us don't find ourselves in such morally obvious situations. Benevolent deception directed to an awkward-looking friend who asks, "Do I look good in this outfit?" may be intended to boost the other's sense of esteem, but this too may have unintended negative consequences. Think, for example, about the way you would feel if you could not trust your best friend to give you an honest appraisal of a situation. Would your truth bias begin to shift to a lie bias? How would such a shift affect the future of your relationship?

> Wilmot's point is that whereas deception is always a choice, it should always be understood as a self-motivated choice rather than one that is other or relationally motivated, as O'Hair and Cody argue. We encourage you to "try on" both of those perspectives and see which one seems most appropriate to you.

Whether you view deception as self or other motivated, patterns of deception are established collaboratively in relationships, and you can choose to sustain them or alter them. You do not have ultimate control over the direction of your relationships' spirals, because it always takes at least two. But your choices do contribute to sustaining, revealing, and preventing deception in your interpersonal relationships. If you are aware of a pattern of deception in an intimate relationship, we think that it would be useful for you to consider the motives for deception and the consequences of it for yourself, your partner, and the relationship. It may be that deception is a way to meet your need for privacy, control, or belonging, but there are consequences for choosing deception as a way to achieve the balance you are seeking. Whether you are the one in the relationship doing more of the deceiving, or the person who has been or is being lied to, you can start to alter the communicative pattern you've helped establish by interjecting more honesty whenever possible. Sometimes revealing a lie and working through its aftermath can lead to relationship development and growth.

We hope it is obvious that we are not advising you to be brutally honest all of the time in all of your relationships. Telling your boss that you think she has a big nose, for example, is irrelevant to the working relationship and could be considered malevolent, to say nothing of how foolish it might be if you are up for review. But when a pattern of deception is present between you and the people closest to you, it is important to identify what is going on and to restore as much of the truth as the relationship can contain. We also hope that you will at least think carefully about our point that deception is a collaboratively created phenomenon. It takes two to develop and maintain patterns of deception, and if you want to change the patterns, you'll need to make a choice to change your role in sustaining them. If you decide not to change the patterns, then at least acknowledge personal accountability for your part in them.

Betrayal

Deception and betrayal are closely related; in fact, some researchers see them as almost synonymous. The difference is that betrayal violates the betrayed person's expectations and can do so even when the person doing the betraying tells the truth. Researchers Walter Jones and Marsha Parsons Burdette define betrayals as "violations of trust or expectations on which the relationship is based" (Jones and Burdette 1994, 244). Their research reveals five important features of betrayal.

First, betrayal appears to be common in interpersonal relationships. Over 90 percent of the participants in one study could easily provide stories of betrayal episodes in which they either did the betraying or were betrayed. As people move from the impersonal end of the continuum toward the interpersonal end, they tend to develop a sense of trust and commitment that grows out of mutual expectations consistently being met, even when some of these expectations remain unstated. It is not surprising, then, that any violation of expectations can be viewed as a betrayal by at least one of the partners.

Many different types of betrayal have been reported, including extramarital and extrarelational affairs, lies, revealed confidences, drinking and drugging, lack of support from a partner, ignoring a friend or partner, criticism, and gossip. Some of the most extreme forms of betrayal reported, and also the most severe, include being abused or abandoned by a parent. Unfortunately, the most painful kinds of betrayal happen in the most important relationships, probably because the expectations about communication and behavior are the highest in relationships that are most important. In relatively impersonal relationships, expectations are more socially shaped, and when social expectations are unmet, the consequences are less profound.

A second feature of betrayal is that the consequences of a betrayal incident differ significantly, depending on whether one is the betrayer or the betrayed. It may seem obvious that those who are betrayed described the relationship as having worsened in the aftermath of the betrayal incident. But it is interesting to note that those who did the betraying generally reported that the relationship had stayed the same or even improved after their betrayal.

Despite this potential optimism, the third feature is that betrayal tends to be followed by relationship termination. This obviously happens in romantic relationships and friendships, which are often referred to as relationships of choice. But even involuntary relationships, such as those between family members and coworkers, suffer serious decline following incidents of betrayal. One major reason is that betrayal involves disconfirmation of expectations, norms of interaction, and, most important, disconfirmation of the other as significant in the relationship. As Jones and Burdette (1994) explain, "The treachery is not just in the actual harm done to another, but also in the fact that betrayals threaten a major source of one's feelings of identity and well-being" (245). That source is the relationship itself. Effects of betrayal can last for a long time, and mitigation often requires help from a counselor, pastor or priest, or a trusted friend.

A fourth finding from studies of betrayal is that gender differences are prominent. Women are more likely to betray and be betrayed by other women, usually when one woman reveals a confidence or secret. Men report betraying their romantic partners more than they betray partners in any other relationship, and most often the nature of their betrayal is sexual. However, men report that they are most often betrayed by coworkers with whom they compete. Men and women also classify incidents of betrayal in significantly different ways. Men are more likely to identify only overt acts or events as betrayals, whereas women are more likely to describe a general lack of emotional support as a betrayal.

Finally, Jones and Burdette conclude that some personality traits may correlate with betrayal behavior. People who are likely to betray others also appear to be generally more jealous, suspicious, envious, and resentful of others. In addition, they tend to have more personal problems, including alcoholism or other addictions, depression, and a self-reported inability to sustain intimate relationships. These characteristics distinguish between those who are more likely to betray others, and they also identify those who are most likely to be betrayed.

Like deception, betrayal involves actions that leave at least one person out of the decision-making loop as the person doing the betraying attempts to control the destiny of the relationship on his or her own. Also like deception, betrayal diminishes trust between relational partners and damages the relationship itself.

When you notice patterns of betrayal in your relationships, it can be helpful to reflect on your expectations of the other person(s) and of the relationship(s). If you can talk to your relational partner and make some of your expectations explicit, then it may be easier for him or her to meet them. You can also discuss what expectations are most important to each of you, because even when people share mutual expectations, the value each places on any expectation can vary dramatically. When you experience incidents of betrayal, you may find it useful to get some perspective on your communication patterns from a third party and to express your feelings about the choices you have made and those that have been made for you.

Applying What You Know

Make a short list of experiences you would describe as betrayals in your life. Identify the type of relationship, the type of betrayal, whether you were the person betrayed or doing the betraying, and the current state of the relationship.

In which kind of relationship have you experienced the most betrayal incidents?

> What similarities and differences exist between incidents when you were betrayed rather than betraying?
>
> If you could replay this situation, what would you do differently now?

Hurtful Messages, Aggression, and Violence

Aggression and violence are two additional relational problems that are influenced by power dynamics. When one party asserts control and influence over the other, patterns of hurtful messages, aggression, and violence may occur. These patterns are not simply created by the person who strikes out in anger or frustration. Like all relational patterns, these are also coconstructed. We definitely do not condone the behaviors of friends, family members, and romantic partners who berate and abuse others. At the same time, we also do not encourage friends, family members, and romantic partners who choose to accept emotional abuse. We acknowledge that sometimes people with less power—children, the elderly, a person in an unfamiliar culture—may not have many choices available. But we urge victims of abuse not to believe that their only option is to accept or reinforce the pattern.

Hurtful Messages. Hurtful messages are one of the ways that people attempt to assert power. Communication teacher and researcher Anita Vangelisti (1994) identified 10 types of hurtful messages people experience in relationships with partners, friends, and family members. The people Anita questioned reported all of the following hurtful messages: *Accusations* about the other's negative behavior ("You are a liar"), *evaluations* of the other person's value as a human being ("You have got to be the most worthless son on the face of the planet"), *directives* or commands ("Just get out of my face"), *advice* ("You really ought to so something about your appearance"), *expressions of desire* ("I don't want to have anything to do with you"), *information disclosure* ("I'm really not attracted to you anymore"), *interrogating questions* ("Were you out with that no-good loser again?"), *threats* ("If you think you can leave me, you have another thing coming"), *jokes* that put down the other ("The way you do that, you'd think your hair was blonde!"), and *lies* ("No, I didn't cheat on you with her last week"). Clearly there are many ways to hurt another person, and the extent of the pain associated with each type of hurtful message depends on the context and the nature of the relationship.

In fact, the experience of hurt is also a relational phenomenon. A message that may be viewed as innocuous from a friend can be very painful when uttered by a family member or romantic partner. Vangelisti (1994) identified three factors that seem to affect how hurtful messages are interpreted: (1) the intent of the person communicating the hurtful message; (2) whether the parties shared a family or non-family relationship; and (3) the level of intimacy. One's overall satisfac-

Attacks on character, ridicule, and profanity are all forms of verbal aggression.

tion with a relationship also influences the extent to which relational partners emphasize hurtful messages. If a relationship is not very satisfying, people come to expect hurtful messages and pay less attention to them. Of course, as hurtful messages increase, overall satisfaction with the relationship decreases, and patterns of put-downs tend to create and maintain degenerative spirals.

When you are angry with someone or frustrated by your circumstances, consider the effects your hurtful messages may have. Many hurtful messages are difficult to repair, and although Vangelisti notes that those in intimate or family relationships may be more forgiving of them, participants in her study reported that it was difficult to forget them. Often they remembered the specific words of a message even years after they were spoken. Hurtful statements have rarely led to positive change in relationships and are often a part of relationship termination.

Verbal Aggression. Two communication researchers who spearheaded the study of verbal aggression noted that when someone uses verbal aggression they attack the self-concepts of other people (Infante and Wigley 1986). Attacks on character, ridicule, rough teasing, and profanity are all forms of verbal aggression. In contrast to content or topic, verbally aggressive messages focus on the identity of the person being attacked. Karen recalls one verbally aggressive message that called into question her identity as a communication professional. An extended family member was frustrated when she felt out of the loop on the timing of a visit from Karen's dad, and rather than strike out at the members of the family with whom she lived, she chose to strike out at Karen by asking, "Don't you ever *use* that communication stuff you teach in your classes? What happened to all that stuff on family communication? Your family doesn't seem to be very good at it!"

As Wilmot and Hocker (2001) note, the forms that verbal aggression take can differ from relationship to relationship and culture to culture. They point out that in cultures that value individualism, verbally aggressive remarks are generally directed against a person (Carey and Mongeau 1996). Examples might include "You are so stupid!" "You're ugly," "I wish you had never been born!" and "You are such a slob." By contrast, verbal aggression in collectivist cultures generally takes the form of attacks against the group, village, tribe, or family the person being attacked identifies with (Vissing and Baily 1996). Examples of verbally aggressive statements toward the group may include "You Irishmen all just a bunch of drunken idiots" or "All Greeks are geeks."

In a study of verbal aggression among college-age couples, Sabourin (1995) found that aggressive partners would attack each other in escalating verbal exchanges in an attempt to gain control. Both would make escalating accusations and assertions in a pattern of domineering talk in which neither would accept the other's desire for control. As Sabourin notes, couples often found themselves stuck in escalating spirals that seemed out of control. She writes,

> The boundaries between individuals and the potential for empathy are lost. The partner is no longer experienced as a distinct individual deserving of respect but instead, as an extension of [the aggressive person]. In the process of escalating aggression, paradoxically, the power of both partners is lost to the pattern between them. (Sabourin 1995, 281)

If you find that you are involved in battles of verbal aggression that seem to be spiraling out of control, what are some of your nexting choices? One effective way to shift away from verbal aggression is to focus on the content of the conflict rather than the character of the other person(s). Remember, verbal aggression is defined in part by the ways it attacks the character and self-concept of the other. Choosing to focus on the issue at hand rather than the identity of the other is one effective way to break degenerative spirals fueled by verbal aggression. If you and your partner do not curb your patterns of verbal aggression, you should be aware that sustained patterns of verbal aggression often lead to episodes of psychological abuse and even to patterns of violence. So, it is definitely worth it to try to intervene.

Psychological Abuse. Psychological abuse, like verbal aggression, can take a variety of forms, and what feels abusive in one relationship may not be interpreted the same way in another relationship. One researcher notes that instances of psychological abuse including the "creation of fear, isolation, economic abuse, monopolization, degradation, rigid sex-role expectations, withdrawal, [and] contingent expressions of love" are widespread enough to occur in some form in all intimate or close relationships (Marshall 1994, 294).

In many cases, psychological abuse, like other forms of aggression and violence, is one way that relational partners assert dominance and control. The individual who chooses this form of verbal aggression is actively engaged in constructing an identity of the other that is subordinate and powerless. When, for whatever reason, their partner accepts this construction of identity, patterns of abuse are likely to continue. Students have reported that when they look back on relationships characterized by psychological abuse, they often wonder why they allowed their partner to define them as dependent when in most other contexts and relationships they were independent or interdependent people. One of the ways to respond to psychological abuse and other forms of verbal aggression is to use perception checking. You may find it helpful to solicit the perceptions of a close friend, family member, religious leader, or counselor to check your own perceptions of yourself and those features of your identity that feel imposed on you by your abusive relational partner.

Physical Violence. You might wonder why anyone would stay in a relationship that is physically violent. Part of the reason may be that, like other forms of violence in relationships, physical violence is often part of a pattern that develops over time, sometimes without the participants being fully aware that they are cocreating it. Most often, however, incidents of relational violence can be predicted by the extent to which verbal aggression and psychological abuse are occurring. Rarely do episodes of physical abuse exist in isolation. Most of the reports of physical violence in intimate relationships indicate that women are more likely to be harmed than men, but both men and women use physical violence as a tactic. Adults are more likely to use physical violence with children as discipline and as a way to assert influence and control.

Unfortunately the occurrence of physical violence as a tactic for negotiating power in a relationship is more common than you might imagine. One report suggests that in dating couples, 30–40 percent report violent incidents, including "pushing, shoving, slapping, kicking, biting, hitting with fists, hitting or trying to hit with an object, beatings, and threats/use of a weapon" (Cate and Lloyd 1992, 97). Most of us have heard reports on the national news of children so determined to save themselves and their siblings from continued abuse by a parent that they feel their only recourse is to murder their mom or dad. Women who murder their abusive spouses have successfully used self-defense pleas to avoid life in prison for terminating abusive relationships by terminating their abusive partners.

Most people will not experience extreme forms of physical abuse in their relationships, but if you or someone you know is in an abusive or violent relationship, on either side of the situation, we hope that the information we have sketched here can help you gain a better understanding of what is happening and provide you with some choices about what to do next. Of course, the abuse will not magically disappear just because you—or others—understand that physical violence is related to verbal aggression or that physical abuse often follows a cyclical patterns of increasing tension, some precipitating event, and a physically violent act, followed by remorse and often some form of restitution. At the same time, you or the person you are trying to advise can make choices about the ways to negotiate power in your relationships so these relationships do not include violence. You may need to change the context in which the relationship is maintained, for example, by putting physical distance between you and your partner. It may also be necessary to seek outside counsel and support from a third party and to learn new patterns of communication using more productive strategies for negotiating power in the relationship. Our point is that one person can choose to alter his or her own behaviors that contribute to the patterns of communication enacted in a problematic relationship and can explore appropriate ways to use the power currencies he or she has in those relationships.

Chapter Summary

All of the relationship problems we have discussed in this chapter are examples of degenerative spirals. If allowed to go unchecked, these patterns usually lead to some kind of relationship deterioration. We've provided descriptions of these patterns not to depress you, but to honestly assess some of the effects of negative power struggles in interpersonal relationships and to provide you with some strategies to respond to them. We also hope that you will be alerted to patterns of communication that have the potential to become destructive in your relationships, and will work to alter them before they get firmly established. Taking the time to metacommunicate about the directions you see your relationships moving is one way to alter the trajectory of degenerative spirals.

Although it may still be tempting to blame another person when something goes wrong, we encourage you to keep in mind that communication in all relationships, whether it is productive or destructive, is collaboratively created. As we've said, the lowest common denominator in your relationships is two, and if you don't like the way things are going, one of you can begin to change them. Fault and blame are likely to be ascribed by others when you experience any relational problems, and we admit that it can be comforting to feel support, even when it comes in the form of someone else blaming your partner for you. But, as we have argued earlier, fault and blame are unproductive strategies for moving the relationship in new directions. We encourage you to focus instead on accountability and response-ability, to use the skills you've been learning and practicing in earlier chapters, and to actively consider your choices about what to do next.

Remember, the quality of your communication is directly related to the quality of your life, and you do have choices about the communicating you experience. When you find yourself faced with a deceptive friend, with the fact that you are verbally abusive to a family member, or with the fact that you are involved in an intimate relationship marked by incidents of physical violence, you do have choices that can improve the quality of your life by changing the qualities of your communication.

In Other Words

In this chapter we have noted the importance of seeking outside counsel as a strategy for responding to problems in relationships. In this excerpt, Shook describes a community-based approach to responding to relational problems. As you read this section, consider the cultural norms of interaction that make this approach (1) possible and (2) productive for the participants. What cultural and/or social norms might inhibit you from participating in such a process? If you were to solicit the support of others outside your relationship for managing the problematic patterns of communication, with whom would you talk? Is it likely that you would have to approach others, or would they approach you to offer their support and insights? To what extent would you be willing or able to accept the perspective of others regarding your relationship? Why?

* * *

An Introduction to the Practice of *Ho'oponopono*

E. V. Shook

A rich body of knowledge about the physical, emotional, and spiritual well-being of an individual in relationship to family, community, and environment has existed in the Hawaiian culture for centuries. One of the specific practices is a complex system for maintaining harmonious relationships and resolving conflict within the extended family; this system is called *ho'oponopono* (pronounced, ho'o pono pono), which means "setting to right." Within the last ten years this concept has become popularized and a number of individuals, mostly within social service programs, have attempted to use this traditional family concept and practice. . . .

A Description

Ho'oponopono is a method for restoring harmony that was traditionally used within the extended family. According to Pukui, it literally means "setting to right . . . to restore and maintain good relationships among family, and family and supernatural powers" (1972, 60). The metaphor of a tangled net has been used to illustrate how problems within a family affect not only persons directly involved but also other family members. The family is a complex net of relationships, and any disturbance in one part of the net will pull other parts. This metaphor reinforces the Hawaiian philosophy of the interrelatedness of all things.

The family conference was traditionally led by a senior family member or, if necessary, by a respected outsider such as a *kahuna lapa'au* (healer). The problem-solving process is a complex and potentially lengthy one that includes prayer, statement of the problem, discussion, confession of wrongdoing, restitution when necessary, forgiveness, and release. An outline of the conditions and steps of *ho'oponopono* and an abbreviated example of a hypothetical ho'oponopono session follow.

The Steps

Ho'oponopono is opened with *pule*, which is prayer conducted to ask God and/or the *'aumakua* for assistance and blessing in the problem-solving endeavor. *Pule* is usually led by the senior person conducting the session. Reliance on spiritual assistance heightens and strengthens the emotional commitment of the participants. Prayer lays the foundation for sincerity and truthfulness, necessary conditions to be maintained throughout the process.

In the beginning phase there is a period of identifying the general problem, known as *kukulu kumuhana*. (This term has two additional meanings that are a part of *ho'oponopono*. *Kukulu kumuhana* is the pooling of strengths for a shared purpose, such as solving the family's problem. It also refers to the leader's effort to reach out to a person who is resisting the *ho'oponopono* process to enable that person to participate fully.) During this initial phase the procedures for the whole problem-solving sequence are also outlined in order to reacquaint all participants with them.

Once the proper climate is set, the leader focuses on the specific problem. The *hala*, or transgression, is stated. *Hala* also implies that the perpetrator and the person wronged are bound together in a relationship of negative entanglement called *hihia*.

Because of the nature of *hihia*, most problems have many dimensions. The initial hurt is often followed by other reactions, further misunderstandings, and so forth until a complex knot of difficulties has evolved. It is the leader's responsibility to choose one of the problems and work it out with the family through the process of *mahiki*, or discussion. With one part resolved, the group can uncover and resolve successive layers of trouble one layer at a time until the family relationships are again free and clear.

The discussion of the problem is led and channeled by the leader. This intermediary function keeps individuals from directly confronting one another, a situation that could lead to further emotional outburst and misunderstanding.

Traditionally, the Hawaiians felt that allowing emotional expressions to escalate discouraged problem resolution. Each participant who has been affected by the problem in some way—directly or indirectly—is asked to share his or her feelings, or *mana'o*. The emphasis is on self-scrutiny, and when participants share they are encouraged to do so honestly, openly, and in a way that avoids blame and recrimination. If in the course of the discussion tempers begin to flare, the leader may declare *ho'omalu*, a cooling-off period of silence. This enables the family to reflect once again on the purpose of the process and to bring then aroused emotions under control.

When the discussion is complete, the *mihi* takes place. This is the sincere confession of wrongdoing and the seeking of forgiveness. It is expected that forgiveness be given whenever asked. If restitution is necessary then the terms of it are arranged and agreed upon.

Closely related to *mihi* is *kala*, or a loosening of the negative entanglements. Both the person who has confessed and the person who has forgiven are expected to *kala* the problem. This mutual release is an essential part of the process and true *ho'oponopono* is not complete without it. The *kala* indicates that the conflicts and hurts have been released and are *oki* (cut off).

The *pani* is the closing phase and may include a summary of what has taken place and, importantly, a reaffirmation of the family's strength and enduring bonds. The problem that has been worked out is declared closed, never to be brought up again. If other layers of the problem need to be worked out, the final *pani* is postponed. Sometimes *ho'oponopono* may take many sessions. Each session has a *pani* about what has been resolved and includes a closing prayer, *pule ho'opau*. After the session the family and leader traditionally share a snack or meal to which all have contributed. This demonstrates the commitment and bond of all who participated and provides a familiar means to move from the formal problem-solving setting to normal daily routines.

In summary, *ho'oponopono* is a highly structured process with four distinct phases: an opening phase that includes the prayer and a statement of the problem; a discussion phase in which all members involved share their thoughts and feelings in a calm manner and listen to all the others as they speak; a resolution phase that enables the exchange of confession, forgiveness, and release; and a closing phase to summarize what has transpired and to give spiritual and individual thanks for sincere participation. . . .

Excerpted from Shook, E. V., *Ho'oponopono: Contemporary Uses of a Hawaiian Problem-Solving Process*, pp. 1, 10–12. Copyright © 1985. Reprinted with permission of University of Hawai'i Press.

References

Andersen, P. 1998. *Nonverbal Communication: Forms and Functions.* New York: McGraw-Hill.

Carey, C., and Mongeau, P. 1996. "Communication and Violence in Courtship Relationships." In D. Cahn and S. Lloyd (eds.), *Family Violence from A*

Communication Perspective. Hillsdale, NJ: Lawrence Erlbaum. Pages 127–150.

Cate, R. M., and Lloyd, S. A. 1992. *Courtship.* Thousand Oaks, CA: Sage.

Deutsch, M. 1973. "Conflicts: Productive and Destructive." In F. Jandt (ed.), *Conflict Resolution Through Communication.* New York: Harper and Row.

Emerson, R. 1962. "Power-Dependence Relations." *American Sociological Review,* 27: 31–41.

Hopper, R., and Bell, R. A. 1984. "Broadening the Deception Construct." *Quarterly Journal of Speech,* 70: 288–300.

Infante, D., and Wigley, C. 1986. "Verbal Aggressiveness: An Interpersonal Model and Measure." *Communication Monographs,* 53: 61–69.

Jones, W. H., and Burdette, M. P. 1994. "Betrayal in Relationships." In A. L. Weber and J. H. Harvey (eds.), *Perspectives On Close Relationships.* Boston: Allyn and Bacon. Pages 245–262.

Marshall, L. L. 1994. "Physical and Psychological Abuse." In W. Cupach and B. Spitzberg (eds.), *The Dark Side of Interpersonal Communication.* Hillsdale, NJ: Lawrence Erlbaum. Pages 292–297.

McGraw, P. 2003. *Relationship Rescue: A Seven-Step Strategy for Reconnecting With Your Partner.* New York: Hyperion.

O'Hair, H. D., and Cody, M. J. 1994. "Deception." In W. Cupach and B. Spitzberg (eds.), *The Dark Side of Interpersonal Communication.* Hillsdale, NJ: Lawrence Erlbaum.

Sabourin, T. C. 1995. "The Role of Negative Reciprocity in Spouse Abuse: A Relational Control Analysis." *Journal of Applied Communication Research,* 23: 271–283.

Vangelisti, A. 1994. "Messages That Hurt." In W. Cupach and B. Spitzberg (eds.), *The Dark Side of Interpersonal Communication.* Hillsdale, NJ: Lawrence Erlbaum. Pages 61–79.

Vissing, Y, and Baily, W. 1996. "Parent-to-Child Verbal Aggression." In D. Cahn and S. Lloyd (eds.), *Family Violence From a Communication Perspective.* Hillsdale, NJ: Lawrence Erlbaum. Pages 85–107.

Wilmot, W. W. 1995. *Relational Communication.* New York: McGraw-Hill.

Wilmot, W., and Hocker, J. 2001. *Interpersonal Conflict.* Boston: McGraw-Hill. ✦

Chapter Eleven

Managing Conflict Effectively

Chapter Objectives

When you complete this chapter, you should be able to do the following:
- Understand how conflict is a natural part of communication that can't be eliminated but can be managed effectively.
- Understand how conflict and culture are interrelated.
- Identify the five features of conflict: expressed struggle, interdependent parties, perceived incompatible goals, scarce resources, and interference.
- Understand the relationship between conflict and communication.
- Identify six potential benefits of conflict.
- Recognize in yourself and others the five common conflict management styles: avoidance, accommodation, competition, compromise, and collaboration.
- Identify the advantages and disadvantages of each style.
- Describe the connection between the collaborative style and nexting.
- List and give examples of 11 conflict management tactics.
- Describe how to approach an apparently irresolvable conflict.

Chapter Preview

This chapter starts by encouraging you to reflect on how you think and feel about conflict. Most people see conflict as a communication problem to be avoided or eliminated. The common view is that conflict creates difficulties in work, family, dating, friend, and international relationships and that the world would be much better off without it. But we encourage you to think about conflict as normal rather than abnormal, as a kind of communicating that has some benefits and that, because it's normal, cannot be eliminated but can be effectively managed.

The second major part of the chapter asks you to review how you personally engage in or "do" conflict. Years of research done in several different Western cultures has identified five basic conflict styles or ways that people communicate in conflict situations. We explore the strengths and weaknesses, advantages and disadvantages of each style. This section illustrates once again the importance of communication *flexibility.* There is no one best way to cope with all conflicts, and the most effective communicators apply a wide range of conflict management resources in different situations.

The third part of the chapter provides you with a number of specific attitudes and skills for dealing with the conflicts you experience. We lay out a kind of "salad bar" of conflict management tactics. You can use your understanding of what conflict is (part 1 of the chapter) and your awareness of own conflict styles (part 2) to choose appropriate specific responses to help you manage your own conflicts (part 3).

Conflict and Culture

Like all kinds of communicating, conflict and culture are interrelated. This means that the cultural environment you grew up in influences how you think and feel about conflict and how you manage conflicts. Overall, we can distinguish between cultures that see conflict as an *opportunity* and cultures that see it as a *destructive force.*

In most Western cultures, at least some people think about conflict as an *opportunity* and a useful process that can result in a renewal and strengthening of relationships. This perspective on conflict admits that there might be people who don't enjoy conflict, but even these people would say that in many cases working through conflict can be a positive thing to do (Canary, Cupach, and Messman 1995). In Western cultures conflict is often regarded as one way of securing your individual rights, executing your right to free speech, and "working things out."

From another perspective, conflict is a *destructive force.* This perspective is rooted in cultural and religious values and often also in a rather strict societal structure. This does not mean that people completely avoid conflict; they just deal with it in different ways. For instance, in many Arab cultures, you won't find children arguing with their parents. In interviews with Iraqi people, Saskia found that the parents try to teach their children to express modesty in front of their parents and not to contradict them because they have more wisdom and deserve children's respect.

This is not to say that conflict is absent from cultures where it is regarded as destructive. However, in these cultures, open disagreement, especially between younger and older people, is regarded as inappropriate. Either the parties avoid it, or they ask a third party—a friend or elder—to help. For instance, what happens in the United States when someone commits murder? If and when the person is caught, the accused is given a trial to determine guilt or innocence and the court provides guidelines for sentencing. In some areas in Palestine, people use a method called *Sulha* to manage disputes. The reading at the end of this chapter talks about *Sulha*, in which the parties who are in conflict use an elder as a mediator. This method helps to diffuse anger and hate, to repair the relationships between the conflicting parties and to reestablish the dignity of the people involved.

Overall, researchers have found that individualistic societies, such as the United States, Western Europe, Canada, and Australia, engage in more conflict than collectivistic cultures, such as those in Asia or most Arab countries. One of the reasons is that the former place more emphasis on individual rights, values, and obligations than on those of the group. In contrast, collectivistic cultures emphasize extended family relationships and contributing to the group. In these cultures, the "us" is more important than the "I." The differences are not this simple, of course, since global travel, communication technology, and the export of Western goods and values exert individualistic influences on collectivist societies. In addition, within any given nation, individuals must negotiate the tensions between their cultural heritage and societal norms.

Generally, however, people from individualistic cultures tend to be concerned with achieving individual goals in conflicts and tend to use more confrontational and solution-oriented conflict tactics (Martin and Nakayama 2000; Ting-Toomey et. al. 1991). Those from collectivistic cultures tend to try to preserve the harmony of the group and the dignity of all people involved by using more avoiding and accommodating conflict styles. The conflict style you choose is affected by your cultural values. It is also influenced by the situation you are in and the relationship you have with the other person. In the next sections of this chapter, we talk mainly about Western conflict management styles and tactics. The reading at the end gives you an opportunity to think about a non-Western approach to conflict.

What Is Conflict?

All five of the communication difficulties we discussed in the previous chapter typically involve conflict. So this chapter, "Managing Conflict Effectively," relates to Chapter Ten as "solution" relates to "problem." You can think of this chapter, partly, as a series of suggestions about how to cope effectively with *deception*, *betrayal*, *harassment*, *co-dependence*, and *breakup*.

But conflict also happens in many less extreme forms and in more everyday situations than those discussed in Chapter Ten. For example, you or someone you know has probably experienced something like the following: A son still lives at home but is planning to move out soon. He wants the freedom of having his own place, and although he appreciates what his family has done for him, he really feels it's time to be on his own. But he can't quite afford it yet. His parents know that he wants to be more independent, and they give him some space by letting his room be private—except when they entertain. Then they want their guests to see a neat and clean house, and his part of it is sometimes not as presentable as they want. As a result, something like this exchange often occurs.

Parent: We're having some people over Saturday night, so I want you to clean your room.

Son: My room is fine the way it is.

Parent: Look, I've made this point a hundred times before: It is not "fine"! You may be able to live in that kind of mess, but most people can't. I don't want my friends thinking our house is a pigpen.

Son: It's my room! Just let me shut the door, and I'll try my best not to shame you!

Parent: Oh, cut the crap! That's not the point. Your room's a mess, and it won't hurt you to clean it.

Son: (Leaving) I'll move enough stuff to get the door closed, but that's it!

Conflicts like this happen every day. Spouses argue about where to spend their vacation, siblings disagree about who should clean up the kitchen, coworkers express different ideas about how best to meet management's production goals, teachers disagree with other teachers about what courses should be offered, students experience conflicts with teachers about grades, and group or committee members clash over who's responsible for which parts of their task. In fact, if you think about what we said about communication in Chapter Two and about interpersonal communication in Chapter Three (and the following chapters), you can see that conflict is a completely normal part of communicating, something that communicators can *expect* to happen fairly regularly.

Here's why: First, recalling Chapter Two, communication is too continuous and complex to go smoothly all the time. No set of events as complicated as human communicating can possibly be completely trouble free, and "conflict" is the general term for these troubles. Second, communication always involves collaboration. This means that it's always a joint action; it's never just a matter of *one* person's inhaling and exhaling. Since it's impossible to completely predict or control—

and sometimes even to understand—another person's thinking, feeling, and acting, there will always be surprises, unexpected turns that can generate disagreement. There's never been a conflict-free time in either local or global human history, and it's highly unlikely that there ever will be. Third, interpersonal communication happens when *uniquenesses meet,* and this is an almost certain recipe for some disagreement. When two or more *different* people connect, eventually their differences will come in contact, and there will be some clash. In fact, it can be said that any two communicators who haven't experienced conflict don't yet know each other very well.

So conflict can be as intense and toxic as our examples of deception, betrayal, and aggression, *and* it can be as normal as the disagreements all of us experience every day. Especially in its milder forms, conflict is an inevitable part of human communicating. It's as much a part of peoples' ordinary experience as changes in the weather. Think how strange—silly even—it would be to try to *eliminate* changes in the weather. They are part of "the way things are." They've always happened, they will continue to happen, and people learn to cope with or manage them by dressing differently, changing activities, altering their environment, or, in some cases, moving to another climate. In an important way conflict is similar. It's most realistic and helpful to see it not as a problem to be avoided but as a common condition that, because it often creates serious problems, needs to be managed effectively.

As a first step toward effectively managing conflict, let's think together about how this common condition can best be understood. Many books focus entirely on conflict management, and they draw from an abundant research literature that defines conflict generally as *an expressed struggle between at least two interdependent parties who perceive incompatible goals, scarce resources, and interference from others in achieving their goals* (Wilmot and Hocker 2001). Let's unpack this definition to see what it's saying.

Expressed Struggle

The definition begins by emphasizing that conflict happens *between,* not *within,* people. Everybody has experiences of indecision, confusion, and worry that we sometimes call *internal conflict.* But this is not what this chapter emphasizes. An interpersonal approach to conflict management focuses on the communicative exchanges that make up the conflict episode. The feelings that people experience are obviously important, and even they are not completely "internal." Feelings are affected strongly by verbal and nonverbal talk—what we hear, whether and how we express what we're feeling, how others respond to our expressions. As a result, much of what follows can change how you *feel* in conflict. But this chapter focuses mainly on what happens in the *expressed struggle*.

In addition, if you take seriously the idea from Chapter Three that humans are "responders," then even the most private and seemingly internal feelings have many social, cultural, or interpersonal dimensions because they are responses to events and experiences that preceded them. The student's internal conflict about what major to declare is strongly affected by past conversations with parents; a dating partner's seemingly private agonizing over whether to have sex echoes conversations he or she has had with friends, parents, and other sexual partners; and inner turmoil about how to spend a large sum of money taps values learned in other conversations. So conflict involves *expressed* struggle, and there are expressed, communicative parts of even the most seemingly internal feelings.

When we define interpersonal conflict as something that occurs *between* individuals and groups, we're also excluding screaming at the wall or pounding a pillow. Some people believe that ventilating or exploding in private can be a useful way to release feelings. Others cite the research that shows how even private violent acts tend to promote further violence, not to reduce it. We agree with authors who emphasize the importance of learning to manage the stress in your life as one way to avoid conflict (Weaver 1990). But we concentrate in this chapter on how to manage it when it occurs, and since ventilating doesn't happen between you and someone else, we don't treat it as an instance of conflict.

Most interpersonal struggles are not expressed in front of signs with a microphone in your hand. But whether it's subtle or overt, conflict happens when struggle is expressed between people.

Notice another way that this part of the definition sharpens the focus of this chapter. Some disagreements are deep and long term. They may have started years ago. We often call them conflicts, too. For example, a supervisor may say that she's had a conflict with the vice president ever since she came to the company. In this chapter we are not talking about the same thing that this supervisor is. We are focusing more narrowly on the specific, concrete communication events where the ongoing hostility actually happens—the exchange of sharp words between the supervisor and the vice president at the planning meeting, or their disagreement over her decision to promote Leroy instead of Sue. Why this narrower focus? Because it concentrates on the communication—the verbal and nonverbal exhaling and inhaling that the people involved can most readily do something about.

This definition basically says that conflict becomes concrete or manifests itself in communication. The verbal or nonverbal "expression" of the struggle may be as subtle as a raised eyebrow or a sarcastic tone of voice. Or it may be as obvious as a shouting match. But whether implicit or explicit, conflict, like all communicating, *happens between people.*

'But . . .' A Student Responds

When you restrict "conflict" to what happens "between" people, you cut out the events that confuse me the most—my internal conflicts. What can I do about them?

First, recognize that the distinction you're making between "external" and "internal" isn't as clear as it might appear. Internal conflicts are affected by all kinds of external events, especially ones involving identities. So if you apply the advice that's given in this chapter, it will help you deal with your internal conflicts.

Second, we're communication teachers, not psychologists or psychotherapists, so we focus on what we know best. You may want to read some clinical psychology books, take a psychology class, or talk with a counselor to develop a response to your question. In fact, the best general suggestion we have for dealing with internal conflicts is to discuss them with someone you trust. They tend to grow and get distorted when you keep them inside. Talking with others can put them in perspective and help you cope.

Interdependent Parties

If Tammy and Andrea are completely *independent,* then nothing either person does affects the other. Tammy can shave off her eyebrows and tattoo her entire face, and Andrea could care less. If Andrea is *dependent* on Tammy, then Tammy's behavior affects Andrea, but not the other way around. But if the two are *interdependent,* then what Tammy does affects Andrea, and Andrea's choices affect Tammy. Conflict happens between parties who are interdependent.

The most important idea that comes from this part of the definition is that *all conflict includes some collaboration.* At this point in this book, this is probably not surprising for you to hear; we've equated collaboration and interdependence before. But it's important to remember that conflict can only happen when the parties involved *agree* to "show up and fight." If they're not actually *inter*dependent, they won't engage with each other. Obviously, people in conflict also disagree, sometimes very strongly. But in order for a conflict to occur, the parties to it also have to agree to participate in the struggle.

Sometimes conflicts are mainly about how interdependent the parties are. Divorced parents in conflict over child custody arrangements usually recognize that their mutual love of their children makes them interdependent, but some want to minimize the amount of interdependence by agreeing to abide by a legal document that contains all the custody schedule and rules. Other divorced parents prefer to work within a general framework but to interdependently discuss month-to-month or vacation-to-vacation issues. But interdependence is an issue in other relationships, too. As you probably recall, research that we cited in Chapter Nine concluded that "independence←——→interdependence" is one of the tensions or dialectics that friends of all kinds are continually managing. This dialectic or tension also affects relationships among family members, spouses, and coworkers.

It's important to remember, though, that harmony or peace is not the only opposite of conflict. Mutual disinterest, apathy, or independence can also prevent conflict from occurring. When you do experience conflict, it can help to remember that the fact that you're disagreeing means partly that both or all of you care enough—or are forced to care enough—to engage with each other, to be interdependent.

The word *parties* is a reminder that conflict can happen between individuals and between groups. Sometimes, in fact, group memberships draw us into conflicts. Role definitions and group allegiances often contribute to struggles between, for example, salespeople and production workers, teachers and students, junior and senior members of an organization, labor and management, dorm or apartment residents, and members of sororities and fraternities. You might find yourself in conflict with a stranger just because you are a Baptist, Young Republican, mountain biker, or vegetarian.

Perceived Incompatible Goals

It sometimes seems like a conflict is only about the past or immediate present—she insulted me, he's too stubborn, she's not being fair, he did not do what he said he'd do. But actions prompt expressions of concern only when they are perceived to be interfering with some short- or longer-term goal. If an insult happened yesterday and affected only the past, I wouldn't bother to complain. But insults hurt because of what they say about how people might treat me *in the future*; they challenge an identity that underlies my communication this afternoon and tomorrow. Stubbornness may have been a problem in the past, but it generates conflict when it is also perceived to be a problem in the continuing relationship. So the phrase "perceived incompatible goals" emphasizes that conflict is prompted, implicitly or explicitly, by what the parties believe will happen next to some goals they are pursuing.

This means that it's important for people in conflict to identify which goals are perceived to be incompatible. Sometimes this inquiry alone can effectively manage the conflict. One influential book about conflict points out that people can sometimes discover that they have conflicting *positions* but compatible *interests* (Fisher and Ury 1981). To explain the difference between positions and interests, this book gives the example of two people quarreling in a library because one wants the window open and the other wants it closed. They bicker back and forth about how much to leave it open: a crack, halfway, three quarters of the way. No solution satisfies them both. Enter the librarian. She asks one why he wants the window open: "To get some fresh air." She asks the other why he wants it closed: "To avoid the draft." After thinking a minute, she opens wide a window in the next room, bringing in fresh air without a draft (Fisher and Ury 1981, 41).

Until the librarian intervened, the two didn't realize that they had competing *positions* but compatible *interests*. In other words, their immediate goals put them in conflict, but they had broader goals that enabled room for agreement. So long as they were perceiving only their incompatible *positions*—"I want the window closed," "I want the window open"—their conflict continued. But the librarian was able to focus on potentially compatible *interests*—"I want fresh air," "I don't mind fresh air, so long as it doesn't come with a draft." As we'll emphasize later in the chapter, people who manage conflict effectively have learned, among other things, to distinguish positions from interests and to focus on interests rather than positions, because they offer the most potential for effective conflict management.

It's also important to realize how *goals* are linked to *identities*. As we mentioned, insults and unfairness generate problems because of what they claim about how certain *kinds of people* (identities) will respond in the future. An insult contradicts part of how I define myself: I'm offended, for example, because I don't see myself as "inconsiderate," "lazy," "forgetful," or "always complaining." Unfairness is similarly resisted because most people want to think of themselves as fair, reasonable, and evenhanded. Notice the ways identities are central in each of these exchanges:

Employee: I can make this decision.

Boss: No, you can't. You haven't been on the job long enough.

Father: What are you doing coming in at this hour? You don't have any business staying out so late!

Son: I can take care of myself!

Jerry: Should I take my break now?

Cicellie: Why do you keep asking me what to do next? I'm not your boss! Schedule your own time!

So the phrase in the definition about incompatible goals can alert you to the identity-management issues that are part of every conflict. Every conflict, in other words, is partly a clash over identities. Goals indicate what people want to or plan to do in the future, and they are tied to how we define ourselves—the kind of person I think I am. Consequently, one of the first questions you should ask about any conflict you're in is, "How are identities being questioned or challenged in this exchange?"

Perceived Scarce Resources

A *resource* is any physical, economic, or social consequence that people perceive positively (Wilmot and Hocker 2001, 46). People engage in conflict when they perceive that there is not enough space, money, attention, or some other resource to go around. As conflict scholars and teachers, Bill Wilmot and Joyce Hocker emphasize, in interpersonal struggles, two resources that are often perceived as scarce are power and self-esteem. When someone complains "she always gets her way," the disputed resource is power. "Why does he have to be so sarcastic?" can be about self-esteem; it's difficult to feel good about yourself around someone who continually makes snide remarks. "I refuse to pay one more penny in child support" can also be a complaint about both power and self-esteem.

Sometimes the problem is not the scarcity of the resource but the perception that it's scarce. Friends sometimes believe that each other's affection is limited, for example, so conflict happens when one friend spends time with someone else. It may help for both to recognize that, while time is a limited or scarce resource, caring and affection are not. In this case the most helpful conflict management move might be to try to change the person's perception of the resource rather than trying to reallocate the resource itself. But, in any case, you'll be better able to manage the conflicts you experience if you understand the perceived scarce resource that the conflict is about.

Perceived Interference

This is the third part of the recipe for conflict between interdependent parties: perceived incompatible goals, perceived scarce resources, and perceived interference in reaching the goal(s) or receiving the resource(s). It would be at least theoretically possible to be interdependent and to have conflicting goals about scarce resources but not to engage in conflict, because you don't perceive the other person to be the one who's interfering. But conflict occurs when the parties do perceive each other as standing in the way of accomplishing their goals. For example, a team leader and a staff scientist at a genetic-engineering firm were in conflict over the scientist's presentations of the results of her experiments and the team leader's management style. The manager wanted different information in the presentations, and the scientist believed that the manager kept shifting his demands. She believed that she could present credible, clear reports if he wouldn't interfere by making unreasonable and constantly changing demands. He believed that the group he managed would be more productive if she wouldn't interfere with their success by giving confusing presentations. They both saw the other person as "causing the problem."

As we've noted, this definition of conflict—as an expressed struggle between at least two interdependent parties who perceive incompatible goals, scarce resources, and interference from others in achieving their goals—can help conflicting parties manage their difficulties by clarifying just what's happening between them. First, those involved can realize that the fact that they're in conflict means that both of them "give a damn." They have at least one important similarity—one way that they are co-labor-ating—and it is that they care enough to express their struggle. Second, they can think about their apparently incompatible goals and can explore whether there are common *interests* hiding behind conflicting *positions*. Third, they can at least notice the differences in identities or definitions-of-selves that are part of the conflict. Fourth, the parties can think and talk about the resources that are at stake. Sometimes—although not always—reframing the ways people are thinking about resources can help the parties understand that both of them can get a lot of what they want. Finally, they can check to be sure that the person they're in conflict with is actually standing in the way of reaching their goals. Sometimes the person you're shouting at *seems* to be the main interference, but when you think about it you realize that they're just a target of opportunity—the one unlucky enough to be in the line of fire. Like other communication difficulties, most conflicts are *not* one person's fault.

One important implication of this definition of conflict is that it happens by way of communication. This might sound obvious, but it's helpful to remember that if you want to do something about the conflicts you experience, you'll have to do something about your *commu-*

nication attitudes and skills. Everything we've said in the first 10 chapters of this book applies to conflict situations.

At the same time, it's important to recognize that all conflict is *not* simply a matter of a lack of communication skills. Some people feel it is. They believe that when people disagree, the problem is poor communication, and that if they communicate better, the disagreement will vanish. But this is a myth. *All conflict does involve communication, but not all conflict is rooted in poor communication.*

Sometimes disagreements *can* be cleared up just by improving the communication between the people involved. At other times, however, two persons—or groups—may communicate effectively and still be in conflict. For example, although many marriages could have been saved by better communication, some divorces occur when the parties finally communicate effectively, accurately, and fully enough to discover that their marriage just won't work. In these cases, good communication clarifies how fundamental the differences actually are. Similarly, when an employee resigns or asks to be transferred because of continual arguments with the supervisor, the problem may not be misunderstanding. The two individuals may understand each other very well and still disagree.

One reason we call this chapter "Managing Conflict Effectively" instead of "Resolving Conflict" or "Conflict Resolution" is that many conflicts cannot be *resolved;* they can't be "put to rest" or "permanently settled." But they still can be *handled* or *managed* interpersonally. While writing this book, for example, the three of us have experienced a working relationship that has included disagreements and misunderstandings, frustrations, and disappointments, but that has so far been free of hostile conflict. This doesn't mean we've avoided all destructive conflicts in our lives. We've been in serious and sometimes toxic disputes with partners, spouses, students, and friends. As conflict managers, we're far from perfect. But our relationship with each other is evidence of the fact that conflict management can enable persons or groups to disagree and still communicate interpersonally.

Benefits of Conflict

As we noted, many people think conflict is bad. When two researchers recorded the spontaneous metaphors people use to talk about conflict, they found that most of them were strongly negative. For example, the central metaphor was that "conflict is warlike and violent." The next four metaphors they discuss are "conflict is explosive," "conflict is an upward struggle," "conflict is a trial," and "conflict is a struggle." As they conclude, "Many images and expressions of conflict cast such a negative tone around the process that creativity stays stifled" (Wilmot and Hocker 2001).

What elements of interpersonal conflict are evident to you in this encounter?

Part of the problem is that when people think about conflict, they think about only part of it. When we dread conflict, it's partly because we remember most vividly the feelings we have *before* and *during* a disagreement and are least aware of our feelings *after the intense part is over*. To be in the midst of a strong disagreement is stressful and threatening. But after it's over, it is often satisfying to notice the understanding that came out of it or to realize that your relationship has survived the difficult experience. Conflict can produce positive outcomes.

Another benefit of conflict is that it can help groups make better decisions. Group communication researchers and teachers have shown how the absence of conflict in a group can be unhealthy, because it can lead to a condition called "groupthink," in which a decision is adopted without alternatives being carefully considered (Janis 1972). Groups work better when the people in them recognize that effectively managed disagreements can lead to better decisions (Fisher and Ellis, 1990). Working through conflicts can bind groups closer together, help members define group structure, and promote helpful associations and coalitions.

Some of this can also happen in legal situations. Most court systems in the Western world are based on the conviction that one way to discover the best solution to a problem is to bring together an advocate for each position and to see what emerges when they clash. This "adversary system" operates on the assumption that truth and justice usually emerge from the crucible of controversy, so long as there are rules

Many people think of conflict as war. If this is your general metaphor for conflict, you will probably not be able to see the positive potential that conflict can bring to organizations, families, friends, and lovers.

that apply equally to both sides. We definitely do not believe that you should treat all your relationships like court battles. In fact, real harm can come to a relationship when each person gets put on a "side" and all work out of a win/lose stance. But if, for example, you are talking with a friend about your plans for buying a new computer, and your friend disagrees with your decision by countering your carefully thought-out plans with expert information, both of you will probably learn from the discussion. Our point is that sometimes conflict can be good because it can help the parties discover the best solution or approach to a problem.

You can identify another benefit of conflict if you think about how, after years of being together, some couples' communication degenerates into monotonous patterns like these:

"Good morning, honey."
"Morning."
"What'd you do with the toothpaste?"
"On the counter."
"Don't forget your keys."
"Yeah. Have a good day."

"You too."
"Hi, honey. How'd it go today?"
"Nothing special. You?"

Some conflict could move the situation out of this kind of rut. We're not saying that you should pick a fight just for the sake of fighting, but that you should be aware of the energy potential that a legitimate disagreement can bring to a relationship.

Conflict is also helpful when it provides a way to get feelings out in the open, where they can be handled. It's often not wise to hide feelings, especially strong ones. But this happens, and it takes a disagreement to bring them out. When feelings are expressed—and not until then—they can be dealt with, and the parties can recognize and figure out how to respond to each other's disappointment, impatience, or fear.

Another way conflict can be good is that, as we suggested, it can help to promote confidence in a relationship. Typically, for example, a couple will spend a great deal of time together before making a commitment or getting married, and although they feel they know each other well, there is still some uncertainty about what the other person would do if things *really* get difficult. Their first serious argument is a major event, but the confidence that follows it can be even more important. Both feel a new sureness, a new secure feeling about the strength of the relationship. And conflict is what helps to promote this feeling. The same thing can happen in your work or living group, in committees and other organizations you belong to, and in your family.

Conflict can also promote genuine interpersonal contact. For example, a person who's always been on the low-power end of a relationship might decide that he or she is tired of being relegated to follower status and might use a disagreement to express a desire to change the relationship. In this case, conflict can be personally empowering. Or, when a friend strongly challenges your job decision or your choice of major, it often provides an opportunity for the two of you to *meet*—to really experience the unique differences between you. If you've thought carefully about your decision and your friend has too, chances are that there won't be a lot of role playing or putting on a front as you argue. You will be *there*, really present, being who you are rather than seeming to be someone else. So will your friend. Of course, this doesn't always happen. Sometimes people respond to conflict by putting up a front and hiding behind it. But conflict can, and often does, help people to make direct, straightforward, genuinely interpersonal contact.

Our point is that from a Western perspective, conflict, whether in intimate relationships, work groups, living groups, families, clubs, or other organizations, can be a positive force. As we've already said, you can never eliminate it so long as people continue to be unique and to communicate. And there's no need to try, because it is not inherently "bad." As a matter of fact, whether it's bad or good depends on how it's handled.

Applying What You Know

Benefits of Conflict

Identify four specific relationships you're in, one with a family member, one with a friend, one with a coworker, and one with a dating partner or lover. For each relationship, recall a conflict you've recently experienced. Then suggest what may have been a *benefit* of that conflict.

1. Family member_____
   Conflict_____
   Benefit of the conflict_____
2. Friend_____
   Conflict_____
   Benefit of the conflict_____
3. Coworker_____
   Conflict_____
   Benefit of the conflict_____
4. Dating partner or lover_____
   Conflict_____
   Benefit of the conflict_____

'But . . .' A Student Responds

Textbooks always seem to make reality so simple and straightforward, but it isn't. Conflict is never easy. It can really get messy "in the heat of the battle." I wish you'd admit this.

You're absolutely right. If you haven't heard us say this before, we'll say it now: Conflict is never easy. All you can do is the best you can do. But you can make improvements if you work at it. As family therapist Virginia Satir used to say, "It works if you do."

Conflict Styles

The term *conflict style* means a person's typical or habitual way of responding to conflict. For example, some people *avoid* conflict at all costs, and others love to *compete*. There has been more research done on conflict styles than on any other aspect of conflict management (Folger, Poole, and Stutman 1993, 182). These and other discussions of

conflict styles note that there are some problems with this research because it often relies on self-reports, the results sometimes give the impression that styles aren't affected by context, and there are strong gender biases in some studies (Wilmot and Hocker 2001).

But we agree with these and other textbook authors that the beginning student of conflict management can still learn a great deal from
reviewing common conflict styles and reflecting on his or her own typical or favorite ways of coping with conflict. Even if the styles research
has some flaws, when you can recognize and label the ways you usually
respond to conflict, you can learn the benefits and limitations of your
own patterns. You can also learn other options, and this is the way to
enhance your communication flexibility. Remember that after we discuss these general styles, we'll outline 11 specific, concrete communication behaviors that can help you manage conflict effectively.

Different researchers and writers label the styles differently, but the
five that are most often identified are *avoidance, accommodation, competition, compromise,* and *collaboration.* You can distinguish among
the five by considering how each is responsive to four elements that are
part of every communication situation: your own goals, the other person's goals, the importance of the issue being discussed, and the health
of the relationship between or among the conflict parties. The following table summarizes the differences, and our explanations and examples will clarify them.

Table 11.1 Conflict Styles					
	Avoid	**Accommodate**	**Compete**	**Compromise**	**Collaborate**
Responsive to:					
My goals	LOW	LOW	HIGH	MODERATE	HIGH
Others' goals	LOW	HIGH	LOW	MODERATE	HIGH
Issue	LOW	LOW	HIGH	MODERATE	HIGH
Relationship	HIGH	HIGH	LOW	MODERATE	HIGH

Avoidance

Avoidance is a style characterized by trying to dodge the conflict by
ignoring or changing the topic, being vague about positions or preferences, or using joking to respond to a challenge, threat, or disagreement. A person using avoidance is showing little concern for his or her
own goals, the other's goals, and the issue and usually a moderate to
high concern for the relationship. A college student in a conversation
with his or her parents, for example, might change the subject when
asked about class attendance because the parents and student have experienced several destructive conflicts about this topic in the past.
Roommates dating the same person may avoid discussions of their

dates, spouses may avoid discussions of old issues that have proven insoluble, and coworkers often steer clear of hot political topics.

Verbally, avoidance is most often characterized by abrupt topic change. The point is *not* to follow a topic to its next reasonable question or conclusion, so the person doing the avoiding will shift focus. An avoidance contribution to a disagreement over a political or religious issue might be, "Did you see Liz the other night? She was dancing with that old guy—you know, the one who wears those ratty sweaters!" If the others pursue that topic far enough to discover another disagreement, the person doing the avoiding would switch again—"Let me tell you what happened at work yesterday! My boss almost killed me!"

Nonverbally avoidance is often marked by random and jerky body movements, inappropriate giggling and laughing, a voice loud enough to force attention toward it, and little direct eye contact. In other words, the mixed and primarily nonverbal behavior is an echo of the verbal—it goes in several directions at once.

Advantages of Avoidance. Avoidance is useful when you believe that the issue is trivial and that other, more important issues warrant your attention. It can also be appropriate when you feel little commitment to or involvement in a relationship. If you are convinced that there is little to be gained from your being engaged in a substantive conversation with someone, avoidance can make good sense. Third, avoidance can buy time to "regroup" or to think of some more developed response to a conflict situation. If you are a low-power person in a relationship, avoidance can also help keep you from harm. Spouses, children, and even subordinates of abusive husbands, wives, fathers, mothers, and bosses often use avoidance to protect themselves.

Disadvantages of Avoidance. When a person practices avoidance because he or she believes the topic is trivial or there is little to be gained from engaging with the other person, this person is sharply curtailing the extent to which the communication can be collaborative. Avoidance is a kind of collaboration, of course. It is one response to a situation and it permits, prevents, and promotes other responses. But when avoidance is based on only one party's preference, it can make it appear that there is little or no *mutual* influence in the conflict. And if the avoidance is effective, the range of possible responses from others is pretty narrow. The person doing the avoiding has decided to privilege his or her perceptions over everybody else's and not to let even that judgment be negotiated. As a result, avoidance can serve to let conflict "fester" without being aired, and sometimes this turns small problems into unnecessarily bigger ones. Avoidance can also reinforce the unrealistic notion that conflict is bad. Parents who habitually avoid conflict can cripple their children's future abilities to cope with the disagreements that they will inevitably encounter. As Hocker and Wilmot conclude, avoidance "usually preserves the conflict and sets the stage for a later explosion or backlash" (Hocker and Wilmot 1995, 140).

Remember that avoidance, like the four other styles, is a communication orientation toward conflict, not a personality type. No one is "an avoider" in all situations. Some people respond with avoidance more often than others, and everyone avoids conflict some of the time. As you read about all five styles, ask yourself which you favor and under what conditions. Then you'll begin to understand how you can increase your range of options to develop more *flexibility*.

Accommodation

Accommodation happens when a person puts away his or her own agendas and concerns in favor of pleasing the other people involved. It shows a low concern for one's own goals, high concern with the other's goals, low concern for the issue, and a moderate to high interest in the health of the relationship. You've probably heard it happen when someone says, "Oh, that's okay; whatever *you* want is fine . . . no problem . . . I don't care what we do . . . it's not up to me to decide." Some people accommodate by giving in—"I don't want to fight about this"—and others by denying their own needs—"I'll be fine here; you go ahead"—or by prioritizing peace above everything else—"Sure I'd like to go skiing at least once this year, but it's more important that you're not upset with me, so let's just go ahead and spend the time at the library." As you may hear in these examples, accommodation is a gendered response option in many cultures. In many Western cultures, women are socialized into both avoidance and accommodation. This is one of the cultural generalizations that we hope you will test against your own experience.

Some communicators also respond this way because accommodation, again like avoidance, is a way to deny and escape conflict and they think of conflict as "inappropriate in public" or simply "bad." At other times, people defer to others because they believe that their relationship "can't survive a fight." From this point of view, conflict may be okay for some people, but *this* relationship is too valuable or too delicate to risk disagreement. In some other cases, accommodating is a strategic attempt to manipulate the other person by making him or her feel guilty enough to let the accommodating person achieve his or her goal. So, for example, Alice might grudgingly permit Britta to engage in a behavior that Alice really doesn't approve of:

Alice: Are you playing golf again?

Britta: Yes, my tee time is eleven thirty.

Alice: Well, have fun, but you could have started earlier.

Britta: I know; maybe I'll call and cancel.

Alice: No, go ahead, you love to golf and you haven't very much lately. (Vangelisti, Daly, and Rudnick 1991, 11)

You can probably hear Alice's wistful, self-deprecating, perhaps even resentful tone of voice as she intones, "No, go ahead. . . ." This is an example of strategic accommodation.

Three communication teachers named Folger, Poole, and Stutman (1993) note that persons who frequently accommodate are often very flexible, are willing to change, and are not as revealing of their individual needs as persons favoring other styles. They may yield in a passive way or concede when they have to.

Advantages of Accommodating. Just about every relationship includes some "quid pro quo" ("this in exchange for that") element, a kind of informal scorekeeping that the parties use to determine how fair or unfair they feel the relationship is. In some relationships this element is dominant; a boss may refuse to be flexible unless an employee has "earned" special consideration, or a spouse may require three special favors for each lapse of memory or may withhold sex until his or her partner has "made up for what you did." Accommodating can be a useful response in quid pro quo situations like these because it can help you build a bank account of "helpful" or "considerate" actions to counterbalance your errors and omissions. Especially if you consider the issues minor, you can sometimes realize a considerable benefit from accommodation without much cost.

Like avoidance, accommodation can also protect a low-power person from harm. In addition, it can reduce the risk of "sticking to your guns" in a conflict with a senior, more experienced person. It may be wisest to defer to the senior person's judgment, especially in the main areas of his or her expertise. Finally, in most long-term relationships, there are times when maintaining harmony is the most important goal, at least in the short term. Accommodation can definitely help keep the peace.

Disadvantages to Accommodation. Wilmot and Hocker point out a possible paradox of accommodation when two parties *compete* over who can be most *agreeable*. As they put it, "People can one-up by showing how eminently reasonable they are" (Wilmot and Hocker 2001, 159). So one person's attempt to avoid competition results in a version of "After you. . . . No, after *you!*" They also point out that if accommodation is overused, the commitment to the relationship, and, we would add, the two partners' communication abilities, are never tested, because one or the other of them regularly gives in. If accommodation is used frequently in a relationship, it also fosters the impression that someone's preferences and ideas don't matter to him or her, and this is almost never true. Most of the time, communicators *care* about their own opinions, ideas, beliefs, values, and choices, and too-frequent accommodation makes it sound as if they don't. So another potential disadvantage of accommodation is that it can create a false harmony, a veneer of agreement covering over various resentments and disagreements. Finally, accommodation can be a signal that the person doesn't care enough about *the relationship* to work through a disagreement. It is sometimes interpreted as a lack of commitment.

Notice that avoidance and accommodation are similar and different. Both are ways to dodge conflict, both can help keep the peace, both can indicate low commitment to the relationship, and both are styles that women are frequently socialized into. But avoidance tries to dodge the conflict entirely, whereas accommodation tries to deal with it quickly by giving in. Avoidance is like the bullfighter flipping the cape in the air and dancing away, whereas accommodation is the equivalent of grabbing onto the bull's neck and struggling to hold on while the bull crashes around the ring with the bullfighter on its back.

Competition

Competition enacts the conviction that conflict is a win/lose game. A person who is competing is responding strongly to his or her own goals, ignoring the other's goals, and is concerned about the issue but not about the relationship.

As a result, competition is characterized by aggressive and uncooperative behavior that pursues the competing person's own agendas at the expense of the other's. A person engaging in competition sees the conflict not as avoidable or as an opportunity for creative problem solving but as a battleground. This style is also gendered in many cultures, and males are most frequently socialized into the competitive conflict style. So sometimes competition is consistent with a "macho" stance—"If you lose a disagreement, you're a weakling and nobody will respect you." In other cases competition grows out of the conviction that "my perceptions are reality" or "the way I interpret it is the way it is." If you begin from this assumption, you'll naturally resist or reject any differing points of view. Competition also makes sense to the person who believes "it's a dog-eat-dog world," and that the basic rule of interpersonal relations is "do unto others before they do unto you."

Blaming and fault-finding are two of the primarily verbal cues common to competition. "Should" is another favorite word—"You should move out of there," "You shouldn't talk to her," "You should change jobs." There is also often a great deal of us-versus-them or polarizing language. Communication scholar Allan Sillars and his colleagues list seven features of the primarily verbal cues of this conflict style:

Faulting—statements that directly criticize the personal characteristics of the partner.

Rejection—statements that indicate personal antagonism toward the partner.

Hostile questioning—directive or leading questions that fault the partner.

Hostile joking—joking or teasing that faults the partner.

Accusation—statements that attribute thoughts, feelings, intentions, or motivations to the partner that the partner does not acknowledge.

Avoiding responsibility—statements that minimize or deny personal responsibility for conflict.

Prescription—requests, demands, arguments, threats, or other statements that seek a specified change in the partner's behavior. (Sillars, Coletti, Parry, and Rogers 1982)

Nonverbally, competition looks and sounds just like you'd think it would. The person often uses posture, space, and eye contact aggressively, talks in a loud, certain voice with few pauses, and points an index finger at those he or she is blaming, accusing, and directing.

Advantages of Competition. Competition can be appropriate and useful when there is little or no time for compromise or collaboration and the conflict cannot be avoided or resolved with accommodation. In other words, in an emergency, competition can prompt a quick, decisive response. Competition can also help create an adversarial relationship that sometimes works positively, as it ideally does in a courtroom, or when there is an arbitrator. When two parties can present equally strong opposing arguments, a third party can often choose the best course of action between them, a course neither party could iden-

This photo effectively captures the disadvantages of competition. So long as people are stuck in this style, progress will probably be difficult.

tify alone. When researchers go after grant funds, for example, they realize that their proposals are in competition with many others for limited funds. Funding agencies see this competition as healthy because they believe it means that only the best projects receive support—"survival of the fittest"—so the limited dollars are allocated in the most effective way. In situations like these, accommodation or compromise could be viewed as out of place or confusingly vague.

Some people are also acculturated by their family, gender mentors, ethnic group, and experiences in sports to thrive on competition, and they are energized and motivated to excel in a win/lose situation. In addition, competition can be useful in situations where the solution or other external goal is more important than the relationship, as when people do not have to meet or work together in the future. Finally, competition can show the other parties involved how important the issue is to the person who's doing the competing.

Disadvantages of Competition. The primary disadvantage of competition is that it prioritizes the specific goal—the topic, policy, or action at issue—over the parties' relationship. As we noted, this may work well when people do not have to work together in the future, but an ongoing relationship can be soured by the narrowly focused aggressiveness characteristic of competition. Each time a person engages in competition, he or she should recognize the potential danger to the ongoing relationship.

Another disadvantage of competition is that parties are almost never really equal in power, and competition can drive the lower-power agenda "underground." In other words, in the face of an aggressive attack, a low-power person may accommodate or avoid, only to surface at a later time in an effort to outflank, surprise, or go over the head of his or her antagonist. Moreover, most competitive conflicts reduce the options to one side *or* the other—"Either you're for me or you're against me." It can be difficult to gain enough perspective to identify fruitful third or fourth options. Finally, although you could argue that apparent success with any of the styles tends to produce more of the same, this is particularly true with competition. Especially if competing helps you get your way once or twice, it is easy to fall into a repetitive pattern of win/lose competing in every situation. Competition can be its own reward; it often feeds on itself and in this way diminishes communicative flexibility.

'But . . .' A Student Responds

When I'm quietly thinking about my conflict style, I recognize that most of the time I attack back—I compete. But I've been doing this for a long time, and when I'm attacked it seems like the only way to respond. Do you really think it's realistic to expect myself to change?

Yes. This kind of change is definitely not easy. But it is possible. You are talking about your conflict *identity*, and identities are always hard to alter. It helps to remember what we've been saying throughout the book about nexting. Regardless of how often you've done it one way, the *next* time you can respond differently. In your case, it might work to think about which style you want to try rather than competing. Just pick one. Then think about how you could verbally and nonverbally apply that style. Then, the next time you get attacked, stop and count to 10. Use the counting time to remember the alternative you've

Compromise

Compromise is a style that results in some gains and some losses for each party to a conflict. You might think of it as a middle style between competition and collaboration. The person who is compromising is involved much more fully than the one who is avoiding or accommodating, and his or her involvement is much more mutually focused than the person who is competing. Below is an example of compromise that illustrates some of its advantages:

Jason and Sarah, ages 8 and 11, both want to play with their new Xbox. Their parents, tired of hearing the kids argue about who got to play first, told the siblings to work out something that was fair. Jason and Sarah decided that if they couldn't decide on a game they both wanted to play, they would take turns, changing who got to choose the game each hour. The strategy worked well after they determined who got to be the first to choose a game to play. While Jason took his first turn, Sarah worked on the computer to make a chart to keep track of turns.

Advantages of Compromise. The most obvious advantage of compromise over the other styles considered so far is that the issue gets addressed without either party being in the unequal power positions that accommodation and competition engender. In most Western democratic cultures there is also a presumption in favor of compromise; it is considered one of the important tools of effective civic leadership. As a result, compromise comes with considerable moral force; it is likely to be thought of as "a good thing to do" by many conflict parties. Although it takes more sustained involvement and effort than the other styles considered so far, compromise can also be easier and quicker than collaboration. The parties can focus their energies on negotiating what each will win and lose, and do not have to deal with the other issues that are often a part of collaboration. Compromise is perhaps most useful as a "last resort." When other attempts to manage conflict fail, parties are often willing to accept a compromise in order to move beyond the issues.

Disadvantages to Compromise. It is often difficult to achieve the power balance that true compromise assumes or requires. Even when

Alternative dispute resolution centers like The Mediation Network encourage collaboration and compromise and divert disputes from overcrowded court systems.

each party has some power over the other, they are seldom complete equals. As a result, the solution that is called a compromise often favors one party and thus resembles the outcome of competition or accommodation. Another disadvantage is that, because both parties have to give up something to achieve most compromises, this style can promote a "lose/lose" feeling. All parties may feel worse off than they were going into the conflict. A third disadvantage is that compromise can become an easy way out, a kind of formulaic solution not responsive to the special demands of the situation. If parties in conflict regularly resort to splitting the difference, they may be covering over aspects of the conflict that could be responded to much more creatively.

Some people believe that deciding by flipping a coin or drawing straws is a form of compromise, but these tactics can be more accurately thought of as a form of arbitration where the arbitrator is chance (Wilmot and Hocker 2001). Compromise requires each party to give up some desired outcome(s) and to get some. It demands deliberation, discussion, and reflection on the desirability and shortcomings of various possibilities.

Collaboration

Since Chapter Two, we have used the term *collaboration* to label a feature of all communication. Conflict researchers, on the other hand, have used the same term to label a specific conflict style. The difference is a matter of emphasis. We want to highlight the joint action that is a part of all communicating, so we foreground the collaborating that goes on when people are avoiding, competing, accommodating, or enacting any of the other conflict styles. You can't have accommodation, for example, unless one party gives up or gives in *and* the other party takes advantage of the action. Conflict style researchers emphasize differences among approaches rather than similarities, so they reserve the term collaboration for a particular, narrow style. For them, collaboration labels an orientation to conflict communication that shows a concern for one's own goals, a concern for the goals of the others involved, a similar concern for the successful solution to the problem, and concern for the health of the relationship.

Many of these researchers also emphasize that, because it manifests concern for all five parts of the process, this style, as a general rule, is the most desirable of the five. In other words, collaboration is the conflict style that does the best job of acknowledging the whole complex, continuous, and collaborative process of communication. People who are collaborating are *aligned* in their common pursuit of mutually beneficial outcomes, even though they may not agree about many specifics. Collaboration happens when parties to a conflict are committed to (1) a thoroughly *mutual* process that (2) produces *emergent* next actions. In other words, *the prerequisite to collaboration as a conflict style is a shared commitment to working together to produce next steps that neither party could envision or accomplish alone.*

Some of the primarily verbal features of collaboration are descriptive statements rather than judgmental or evaluative ones; appropriate disclosure of one's perceptions, goals, and feelings; and genuine questions about the others' opinions and preferences. One difference between compromise and collaboration is that in compromise the parties look for some easy intermediate position that partially satisfies them both, while collaboration involves them in a creative project of finding a solution that will maximize goals for all. Mixed and primarily nonverbal collaboration cues include inquiring and tentative tones of voice, open gestures, positive rather than negative intensiveness, and appropriate silence to let all the parties think and feel about what's been said.

Advantages of Collaboration. As we've already said, there are definite advantages to each of the other four styles, *and* there are some especially important advantages to this one. Research indicates that collaborative styles result in better decisions and greater satisfaction with the other parties to the conflict (Tutzauer and Roloff 1988). When collaboration works, the conflict event is not concluded until everyone is reasonably satisfied and can support the agreed-upon next step. As a result of collaboration, relationships are better rather than worse than they were when the conflict began. Since no one person ends up feeling like he or she has "won," no one also feels like he or she has "lost." The parties have identified common interests—and at least overlapping positions—and they are often energized by the conflict. In short, collaboration requires all the parties' best communication efforts, but it also offers the greatest reward for the effort invested. When it works, it replaces aggression, harassment, and violence and helps the parties experience how conflict can be genuinely productive.

Disadvantages to Collaboration. Collaboration takes time, energy, and skill. It is neither easy nor efficient. As a result, when people have a low investment in the relationship or the topic, collaboration is not worth the effort. It works best in long-term relationships in which the parties have a considerable stake in continuing together. In addition, some collaborative communication techniques can be used by glib people with power to force submission or generate guilt because the other person "isn't being reasonable." This kind of pseudo-collaboration is really a form of manipulative competition, but it illustrates how a commitment to collaboration can increase your vulnerability. Another disadvantage is that genuine collaboration requires that power actually be shared, and when it isn't—even though the rules say it should be, or one party thinks it is—the low-power person can suffer more than in straightforward, open competition. Finally, one avoider can frustrate the good intentions of four or five collaborators, and in this sense collaboration is a weak style.

'But . . .' A Student Responds

How do arbitration and mediation fit in? There's an Alternative Dispute Resolution Center in town that provides mediation services, and I hear about business and labor-management conflicts that are resolved by an arbitrator.

If this were a book on conflict, we'd discuss arbitration and mediation in detail. Both are ways to manage conflict. Arbitration is a process in which a disinterested third party listens to the two or more conflicting parties and then hands down a decision that may be binding. Mediators, on the other hand, help the conflict parties themselves work through their difficulties to some sort of resolution. Mediation requires collaboration, and arbitration usually demands a lot of competition and some collaboration. The center you mention is designed to keep some disputes out of the overcrowded courts. If you're interested in these topics—for a paper or class assignment or as a possible career—we encourage you to consult *mediation* and *arbitration* entries on the Internet, in your library catalog, or at your local bookstore.

Many of the communication attitudes and behaviors that have been highlighted in previous chapters can contribute to collaborative problem solving. For example, it's vitally important to remember that all the parties to the conflict are selecting, organizing, and interpreting what they perceive (Chapter Five), and that differences among these processes are often at the heart of the conflict. Both parties also need to be aware of how their own facial expression, tone of voice, gestures, movements, and proximity (Chapter Eight) are affecting the communication. Collaboration works best when the parties respond with open sensitivity, although open stereotyping and closed sensitivity can also help along the way (Chapter Four). In addition, the empathic and dialogic listening skills discussed in Chapter Six are powerful and important elements of collaboration. Dialogic listening especially enhances the parties' abilities to find creative mutual solutions. Collaborative conflict management, in other words, can test all your communication competencies. Conflict is the greatest challenge to moving your communication toward the right-hand end of the impersonal←——→interpersonal continuum, and collaboration is the style that can best help you encourage this move.

Conflict Management Tactics

In addition to all the attitudes and skills from other chapters that can also be applied to conflicts, there are several communication techniques designed specifically for managing conflict effectively. We call these *conflict management tactics* even though we realize that the term *tactics* may sound manipulative. Here's why we use this term: We want to emphasize that effective conflict management takes planning, practice, and flexibility. You won't get better at it until you approach it intentionally, consciously working to improve. Even if some of the suggestions in this section sound or feel strange at first, we encourage you to try them to find which work best for you. As your conflict management abilities mature, some of the actions that initially feel artificial or "too much like techniques" will become part of your natural way of responding genuinely to conflict.

Our second reason is to exploit the distinction between more general strategies and more specific tactics. The five styles that we've already discussed set the general tone for your conflict management efforts. Avoidance, accommodation, competition, compromise, and collaboration are labels for conflict management *strategies*. This section outlines eleven *tactics*, specific communication moves you can make in order to deal with different parts of the conflict process. As we've suggested before, approach what follows in this section as a salad bar. With few exceptions, specific tactics do not exclusively go with specific strategies. Select the tactics that work for the particular situation and leave the rest. We've included only communication moves that we've tried and those that research has also found effective.

1. Fractionate. Fractionating means breaking a conflict down from one big mass into several smaller, more manageable pieces (Fisher 1971). The process does not do away with conflict, but it can make it more approachable by reducing the threat or challenge that the parties are facing. Here's an example of fractionating between two roommates:

> *Carrie*: I don't like your attitude. You're always so negative and sarcastic about everything. I'm thinking I should look for another roommate. [Sounds like the problem is "global," a huge one to solve.]
>
> *Amy*: I didn't realize I was getting on your nerves so much. I don't understand what you mean, anyway. What do you mean "negative"? [A request that asks for a specific problem to address—fractionating the conflict.]
>
> *Carrie*: As soon as you walked in the door today, you started complaining about the mess everything was in and how everything is screwed up at work. I'm tired of listening to all that. A simple "Hi, Carrie" would be a whole lot nicer. [A relatively easier, much more narrow request.]
>
> *Amy*: I guess I have been pretty short-fused lately. I've been really worried about work, and I've started bringing that home.
>
> *Carrie*: Well, you aren't *always* negative, and I know things have been going really rough for you at work. I guess I get a little stressed when you unload.
>
> *Amy*: I really needed to talk about it with somebody, but I have a hard time asking for that, I guess. So I just took it out on you instead.

As this example shows, fractionating can significantly affect how people respond to conflict. Usually this "sizing" process can make smaller conflicts out of larger ones. But even when the overall magnitude of the conflict is not reduced, this strategy can divide it into manageable parts.

2. Isolate the Trigger. As you work to identify the central content issue you're disagreeing about, also be sure to distinguish it from the conflict's *trigger*. By trigger we don't mean cause. Triggers are precipitating events, the actions or words that mark when a given discussion escalated. It's helpful to identify the trigger because it often *seems* major, even when it is minor compared with the underlying problems that need managing. In terms we introduced earlier, triggers are usually about *positions* and not about *interests*. Unfortunately, parties to a conflict often forget that the trigger is "the last straw," and they focus on them as if they were "the first straw." For example, an employee's late arrival may trigger an argument between the employee and the boss, but the disagreement may not be over the tardiness so much as over what the boss believes are the employee's negative, careless attitudes about the job. That issue won't surface until both parties recognize that although the late arrival is the trigger, it isn't the key issue.

Often, noticing the triggering event can help clarify the identities that are involved in the disagreement. This process, in turn, can help you put the conflict in perspective. For example, although a son or daughter's coming home two hours late seems like a legitimate reason for a disagreement over priorities, the nature of the conflict itself can change if the parent recognizes that tardiness is just the trigger and that the central issue or topic involves identities. The parent may be defining him or herself as (1) responsible for the son or daughter's safety ("I must protect you"), (2) being watched by other adults ("People will think I'm a poor parent"), (3) the enforcer of agreed-on family regulations ("There have to be some rules around the house"), or even (4) frightened ("Kids are getting kidnapped every day"), or (5) rejected ("I see myself as an authority, and I feel you're rejecting that"). The son or daughter may also come to understand what's happening more clearly by examining what the triggering event reveals about his or her identity.

3. Avoid Gunnysacking. As you probably know, a gunnysack is a big burlap bag used to hold potatoes, peanuts, or some other bulk commodity. Gunnysacking occurs when a person stores away weeks, months, or even years of resentments and then uses a particular conflict as an opportunity to bring up all the bruises he or she has been nursing and to dump them on the other person. The most vivid example of gunnysacking we've read comes from a novel called *The Shadow Knows* by Diane Johnson:

> The fights were all conducted in the same phrases but each phrase was just a formula, stood for pages and pages, a very long list, of hate and pain. I didn't understand this at the time, I admit. I didn't understand for example, that every time Gavin said, "And then you bought that fucking chair," which he did say obsessively in the course of every fight, he really meant, "You defied me and went and did what you wanted just as you always do, causing me to feel unimportant and wretched and unattended, unlike my mother, who does what I want, which makes me feel manly and, because it is an ugly chair which I hate, you are also assailing my comfort and my position in the household, making me feel unwanted and uncomfortable here; and by buying that hideous old secondhand chair when I had said not to, you were reproaching me financially, you were complaining that we couldn't afford a new one, another way of saying, as you constantly seem to, that now that we have all these loathsome brats I ought to disregard my personal develop-

ment and think about earning money for them, something a man is not obliged to do, as I infer from my own family, where my father's career was sacrosanct and my mother's whole concern was my father, and instead you stick me with all these brats whom you don't even take care of properly, witness their dirty faces and wet pants, and have the nerve to complain to me about needing help and freedom when I did not ask you to bring all these brats into the world and when I did, good-naturedly, help you bring the chair home and help you upholster it, that's when I stuck the upholstery needle in my eye you were not sorry although I could have been blinded which is another way of saying castration which is really your game isn't it, isn't it? (Johnson 1974, 220–221)

Gunnysacking occurs when a bag of old resentments like these are "dumped" in the middle of a conflict. Rather than filling a gunnysack with complaints, it's much healthier to try to deal as much as you can with controversial issues as they come up. This can keep a disagreement triggered by one event from becoming the occasion to air every doubt and hurt you've carried for weeks—or even years. The often-repeated advice to couples to "not go to bed angry" is another way to say, "Avoid gunnysacking" or "Keep current; don't let resentments build."

4. Address What You Want to Have Happen. A fourth way to handle content conflict is to combine criticisms with positive suggestions for change. Occasionally, your main goal in a conflict may be to simply dissuade the other from taking some action, but usually a disagreement involves not just stopping one kind of action or plan but also starting a different one. As a result, persons involved share the responsibility for developing solutions. Disagreements often dead-end in such statements as "Well, you just have to grow up!" "Stop being so radical!" "Be nice to me!" or "Stop wasting so much time!" These orders are dead ends, not only because their tone tends to create defensiveness but also because it's next to impossible to comply with them. Do you mean by "growing up" that you think it would help for the other person to be on time more often, or to take more responsibility for his or her comments about others, or to stop putting off term papers until the last minute, or what?

One way to apply this advice is to ask your conflict partner, "What do you want to have happen?" Another way is to respond to this question yourself by suggesting alternatives that describe what you want to have happen next, or what you'd prefer instead of what's been happening. It's most important to be willing and able to collaborate with your conflict partner to define these alternatives.

Couples therapist Richard Stuart's Conflict Containment Model is one way to summarize these first four tactics. Based on several years of experience, Stuart recommends three guidelines for containing and regulating conflict exchanges:

- Emphasize a present orientation—focus on the present rather than the past. Substitute "how" questions for "why" questions.

- Adopt a "conciliatory set." Label the behavior of the other in the most positive light and plan your own moves to "resolve the issue equitably" rather than by winning.

- Seek solutions in small steps—use fractionating to address issues one at a time and sequentially. (Stuart 1980, 290; cited in Wilmot and Hocker 2001, 260)

'But . . .' A Student Responds

When I try applying some of these suggestions, I feel and sound mechanical and phony. And the people I'm in conflict with obviously know that I'm trying something new on them. So these tactics or techniques really don't help. Sometimes they even make the person more angry!

This happens because the suggestions are new. The more you apply them, the more natural they will get. Remember that these are not just ideas we've pulled out of the air. The attitudes and behaviors we've discussed have been tried in practice, validated, and found to be effective. They've worked in our experience or we wouldn't have included them. They've been studied by social scientists and other communication researchers. None of them is a surefire panacea for all your conflict problems, but we encourage you to try them out, adapt them to your own communication style, and don't give up after the first time.

---

5. *Identify Conflict Identities.* Every conflict includes differences over identities. The parties disagree about who is innocent or guilty, who "started it" and who is "just responding," who "intends harm" and who "is just trying to protect her- or himself." Especially when emotions are strong, these identities can seem set in stone—if not for all time, at least for this conflict. Throughout this book, though, we've been showing how identities are constructed in each interchange. There are favorite and typical patterns, but they also change in each communication event. Effective conflict managers take advantage of this flexibility. They are aware of the identities they bring into a conflict, recognize alternative identities, and are willing and able to change and to have some *flexibility,* even in long-standing self-definitions.

The first step is to become aware of your own conflict identities. Although generalizations obviously won't cover all your unique responses, you can get some insight into your typical self-definitions by reflecting on your responses to the statements in the following box.

Applying What You Know

Your Conflict Identities

How do you respond when you disagree with persons who are older than you? Younger? With superiors? With your partner or parents?

For each of the situations described below, note how you usually or typically define yourself. For example, do you see yourself as more competent than the other person, less competent, or about as competent? Is your first inclination to define yourself as innocent or guilty? Flexible or rigid? Well informed or uninformed? As one who needs to defend a position or as a collaborator on a solution?

1. When I disagree with a friend who is my age, I usually define myself as

   _____.

2. When I disagree with my partner, lover, or intimate friend, my typical identity is _____.

3. When I disagree with my parent or an adviser, my typical identity is

   _____.

4. When I disagree with a job supervisor, I usually see myself as

   _____.

You can use this information in a couple of ways. First, it can help you to understand how others might respond when in conflict with you. If you define yourself as more competent, for example, the other person may well respond with resentment, increased antagonism, or capitulation (depending on his or her own self-definition). Your responses to these questions can also help you understand why you might dread conflict with your partner or lover ("I usually feel inferior and tend to respond by giving in") whereas you welcome a

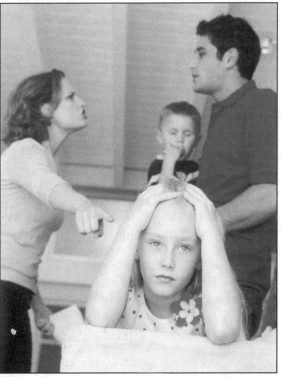

Who are the victims here? Who might be the rescuer? What other conflict identities are visible?

disagreement with a friend your own age ("I usually feel equally competent and tend to assert myself").

In addition, this kind of analysis can give you information about your conflict identities that can allow you, at least in your long-term intimate relationships, to set *belt lines* below which you and your partner agree not to strike. As two conflict teachers explain, "Everyone has such a belt line—a point above which blows can be absorbed, thereby making them tolerable and fair; and below which blows are intolerable and therefore unfair" (Bach and Wyden 1968). In other words, each person has spots of intense vulnerability where a blow can seriously damage his or her self-definition.

One reviewer of these materials shared some examples of his own especially touchy topics. "Most of my below-the-belt areas," he wrote,

> involve characteristics or behaviors over which I have little control: the size of my ears, the fact that I blush, that I tend to get tongue-tied when highly excited. When my "opponent" points to these things during an argument, I am really wiped out. I see this sort of thing happening often in arguments between people.

It can help for intimates to disclose these sensitivities to each other and to mutually agree on belt lines so that their arguments will not become person-destroying.

A third way you can use these insights into your conflict identities is to remember that, since they're coconstructed, they are changeable. This is probably the most difficult and most potentially useful place to apply *nexting*. Even though your typical identity in this situation is defensiveness, you can respond less defensively this (next) time. Even though you and your conflict partner have a long-standing pattern of dependence-codependence around holiday preparations, this time you could change. And so on. The basic tactic is to be aware of the identity you're bringing to the disagreement and then to be willing and able to keep it flexible so it can change in ways that help manage the conflict effectively.

6. The X-Y-Z Skill. A book called *A Couple's Guide to Communication* offers a technique called the "X-Y-Z skill." The principle is simple: You make a statement of the form, "When you do X in situation Y, I feel Z" (Gottman, Notarius, Gonso, and Markman 1976, 37). So a spouse might say, "When you talk with someone else about a private conversation you and I had, and I'm there listening, I feel embarrassed." This statement is much more likely to promote effective conflict management than if the spouse said, "Why do you always embarrass me in front of them!?" or "Isn't there anything private between us?" As Wilmot and Hocker point out, the X-Y-Z statement can both help clarify the issue of concern for the listener and help the speaker remember to take responsibility for his or her emotional response (Wilmot and Hocker 2001). The statement does not prescribe a desired change, but it does clarify the complaint in a specific, descriptive form so that the hearer can respond with minimal defensiveness.

7. Relationship Reminders. Relationship reminders are references to the history that's shared by you and the persons(s) you're in conflict with. The purpose of these reminders is to keep the disagreement in perspective, to remind the parties that this specific conflict exists in a broader context of mutual commitment and respect. A relationship reminder is a kind of *metacommunication* because it is a comment about your relationship or how you're communicating. "Let's remember we're on the same side here," "Remember, we've got a long history together," or "I love you and I don't want to fight about this" are all relationship reminders.

In some cases you can best communicate this kind of confirmation by saying something like "I love you, honey, and I really disagree" or "I hear what you're saying, and I can't accept your conclusion." When disagreeing with a friend, it might be most accurate to say, "Look, the reason I'm disagreeing with what you're doing is because I'm afraid of what's going to happen to you."

It's crucially important that relationship reminders be genuine rather than devices or gimmicks. Most persons are sensitive to this kind of phoniness, can readily spot it, and get angry when it happens. It's easy to see why. Phony confirmation is manipulative, and nobody likes to be a puppet on somebody else's strings. So try not to fake relationship reminders. If you honestly cannot see worth in the other person or value in your relationship, it would probably be best to postpone your discussion until you can.

Results of a study done by counselor David Johnson indicate that people respond positively when a person they're disagreeing with combines genuine expressions of confirmation and warmth with expressions of anger. Johnson trained persons to express anger and warmth and then asked them to communicate with another person in a negotiating context. Some of the experimenters (trained persons) communicated "all anger," some communicated "all warmth," some communicated "anger followed by warmth," and some communicated "warmth followed by anger." The study generated the following conclusions: (1) The participants *liked* both the experimenters communicating "all warmth" and the ones communicating "anger followed by warmth"; and (2) the expression of anger followed by warmth seemed to lead to the most agreements on the negotiated topics (Johnson 1971a).

8. Circular Questioning. This kind of circular questioning is not the logical fallacy you might have studied in argumentation or philosophy. We use this term to label a kind of inquiry that accepts and builds on a person's view of a situation in order to explore possible alternative views. It is a technique used by some therapists to help families change, but it can also be applied by nontherapists to conflicts at work, in organizations, in living groups, or between dating partners (Tomm

1985). The "circle" in circular questioning is the other person's reality or world. The point is to ask a question from inside rather than outside this circle.

Someone trying to help a married couple, for example, could respond to a wife or husband's complaint in two different ways. When the wife says, "My husband is always rejecting me," the helper (friend, counselor, therapist) might try to get the wife to *change* her definition of the situation—"It doesn't seem to me like he's rejecting you" or "It seems to me he's just asking for more explanation. What do you mean 'rejecting' you?" These responses come from *outside* the wife's world, or "circle." On the other hand, the helper could *accept* the wife's characterization of the relationship *and probe it,* and these are the keys to circular questioning. So the helper might ask, "When is your husband most likely to reject you? Are there times when he doesn't reject you? What are you most likely to be doing at those times? If you knew he was going to reject you, do you think you would be able to prevent him?" (McNamee and Gergen 1996, 59). These are circular questions because they enter the circle of the wife's world and probe it, rather than trying to change the wife's reality. As the wife in this example responds to these questions, she might recognize that what she experiences as "rejection" is not just something that her husband "does to her," but that it is a mixture of his actions and her interpretations, a *collaboration.* In fact, this is the primary point of circular questioning—to foreground the collaborative quality of the difficulties that generate conflict. When people see how they are collaborating, this can often reduce the amount of blaming and fault-finding and help the people involved manage the conflict more effectively.

It's easiest to use circular questioning when you're functioning as a third party to the conflict—as a mediator or "referee." But circular questioning can also be a powerful tactic for a person directly involved in the conflict, because it can open the door for *both* parties to change in positive ways. It takes some communication ability and some confidence, but you can respond to an accusation, for example, with circular questioning. When your partner accuses you of always criticizing him or her, you might ask, "When do you feel most criticized? What topics do you feel like I criticize you the most about? Are there times when I don't criticize you at all?" And you can pay close attention to what the responses tell you about your part and the other person's part of the problem. Circular questions by either party can help both the questioner and the questioned recognize how they are collaborating on the definition, intensity, and continuation of a conflict.

9. Role Reversal. Sometimes the most effective way for disagreeing individuals to consider the legitimacy of their opponent's position is to agree for a few minutes to take the other's place in the conflict. When you are forced to act out the other person's responses, even though it's "only pretending," you can often get an unusually clear picture of the other's understanding of the situation. This is another technique often used by mediators and other third-party conflict managers. But colleagues, superior-subordinate pairs, and intimates can also build into their relationships the possibility for role reversal. It usually works best for them to agree when there is no conflict that they will try this tactic the next time they experience a disagreement. Then, in the midst of a conflict, they can refer back to the agreement.

David Johnson also studied how role reversal works. In one study he found that except when two persons' positions are mutually exclusive, role reversal significantly helps the disagreeing persons to understand each other (Johnson 1967). The results of a later study validated the conclusion that the accuracy of understanding created by mutual role reversal significantly helps people reach agreement (Johnson 1971b). Role reversal is definitely not easy to do, but it can help antagonists understand each other's position.

10. Defusing. These two final suggestions work best when a conflict seems irresolvable. Especially when identities are really on the line, and they often are, people may take exaggerated, hard-and-fast positions that they're actually willing and able to modify. Defusing can help this happen. Defusing means pulling the fuse out so the dynamite won't explode, or in this case reducing the intensity of a disagreement so that the people involved can cope more effectively.

You can *defuse yourself* by asking yourself seven questions:

1. *"What are the potential advantages or benefits of this conflict?"* If you can remind yourself that this disagreement may be good in some ways, it's often easier to reduce the intensity of your own feelings and actions.

2. *"Am I remembering that other people don't perceive things exactly the way I do?"* From *their* point of view, the other person's actions and opinions make sense. *They* think and feel that they're being reasonable. Are you remembering this?

3. *"Do I understand their position? Have I listened carefully and thoroughly enough to understand what they're saying and feeling?"*

4. *"What am I doing to help intensify or prolong this disagreement?"* This is the most important of the seven questions. The natural tendency is to blame the other person or the circumstances for a conflict. But we know that communication is complex, continuous, and collaborative: I'm not just a passive recipient of what's going on, but I am contributing to it—to the hurt, the disappointment, the fear, and so on. This does *not* mean it's all my "fault." We're in this *together.* But since my natural inclination is to forget this, it can help for me to ask myself—out loud even—"What am I doing to pro-

long the conflict or to make things worse?" Then I often can see ways to handle it more effectively.

5. *"Am I seeing myself as the target of their upset?"* Are you taking on personal responsibility for what may be an impersonal, diffuse frustration that they're experiencing?

6. *"Are my goals realistic?"* Remember that there's a close relationship between the amount of success people experience and the goals they set. One sure way to fail is to set unreachable goals. Is your goal to make the other person feel good about doing what you want to and he or she doesn't? If so, you'll probably fail. If you set achievable, realistic goals, you can probably succeed, and that success is likely to produce more of the same.

7. *"Am I trying to win this one?"* Are you doing all you can to promote a competitive atmosphere? If so, you probably won't be able to handle this conflict effectively.

You can help to *defuse the other person* if you do three things: (1) Listen dialogically, (2) explicitly identify areas of agreement, and (3) maintain your nonverbal cadence. People often assume that the most important thing they can do in a conflict is to *say* the right thing. They overlook the fact that how you listen is at least as important, probably more so. The other person will almost always be more reasonable, open to alternatives, and willing to change if he or she feels listened to. And that's something you can do something about.

Second, don't assume that everybody is remembering what keeps the people together, what keeps you arguing instead of just terminating the relationship. Make these agreements explicit. Remind yourself and the others of the points at which there is no conflict.

Finally, maintain your own nonverbal cadence. We have found this to be especially important in superior-subordinate communicating, but it also applies to communication among family members and friends. Frequently, the other person will respond strongly and negatively to abrupt or significant changes in the way you are standing, sitting, or gesturing, or to obvious changes in your voice, eye behavior, or facial expression. We're not saying that you should hide your feelings. But it works better to express them in words that others can interpret and respond to rather than in ambiguous nonverbal cues. Try not to fan the flames of the disagreement by abruptly frowning and rolling your eyes, turning your back, or making dramatic, "How can you believe that?" movements and gestures.

You can *defuse the situation* by moving away from anyone who might be seen as an "audience" and by dealing with as many contextual barriers as you can. If the immediate situation creates "listeners" for an argument, all parties will to some degree be performing. Move to another location or reschedule the discussion if you can.

You can also usually do at least something about interruptions, time pressures, or other distracters. You may often feel as though "This is too important to postpone or move; we'll just have to do the best we can here." And sometimes that may be true. But often it isn't. And the conflict can be handled much more productively after only the brief pause created by the move to another place or time.

11. Quiet Time. This brings up our final point. If all this doesn't help, try a quiet time. Call a moratorium on the disagreement, and do something else for awhile—an hour, a day, maybe several days or a week. Give everyone involved time to think and feel things through. Don't wait so long that the issue gets ignored; this can create a festering wound that will get more and more difficult to heal. But when the situation seems to require it, build into your disagreeing some breathing space, some time to put things into perspective.

Applying What You Know

Practicing Conflict Management Tactics

As we suggested, think of these tactics as a salad bar—you can pick and choose the ones that feel right or that fit the situation, but you never use all of them at once. Practice choosing the best ones by responding to the following scenarios:

1. A good friend has failed to repay some money you loaned him. After waiting an extra two weeks, you ask him when you can expect to get it back. He gets defensive and says, "Just get off my ass! I'll pay you when I can!" What two or three tactics might you apply here?

2. Work hasn't been going well for a couple of weeks. Your energy's been low because you haven't felt well, you came in late a couple of times because you got stuck in traffic, and you've been distracted by worries about school. A coworker has just complained bitterly: "I'm sick of having to do your work and cover for your screw-ups!" What two or three tactics might you apply here?

'But . . .' A Student Responds

How am I supposed to remember all these labels and lists? There are so many different suggestions in this chapter that it's just a big blur!

Some salad bars or dessert buffets can look overwhelming, too. But just as you don't put some of everything on your salad plate, you don't have to follow every suggestion or use every technique in this chapter every time you experience a conflict. Just pick and choose those that apply to the situation and work for you.

If you're asking about how to pass a test over this material, we suggest, again, that you (1) break it down into the sections designated by our major headings, (2) talk about it with others, and (3) go over it more than once.

Remember that if you experience a genuinely irresolvable disagreement, you can still "agree to disagree." Some differences between unique persons are irreconcilable. But the aspect that is never irreconcilable—the element that is always shared in common—is their humanity. And the living possibility always exists for two combatants to meet on this ground.

When you're in an irresolvable conflict, remember that sometimes the best you can do is to recognize clearly the point at which you disagree and to do so in a way that maximizes the presence of the personal. Sometimes the most you can do is interpersonally agree to disagree.

'But . . .' A Student Responds

Why is this chapter so long? Wouldn't it have worked better to divide it into more than one chapter?

Conflict provides the hardest test for any approach to communication. When people get into a hot disagreement, most of their good intentions, positive attitudes, and helpful skills go out the window. So we're trying to provide as much substance as we can to help you deal with these difficult situations. You might want to digest this chapter in chunks, rather than all at once. Besides breaking it into smaller parts, another way to deal with its length is to read it more than once.

Chapter Summary

Conflict is an expressed struggle between at least two interdependent parties who perceive incompatible goals, scarce resources, and interference from others in achieving their goals. This means, in part, that conflict is a normal, natural part of all human relationships. The point is not to try to eliminate it or even to resolve every conflict, but to manage conflicts effectively. You can also use this definition to help define what a conflict is about and to begin to identify how to manage it. Although we emphasize that conflict happens in communication, all conflict is not just a matter of "poor communication." Often people communicate very well and still experience conflict. It is also important to remember that conflict is not necessarily bad; it can (1) move a relationship out of a rut, (2) help people discover the best solution to a problem, (3) get feelings into the open, (4) promote confidence in a relationship, and (5) be a site for genuine human contact.

People respond to conflict in five general ways: by accommodating, avoiding, competing, compromising, or collaborating. Most people have their preferred styles, but just about everyone engages in each of these styles in different situations. Each style has advantages and disadvantages for the pursuit of your own goals, the other's goals, the topic, and the relationship between conflict partners. Collaboration is the style that can do the most to move your communicating toward the right-hand end of the impersonal←—→interpersonal continuum.

One textbook discusses over 60 specific tactics for responding to conflict. We limit ourselves to 11 that have some research support and that we've found to be helpful. *Fractionating* divides large, conflicts into smaller, more manageable parts. *Identifying the trigger* can help distinguish key issues from less important ones. It's important to *avoid gunnysacking.* You can help negotiate creative responses by identifying *what you want to have happen.* Effective conflict managers *identify identities,* set and observe *belt lines,* and apply *nexting* to conflict identities. Couples can apply the *X-Y-Z skill. Relationship reminders* are useful in all conflicts. *Circular questioning* can empower people to respond when they feel "stuck." *Role reversal* can be enlightening. And, especially when conflict seems irresolvable, you can try *defusing yourself,* especially by asking, "What am I contributing to this?" You can also *defuse the other* by listening, identifying areas of agreement, and maintaining your nonverbal cadence, and *defuse the situation* by avoiding any audience and choosing a setting where all persons can see, hear, and concentrate. If all this fails, try a *moratorium,* a quiet time.

In Other Words

At the beginning of this chapter we said that the culture you grew up in can influence how you approach conflict. By now you are familiar with conflict styles and tactics that will help you to become better at managing interpersonal conflicts. However, as we said at the beginning, most of these styles and tactics are based on Western approaches to conflict management. The following reading will give you insight into a non-Western approach to conflict management, called *Sulha. Sulha* is a type of mediation practice that is used in Arab villages in Israel, Palestine, and many other parts of the Middle East. *Sulha* is a tradition that dates back to pre-Islamic societies and is seen by Arabs in Palestine and Israel as one alternative to resolving conflicts in courts. The *Sulha* process involves some ritualistic practices, and the goal is that the involved parties should come to forgive each other. Although the article gives examples for how *Sulha* is used in the case of killings, *Sulha* is practiced in several types of conflicts, from struggles over pieces of land to marital problems.

After reading the text, you should be able to respond to the following questions:

1. What are characteristics of *Sulha?*
2. In your opinion, what are the advantages of this type of mediation for interpersonal relationships?
3. What are the disadvantages of *Sulha* that you see?
4. Compare *Sulha* to the conflict management styles that we talked about in Chapter Eleven. Which conflict style does *Sulha* resemble most?

* * *

Sulha Peacemaking and the Politics of Persuasion

Sharon Lang

Reconciliation Instead of Revenge

Throughout the Galilee, as in many parts of the Middle East, the Arab population has traditionally practiced a ritualized process of conflict resolution known as *sulh*, a term glossed by informants as "reconciliation," "cooperation," or "forgiveness." Any specific case of *sulh* is referred to as a *sulha*, as is the formal public ceremony that marks the culmination of the peace-making negotiations. Mediation is employed widely to resolve disputes, however trivial or serious, between (and sometimes within) families, but this article deals with only one type of *sulha*, the lengthy reconciliation process that follows a murder. Murder always entails immediate and active *sulha* responses on the part of interested parties—offenders, victims, and the notables and local leaders acting as mediators—setting in motion a resolution process that aims to restore peaceful social relations in the community. In the case of a murder, anywhere from six months to several years is typically required before the final peace agreement is sealed.

Certainly, in Israel, as elsewhere in the Middle East, crimes today are regulated by law and the state. Yet, rather than being replaced by the state, *sulha* has proven to be a tradition that works in tandem with the civil and state justice system. And while informants claim that *sulha* is currently in rapid decline, especially in urban areas, major *sulhas* involving hundreds and even thousands of men continue to occur each year in Arab villages among Bedouin, Druze, Muslims, and Christians; participants even keep written and audiovisual records of *sulhas*. Although *sulha* is often seen by the young as being out of step with modern life in Israel, most informants consider this pre-Islamic custom a positive tradition that bolsters Palestinian identity in Israel by unifying and incorporating Arabs of various religious backgrounds and ethnicities. . . .

[W]ithin twenty-four hours of a killing, close male relatives of the aggressor go to the homes of influential notables in the village and surroundings to ask them—even plead with them—to form a committee of mediators to calm the aggrieved and enraged family and induce them to engage in the *sulha* process instead of taking revenge. The initiative is supposed to come from the aggressors who, whatever their reasons for wanting to end the conflict, voluntarily approach the *rijal kibar* ("big men") and, shedding their pride, stand before them *'ara'ya'* ("naked"), *rijal sighar* ("small men"). These humbled aggressors, according to the traditional account, employ set phrases, such as "I am in your house and you must help me; I am in serious trouble and I am in your hands."

There is always a certain disjunction between actual social practice and the idealized models elaborated by interested social actors. Thus, the repentant gesture described above may amount to little more than a phone call from the patriarch of one family to a leading notable. Indeed, in some instances the *jaha* assembles spontaneously, without the aggressor's request, though it is important for the *sulha's* success that such divergences from the official narrative be elided. In one case, when it became known that the *jaba* had acted on its own accord and that the accused family had not begged or even phoned for assistance, the revelation led to a complete breakdown of the *sulha* process, for the symbolic gesture of supplication by which the aggressor's family begins ritually to express remorse is necessary to set in motion the process of mending social relations.

In the hours after a killing has taken place, notables visit the home of the bereaved family. The purpose beyond offering condolences is to secure *hudna*, a promise of cease-fire. *Hudna* checks the potential destruction and violence of *fawrat al-dam* (literally "the eruption of blood"), the period immediately after a killing, when the victim's family may legitimately exact revenge under local custom. During *fawrat al-dam*, and generally for an extended period thereafter, the male kin of the killer flee their homes to seek refuge with relatives or friends. This departure may be more symbolic than real, since often the killer's family simply relocates to another part of the village, where those seeking revenge can easily follow. This "exile" is another gesture to the aggrieved family; attackers show humility and remorse by demonstrably staying out of sight of those they have offended. As an informant explained, "By moving away from the (victim's) family, the killers are saying, 'We are not proud of what we did, and we do not want to hurt your feelings further.'" Through debasing steps such as voluntary exile and requesting a *jaha*, the family which prior to the *sulha* process was "on top" is brought down in terms of *sharaf* and set on par with the subordinate side.

The *jaha*, made up of the community's most prestigious men, supplicates the victims to agree to a suspension of hostilities and later to accept a *diyyah* (monetary compensation for murder or injury) instead of taking another life. This begging of favors from the family of the victim exemplifies the reverse patron-client strategy, or reverse *musayara*, described above. Yet *budna* is not always attained so easily, and the *jaha* may have to deploy persuasive powers that test the members' own *sharaf* abilities. At this point in the *sulha*, oral performance comes to the fore: it is not merely who is speaking and what is said, but the way the *jaha* communicates—its skill in playing upon the *musayara* tradition of "polite speech"—that is crucial. As one *jaha* member described the process:

> We make every effort to get the victim's family to agree. . . . We use the
> beautiful language (*hilwa*). We appeal to their sense of goodness and what is
> right, and we do not leave until the family agrees. But if they really refuse, we
> keep trying. We come back day after day. We speak to them each time with
> all the politeness and respect in the Arabic language. We beg them to be so
> kind, so honorable as to do us the favor, until finally they cannot refuse us.

From first contact until the *sulha* process is completed, the *jaha* treats the family of the victim with inordinate respect and consideration, never failing to use
"beautiful" or "sweet" language.

The offended side—particularly if they are powerful themselves—may be
reluctant to grant a cease-fire and may provide a list of demands that may well
be humiliating to the attacker's side. The attacker's side may have no choice
but to cede to the victims' demands if they wish to resolve the conflict. If the
jaha's initial effort is unsuccessful, they return repeatedly and add to their collective weight by bringing additional notables in each successive visit to join
the chorus calling for peace. Eventually the disgrace of refusal reaches an intolerable point, and the victim's family cedes. . . .

If the *jaha* secures a cease-fire, the *sulha* process goes forward. The next
step, according to the official narrative, is for the arbitration committee to
make a ruling on the amount of *diyyah* to be paid by the attacker's family to the
victim's family. *Jaha* elders claim that the *diyyah* in any particular case corresponds in value to the *diyyah* paid in previous cases involving similar crimes.
The figures reported to me were consistently in the range of NIS 100,000 (at
the time approximately $30,000) for a murder. Killings that entail disfigure-
ment or any bodily desecration, however, demand additional payment. Apparently impartial *diyyah* decision making hides a process of haggling and negotiation between the family of the victim and the family of the attacker, mediated
by the *jaha*, who themselves have personal interests. The latter covertly moderate how much the victims rightfully can demand and how much the aggressors will suffer. Any public discussion concerning the size of the *diyyah* or other
conditions would undercut the *jaha's* image as a wise and unified body that unilaterally makes its ruling in light of custom and precedent.

With the amount of *diyyah* and any other conditions determined, the *sulha*
ceremony is arranged. All men of the village and notables from other villages
are sent invitations announcing the formal reconciliation of the two families.
One person, who may or may not be part of the *jaha* , is generally designated
to send invitations and coordinate the *sulha* ceremony. It is important that an
adequate number of dignitaries attend the ceremony to confer *sharaf* on the
family of the victim and help restore their shattered dignity. There have been
cases where a family refused to engage in *sulha* until they were assured that a
number of prestigious figures would attend.

The *sulha* ceremony takes place outdoors, in the village center, in front of
the municipal building, or in another central space, as *sharaf* relies on public
view. The *jaha* initiates proceedings by having an influential member of the offended family, usually the father of the victim, tie a knot in the *rayah* (banner).
This symbolic gesture indicates that the victim's family is ready for reconciliation and that it is safe for the family of the killer to proceed. The members of

the *jaha* then take the white *rayah* to the killer and his family in another part of the village. "The *rayah* is white and clean," a *jaha* member explains, "the *rayah* has no spots—as if to show that the problem has been cleansed." The *jaha* proceeds through the streets to meet with male members of the victim's family who are lined up in the place where the ceremony will be enacted. There may be as many as several thousand men attending the *sulha*—all watching with solemn anticipation. Women and children's viewing is limited to what can be seen from windows and the sidelines. The *jaha* surrounds the killer to shield him from possible attack. "No one, particularly not the attacker and his family, dares to utter a word," explained a *jaha* member. "Everyone senses that the less people speak the better—one wrong word might ruin everything. So there is a heavy silence." Again, it is the enactment of rituals and not the words per se that is efficacious.

The final *sulha* ritual is a scene of temporary humiliation, or *sharaf* lowering for the offenders. Whatever the genuineness of the humility, the offenders must publicly go through the prescribed steps conveying shame and remorse. If they perform their moves adequately, the victims will feel assuaged and the egalitarian balance of *sharaf* will be restored. The waiting family of the victim is lined up in the prescribed place outside the municipality or local council building or in a central public space. The killer and all his male relatives arrive and move down the line, shaking the hands of each and every member of the victim's family. "When they put their hands together, the tension must ease," explained a *jaha* informant, who added that this is potentially the most volatile moment of the *sulha*. In one case, the brother of the victim pulled out a knife that had been hidden in his sock and stabbed his brother's murderer at the very instant when he was expected to shake the killer's hand and forgive the deed. In the vast majority of cases, however, the tense moment passes without incident.

After the shaking of hands, the *diyyah* is passed from the family of the attacker to the family of the victim. According to *jaha* informants, it is crucial that these monetary exchanges take place in front of many witnesses (today, the *diyyah* is commonly placed in a transparent plastic bag), since promises made before the tribunal of the community are likely to be kept. . . .

The *sulha* ceremony ends with the signing of an official peace agreement by leaders from the two warring families, members of the *jaha*, and some of the other dignitaries present. The signatures of the notables give the accord a weight it would not have if only the two families signed it. To break such an agreement is not only to go back on one's publicly given pledge, it is also a direct insult to the important men who mediated the *sulha* and signed the agreement. It is important not to have too many dignitaries sign. If every one's *sharaf* is at risk then, in effect, no one's is: breaking an agreement that a very large number of people have signed is not a direct affront to any one person's *sharaf*. If, on the other hand, only a few select notables have signed, then breaking the contract would be a clear insult to them. With these high stakes, the two sides are under great pressure not to disrupt the peace.

When the ceremony is over, certain actions are still required before villagers consider that relations have "returned to normal." The penultimate step is that the killer and his kin are taken to the home of the victim to drink bitter coffee, traditionally offered to guests as a symbol of hospitality. It is significant that the attackers go to the home of the victim for coffee because being hospitable is always *sharaf* heightening for the host. By placing the two sides in the positions of host and guest, the victims' *sharaf* is raised, and the aggressors' *sharaf* decreased one last time.

The family of the killer then invites the victim's family to share a feast at their home. If it is considered an honor to be the host, it is a still greater mark of prestige to have a costly and substantial meal arranged solely on one's behalf. Thus, after sipping the bitter coffee a respected elder of the aggressor's family will say, "In the name of God, I invite you to eat with us today." The men of the entire extended family of the victim and all the invited notables—a number which runs to hundreds, sometimes even thousands, of people—will go directly to the killer's home and eat a meal that usually consists of rice and lamb. Each man tends to eat only a few bites as a symbolic gesture before he gives his place to one of the many who are waiting. This feast completes the peacemaking ritual; it is the final *sharaf* transfer. The victim's family [is] shown respect as guests for whom this lavish feast was prepared, and the aggressors, though forced to pay for this costly affair, are compensated somewhat by having what is considered the honor of preparing the meal. . . .

Copyright © 2002 by Institute for Palestine Studies. Sharon Lang, "*Sulha* Peacemaking and the Politics of Persuasion." Reprinted from *Journal of Palestine Studies*, Vol. 31, No. 3, Spring 2002, pp. 53, 56–57, 58–59, 60–61, by permission.

References

Bach, G. R., and Wyden, P. 1968. *The Intimate Enemy: How to Fight Fair in Love and Marriage.* New York: Avon.

Canary, D. J., Cupach, W. R., and Messman, S. J. 1995. *Relationship Conflict.* Thousand Oaks, CA: Sage.

Fisher, B. A., and Ellis, D. G. 1990. *Small Group Decision Making: Communication and the Group Process.* New York: McGraw-Hill.

Fisher, R. 1971. "Fractionating Conflict." In C. Smith (ed.), *Conflict Resolution: Contributions of the Behavioral Science.* Notre Dame, IN: University of Notre Dame Press.

Fisher, R., and Ury, W. 1981. *Getting to Yes: Negotiating Agreement Without Giving.* Boston, MA: Houghton Mifflin.

Folger, J. P., Poole, M. S., and Stutman, R. K. 1993. *Working Through Conflict.* 2nd ed. New York: HarperCollins.

Gottman, J., Notarius, C., Gonso, J., and Markman, H. 1976. *A Couple's Guide to Communication.* Champaign, IL: Research Press.

Hocker, J. L., and Wilmot, W. W. 1995. *Interpersonal Conflict.* 6th ed. New York: McGraw-Hill.

Janis, I. 1972. *Victims of Groupthink: A Psychological Study of Foreign Policy Decisions and Fiascos.* Boston, MA: Houghton Mifflin.

Johnson, D. W. 1967. "The Use of Role Reversal and Intergroup Competition." *Journal of Personality and Social Psychology,* 7: 135–141.

———. 1971a. "Effects of the Order of Expressing Warmth and Anger on the Actor and the Listener." *Journal of Counseling Psychology,* 18: 571–578.

———. 1971b. "Effects of Warmth of Interaction, Accuracy of Understanding, and the Proposal of Compromises on Listeners' Behavior." *Journal of Counseling Psychology,* 17: 207–216.

———. 1974. *The Shadow Knows.* New York: Alfred A. Knopf.

Martin, J. N., and Nakayama, T. K. 2000. *Intercultural Communication in Context.* 2nd ed. Mountain View, CA: Mayfield.

McNamee, S., and Gergen, K. J. 1996. *Relational Responsibility.* Thousand Oaks, CA: Sage.

Sillars, A. L., Coletti, S. F., Parry, D., and Rogers, M. A. 1982. "Coding Verbal Conflict Tactics: Nonverbal and Perceptual Correlates of the 'Avoidance-Distributive-Integrative' Distinction." *Human Communication Research,* 9: 83–95.

Stuart, R. B. 1980. *Helping Couples Change: A Social Learning Approach to Martial Therapy.* New York: Guildford.

Ting-Toomey, S., Gao, G., Trubisky, P., Yang, Z., Kim, H. S., Lin, S. L., and Nishida, T. 1991. "Culture, Face, Maintenance, and Styles of Handling Interpersonal Conflicts: A Study in Five Cultures." *International Journal of Conflict Management,* 2: 275–296.

Tomm, K. 1985. "Circular Interviewing: A Multifaceted Clinical Tool." In D. Campbell and R. Draper (eds.), *Applications of Systemic Family Therapy: The Milan Approach.* London: Grune and Stratton.

Tutzauer, F., and Roloff, M. E. 1988. "Communication Processes Leading to Integrative Agreements: Three Paths to Joint Benefits." *Communication Research,* 15: 360–380.

Vangelisti, A. L., Daly, J. A., and Rudnick, J. R. 1991. "Making People Feel Guilty in Conversations: Techniques and Correlates." *Human Communication Research,* 18: 11.

Weaver, R. 1990. *Understanding Interpersonal Communication.* 5th ed. New York: Scott Foresman.

Wilmot, W., and Hocker, J. 2001. *Interpersonal Conflict.* 6th ed. Boston: McGraw-Hill. ✦

Chapter Twelve

Relating Interpersonally in Cyberspace

Chapter Objectives

After reading this chapter, you should be able to do the following:
- Give reasons why studying communication in cyberspace is important.
- Explain how online identities are constructed.
- Explain features of verbal and nonverbal communication online.
- Demonstrate an understanding of romantic and friendship relationship development and maintenance online.
- Provide examples for flaming.

Chapter Preview

What Is Cyberspace and Why Study It?

Online communication has become an important kind of daily interaction for many people. Popular venues include e-mail exchanges, chat rooms, newsgroups, instant messaging, and blogging. One woman writes,

> I consider the people in my newsgroup to be an extended family. I live by myself, and it's a wonderful feeling to be able to go somewhere at any time of the day or night where you know people, and they know you to some extent or other. It's weird. There are a few people I routinely greet warmly, with whom I feel a kinship, and I don't even know if they're male or female. (Morrison 1995, 220)

You might wonder about two things this woman says. First, why does she say, "go somewhere," even though she does not physically move in her apartment? And second, how is it possible that she can feel "a kinship" with people she doesn't even know are male or female? Have gender, ethnicity, race, class, and level of education become unimportant in cyberspace?

Let's explore these questions by reviewing how cyberspace communication works. *Cyber* comes from the Greek word *kubernetes*, which means steersman and is related to the ways message flow and direction are electronically controlled in cyberspace (Wood and Smith 2001). There are basically five ways to exchange messages online: electronic mail, bulletin board systems, Internet relay chat, multiuser domains, and the World Wide Web. You may be involved in some or all of these. E-mail is probably the most popular and familiar form of communicating, and a very high percentage of college students, faculty, and staff—and their families—are regular e-mail senders and receivers.

Bulletin boards function like the large boards with messages that you see around campus. Someone sends a message to a single computer address, it gets posted, and people can access it whenever they want. Bulletin boards are organized according to special interest groups, called newsgroups.

Internet relay chat is what takes place in chat rooms. People "enter" these rooms to talk about special topics in real time. Multiuser domains (MUDs) also enable people to have synchronous (real-time) interactions. In MUDs and their diverse offspring, such as "MUDs object oriented," or MOOs, people come together to create virtual realities through talk. Words and imagination are all you need to build a house or take a walk with your cat in these virtual spaces. Finally, the World Wide Web is becoming more of a tool to access the four other forms of communicating and to retrieve information about almost any kind of topic you can imagine.

Why do people communicate in cyberspace? Some want to talk with people with similar interests, some want to keep in touch with friends or the family, some want to hang out with people without getting judged immediately on their looks, some are interested in finding a friend or a romantic partner, and some simply want to surf around because they have nothing better to do. This variety is one reason why studies of the effects of the Internet on its users are sometimes contradictory. For instance, the Stanford Institute for the Quantitative Study of Society found that as Internet use grows, Americans report spending more time working for their employers and less time watching TV or associating with family and friends. Almost 60 percent of adult Americans reported that when they spend more time on the Internet they spend less time with friends and family. Almost 50 percent say that computers have given people less free time, but 24 percent believe the contrary (Nie 2001). Another study reported that Internet use is associated with spending more, not less, time in face-to-face interactions with family and friends (Kraut et al. 2002). This study also found that the Internet has overall positive effects on the social involvement of users and on their psychological well-being. Studies also show a strong relationship between Internet access, income, and education. As of 2001 in the United States, just over 50 percent of those without a high school diploma and 53 percent of high school graduates use the Internet, whereas 86 percent of college students are users (Nie 2001). In addition, 90 percent of 16–18-year-olds were Internet users in 2001, and only 25–30 percent of the people older than 66 years were surfing the Web (Nie 2001).

The fact that over 85 percent of college students have access to or use the Internet makes it highly likely that, as we said, you are a user and that this is one element of your world of meaning. As we said in Chapter One, technology is one important dimension of peoples' worlds of meaning, along with physical environment, time, relationships, spirituality, vocation, and language(s). These dimensions operate in some interesting ways when you enter cyberspace.

For instance, as the quotation above indicates, the concept of "space" changes. In the natural or "real" world you can physically move from your desk to the coffee shop to meet your blind date. In cyberspace you don't experience this same bodily activity, but the space idea still operates. Strategically designed collections of digital data in bytes and gigabytes make up what every one who uses them call "places"—"sites," "rooms," and "domains" that are "opened," "closed," "entered," "visited," and "blocked." These spatial terms are used metaphorically in order to help make the strange more familiar. In other words, people think and talk about certain computerized phenomena as *places* in order to understand and use them more easily.

Your online experience of time might also be quite different from what it is in the natural world. For example, when you discover that the blind date you meet in cyberspace is really hip and beautiful but from Portugal, you end up calling twice a week, which generates a huge phone bill and chronic fatigue, because you have to call in the middle of the night. So you start using e-mail, and although you can no longer listen to his chuckle, you can save money and sleep. You can write e-mail messages at any time of the day and your friend can read them and reply at any time. This is called *asynchronous* rather than synchronous or real-time communication, because your sending happens at a different time from his receiving.

Verbal and nonverbal communication play important roles in cyberspace as well, and again with some differences. You have to rely mainly on the verbal channel online and do not have the help of most visual and aural channels. Emoticons, such as a smiling or winking face, can help. Plus, it's important to be careful. Recently Saskia accidentally pushed the caps lock key and the classmates she e-mailed thought she was screaming at them. She learned from their responses that they didn't appreciate it. Instead of using emoticons or caps, you might play with underlines, abbreviations, and acronyms like the ones we discuss later in this chapter. But clearly, even though online messages are written, nonverbal features of oral communication are important parts of the shared meanings that are created in cyberspace.

This chapter about relating online will help you to understand how people negotiate cultural identities online, what it means to form relationships in cyberspace, and how relational problems can occur there. We begin each topic with a brief story written by a student like you who is engaged in cyberspace communicating.

Inhaling and Exhaling Online: Perception and Constructing Selves

> My very first screen name I had made for myself was "Physiman." I had already understood that I wanted something unique and relevant to myself. At that point in my life I had a great interest in physics and I wanted to portray an air of being a superhero, thus the "man" tacked on at the end of a chopped off word. As luck would have it, no one else had taken that name, so it was all mine. It was quickly to my dismay, in my involvement with the chatrooms, that people in general assumed my name meant "physical man" or something with more reference to athletic ability. They constantly asked me questions that I felt embarrassed to answer. I found myself forced to act older than I was in order to maintain respect. I often lied about my age, saying 16 or 15. I remember one day in particular, when a random person privately messaged me, saying "I can make you the luckiest man west of the Mississippi!" It was then that I promptly changed my name to something less provocative.

In Chapter Four we talked about how identities appear and are worked out in verbal and nonverbal talk. We also said that some of the most important meanings people collaboratively construct are their identities. All communication involves constructing identities or selves. In addition, people continually negotiate identities. This means that, as we communicate, we are choosing one identity over another. As you remember, this is a process that happens *collaboratively,* outcomes are *not predetermined,* and identity construction is made up of *reactions and responses.* Let's see how these characteristics fit relating in cyberspace.

One characteristic of communicating in cyberspace is that people think they have more control over how they are perceived than they actually have. This perception is based partly on the assumption that one can log on whenever he or she wants to and exit at will, without affecting others online.

But assumptions about how others view you can be inaccurate. In one study (Sherman et al. 2001), people who had constructed home pages assumed that the impressions that they made with these home pages were more positive than they actually were. Visitors had varied reactions to what they found online, and more positive impressions were developed on the basis of brief face-to-face encounters than via home pages. Home page authors might believe that they can control others' perceptions, but identities are *co*constructed in cyberspace just as they are off-line.

In the "physiman" story, the young man was surprised when he received messages with sexual implications. This happened because, as others perceived him, they were selecting, organizing, and inferring from the cues he provided. Physiman himself wanted to exhale the identity of an intelligent superhero. Others, however, inhaled the identity of an athletic male. Why? Because in their world of meaning, the combination of "physic" and "man" meant a male with athletic abilities, not one who loved studying physics.

Clearly, selves are constructed online and offline in similar ways, but cyberspace has some features that lead one author to call it "an identity workshop" (Bruckman 1992). This means in part that people can be in cyberspace what they can't be in the other parts of their world. For example, someone who grows up as a male but who feels like he wants to be female, and whose family and friends believe that gay or transgendered people are "wrong" or "immoral," will either suppress his identity questions or look for ways to enact an alternate identity. Online communication might provide these possibilities. The person might engage in newsgroups that discuss traditionally feminine issues, such as how to learn self-defense, how to get your husband to talk more with you about his problems, or where to find a good midwife. By doing so, he may connect with other like-minded people and get a sense of what femininity feels like.

One advantage of using cyberspace as an identity workshop is that people can put themselves into the shoes of others. The disadvantages are, as you might guess, that people can deceive each other and interact unethically. An extreme example is the character "Mr. Bungles" (Dibbell 1993). In the mid-1990s, someone going by this name disrupted the conversation in a multiuser domain (MUD) with vulgar statements. He also used the graphic of a voodoo doll to make other users of the MOO appear on the screen in sexual acts as though they wanted to be there voluntarily. He ignored the protests of the others until one was able to block Mr. Bungles's access to the group. Interestingly, the people who witnessed Mr. Bungles's communication described it as "rape" even though the events had only taken place online. People felt that their virtual selves were violated, and this was almost the same as a physical assault (Dibbell 1993). The example of Mr. Bungles illustrates that ethical standards applied in "real life" are also important in the virtual world. It also illustrates again how perception

These women are working hard to create on-line identities and may be unaware that they have less control over how others define them than they think.

processes online and offline are similar. In the next couple pages, we'll talk more about some of the specific characteristics of relating verbally and nonverbally online.

Characteristics of Cyberspeak

> Dear members of this newsgroup,
>
> I am a new member of your group and just wanted to introduce myself. My name's Nina Miller. I still feel a little homesick but have met some really nice people in my school. I like going tango-dancing and reading. I want to get to know some people in this newsgroup cause I sometimes feel lonely. Please give me your addresses and phone numbers so we can start hanging out. By the way, what does JK mean?

How would you describe this person? If you are familiar with on-line communication, you might infer that she is a newcomer to cyberspace because she uses rather formal written English to express herself, she addresses the newsgroup as if she were writing a letter, and she does not know what JK means. You might also disapprove of her immediate request for addresses and phone numbers "so we can start hanging out."

In some negative ways, this example highlights a couple of important characteristics of cyberspeak. The first is its *orality*. Spoken language has mostly been associated with face-to-face interactions. Spoken language has also usually been contrasted with written language in some fairly clear ways. But in cyberspace, the distinctions begin to blur. Communication in newsgroups and bulletin boards has many characteristics of oral interaction. People use pause fillers, use lower case instead of upper case letters, omit verbs or use colloquialisms, like "nope" and "yeah" (Lewin and Donner 2002). All these are features of oral communication. Consider the following exchange:

> adz46: hows you
>
> pintsize: fine thanx u?
>
> adz46: great
>
> pintsize: cool wot u up2?
>
> adz46: not A LOT (Merchant 2001)

The form of this exchange is more like oral conversation than like writing. In exchanges like this, people also use pause fillers, such as "hm"; words for laughter, such as "heh" or "haw"; run-on sentences without punctuation; and acronyms such as "bc" for "because." Cyberspeak texts often create the impression that someone is actually talking with you.

Two other characteristics of cyberspeak are *creativity* and *economy*, and they go together. Vocabulary in cyberspace is similar to slang that is created and used by particular cocultures, such as surfers, skaters, gays and lesbians, or gamers. The online environment is changing rapidly, and people enter and exit newsgroups and multiuser domains at a rapid rate. Therefore, new terms come up continually, and people who log onto certain forums learn quickly how to participate in the discussions. Many words have either been invented for the online medium or recreated in the form of acronyms or combinations of letters and numbers, such as in "up2." Examples for words with new meanings include *flame*, an ill-considered e-mail or Usenet retort, *troll* for deliberately posting false information to a newsgroup in hopes of tricking, or *ego-surfing*, which means searching the Internet for one's own name. You are also probably familiar with words like *virus*, meaning a computer program that drives your computer insane, or *spam*, which is unsolicited junk mail. Often, words are taken from offline talk and used with shifted meanings in online talk. Examples include *worm* and *Web*. People who are able to write and interpret the new word correctly and use acronyms and combinations of words and numbers correctly, are regarded as cyberspace insiders. This is another example of how language creates identities, because your correct use of cyberwords identifies you as a member of the online community.

Many of the new language creations pack as much meaning as possible into the fewest possible characters or letters. This is called *speech economy*. Acronyms are a commonly used feature of cyberspeak and a good example of how people can say things with the fewest words or letters. Here is a list of commonly used acronyms, and you probably know many more:

Acronyms

BCNU: Be seeing you

BTW: By the way

FYEO: For your eyes only

FYI: For your information

ROTF: Rolling on the floor

OBTW: Oh, by the way

WTH: What the hell

F2F: Face to face

PANS: Pretty amazing new stuff

EOM: End of message

The fact that language is manipulated in these ways online emphasizes how, as we said in Chapter Seven, language is the human's way of being. People invent new words and play with grammar conventions as we go. The fact that Web users creatively invent words in cyberspeak and use spoken communication in written form demonstrates again how humans are linguistically productive beings who continually adapt our language to new circumstances.

Nonverbal Relating Online

Online communication involves not only verbal language but also nonverbal cues that emphasize, support, and clarify the verbal message. As one user wrote,

> I think there are ways to create a computer identity that is recognizable and comforting to people. One time I was using AIM, and I had just gotten my new laptop so I was downloading it on my comp. . . . I was trying to set up my preferences, and when I Imed my friend in blue Arial rather than purple, he was like, "What's going on? This isn't Tara. Change the color back!" As strange as it is, purple Arial is my online identity. Also, you can keep your personal style when writing e-mails. Emoticons help, although sometimes meanings are lost. You can IMAGINE people laughing, or the faces they'd be making when they say something in their e-mail . . . but maybe I can do that because I know my friends so well.

This woman knows that both verbal and nonverbal cues are important in cybercommunication. As we said in Chapter Eight, facial expressions, posture, paralinguistics, and eye contact are all very important in face-to-face communication. What changes when we communicate in a medium that allows only for restricted use of nonverbal cues? Of course, webcams and other devices allow us to add the visual to the verbal channel. However, despite all these visual aids, many people still think that cyberspace is an impersonal medium because you can't exchange the rich nonverbal cues that occur in face-to-face communication.

But there are at least four ways that people flesh out their online verbal communication with nonverbal elements: *onomatopoetic words, narrations of physical actions, forms of emphasis,* and *emoticons.*

The first strategy is to write out vocal utterances, such as "hahaha" for laughter. This technique exploits sound the same way a poet or novelist does when she uses onomatopoeia—words that sound like what they mean. You can also use acronyms to express a particular emotion online, such as HHOJ (ha-ha, only joking) or LOL (laughing out loud).

A second way to add nonverbal elements is to narrate physical actions to create a word picture for your communication partner(s). For example, you might write *I was rolling on the floor with laughter* or [Here I shut and locked my door]. These narrations are set off with asterisks or brackets to clarify that they are metacommunicative—they communicate about the communication itself. Even though they take the form of words, they function like nonverbal cues—tone of voice, facial expression, and so forth—to tell others how you want your written message to be interpreted.

Emphasis by capitalization, underlining, or boldface type is another way people introduce nonverbal cues into cyberspeak. Notice how differently you would interpret "I screamed at him" and "I SCREAMED at him!"

A fourth way to express emotions online is by using emoticons. As you probably know, emoticons are icons or abstract pictures that you can produce on a keyboard and that can also be used as metacommunication. Here are several examples and, again, you probably know many more.

Table 12.1 Common Emoticons			
:-) grinning	:(sad	%*} very drunk	5:-) Elvis Presley
;-) winking	:P happy with a tongue	(!) Hamburger	:-0: Please be quiet

Source: Sanderson 1997.

A comparison between the German (Sanderson 1997) and the U.S.-American keyboard characters for happy or sad shows that the expressions are the same in both languages. These are German emoticons:

:) or :-) for happy

:(or :-(for sad

:-D laughing

This comparison underscores the point made in Chapter Eight that there are some universal emotions recognized across cultures.

Finally, recognize how nonverbal cues, such as emoticons, help you to construct a certain identity online. If you want to be perceived as a "faceless" user who is just popping into a chat room but doesn't intend to participate, you probably won't take the effort to use elaborate emoticons to express your feelings. But when you e-mail your older brother who is also your best friend, you might use underlining and capital letters to drive a point home and emphasize that, even though he has more experience, you have a position of your own to express. When your older brother writes an e-mail to his boss, he won't use underlining, caps, or emoticons because this would be inappropriate. He assumes the identity of an employee who does not want to disclose too many emotions, and his communication becomes more *impersonal*. In fact, the more emoticons you use, the more you move your part of the communicating toward the *interpersonal* side of the continuum.

In Summary So Far

At this point we've made four main points about online communicating. First, identities are constructed collaboratively online, and, just as in offline communication, you cannot completely control the outcome of your interactions. Second, online identities are constructed using verbal and nonverbal cues. Third, cyberspeak or online language has many oral characteristics, even though it is written. And fourth, nonverbal cues are used online to accentuate and reinforce verbal messages and to make them less ambiguous.

Relationship Development and Maintenance Online

In Chapter Nine we discussed types of relationships and models of relationship development and maintenance. So far, studies of relationships in cyberspace have mainly examined how friendships and romantic relationships form online. We summarize and apply some of what's been learned here.

Online Friendships

As you remember, friendships are voluntary and personal. You choose your friends on the basis of common commitments, usefulness, or just to have fun. In all cultures there are universal rules for friendships, and in many cultures these include respect for the other's privacy, looking the other person in the eyes during conversation, avoiding sexual activities with them, repaying debts and favors promptly, and avoiding public criticism of the other person. You might ask how all this works in cyberspace. For example, usually physical proximity and frequent interactions are necessary to start and deepen friendships, so, is it possible for friendships to develop online? Some researchers are skeptical. They believe that online relationships are shallow and impersonal, and that the idea of making friends online is just an illusion (Stoll 1995). This view is also supported by some Internet users, one of whom wrote, "Online relationships, in my experience, have about a 60–75 percent turnover rate, whereas more intimate communication tends to last a lifetime."

Others believe that cybercommunication liberates people from the constraints of locality and the pressure of physical attractiveness and therefore creates opportunities for genuine friendships (Rheingold 1993). Most of the findings from early studies emphasized the social disadvantages of online friendships and suggested that personal relationships develop more successfully in off-line settings. In the early 1990s, for example, researchers found that people engage more in verbal aggression and blunt disclosure in online groups than in off-line groups (Dubrovsky, Kiesler, and Sethna 1991). They speculated that this behavior might be due to the relative anonymity of the Internet and to the missing relational cues, such as vocal qualities, body movements, facial expression, and physical appearance. But those who don't believe online friendships can work have been challenged by evidence that people are very willing and able to use the Internet according to their needs.

In other words, recent research shows that close and meaningful relationships can develop online. Malcolm Parks and his associates have found that those who are able to better express their feelings over the Internet are more likely than others to have formed close online relationships. These relationships do not stay in cyberspace but can move to face-to-face interactions and can therefore be relatively stable (Parks and Floyd 1996; Parks and Lynne 1998). Other studies demonstrate that Internet relationships tend to develop closeness and intimacy more quickly than do real-life relationships (McKenna, Green, and Gleason 2002).

At least three characteristics of online communication make it possible, and even easy, to form friendships there: the disclosure dynamic, the absence of gatekeepers, and common interests.

Self-Disclosure. You probably remember our earlier point that self-disclosure begets self-disclosure. In romantic relationships this means that partner disclosure and self-disclosure increase the experience of intimacy. Of course, there are risks involved when you disclose information about yourself and your feelings, such as getting hurt, being ridiculed, or being talked about. Since one characteristic of the Internet is its relative anonymity, studies show that these risks are reduced online because people can share intimate aspects of their lives without high levels of fear of disapproval or immediate sanctions (McKenna and Bargh 2000). Why do people have less fear? It's like the stranger on the plane phenomenon. People sometimes tell complete strangers their life stories because they know that the listener does not have access to the social circles the speaker is moving in. But in contrast to a conversation with an airplane seatmate, online interactions are often repeated. Open and free self-disclosure can therefore be a foundation for continuing, close online relationships (McKenna, Green, and Gleason 2002).

Absence of Gatekeepers. Another reason for increased willingness to self-disclose is the lack of the ability to perceive physical appearance, attractiveness, or many types of social stigma, such as having a lisp, age, disfiguring features, disabilities or, in some cultures, skin color. Because these gatekeepers are not obstructing first impressions online as they do in face-to-face relationships, people are better able to focus on getting to know each other.

Common Interests. Common interests also obviously play a significant role as well in getting to know someone else, and these can easily be identified online. You might get a sense of shared interests when you chat with someone in a newsgroup about traveling to Alaska or when you follow a person in a multiuser-domain and find her fantasy-world attractive.

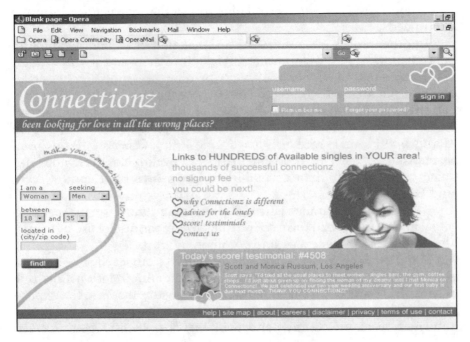

We now know that the early critics of cyberspace painted a too gloomy picture about the shallowness of virtual friendships. Although online friendships might be restricted to online settings and might not last as long as "real-life" friendships, there are some characteristics that are similar between them. Cyberspace is, in part, just another setting for people to have fun and socialize with people they like. It provides an often—though not always—safe place to get to know people, to play together, and to communicate with people of the opposite sex without the obligation to proceed to a romantic relationship.

But, you might ask, what about developing romantic relationships online? As one student said:

> I don't think you can do that [develop a romantic relationship online]. There is so much stuff involved, when I get to know someone, like looks and the way he or she dresses, the kind of people he or she hangs out with, and so on. How can it be possible to date someone whom I only know through his or her verbal messages and a couple of emoticons?

Relating Online With Romantic Partners

The common impression is that it is hard to meet someone online and become romantically involved. However, there is evidence that people do meet there, fall in love, and live as couples. Findings indicate that relationships online do not develop that differently from offline relationships. What is most important is the *quality* of the communication the participants experience.

One study found, for example, that couples who took a lengthy period of time to get to know each other online before meeting face-to-face and who postponed sexual involvements tended to have longer relationships than those who were sexually active early in their face-to-face relationships (Baker 2000). The same researcher found that people who learned to solve conflicts online before meeting face-to-face were more satisfied with their relationships than people who did not learn to cope with difficulties before meeting (Baker 2000).

As we've already noted, self-disclosure is a key element of online relationship development. In online settings, people communicate using verbal and nonverbal cues rather than by participating in shared activities like dinners, sports events, or movies. In fact, people exchange four times as much information online as they do when they spend a weekend together engaging in various activities (Joinson 2001).

This often-intense exchange of online messages also enables couples to move through many of the turning points that are important in all romantic relationships. Getting-to-know time, quality time, and physical separation are all important turning points in the development of a romantic relationship—as we explained in Chapter Nine. All these events can and do happen online.

Aspects of Baxter and Montgomery's relational dialectics help explain why and how this occurs (Baxter and Montgomery 1996). As they develop relationships, people fluctuate between the needs for *separateness and connectedness, privacy and disclosure,* and *certainty and uncertainty.* The Internet provides a very good playground for engaging these tensions or polarities before one makes a serious commitment and meets face-to-face. For instance, imagine that a heterosexual man meets an interesting woman on the Internet and realizes that the two of them have similar interests. In the initial stages of the friendship, he might connect fairly intensely through a daily narration of what he did and how he felt. However, he has a great deal of control over when to exit the discussion in order to meet his need for separateness, for example, after a very tiring day. He can also choose what to disclose and what he'd like to keep private. All this information creates some certainty in the relationship, but there is still uncertainty, for example, about exactly how she looks, the friends she hangs out with, and where she lives.

MOOs are an online environment where personal relationships often form. Meetings are made relatively safe because age, race, education, and other social factors do not limit the initial contact between users and are often subordinated to other concerns. Personal relationships develop very often in these environments. This occurs partly because many persons' "natural" environments do not expose them to people from as many different social classes, ethnicities, and races as they can meet online. In addition, part of the culture of MOOs is that relationships there are often characterized by high disclosure.

Despite the potential of online relationships, there comes the point when people who have developed some commitments to each other want to meet face-to-face and explore actual rather than virtual meeting. Ultimately, a successful romantic relationship is one where people talk with each other face to face and spend time in physical closeness and intimacy. But there is ample evidence that online venues can be places where long-term relationships can begin and can even mature.

Flaming

According to O'Sullivan and Flanagin (2003, 84) " 'flames' are: intentional (whether successful or unsuccessful) negative violations of (negotiated, evolving, and situated) interactional norms." Here is an example that is tame enough to be reproduced in a textbook:

> See, before folks like you and me decided to lace up our online high-tops and hit the virtual hardwood, jerks who made my life miserable when I was a kid were surfers on the electronic tsunami of data. They spoke an arcane, flavorful dialect of a mysterious language called Unix. It was their own clubhouse to enjoy with

each other. All of a sudden there are a lot of normal people around. Idiots who don't know the argot, who stumble around with improper protocol, trampling on the interactive lawns. Ew! Real people! Pfui! Get'em out of here! And so they flame us. Insulting our intelligence. Urging us to get lost. They screech with contempt, these flaming loudmoths. Worst of all, they think they're cute. They think they're funny, piling onto poor, unsuspecting America Onliners, making them feel bad about their cyberselves. Well, flame you, bozos. You're not cool. You're yesterday's news. Flame all you want. We won't burn. And we won't go away, either. It's kind of Internice around here. (Schwartz 1994, 38)

One student who is a frequent and competent online user said that flaming is mainly a result of the anonymity of the author and the impersonal setting. He said that "you don't have the same repercussions from making a Website as you do holding a sign and yelling in the streets." In other words, since more is possible in an anonymous—and therefore impersonal—setting, some people take advantage of it.

Many people think of flaming as one type of hurtful messages that Vangelisti identified (see Chapter Ten). "Flames" can be highly negative messages that can burn a person, metaphorically speaking. Some researchers who have studied flaming have concluded that the reduced impact of social norms on the Internet and the reduced impact of politeness expectations make the medium highly susceptible to damaging flaming (Sproull and Kiesler 1991). Those who believe this to be true for the Internet also believe that it fosters impersonal communication.

However, the idea that inherent features of the Internet attract and cause damaging verbal aggression is challenged more and more. Some critics of this view point out that what scholars have regarded as verbal aggression might not appear to be aggressive to the people for whom it was originally written. If I call my best friend names, like "stupid you," or something much worse, she may take the labels as intimacy markers rather than ridicule. It depends on the teasing conventions that have developed along with our friendship. Those who view flaming as negative are often judging it from the outside. Their interpretations might be different if they were to apply the context that is understood by the people sending and receiving the messages.

Another response to the negative view of flaming is that sometimes messages laced with profanity, name-calling, or impolite language can be a way people create bonds and also affirm close friendships (O'Sullivan and Flanagin 2003). Flaming can be understood as part of the creation and maintenance of identity (Plotz and Bell 1996). In the excerpt above, the person is trying to maintain her identity as being different from the "jerks" who made her life miserable in high school and now in cyberspace. The person presents herself as different from one of the know-it-alls who look down on others and belittle them. And the person is not going to submit to these people. She creates the image of a strong, outspoken, funny person who does not hesitate to use threats to assert herself.

One of the prototypes of flaming, which was created as a response to increased incidents of flaming online, is the newsgroup alt.com. People who insult others in the alt.flame newsgroup do so to perform identity. In a way that echoes some rap artists, some flamers call themselves "Usenet Performance Artists" or "Net Entertainers" (Vrooman 2002). They use flaming to insult each other and to test their verbal intelligence. Just as in some verbal exchanges between young African Americans, it is important online to be cool, funny, and more quick-witted than the others. Interestingly, there are limits. Flamers in this newsgroup usually shoot down racist, sexist, and homophobic flames as "lames." Clearly, this verbal aggression has its limits, and the people who participate in it in the newsgroup know these limits (Vrooman 2002).

As with many other parts of human communication, flaming is more complicated than it might first appear. It is important to interpret messages that appear to be flames in their natural *context* (Lea et al. 1992; O'Sullivan and Flanagin 2003; Vrooman 2002). It is also important to acknowledge the identity work that is often being carried out via flaming.

All this does not mean, however, that flaming is a wonderful thing. Scholars are just saying that equivalents of flaming have existed for centuries in face-to-face communication, and that the impact of flaming depends on where it happens and who's involved. In this way it is similar to the other messages that Vangelisti (1994) calls "hurtful." The potential for damage is undeniable, *but* some flaming is benign and other flaming even strengthens interpersonal bonds.

Applying What You Know

1. Do you agree or disagree with the following statement? Give an example to support your response: "Face-to-face communicating easily wins out by a long way over online relating. Much more communication is possible during direct contact because voice, posture, and gestures add enormously to information content." What do you think?

2. "Online relationships, in my experience, have about a 60–75 percent turnover rate, whereas more intimate communication tends to last a lifetime." Do you agree or disagree? What is your experience?

Chapter Summary

There is still a lively discussion about whether cyberspace communication keeps people from developing meaningful face-to-face relationships or whether it actually helps people to engage with each other more easily. This chapter might help you to reflect on these questions. As you have learned, it is possible in cyberspace to express your identity by using verbal and nonverbal cues creatively. It is also possible to develop meaningful relationships that can either stay in the virtual medium or move to face-to-face interactions. This said, online communication does not protect you from relational problems, such as verbal aggression or even identity fraud. And because we only have written verbal and nonverbal cues to form impressions about other people, we sometimes have to take risks when relating online. So when you write your next blog entry or have your next Internet chat, take a minute and think about how you present yourself, perceive others, and relate to others in cyberspace.

In Other Words

In Chapter Twelve we discussed how people can relate in cyberspace and which verbal and nonverbal means of communication they can use to construct meaning together. The following reading adds to our discussion in that it illustrates the importance of technology in our daily lives and how our work life has become dependent on the use of computers. After reading this essay, you should be able to discuss the following questions:

1. In what ways does new technology contribute to making the boundaries between work life and private life more fluid?

2. Discuss how cyberspace affects the relationships that you have with people at work and the relationships that you have with friends, parents, or romantic partners. Do you think that cyberspace provides you with more opportunities to connect with people in both the public and private sphere? Or not? How so?

3. Do you see any differences in opportunities between people who are using new technology extensively and those who do not or are not able to do so, such as some elderly people or people with less money? If so, please discuss these differences.

4. Think about the impact that cyberspace has on your daily life. Describe a day in your life in which you use online communication and imagine the same day without it. In which situations would you feel constrained if you were not able to engage in online communication?

When Amy Bruckman wrote this she was a doctoral candidate at the Media Lab at M.I.T., where she specialized in virtual communities. She created several role-playing games that take place in imaginary or virtual spaces on the Internet. These include MediaMoo, a MUD (multiuser dungeon fantasy game) designed for media researchers, and MOOSE Crossing, a MUD designed to serve as an innovative learning environment for children. The following essay originally appeared in the January 1995 issue of *Technology Review*.

The extent to which our everyday lives are dependent upon computer technology becomes more comprehensible when we consider how ubiquitous electronic communications have become and consequently how hard it is to unplug from the Net. This is exactly Bruckman's predicament when she decides to leave her laptop behind to visit her parents during Christmas in Miami. As a result, she has to reevaluate her obsessive reliance on its "seductive, engrossing world."

Have you become addicted to e-mail and chat rooms to the point where you cannot conceive of taking a vacation without taking your computer with you?

* * *

Christmas Unplugged

Amy Bruckman

If I had a network link, I'd be home now.

From my chaise lounge on the terrace of my parents' Miami Beach apartment, I see a grid of four-lane roads with palm-treed median strips, yachts moored on the inland waterway, a golf course, and a dozen tall white condominiums. The hum of traffic is punctuated by the soft thunk of racquets striking tennis balls somewhere below. The temperature is in the 70s and a breeze blows through my toes. I am a long way from Boston. If I had a net link, I'd know exactly how far.

I'd know the weather forecast for Miami, and, if I cared, for Boston too. Just about anything you might like to know is out there on the worldwide computer network—the Net—if you know where to look.

It's Christmas day in Miami, but I'm not sure it would really be Christmas or I would really be in Miami if I were plugged into the Net. I would be in my virtual office, a "room" in the text-based virtual reality environment where I do most of my work. I have a desk there, piled with things to do, and a fish tank—just like my "real" office. Except that the virtual fish don't need to be fed—they're just a program I created one day while procrastinating from real work. My virtual office is just some data on a computer housed at MIT that I can tap into from anywhere, but it is a place to me. When I log onto the network, I am there.

And I would be there right now, if not for a difficult choice I made two days ago. I was packed for my trip south and had called a cab. I had the important things: airline ticket, wallet, bathing suit. I stood in the hall staring at a padded gray bag, the one containing my Macintosh PowerBook computer. I grabbed the bag, double-locked the door, and started to walk down the hall. I stopped. I went back, opened the door, and put down the gray bag. I stood in the doorway, feeling foolish. The taxi honked. The honk gave me courage: I locked up again, leaving my computer—my office—behind.

A vacation should be about escaping from routines; going somewhere else provides a new perspective. But when I travel with my PowerBook, I bring many of my routines with me. I can readily gain access to all my familiar tools for finding information. It's as if I never left. And that's the problem. Had I brought my computer, I would not have written this essay (for which I am using a pencil). Instead, I would have logged onto the network and entered its seductive, engrossing world. By now I would have read the newswire and Miss Manner's column, answered a dozen questions from friends and colleagues, and possibly posted my thoughts on a movie I saw last night to a public discussion group. It would be as if I never left home.

The network destroys a sense of time as well as place. Daily and seasonal rhythms are subtle at best. As morning turns to evening, I am more likely to bump into my friends in Hawaii, less likely to encounter my friends in England. In the summer, things quiet down. April 1st is the only real network holiday—don't believe anything you read that day! Beyond that, life on Ac Net proceeds at an even, unpunctuated pace. There are no holiday decorations on the Net.

On my flight down here I saw a young boy carrying a sleek black bag on his shoulder. He held it naturally, but with a hint of importance. It took me a moment to see the logo: it contained his Nintendo Game Boy. His generation sees nothing remarkable about traveling at all times with a computer. It is already possible to connect to the network from a palm-sized computer with a cellular link. As computers get smaller and cheaper, we will lose even the excuse of the weight of that black bag or the cost of losing it.

The Net is becoming an important part of the lives of a broader segment of the population. Its spread presents a worrisome challenge: is it ever possible for us to take uninterrupted time off any more? The new technologies of connectedness are pushing people to blend their many roles into one: personal mail is mixed with professional correspondence, and work crises arrive on a cellular phone during leisure time. If our coworkers and competitors have made themselves perpetually available, we feel all the more pressure to do the same, lest we be left behind. One of my colleagues deliberately vacations in places so remote that getting a Net connection is almost impossible—it's the only way she can get a real break, and, for a little while at least, be a carefree newlywed instead of a world-renowned researcher. But such exotic locales are getting harder and harder to find.

I love the network and the people and places I find there. But sometimes I find it important to disconnect—to leave the cellular phone and the beeper in a desk drawer, leave that padded gray bag at home. To be out of touch, not for hours but for days. To leave behind routines, both virtual and real.

Excerpted from Bruckman, A., *Christmas Unplugged.* Copyright © 1999. In S. Hirschberg and T. Hirschberg (eds.), *Reflections on Language,* New York: Oxford University Press. Reprinted with permission from Republication Licensing Service.

References

Baker, A. 2000. "What Makes an Online Relationship Successful? Clues from Couples Who Met in Cyberspace." *Cyberpsychology and Behavior,* 5: 363–375.

Baxter, L., and Montgomery, B. 1996. *Relating: Dialogue and Dialectics*. New York: Guilford.

Bruckman, A. 1992. "Identity Workshop: Emergent Social and Psychological Phenomena in Text-Based Virtual Reality." Unpublished manuscript. MIT Media Laboratory, Cambridge, MA. Available via anonymous ftp from media.mit.edu in pub/MediaMOO/Papers/identity-workshop.

Dibbell, J. 1993. "A Rape in Cyberspace: Or, How an Evil Clown, a Haitian Trickster Spirit, Two Wizards, and a Cast of Dozens Turned a Database into a Society." *Village Voice*, December 21, 36–42.

Dubrovsky, V. J., Kiesler, S. B., and Sethna, B. N. 1991. "The Qualization Phenomenon: Status Effects in Computer-mediated and Face-to-face Decision-making Groups." *Human-Computer Interaction*, 6: 119–146.

Ekman, P., and Friesen, W. V. 1995. "Universals and Cultural Differences in the Judgments of Facial Expressions of Emotion." *Journal of Personality and Social Psychology*, 53: 712–717.

Joinson, A. N. 2001. "Self-Disclosure in Computer-Mediated Communication: The Role of Self-Awareness and Visual Anonymity." *European Journal of Social Psychology*, 31: 177–192.

Kraut, R., Kiesler, S., Boneva, B. Cummings, J., Helgeson, V., and Crawford, A. 2002. "Internet Paradox Revisited." *Journal of Social Issues*, 58: 49–74.

Lea, M., O'Shea, T., Fung, P., and Spears, R. 1992. " 'Flaming' in Computer-Mediated Communication: Observation, Explanations, Implications." In M. Lea (ed.), *Contexts of Computer-Mediated-Communication*. New York: Harvester. Pages 89–112.

Lewin, B. A., and Donner, Y. 2002. "Communication in Internet Message Boards." *English Today*, 71: 29–37.

McKenna, K. Y. A., and Bargh, J. A. 2000. "Plan 9 From Cyberspace: The Implications of the Internet for Personality and Social Psychology." *Personality and Social Psychological Review*, 4: 57–75.

McKenna, K. Y. A., Green, A. S., and Gleason, M. E. J. 2002. "Relationship Formation on the Internet: What's the Big Attraction?" *Journal of Social Issues*, 58: 9–31.

Merchant, G. 2001. "Teenagers in Cyberspace: An Investigation of Language Use and Language Change in Internet Chatrooms." *Journal of Research in Reading*, 24: 293–306.

Morrison, J. 1995. "Welcome to Cyberspace." *Reader's Digest*, 146: 219–228.

Nie, N. H. 2001. "Sociability, Interpersonal Relations, and the Internet: Reconciling Conflicting Findings." *American Behavioral Scientist*, 45: 420–435.

O'Sullivan, P. B., and Flanagin, A. J. 2003. "Reconceptualizing 'flaming' and Other Problematic Messages." *New Media and Society*, 5: 69–94.

Parks, M. R., and Floyd, K. 1996. "Making Friends in Cyberspace." *Journal of Communication*, 46: 80–97.

Parks, M. R., and Lynne, D. R. 1998. " 'Making MOOsic': The Development of Personal Relationships On-line and a Comparison to Their Off-line Counterparts." *Journal of Social and Personal Relationships*, 15: 517–537.

Plotz, T., and Bell, E. 1996. "Invisible Rendezvous: Mapping the Music and Community of Computer-Mediated Communication Through Performance." *Text and Performance Quarterly*, 16: 172–188.

Rheingold, H. 1993. *The Virtual Community: Homesteading on the Electronic Frontier*. Reading, MA: Addison-Wesley.

Sanderson, D. 1997. "Lexikon der Emotikons." *Zeitschrift fuer Semiotik,* 19: 307–315.

Schwartz, G. 1994. "Flame off Internazis!" *Computer Life,* 1: 38–39.

Sherman, R. C., End, C., Kraan, E., Cole, A., Campbell, J., Klausner, J., and Birchmeier, Z. 2001. "Metaperception in Cyberspace." *Cyberpsychology and Behavior,* 4: 123–129.

Sproull, L. and Kiesler, S. 1991. *Connections: New Ways of Working in the Networked Organization.* Cambridge, MA: MIT Press.

Stoll, C. 1995. *Silicon Snake Oil.* New York: Doubleday.

Vangelisti, A. L. 1994. "Messages that Hurt." In W. Cupack and B. Spitzberg (eds.), *The Dark Side of Interpersonal Communication.* Hillsdale, NJ: Lawrence Erlbaum. Pages 53–82.

Vrooman, S. S. 2002. "The Art of Invective: Performing Identity in Cyberspace." *New Media and Society,* 4: 51–70.

Wood, A. F., and Smith, M. J. 2001. *Online Communication: Linking Technology, Identity, and Culture.* Mahwah, NJ: Lawrence Erlbaum Associates.

Recommendations

Books

Markham, A. N. 1998. *Life Online: Researching Real Experience in Virtual Space.* New York: Altamira Press. The author immersed herself in online reality to understand Internet users. This is a very helpful book to understand the complexity and diversity of Internet realities better.

Nakamura, L. 2002. *Cybertypes: Race, Ethnicity, and Identity on the Internet.* New York: Routledge. This book critically examines the construction of race and ethnicity online.

Movies

Cronenberg, D. 1999. *Existenz.* This movie is peculiar but a good example of interaction through technology.

Sena, D. 2001. *Swordfish.* This movie is a cyber-thriller story. It gives examples of how the Internet can affect interpersonal relationships.

The Wachowski Brothers. *The Matrix* (1999), *Matrix Reloaded* (2003), and *Matrix Revolutions* (2003). These are fictional examples of human interaction through a technology-based medium.

Winkler, I. 1995. *The Net.* This is one of the first mildly good Internet thrillers.

Links

Definitions and examples for Cyberspeak can be found in a high-tech dictionary under the following link: <http://www.computeruser.com/ resources/dictionary/noframes/index.html>. ✦

Photo Credits

Chapter One
Page 3—Tim Melander; page 12—Tim Melander.

Chapter Two
Page 21—Roxbury; page 30—Tim Melander; page 40—Shehzad Noorani/ Woodfin Camp & Associates; page 48—Fotosearch/Brand X Pictures.

Chapter Three
Page 61—Roxbury; page 71—Roxbury; page 76—Roxbury.

Chapter Four
Page 93—Tim Melander; page 96—photo illustration by James Darsey; page 106—Roxbury; page 113—*Daily Bruin*.

Chapter Five
Page 130—Corbis; page 139—Tim Melander; page 141—Tim Melander; page 144—Fotosearch/Brand X Pictures.

Chapter Six
Page 158—Roxbury; page 164—Roxbury; page 168—Corbis; page 176—Roxbury; page 181—Corbis.

Chapter Seven
Page 195—Tim Melander; page 202—Sherry Steinbeck.

Chapter Eight
Page 221—Corbis; page 228a—Roxbury; page 228b—Roxbury; page 229—Corbis; page 230—Carl Wilson; page 232—Roxbury; page 241—Tim Melander.

Chapter Nine
Page 255—Tim Melander; page 272—Roxbury; page 279—Roxbury.

Chapter Ten
Page 295—Corbis; page 300—Corbis; page 307—AP Worldwide/ Jeni Rosenthal.

Chapter Eleven
Page 320—courtesy of Feminist Majority Foundation; page 327—Corbis; Fotosearch/Digital Vision; page 336—Roxbury; page 339—courtesy of Mediation Network of North Carolina; page 347—Fotosearch/Goodshoot.

Chapter Twelve
Page 368—Roxbury. ✦

Glossary

A, B

accommodation. One of five conflict styles. It happens when a person puts aside his or her own concerns in favor of pleasing the other people involved and preserving the relationship(s). (Chapter 11)

acronym. A word that is formed from the initial letters of each part of a compound term (e.g., btw: by the way) or the initial letters of each syllable of a word (e.g., bc: because). (Chapter 12)

addressability. One of the five features that distinguish persons from other animals. It means linguistic responsiveness; beings that are addressable can recognize when they are called or spoken to in language, and can also respond in language. (Chapter 3)

alienation. In the helical model of relational change, the period of alienation is marked by estrangement of both partners as they cope with the disintegration of an earlier security in their relationship. The helical model predicts that alienation can be followed by a period of resynthesis and a new security. (Chapter 9)

analytic listening. The type of listening that emphasizes the listener's desires not to be taken advantage of or lied to and the listener's determination to analyze and test what is heard. This type of listening helps the listener to respond critically to a speaker's perspective rather than simply reacting to it. (Chapter 6)

asynchronous communication. Communication in which participants don't interact in real-time. Examples are email in online communication and writing letters in offline communication. (Chapter 12)

attachment. The type of bond established between a child and the primary caregiver. Overattached children have demanding, controlling, and overprotective parents. The children are often observed to be both anxious and ambivalent. Underattached children have parents that spend little time encouraging frequent or prolonged periods of interaction. These children are "avoidant" in their responses. Children who are securely attached have parents who effectively balance periods of intense interaction with periods of "alone time." (Chapter 9)

attribution. A type of perceptual inference in which people develop reasons or explanations for another person's behavior. Attributions can be internal (the source of the behavior is interpreted as coming from the psychological make-up of the person) or external (the source of the behavior is interpreted as coming from the situation or factors outside of the person). (Chapter 5)

availability. This attitude accompanying self-expression means (1) bringing some relevant aspects of a person's self to the conversation, and (2) being present to the other person and being open to some of the other person's concerns. Another term for it is "mindfulness." (Chapter 7)

avoidance. One of the five conflict styles. Avoidance is characterized by trying to dodge the conflict by ignoring or changing the topic, being vague about positions or preferences, or using joking to respond to a challenge, threat, or disagreement. In these ways, avoidance privileges the other person's goals and the relationship over the avoider's goals and the issue. (Chapter 11)

avoiding. One of Knapp and Vangelisti's stages of "coming apart." In this stage, people attempt to distance themselves from each other by minimizing contact. (Chapter 9)

avoiding gunnysacking. A conflict management tactic in which a person refrains from dumping all past resentments experienced in the relationship during a specific conflict. (Chapter 11)

avoiding overload. A type of listening problem which occurs when a person attempts to reduce the continuous bombardment of messages in the environment by tuning out some of this information. (Chapter 6)

belt lines. As part of managing conflict, a person establishes limits about what topics can be discussed. (Chapter 11)

benevolence. In deception research, this is one of the motives for deception. Refers to using deception to protect the self-esteem, safety, and/or general well-being of the other person. (Chapter 10)

bonding stage. One of Knapp and Vangelisti's five stages of a relationship's "coming together." This fifth stage is marked by the enactment of a private or public ritual to define the permanence of the relationship. (Chapter 9)

bottom line statement. A single, simple, concrete, vivid statement that captures the essence of what a person is saying. (Chapter 7)

C, D

circular questioning. A conflict management tactic in which one person adopts a kind of inquiry that accepts or builds on a person's view of a situation in order to explore possible alternative views. (Chapter 11)

circumscribing. One of Knapp and Vangelisti's stages of "coming apart." In this stage, people mutually limit the contexts in which they are together in favor of contexts in which they are separate. (Chapter 9)

closed families. Families which prefer activities limited to family members and restrict social contact; low in adaptability and, in extreme form, rigid. (Chapter 9)

closed sensitivity. An identity negotiation response option in which the person expresses only social characteristics while perceiving and responding to some personal features of the other person. (Chapter 4)

closed stereotyping. An identity negotiation response option in which the person expresses social characteristics of self while perceiving and responding to only social characteristics of the other person. (Chapter 4)

collaboration. Joint action. As a general term, collaboration is central to the entire approach to communication explained in this book. (Chapter 1) Collaboration is also one of five conflict styles. It happens when participants are committed to a thoroughly mutual process that produces emergent next actions that neither party could envision or accomplish alone. (Chapter 11)

communication. A general term used to label the process through which humans collaboratively construct meaning. It is the continuous, complex, collaborative process of verbal and nonverbal meaning-making and the negotiating of identities or selves. (Chapter 2)

competition. One of five conflict styles. Interprets conflicts as "win/lose" or "zero sum games." Puts own agenda first, combats the other's agenda, and deemphasizes the importance of the relationship. (Chapter 11)

compromise. One of five conflict styles. Each party gives up something desirable in an attempt to balance power in the relationship. It is more other-focused than competition, but more self-focused than avoiding or accommodating styles. (Chapter 11)

confirmation. The opposite of disconfirmation. Confirmation occurs when communication acknowledges the other person's existence and significance. Different from agreement; confirmation can occur when there is disagreement. (Chapter 4)

conflict. An expressed struggle between at least two interdependent parties who perceive incompatible goals, scarce resources, and interference from others in achieving their goals. (Chapter 11)

conservative attributions. The perceptual problem which results from the tendency, when explaining someone's actions, to rely heavily on existing beliefs, attitudes, and emotions, and underutilize new information. (Chapter 5)

constructing selves. The process of mutually building identities that happens in all communicating. The process of constructing selves is collaborative, the outcomes are emergent, it includes giving out and taking in, and it happens in and out of awareness. This term appears frequently throughout the book but is discussed at length in Chapter 4: Identity Construction.

cosmopolitan communication. The type of communication which underlies dialogic listening. The listener adopts an inclusive orientation toward ideas and experiences. The main goal is to work toward alignment or coordination rather than agreement among all perspectives. (Chapter 6)

culture. A group identity, the shared ways of living that produce and reflect this identity, and the transmission of this identity from one generation to the next. (Chapter 2)

cyberspace. Electronic space that is created through computer networks. (Chapter 12)

cyberspeak. The jargon that is used in online communication. (Chapter 12)

deception. A complex communication pattern in which at least one participant is misled by a false appearance or statement. There are at least six different types: lies, fictions, playing, crimes, masks, and unlies. (Chapter 10)

defusing. A conflict management tactic that reduces the intensity of a disagreement. Various communication tactics can work to defuse oneself, the other person, or the situation. (Chapter 11)

descriptive communication. Increasing flexibility by focusing on observations of behavior as opposed to expressing evaluations or judgments. (Chapter 7)

dialectical model of relational change. The perspective that relationships change over time as a result of the tension between opposing needs. (Chapter 9)

dialogic listening. A type of listening that explicitly enhances processes that result in meanings being collaboratively co-constructed by all participants. (Chapter 6)

differentiating. One of Knapp and Vangelisti's stages of "coming apart." In this stage, people begin to move away from each other, seeing themselves as independent more than a "partner" or part of a "couple." (Chapter 9)

disclosure. The process of revealing one's social, cultural, and/or personal self. Some disclosure happens every time you communicate. When you disclose information about your personal self, you tend to increase the level of intimacy between you and the other person. (Chapter 7)

disconfirmation. A type of closed stereotyping in which one person communicates in ways that deny the other person's existence or significance. (Chapter 4)

discrimination. Attending to unique or distinctive features of the sensory information that is received in the process of perception. (Chapter 5)

disengaged families. Families who emphasize autonomy and separateness in setting boundaries and resist any change within the family structure; low in cohesiveness. (Chapter 9)

disintegration. In the helical model of relational change, this is the first period of uncertainty that replaces an established security. Followed by alienation. (Chapter 9)

E, F

egoism. In deception research, this is one of the motives for deception. Refers to using lying to protect or promote the deceiver's positive self-concept. (Chapter 10)

emoticon. Icons that you can produce on a keyboard (letters, numbers, symbols) and that express the feelings of the writer of a message. Emoticons often emulate facial expressions and can be used to complement verbal messages and make them less ambiguous. (Chapter 12)

empathic listening. A type of listening most closely associated with the closed sensitivity response option discussed in Chapter 4. The listener is receptive or sensitive to a full range of social, cultural, and personal characteristics shared by the other person, but responds only with social and/or cultural characteristics. (Chapter 6)

encouraging skills. A set of skills used in empathic and dialogic listening which are designed to "pull" more talk from the other person. The goal is to understand what the other is saying more completely and clearly. (Chapter 6)

enmeshed families. Families who do not develop clear boundaries about possessions, activities, and behaviors; dangerously high in cohesiveness. (Chapter 9)

entertainment factor. A type of listening problem which results from becoming accustomed to getting information in entertaining packages. Listeners tend to demand to be entertained. (Chapter 6)

ethics. Standards for judging communicative behaviors as good or bad; right or wrong; appropriate or inappropriate. Moral and ethical judgments are based on socially constructed and sustained ideals of right and wrong rather than "absolute truths."

ethnocentric communication. Communicating with the assumption that one's own culture is the preferred or "right" perspective from which all other cultures should be viewed. It emphasizes coherence, or the process of making new information fit familiar and comfortable attitudes, rather than attending to and valuing novelty. (Chapters 6 and 7)

exhaling. The "giving out" part of the communicating process-making available primarily verbal, mixed, and primarily nonverbal cues. (Chapters 7 and 8)

exiting. A terminating strategy in which the relationship is ended by breaking contact, formally separating, moving out of a joint residence, or getting a divorce. (Chapter 9)

experimenting stage. One of Knapp and Vangelisti's five stages of a relationship's "coming together." During this stage, people get closer by using small talk to reduce the uncertainty they have about each other. (Chapter 9)

expressive communicating. A developmental stage of communicative competence in which the communicator treats communication primarily as a way to express thoughts and feelings. Normally followed by the development of rule-governed communicating and then negotiation. (Chapter 3)

exploitation. In deception research, this is one of the motives for deception. It refers to using deception to gain some useful, personal advantage. (Chapter 10)

family of origin. The family unit in which a person spent the first five to seven years of life. (Chapter 9)

fast thinking. A problem with the selecting part of the perceptual process in which a person can become sidetracked in attention by the extra time between thinking speed of the person listening and conversational speed of the speaker. (Chapter 5)

flaming. Messages that intentionally violate norms for social interaction in online communication. (Chapter 12)

flexibility. We refer to this term many times throughout the book. In Chapter 3, we mean developing the skills necessary to be able to move your communication toward the interpersonal end of the continuum. In Chapter 7, we explain how it is related to becoming descriptive, spontaneous, and provisional. (Chapters 3 and 7)

focusing skills. A set of listening skills used in empathic and dialogic listening in which the listener orients to or concentrates on the other person. (Chapter 6)

fractionate. A conflict management tactic in which the conflict is broken down from one big mass into several smaller, more manageable pieces. (Chapter 11)

framing. Any part of the communication process which helps one person interpret or understand the perspective of the other person. See metacommunication. (Chapter 7)

fundamental attribution error. A perceptual problem in which a person tends to underestimate the impact of situational or external factors which contribute to another's behavior and to overestimate the role of personality or internal factors. The reverse process occurs when attributing reasons to the person's own behavior. (Chapter 5)

G, H

generalization. In the process of perception, generalizing is scanning incoming sensory information for the purpose of categorizing it. It is one kind of stereotyping. (Chapter 5)

gunnysacking. Collecting resentments and then dumping them all in the middle of a conflict. One strategy for effective conflict management is to avoid gunnysacking. (Chapter 11)

helical model of relational change. This perspective assumes that relationships undergo periods of stabilization and change characteristic of the type described in the dialectical perspective. This view also assumes relationships have direction best characterized by spirals which lead to more positive or negative beliefs about the relationship. (Chapter 9)

hurtful messages. A type of negative message which varies in intensity depending on the intent of the person saying it, the relationship the two share, and the level of intimacy in that relationship. Examples include: accusations, evaluations, directives, advice, expression of desires, information disclosures, interrogations, threats, jokes, and lies. (Chapter 10)

I, J

idea-transmission view of communication. A "hypodermic needle" view of communication in which it is assumed ideas are injected from the head of one person into the head of another through the process of communication. Definition and model are in Chapter 2.

identities or selves. Who a person is grows out of how that person talks and listens to and with others. The responding "self" is relational rather than individual, emphasizes both choice and connection to others, is multidimensional and changing, and is developed in past and present relationships. (Chapter 4)

implicit personality theory. The process of making a series of related internal attributions about someone's behavior which serves as a "theory" about that person's personality based on qualities or characteristics that are implied by his or her behavior. (Chapter 5)

independents. One of three marital couple types; independents are unconventional, openly and freely engage in conflict, and highly value autonomy, honesty, and change. (Chapter 9)

inference making. One of the three subprocesses of perception that refers to the way people go beyond all sensory cues they select to their interpretations of those cues. (Chapter 5)

inhaling. The "taking in" part of the communicating process including noticing, being aware of, perceiving, and listening. (Chapters 5 and 6)

initiating stage. One of Knapp and Vangelisti's five stages of a relationship's "coming together." In this first stage, people meet, greet, and typically make arrangements to meet again. (Chapter 9)

integrating stage. One of Knapp and Vangelisti's five stages of a relationship's "coming together." During this fourth stage, people begin to see themselves as a "couple" or "partners." (Chapter 9)

intensifying stage. One of Knapp and Vangelisti's five stages of a relationship's "coming together." In this third stage, people move significantly closer and become intimate. (Chapter 9)

interpersonal alignment. Mutual understanding that happens in communicating when people recognize they share a set of goals; they are "collaborating." (Chapter 3)

interpersonal communicating. Communicating that maximizes the presence of the "personal," comprised of five characteristics: unique, unmeasurable, responsive, reflective, and addressable. It represents one end of the "qualities of communication" continuum. (Chapter 3)

intimate distance. The distance that, in a given culture, indicates that the people communicating have an intimate relationship. Contact to 18 inches in most Western white cultures. One of E. T. Hall's proxemic categories. (Chapter 8)

isolating the trigger. A conflict management tactic in which a person tries to identify the precipitating event, action, or words where discussion escalated to a conflict. The trigger is not the "cause." (Chapter 11)

jargon. A specialized "in-group" vocabulary used to help social, professional, cultural, and political groups define themselves. (Chapter 7)

K, L

leakage. Nonstrategic cues inadvertently given by a communicator, especially one who is in the process of deceiving another person. (Chapter 8)

love. A complex set of beliefs, emotions, and attitudes constructed by persons in close relationships. At least six different types have been identified: eros (sexual love), ludis (playful love), storge (companionate love), mania (obsessive love), pragma (realistic love), and agape (altruistic love). (Chapter 9) *loyalty.* A terminating strategy in which one partner hopes to reverse ending the relationship by waiting for things to improve, supporting the partner in the face of criticism, and believing that the relationship will improve. (Chapter 10)

M, N

malevolence. In deception research, this is one of the motives for deception. Refers to using deception to intentionally hurt the other person. (Chapter 10)

metacommunication. Communication about (behind) communication that often helps to clarify one person's meaning. May be implicit or explicit, verbal and/or nonverbal. (Chapter 7)

metaphor. A comparison, a phrase, description, or story that connects one well-known event or idea with another that is less well known for the sake of increasing clarity. (Chapter 7)

mirroring. A listening skill in which key words or phrases of the other person are repeated with a questioning inflection for the purpose of requesting an elaboration of meaning. (Chapter 6)

neglect. A terminating strategy in which the relationship is allowed to "die" by spending less time with one's partner, refusing to discuss problems, complaining about its state without offering solutions, and, in some cases, developing a new relationship. (Chapter 10)

negotiation. Mutual construction of identities and meanings. Negotiation is also a term used for a developmental stage in which a person views communicating as a process in which who the participants are and what they are doing are constructed in the communication occurring between them. (Chapter 3)

nexting. The process of doing something helpful next, responding fruitfully to what's just happened, taking an additional positive step in the communication process. It can be used as a more effective means of self-expression and as part of managing conflict more effectively. (Chapters 2, 7, 11)

noise. Any type of interference that compromises a person's understanding. There are three types: physiological noise (internal physical interference), emotional noise (strong opinions and feelings about an issue that prevent a person from listening effectively), and environmental noise (situational factors that interfere with understanding). (Chapter 6)

O, P

online identity. The self that a person constructs through verbal and nonverbal means when communicating online. (Chapter 12)

onomatopoeia. Words that sound like what they mean. (Chapter 12)

open and closed questioning. Asking open questions is an encouraging listening skill in which the question simply identifies a topic area and asks the other person to talk about it. This technique is contrasted with closed questions that call for a yes/no, single word, or simple-sentence answer. Closed questions provide minimal help in clarifying the other person's perspective. (Chapter 6)

open families. Families that develop fluid boundaries with the outside world, encouraging participation in many activities and relationships outside the family, are highly adaptive and, in extreme forms, chaotic. (Chapter 9)

open sensitivity. A negotiation response option in which a person expresses personal characteristics and perceives and responds to personal characteristics of the other person. (Chapter 4)

open stereotyping. A negotiation response option in which a person expresses personal characteristics while perceiving and responding to social characteristics of the other person. (Chapter 4)

organizing. One of the three subprocesses of perception that describes the way a person constructs and imposes patterns or structure onto the stream of sensory cues received. (Chapter 5)

paralinguistics. The nonverbal, vocal aspects of language that include rate of speech, pitch variation, volume, and vocal quality. (Chapter 8)

paraphrase. A skill in which the listener restates the other's meaning in the listener's own words with a verification check. (Chapter 7)

paraphrase plus. A paraphrase that includes a statement about the paraphraser's perspective on the topic and then encourages the conversation partner to reply. It is a listening skill particularly associated with dialogic listening. (Chapter 7)

perceived incompatible goals. One reason for conflict. Conflict sometimes occurs when positions and interests are confused. Positions are immediate goals; interests are broader goals. Often, conflict ends when people discover they have compatible interests even if their positions differ. (Chapter 11)

perceived interference. One reason for conflict. Conflict occurs when a person perceives the other as standing in the way of achieving some goal. (Chapter 11)

perceived scarce resources. One reason for conflict. Whenever resources are lacking, conflict can arise. The conflict is managed if it is found that the problem is the perception of scarcity rather than an actual lack of resources. (Chapter 11)

perception. The basic "taking in" or inhaling process of communicating where one becomes aware of and listens to others. It is comprised of three basic subprocesses: selection, organization, and inference making. (Chapter 5)

personal distance. The distance preferred by most Western Caucasians in conversation: 1.5 to 4 feet. One of E. T. Hall's proxemic categories. (Chapter 8)

person-centered communication. The type of communication that is likely to be constructed by people who make more frequent use of discriminating, or who make distinctions about the unique features of others. (Chapter 5)

person prototype. A generalized representation of certain types of persons usually based on experience and repeated interaction. Person prototypes include information about traits and characteristics you believe about a particular type of person—drag queen, professor, lawyer, homeless person, mother. (Chapter 5)

primarily nonverbal aspects of language. Elements of communication that can occur without words such as gestures, eye gaze, facial expression, touch, and space, but are usually interpreted in the context of spoken words. (Chapter 3)

primarily verbal aspects of language. Written words. The words are still composed of nonverbal "space" on a page, appear in a particular font, etc. (Chapter 8)

provisional communication. Increasing flexibility by being willing to explore and experiment with ideas, beliefs, attitudes, and behavior (as opposed to being certain that one's own perspective is most truthful and relevant). (Chapter 7)

proxemics. The study of the communicative effects of space or distance. (Chapter 8)

pseudoquestions. Judgments or opinions masquerading as questions. This type of question is often an attempt to soften negative evaluations. (Chapter 6)

public distance. This range is typical of one-to-many communication situations, such as teachers lecturing or a public speaker giving a speech. In most Caucasian cultures, this is 12 to 25 feet. One of E. T. Hall's proxemic categories. (Chapter 8)

Q, R

quiet time. A conflict management tactic where one or all participants call a moratorium or "time-out" from the disagreement for the purposes of gaining a fresh perspective and finding temporary relief. (Chapter 11)

reflecting skills. A set of listening skills associated with empathic listening that emphasize mirroring or restating the other person's perspective. (Chapter 6)

reflective. One of the five features of communicating that distinguishes persons from non-persons. Reflecting basically means being aware that you are aware. Persons reflect when they think about what they have said or done, speculate or plan the future, consider alternate courses of action, etc. (Chapter 3)

reflective listening. The kind of listening that intensifies and applies the human capability to concentrate, study in depth, and question what is heard. Reflective listening includes various forms of meditation and listening for enjoyment. (Chapter 6)

regress. In deception research, this is one of the motives for deception. Refers to using deception to stymie, damage, or terminate the relationship. (Chapter 10)

relational dialectics. The perspective in communication theory that assumes people define themselves personally and socially in communicating, relationships are constructed from the tension of opposing needs, relationships exist in time and space, and communicating requires at least two distinct voices which each become reference points for the other. (Chapter 9)

relational violence. The use or threat of physical force or restraint by a person who intends to cause pain or injury to the other person. Chapter 10)

relationship. A coherent pattern of communicating between people. (Chapter 9)

relationship reminders. References to the history that is shared by you and the other person for the purpose of keeping conflicts in perspective. (Chapter 11)

resource. Any physical, economic, or social consequence that people perceive positively. (Chapter 11)

responsive or response-able. From a tensional view of communication, to be "response-able" means having the willingness and the ability to contribute in some way to how events are unfolding. Being able to make choices about the way one responds is one of the five features of communicating that distinguish persons from non-persons. (Chapter 3)

resynthesis. In the helical model of relational change, this period occurs when both partners overcome alienation by redefining part of their relationship. The helical model predicts that resynthesis leads to a new security. (Chapter 9)

role-reversal. A type of conflict management tactic in which one person considers the legitimacy of the other person's perspective by taking the other person's place in the conflict. (Chapter 11)

rule-governed communicating. A developmental stage in which communicating is viewed as a game to be played by following social rules. Contrasted with expressive and negotiation stages of communication development. (Chapter 3)

run with the metaphor. A dialogic listening skill that can help the sculpting process happen. The listener weaves one of the speaker's metaphors into her or his listening responses in order to connect with the speaker's meaning. (Chapter 6)

S, T

scripts. A type of cognitive schema that helps make sense of sequences of actions. Based on experience, scripts help an individual to anticipate what is likely to happen next in routine or patterned interaction. (Chapter 5)

sculpting skills. A set of skills associated with dialogic listening that focus on the collaborative process of constructing or "sculpting" meanings together. (Chapter 6)

security-1. From the helical model of relational change, these terms refer to periods of relational stability. Security-1 is an initial stability that eventually disintegrates, produces alienation, then leads to resynthesis, which in turn leads to security-2. (Chapter 9)

selecting. One of the three subprocesses of perception in which a person decides at some level of consciousness what sensory cues to pay attention to. (Chapter 5)

separates. One of the three types of marital couples; separates express little interdependence, engage in activities alone, avoid conflict, and enjoy separate physical space. (Chapter 9)

sexual harassment. Unsolicited, unwanted attention paid to one's sexual characteristics. (Chapter 10)

snap judgments. The most limited stereotype we make about others we perceive. Snap judgments are immediate and do not involve complex cognitive processes. (Chapter 5)

social distance. This distance is usually reserved for more impersonal business such as people who work together or who are attending a social gathering, and ranges from 4 to 12 feet in most white cultures. One of E. T. Hall's proxemic categories. (Chapter 8)

speech economy. To convey meaning with the least amount of verbal means. (Chapter 12)

spirals. Repetitive patterns of communicating in relationships. There are two types: generative spirals (which lead to more positive attitudes, feelings, and beliefs about the relationship), and degenerative spirals (which lead to increasingly negative attitudes, feelings, and beliefs about oneself, the other person, and the relationship). (Chapters 9 and 11)

stage model of relational change. The perspective that relationships change and develop in discrete stages or phases that are identifiable as discrete and separate. Change can be either toward "bonding" or toward "terminating." (Chapter 9) *stagnating.* One of Knapp and Vangelisti's stages of "coming apart." In this stage, the individuals' communication becomes mostly repetitive, established patterns. The relationship has stopped growing. (Chapter 9)

stereotyping. This term has two meanings: (1) a type of inference in the process of making sense out of what we perceive by categorizing or generalizing it, and (2) an oversimplified way of labeling people which is designed to categorize them by various characteristics. (Chapters 4 and 5)

synchronous communication. Communication in real-time (e.g., chat rooms). (Chapter 12)

tensional view of communication. A relational, dialectical, or dialogic view of communication that assumes that meanings are continually unfolding, developing, and in-process, partly stable and partly changing, and that communication is the process of mutually constructing meanings. (Chapter 2)

terminating. One of Knapp and Vangelisti's stages of "coming apart." In this stage, the people separate, break up, divorce, or otherwise define their relationship as finished. (Chapter 9)

territory. An identifiable geographic area that is occupied, controlled, and often defended by a person or group as their exclusive domain. (Chapter 8)

traditionals. One of the three types of marital couples; they favor conventional ideas about marriage, highly value mutual sharing, and emphasize stability rather than change. (Chapter 9)

turning points. A term for a critical event in the life of a relationship. Turning points are the points at which the relationship undergoes a significant change from, for example, superior-subordinate to friends, or close friends to lovers. In dating relationships, examples of turning points include the first date, quality time, meeting the family, and first kiss. (Chapter 9)

U, V

uniqueness. One of the five features of communicating that distinguish persons from non-persons. Our one-of-a-kind-ness; the fact that no person exactly duplicates any other, even if they're clones. (Chapter 3)

unmeasurability. One of the five features of communicating that distinguishes persons from non-persons. Persons have qualities that cannot be measured, that is, they are intangible and cannot be described fully in space-time terms (weight, length, width, etc.). (Chapter 3)

utility. In deception research, this is one of the motives for deception. Refers to using deception to improve, enhance, escalate, or repair the relationship. (Chapter 10)

verbal aggressiveness. Communication which attacks the personality or character of the other person. (Chapter 10)

W, X, Y, Z

world of meaning. A person's "reality" or overall view of the way things are. The more-or-less coherent spheres of sense, significance, or interpretation that each human inhabits. It is composed of at least seven elements: physical environment, time, relationships, spirituality, vocation, language(s), and technology. (Chapter 2)

X-Y-Z skill. A conflict management tactic in which one person uses the form "When you do X in situation Y, I feel Z" to describe what is happening from that person's perspective. (Chapter 11) ✦

Name Index

Subject Index